I SURVIVED MYSELF

I SURVIVED MYSELF

BY PETER "PERU" CHRZANOWSKI

Degan Media, Inc.
Campton, New Hampshire
USA
https://dan-egan.com/

Publishers
Degan Media, Inc.
Campton, New Hampshire
USA
https://dan-egan.com/

Title: *I Survived Myself*
copyright txt © by Peter Chrzanowski 2023
copyright book © by Peter Chrzanowski 2023
All rights reserved

First edition, 2023, second print run 2025
No part of this book may be reproduced in any form,
or by any electronic m mechanical, or other means,
without permission in writing from the author/publisher.

Supervising editor: Roman Gołędowski
Copy Editors: Rod Drowne, Chris Lockhart, Simon Bedford
Editorial Cooperation: Peter Shrimpton, Evelyn Stypulkowski,
Karen Love, Matthew Hayto

Cover Design: Mylinh Huynh
Cover illustration: David Clarke
Back Cover illustration: Mauro Sierra – Peter paragliding Peru,
Malcom Parry – small Peter blue shirt pic.
Formatting: drukujz*sense*m.pl, Roman Gołędowski, Sammy Blair

ISBN: 9781736492789

Peter Chrzanowski, EXTREME EXPLORATIONS
Box 1005, 1740 Reid Rd
Mt Currie BC CANADA, V0N 2K0
tel. +1 604-894-2492
e-mail: petercperu@hotmail.com
www.facebook.com/petercperu

Sponsored by: INTUITION LINERS www.intuitionliners.com
Robert Jungman www.Jungmaven.com

CONTENTS

Introduction – the Young Rebel	11
1. MY PRE-EXTREME 1970's	37
2. IN TROUBLE AGAIN; PERU, COLOMBIA TO FRANCE	53
3. THE DAWN OF MY RADICAL 20's	67
4. MY TRULY EXTREME 80's	91
5. SURVIVING MT ROBSON, SIMON FRASER UNIVERSITY AND EARLY DAYS OF FILMMAKING	107
6. MATURING WITH MOUNTAINS AND WOMEN	125
7. FROM EASY LIVING TO FREE FLIGHT	163
8. THE CONTINUING MOUNTAIN MADNESS OF THE 90's	185
9. THEN, THERE WAS FILM	203
10. DIRTBAGGING IT	221
11. SURVIVING THE MILLENIUM AND BEYOND, THE 2000's	257
12. BACK TO PERU	279
13. AIR HEADS TO X-ANDES	307
14. CUBA AND BEYOND	321
15. MORE TIME SPENT SOUTH	341
16. MORE ACCIDENTS, LIABILITY, AND NOSTALGIA	353
Epilogue	379
Acknowledgments	415
Photo credits	418
Interesting links – videos	419
Interesting links – news/articles	421
Opinions about the author and his book	422

*To my dearest Mother
as well as to all those friends
that had left us till now.*

Extreme sports such as paragliding, extreme skiing, mountain biking and others can cause severe injury or death. By no means the author intends to encourage youth to practice these activities and only presents things as his choice in life.

Peter is long-time friend. He helped in many occasions and I will always be grateful to him. The title of his book: I Survived Myself could not be more accurate. Peter is what we call in French «a locomotive», an adventurer always ahead, always launching new projects and arousing enthusiasm. Things have not always follow the direction he wanted, but he never gave up, and when down, he would revive like the Phoenix and start again. He has an incredible resilience, an example for today's youth.
He is the kind of person who always speaks the truth. Indeed a strong-minded man, a man who never does things by halves.

Peter, I wish you a lot of success with your book, you deserve it!

Sylvain Saudan
Skier of the Impossible
Chamonix, France

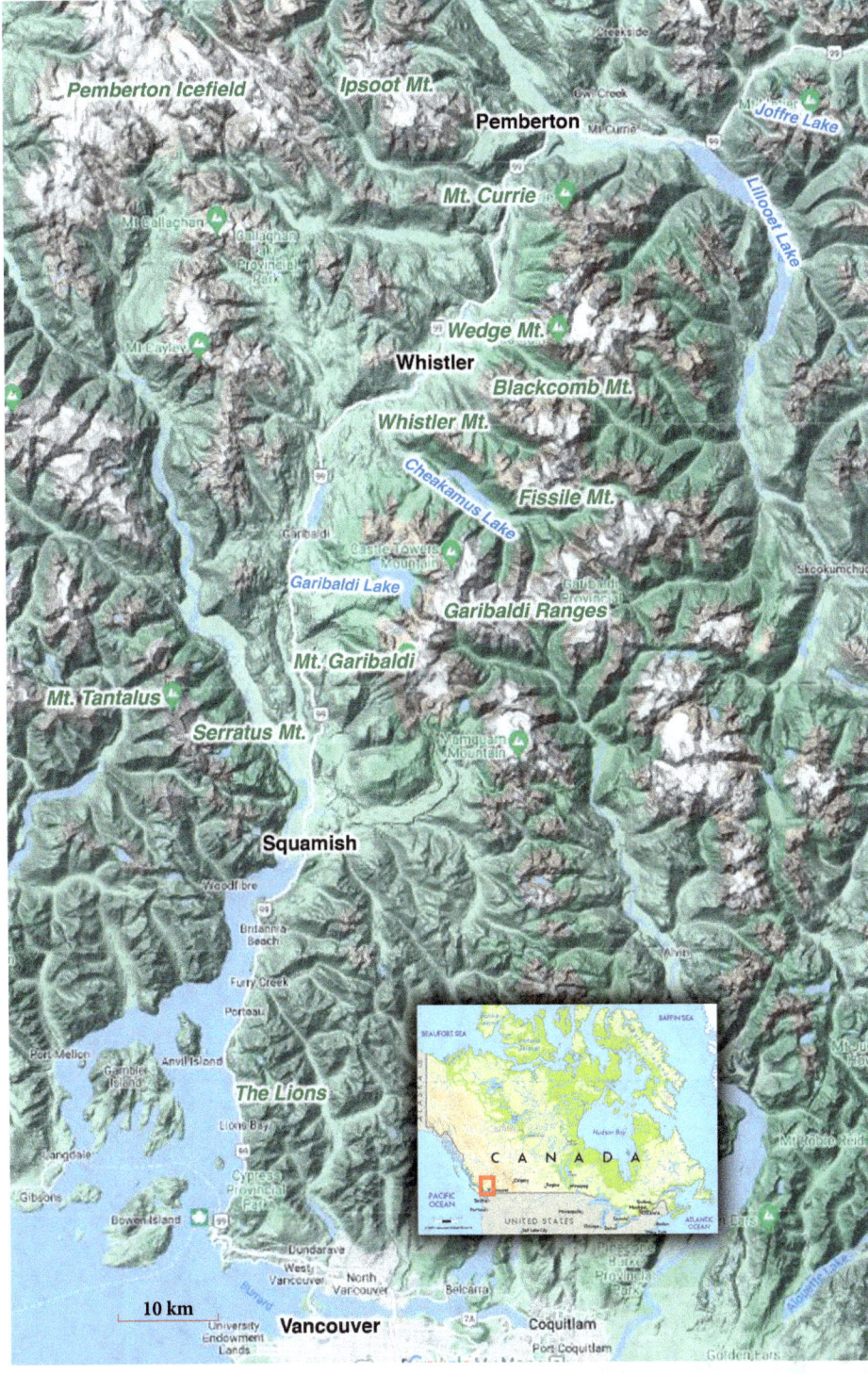

INTRODUCTION – THE YOUNG REBEL

July 1979, Huaraz, Peru, A glacier, somewhere in the Cordillera Blanca.

I opened my eyes and for a while saw nothing but darkness. I didn't know where I was or how I'd got there, but it was cold and dark. As I moved my head, a beam of daylight hit my eyes from above. I then looked down towards my feet, and for some reason I seemed to be barefoot, which was odd because I was wearing a pair of ski pants. I seemed to be wedged into a narrow, snow-filled crevasse, and I had come to a rest two metres below the entrance and was lying on a sort of shelf. Phew! That was lucky, I thought. I can just about climb out of this hole without too much trouble. I then instantly freaked out when I looked around to check out the rest of my surroundings. I wasn't in a comfortable position at all, as I was literally lying inches from the edge of a gaping abyss that appeared to have no bottom. The walls of ice which surrounded formed the top of a vast chamber. They were deep blue at my level, but they quickly became darker as they fell away, until there was nothing but pitch black in the void. Panicked by the view, I frantically clawed my way up towards the daylight above me, and I now noticed I'd lost my gloves as well as my boots as my frozen fingers tried to get a purchase in the hard icy snow. Somehow I managed to claw my way through the soft snow that rimmed the crevasse, and crawled out onto the slope of the glacier where I collapsed in a heap. After a while, and I don't know how long I lay there, I recovered enough to get up on my knees and start yelling for help as loudly as I could. I was in a totally disoriented state, but some flashes of memory began to come back. Yes, I was aware I was in Peru. I remembered climbing this mountain called Ranrapalca, which, at 6,162m, was a rarely visited, high and secluded Andean peak. It had a reputation for being a very technical climb, but I had not only achieved that goal, I was also attempting to claim the first ski descent of it as well. Solo. As the fog cleared and my mind began to function again, I had no idea how long I had been lying there unconscious.

I realized that I must have fallen down the full 900 meters of the 55 degree south-west face of the mountain, and had fallen into the crevasse at the base. By some miracle I appeared to be alive and not too badly hurt. I remembered I had made a short traverse at the top before trying a couple of hesitant turns on snow that was harder than I had expected, but then nothing more. Now I felt all around my body for evidence of any breaks or fractures, and I could not believe I had survived. Not only that, but I could also move and all my limbs were working. Whew! I was alive, and seemingly unhurt! A miracle!

Little did I know that this marked the beginning of a life that has been filled with many more adventures and mishaps, and that I would experience this exhilarating rush of survival under the most unlikely circumstances over and over again, as I would go on to log many more crashes while skiing, and then paragliding my way through life.

So here is my story.

*　*　*

WHISTLER, British Columbia, April 2017.

Fast forward 38 years, on a glorious spring afternoon, I was skiing with my good friend Doris Spika on Blackcomb Mountain in British Columbia. It was one of those special spring afternoons. We had just skied down Blackcomb Glacier early enough, just before brilliant sunshine began glittering on the light powder snow. We managed the traverse out at the bottom of the run when, out of nowhere, a familiar face appeared where skiers converge at a sign board, a place where old friends from past skiing ventures often meet.

This was someone I knew from my old ski-bumming years at Blackcomb, but I could not really place the name. He was a blond good-looking guy, around my age, with a well weathered face like mine. He skied up to me while my mind raced trying to put a name to his face. He took off his ski glove, put out his hand and said,

"Hey Peter Peru, I just want to congratulate you on surviving your lifestyle."

I must admit I was a bit stunned. We shook hands and Doris and I skied off again. It was not till much later when we both looked back at this particular incident and giggled. So this was it – the quote which prompted me to document my life in these memoirs.

* * *

My nickname is "Peter Peru", but I didn't earn that name until many years later. I was actually born in Poland in the wee hours of the morning in a state hospital in Krakow, Poland on November 5, 1957 – a place that is very far from Peru. My parents, Adam and Maria "Nina" Chrzanowski, did not realize at the time what a deviant they had brought upon themselves and into this world.

I didn't learn the meaning of the word "extreme" until much later and was not dubbed "Peter Peru" until the seventies. The nickname had many various and strange origins. While I cannot peg exactly when, why or how it arose, it may have originated following a few outlandish incidents in Whistler, at the time an emerging Canadian ski resort in the incredibly beautiful province of British Columbia. When I arrived in Whistler in November 1979, full of wonder and excitement, and with a little piss and vinegar added. Everyone in town learned about my expeditions in Peru through two articles I had recently managed to have published: "Peruvian High", in Powder Magazine, which was the bible of serious skiers around the globe, and "I skied Huascaran", in Ski Canada, Toronto's premier ski magazine. These and other stories shared at skier parties about my misconducts in Peru undeniably contributed to my nickname. Peru was then still considered exotic and mysterious, as not many people had made the long trek to ski there. As for me, I could really relate to the nickname and I adopted it wholeheartedly. No question, I had been born to adventurous parents, and undoubtedly this became an overwhelming influence on my outlook on life and included my love and craving for adventure. Other influences included the fact that as a child I had no hair until the age of three, and this may have developed in me a sensitivity towards my looks at that time. Also, being an only child, led me to be the self-centered, sometimes egotistical and overly optimistic person that I am today.

My parents loved extreme sports even at a time when no one knew what "extreme" meant. They practiced everything from river kayaking to ski touring and rock climbing. They took me along on many of their trips, but I cannot have been the easiest child to handle. I still recall a trip on our little scooter when we went on a picnic. I was about three years old and the minute my parents turned their backs, I approached a line of parked scooters and motorcycles, and pushed one of them over. This caused a domino effect and, before I knew it, about 10 motorcycles and scooters came crashing down. That kind of sums up what kind of a youngster I was.

I was blessed with the greatest grandparents one could have. While my parents worked in Krakow city centre, I grew up under the doting eyes of my maternal grandparents in the outskirts of Krakow, in a little suburb called Prokocim. While my parents worked in the city centre, my paternal grandmother, who lived in central Krakow, would take me for excursions downtown. A real urban experience and an always different treat.

My maternal granddad was an avid sportsman in his own right. He played soccer every weekend and had ridden a Harley-Davidson motorcycle earlier in life. He insisted on teaching me to learn how to ski. I can still recall how I gingerly climbed the little hill just a block away from our house in our little suburb – eagerly sidestepping clumsily upwards and making my first tiny snowplow ski turns.

I still smile to myself when I think of my first ski trips with my parents. These were often to Gubalowka, Zakopane or Bukowina in southern Poland. I started skiing at a very early age around three. I remember my first little skis. They were red and had permanently attached bindings made of leather shaped like water ski boots with straps to ensure a snug fit over kid ski boots.

Unfortunately, I have been told I could be a nasty little boy and hardly ever gave my parents a chance to be alone. I loved it when they took me on these cherished ski trips. I laugh when I recall one particular incident when my parents left me so they could have a few runs on their own. They left me with friends, who placed their skis in front of mine so I would not follow my parents but that did not deter me. I just rode straight across their skis to follow my parents and I caught up with them in no time at all.

I was also quite a bookworm in my youth. From about the age of seven, I swallowed books, without an end in sight. Both my parents and my grandparents greatly encouraged me to read. My grandfather recounted many war stories and had me read a little series of books called the "Tiger Series" from World War II. He was a veteran of two world wars and his stories never seemed to come to an end, as he sat with me before my bedtime and numerous other occasions we were able to enjoy together. Grandfather had been awarded several medals, having fought for Polish independence against the Russians long prior to World War II. He was a warrior and always gave me the inspiration to be one too.

The books I devoured by the volume ranged from Jules Verne to Mark Twain and so many other inspiring adventure travel writers. I just wanted to experience more, to be an explorer, and to have sporting thrills – an ambition which later turned into a lifelong extreme quest of sorts. Even 40 years later, I thoroughly enjoyed a purely adventure-style book which chronicled an incredible trip by a Canadian father and two sons. "Paddle To The Amazon" told the wonderful story of them embarking in a large Canadian First Nations canoe, with the aim of paddling all the way down the Mississippi and then along the entire Mexican and Central American Atlantic coast. One son gave up and withdrew from the expedition in Mexico and flew back to Canada, as he had found the trip was too harsh. But the father and other son continued their way down to Venezuela, up the Orinoco River and then took the Rio Negro connecting with the Amazon which they then took all the way to its mouth and the city of Belen in Brazil. A two year journey.

Few books have instilled the spirit of adventure in me as this one did. Since childhood it was engrossing books and singularly minded people like these that inspired me. As cliched and corny as it sounds – I guess I always wanted to be an "explorer."

I grew up in a very Catholic household, looked after by my maternal grandparents, who were very religious. In contrast, my paternal grandmother, Janka Ziemborak, was not as religious, and was quite cosmopolitan. She loved to socialize in the many popular cafes and restaurants which Krakow had to offer. My mother used to point out that some of my less desirable traits must have been inherited from Janka's side of the family. My Ziemborak grandmother was said to have been great at delegating rather than doing things herself, and my personality supposedly somewhat followed her footsteps. Perhaps, that's where I got my knack for delegating work to others, for organizing kids to do things and, later, for directing films and expeditions as a rebel ringleader from an early age.

Grandma Janka lived in a six centuries-old apartment block situated on one of Krakow's oldest streets, called Florianska. She would sometimes take me to her place on weekends, which I found really great as a child. I would accompany her to one of her favourite pastimes – parties at various cafés and restaurants around Krakow. She would feed me pretzels from the food vendors and, to help me sleep at night, would sometimes give me sips of liquor, wine or beer. Janka had a companion named Kazek, who drove a Russian Moskwicz car rather wildly and cursed a lot at other drivers (which always entertained me!). He often took my grandmother and me for rides in and around the old city. I always had an overly big mouth, so when I recounted my escapades with my Krakow grandma, my more conservative, God-fearing grandparents in the suburbs were often outraged. However, in the end, I knew that all of my grandparents loved me very much and I have fond memories from each and every one of them.

I was even a rebel when attending Sunday school. After class got out a group of us children would have chestnut fights. Once, I made it a point to hit a particular priest in the head with one and he never forgave me for that. Poland was 98% Catholic, and my mother, having been brought up as a devout Catholic, was riddled with guilt, as that's how the church and organized religion always ruled over its victims – with abundant fear and guilt. As things got out of control around the world with the paedophillia scandals, my mother left the church officially, choosing instead to visit its temples just for meditating in a quiet and spiritual place. I had left the church much earlier, due to my dislike of its endless rituals, which I felt were all about control rather than genuine goodness.

For me, organized religion had had its place in medieval times, as did the Bible, but the latter had been rewritten so many times, with so many different agendas along the way, that I felt the necessity for both in my life left me long ago. Gradually over time I would come to believe, out of personal experience and the many accidents I had survived, that there is a God but it is in our hearts and in the universe all around us. I felt we will probably never know the true creator until we die. During one of my accidents on Huaraz, I tumbled into a crevasse, an event which mirrored Joe Simpson's fall in his epic book of survival "Touching the Void". During my own hell I too would feel that I had visited that place we are all headed to – the so called Land of Blue Lights. Joe Simpson, who won a Pulitzer for his story, was one of the main inspirations for me to document my own life.

Anyhow, here is my two cents worth regarding not only Catholicism, but all organized religion as a whole: I have found that when one mixes church and state especially, only disaster and fanatical fundamentalism result. Of all the world religions I think Buddhism, with its "karma" is the nicest and most positive spiritual belief. In other words, "What comes around goes around." Also, I do have to believe in guardian angels. Otherwise how would I still be here?

Life was not easy in Communist Poland in the 1950's and 60's. Poland was still part of the post-World War II Soviet sphere of influence in Eastern Europe. In practical terms this meant that the Soviet Union exercised a smothering degree of control over Poland's politics and economy. The majority of Polish products were diverted to the Soviet Union, thereby causing scarcities in Poland, and this generally restricted Poland's ability to engage in other more profitable trade and help raise the living standard of everyone. Even the most basic foreign goods were in short supply. What I remember most from my childhood was how fruits such as oranges and bananas were rare commodities and their scarcity, although trivial, was depressing. So I was really happy that my father announced that we were to move to Canada in 1965.

My mother was a geologist, and my dad a survey engineer so both had good skills and Canada was keen to have such experts in their fields come to live and work. Father left Poland first and my mother and I followed in his footsteps two years later. We took the Polish ocean liner "Stefan Batory" from Gdansk to Quebec City arriving in 1967. A combination of events and circumstances enabled my father to leave Poland, the most enabling factor having been his receipt of a stipendium or scholarship to enable him to undertake postgraduate studies in Canada at the University of New Brunswick. At this point my father played a ruse that was to have lasting consequences. Because of strict communist rules, my father had sent my mom an official invitation simply to visit him for a brief stay. This was allowed by the authorities and even my mother was tricked, because she was certain that we were to return to Poland and informed her family and friends accordingly. So we travelled with little except what we needed for a short holiday, and we arrived with only a few suitcases. We were astounded when my father announced we were here in Canada to stay. The fact that my mother had been so earnest in telling everyone that we would have gone back to Poland may have helped in convincing the Polish authorities that would be so. As was the way in Poland in those days, there had been backroom deals made by friends of Communist party friends: gifts and dinner invitations were given here and there to clinch a deal to obtain passports for our trip to Canada. My grandmother Janka, who was a Krakow socialite, had a good friend whose son was positioned high up in the Communist party, and she lobbied her son to intercede on behalf of my mother's application to get the passport for us. We had to have pictures taken together for the documents which represented us as one unit. Unfortunately the friend's son who helped get us the passports eventually got in trouble because my mother and I remained in Canada with my father, but my parents never regretted their decision. "He joined the Communist party after all, did he not?"

my mother would always say when referring to the son of grandma Janka's friend.

So we eventually sailed out of Gdansk and briefly stopping in Copenhagen, Denmark, crossed the big Atlantic pond and arrived in Québec City in March after two weeks at sea. There must have been violent waters on the Atlantic that spring because what I remember most of the trip is that the boat stank of vomit. However, I had no problems and tried making new friends, playing and just enjoying the voyage, while everyone was seasick around us.

One thing that was hard about leaving Poland at the early age of eight was that I didn't finish my grade two in primary school due to our winter departure. Also as a child, I really missed all my many friends I had left behind. Getting accustomed to a totally new life in Fredericton, New Brunswick was not going to be easy. On our arrival, I was the only Polish speaking kid in town, and I spoke no English. My parents perceived Fredericton as "The end of the earth". It was the capital of the province of New Brunswick, as well as the home of the University of New Brunswick. At the time, the town had a population 25,000. It is situated in the rather impoverished Maritime or Atlantic provinces of Canada and about an hour's drive from the Atlantic coast. The people were mainly small town folk, with a few snobs who thought they were better than most, and spoke in fake British accents to emphasize their British Loyalist roots. It was a far cry from cosmopolitan Montréal, which was an 800 km drive west, or from the culturally rich Krakow that my parents were used to. At least my father had the opportunity to travel away from the town for his work so it was not that painful for him to live there. Mother initially suffered from the inevitable culture shock after leaving Poland under such unusual circumstances, but eventually they came to love the town and both of my parents made some life-long friends within the University faculty. I found learning English not to be an easy task, so for about three months all I seemed to do was fight with other kids in my new school to make up for my complete lack of language and proper communication. The whole nightmare of being different and not speaking English when I came to Canada probably contributed to my becoming a bit of a freak later. Anyway, I showed off the best I could to my new friends, thus making up for the immigrant complex I surely displayed back then.

On one school outing into the forest the teacher asked all the kids to bring back a little animal. The other children all brought back bugs, frogs, and other little critters. I wanted to outdo everyone else and spotted a raccoon and chased it up a tree. Caught by the tail, it had angrily bit my hand when I brought it back for the teacher to see. The result was panic amongst the teachers and I was rushed off to the hospital for rabies shots. Hey, I certainly did bring back the worthiest trophy. This was just one example of how I tried to impress the other kids to make up for this inability to communicate properly in English. Also, I have a lisp which the other kids made fun of, and this probably also spurred a complex in me. Later in life, I took therapy courses to correct my speech, but even today some so called "friends' make fun of my lisp, imitating my speech when they see me. It seems not only kids can be cruel sometimes.

My father, having arrived in Canada two years earlier experienced some incredible adventures of his own. I was so proud when I heard that he had been invited to join the 1965 Mount Kennedy expedition, organized by the National Geographic Magazine to rename one of the highest peaks in the St. Elias range after President Kennedy. President Kennedy's brother Robert Kennedy had flown in to join the team to do a symbolic climb to the 4,300 metre (14,000 ft) summit. This climb was recorded by Life Magazine and it even made the front cover, which at the time was a worthy accolade.

Coming from Poland with their European cultural background did not make it easy for my parents to adjust to life in conservative Fredericton. It had originally been the heartland of the old Loyalists, ex-Brits who were loyal to the Crown. They had rejected the ideology of the American Revolution and moving north had remained loyal to the British Crown. So many of these Loyalists ended up in what is now the province of New Brunswick and its capital Fredericton. Unlike the Loyalists who can be a bit stuck-up, Polish people are really quite light hearted; they like drinking and partying without too many inhibitions. The men often fraternize and flirt with each other's wives at gatherings, which is behaviour that is considered unacceptable in uptight Fredericton.

Not being aware of Fredericton's conservative characteristics, my parents went through some embarrassing experiences at a couple of parties they hosted for parents of my school mates and had just wanted to get to know them better. The university crowd my parents usually hung out with, and invited to their parties, tended to be European, including Dutch, Spaniards, Germans and other nationalities as such it was more liberal than the Victorian Loyalist-minded locals. Perhaps these people also knew how to handle their liquor better. They simply enjoyed my parents' parties and there were never any fiascos as a result. As the liquor always flowed openly, often the husband from the established Fredericton crowd and father of one of my friends would get drunk and flirt with other women, because the vibe and atmosphere was always loose. This would royally piss off his wife who in turn would often leave early or sit sulking in her car till "hubby" begged for forgiveness – or slept on the couch that night! This happened on more than one occasion that I remember. There was a big gap in social behaviour between Europe and conservative Canada in those days and this was especially true of Fredericton.

My parents started me off skiing as soon as we arrived in Canada. My first memories are of going to a small hill with a single rope tow. Later we started spending our weekends on the local ski hill called Crabbe Mountain. Initially, there were also a two-rope tows which stretched along the mountain's entire 1,000 foot vertical. Although tiny compared to the big mountains I would get to know out west, the hill presented quite a few challenges and had a steep racing trail. Later the rope tows were replaced by a much more modern T-bar.

My skiing friends were mainly the sons of doctors or lawyers but that is not unusual as skiing has always been more of a white-collar sport. As a teenager when I was 16 and 17 old, I was totally taken by freestyle skiing. My friends and I did mountain jumps and other sorts of aerial maneuvers, copying from what we saw in ski magazines and freestyle exhibitions on television. I also took up racing with the Crabbe Mountain Ski Club, and we went on many road trips each weekend to other hills around New Brunswick. I made it to the Provincial level of racing, and the highlight of my career was when I represented New Brunswick at the prestigious Pontiac Cup downhill race at Mont-Sainte-Anne, Quebec. I didn't do so well in the downhill as I had absolutely no experience from just skiing tiny Crabbe Mountain, but it was a great experience and I was happy to have reached that far in my ski racing career. I was never a great team player, but I did take to ski racing, if only for the trips and the partying with friends in motel rooms.

Around that time, the mid-seventies, I read about the extraordinary exploits of Yuichiro Miura, who was The Man Who Skied Down Everest, or rather fell down it with the aid of a parachute. French skiers Patrick Vallencant and Jean-Marc Boivin were also just beginning their careers of extreme skiing descents in the Alps. Then there was Sylvain Saudan, the Swiss skier from Geneva, who was later crowned the true originator or grandfather of extreme skiing. In 1967, he made his first descent down an unnamed couloir from the top of the Rothorn down to the village Arosa (2895 metres), when I was just eight years old and moving to Canada. Before then slopes of 55 degrees were deemed impossible to ski and only fools would risk their lives on such slopes. Little did I know that our paths would cross many years later, and my dreams were to strive for similar adventures. Saudan's skiing was lonely or solitary world as one of the extreme pioneers, and I liked the idea of following his style more than listening to a coach. These skiers skills were self-taught, and their experience acquired the hard way. Mistakes on slopes as steep as these mean certain death. This was real ski mountaineering, and to me it seemed much higher and more prestigious in the ski world food chain.

There was great competition in the extreme skiing world between the huge egos of extreme skiers such as Vallencant, Boivin and Saudan. Saudan was criticized by Vallencant who accused him of not being pure and for taking helicopters or an easy climbing route to reach the top of his first ski descents. But Saudan countered that he was the originator of the sport and thus kept his head high. Two of my friends, Steve Smaridge and Trevor Petersen, sided with Vallencant for the 'pure' way he insisted on climbing all his ski descents first. It made sense as the climber then got a good look at the slope with the exposure and how the snow changed progressively on his way up. On the other hand, the climber was also exposed to the risk of avalanche, rock fall or cornices breaking off above him making for a rather unnerving experience. I have tried to follow Vallencant's example on most of my first descents, although in Alaska we did use a helicopter later on. Sylvain Saudan's last big descent was from the top of Pakistan's Hidden Peak, which is also known as Gasherbrum I and at 8,080 metres is the 11th highest peak in the world. Since that last first descent he has occupied himself by giving motivational talks and lectures. Saudan may have earned some unwarranted criticism for his style of approaches, but unlike Vallencant and Boivin who both perished in accidents, he is still alive and kicking in his '80s, and still skis 80 days a year in Chamonix, France, the world centre of steep skiing.

When I read about the exploits of these daring athletes, I felt that this sport had an irresistible draw for me because all the responsibility was on my head. There was fear, of course but they had proved that you could use and harness this emotion positively.

One time back in my Fredericton days, a really interesting thing happened to me while I was hitchhiking from Québec city to Mont St. Anne for a ski race there. I was picked up by Rene Levesque, a real political celebrity who was driving his own limousine. He was leader of the Quebec Separatist party at the time; I had a very interesting conversation with him. I remember being quite surprised at his comments when he asked me where I was from. I said I was Polish-Canadian. He appeared to bark at me that everybody should say they are Canadian no matter what the country of their origin was. This kind of surprised me at the time. If he was such a Canadian patriot, why was he insisting on having Québec separating from Canada? I never understood some of the Canadian politics that took place back then. Maybe Rene enjoyed talking with and teasing teenage boys but I will never know.

Later, while attending the University of New Brunswick, I was part of the UNB ski team and I have many great memories of skiing with my friends at Crabbe Mountain. Occasionally we would even skip school and ski Fridays at Crabbe with some of my renegade friends. When there was fresh snow, we would seek out the little fresh powder that was around. Our favourite powder run was to ski down the T-bar line when nobody else was skiing it – and this was strictly prohibited. Virtually everywhere skiing the T-bar line was a no no at ski resorts and prohibited by the mountain management. I remember showing off and doing slalom between people on the T-bar race through about a foot of fresh light powder snow.

There were a lot of politics at the ski hill. I feel that I was unfairly punished for being a rebel skier, and perhaps this was why I was failed on my Level I ski instructor's exam. Although I was an enthusiastic athlete in freestyle and ski racing, from an early age I think I just really wanted to ski those slopes untouched by humans. I remember that I would always go off the groomed runs into the forest seeking out the little powder that there was and I remember doing that at the age of seven while skiing in Bukowina, Poland. I would venture off into the woods and come out again at the bottom of the rope tow, giving my parents or guardians a good scare. Later my favourite run at Crabbe Mountain was another little narrow run through the forest out of which one had to traverse back to the lift, called "Tippy Canoe." It was that one silly run which wound and meandered its way off the regular piste, through bushes and trees, over some "whoop-de-doo rollers or uneven terrain, which made me start dreaming of the outback and back country skiing, which I would also read about in ski magazines as a teen years later.

During spring break, my family and I would venture southward across the border into Maine and spend a week skiing Sugarloaf Mountain. The peak was one of the more challenging areas back East. It even had some snowfields above the tree line, which were famous for sometimes harbouring powder. It was a thousand metres high and had close to that in vertical drop, so compared to what I was used to at Crabbe Mountain, it was Himalayan in scale. Later I would do the same trip with friends and because it was located in the state of Maine, which to us was the land of cheap beer and loud American girls, Sugarloaf was a ski resort, then loved by us teenage Canucks ready for anything. We also frequently skied Mont-Sainte-Anne in Québec. My parents were also both good skiers who loved very fast ski groomed runs. As a result, my mother shattered a knee schussing down one of the runs with a friend. She does not ski downhill anymore, because she needed a knee replacement. She still continued with cross-country skiing however despite the old injury, with strong advice from her doctors to be careful.

Of course, all the more affluent kids skiing Crabbe Mountain had the latest state-of-the-art ski equipment. The big craze then featured the then-trendy Head or Hart metal skis, as well as yellow Nordica "banana" ski boots, which were worn with plastic, strap-on spoilers or "jet sticks". These enabled one to sit back on the tails of your skis and wiggle your turns. My parents had to economize, as their salaries were not on par with the lawyers and doctors whose kids I was skiing with. Instead of buying the well-known local brands of skis, they imported our ski gear from Poland. In my opinion my Polish metal skis were just as good as the US-made Heads or Harts. I remember well how the kids made fun of my Polish "Rysy Zakopane" metal skis. Also, instead of the expensive yellow banana Nordicas, my parents bought me yellow San Giorgios, a brand that was far less expensive, and the kids also made fun of those. Kids really can be so cruel to each other, as I experienced firsthand, even at the ski hill in New Brunswick. My parents had really arrived to Canada with nothing. They started with some basic furniture, but I remember my father buying an entire set of The Encyclopedia Britannica which stood on the living room shelf unit as our symbol of being a "literate" family. I pored over and loved these books, the volumes letting my mind drift away to foreign lands and places to seek out new exotic mountain places where one could ski. Otherwise, our home was sparsely furnished but my mother always had a knack of making our home look nice and came up with some very innovative ideas. She would put up an empty picture frame on the wood paneled wall and fill it by gluing colorful stamps and coins from different countries. She also took up pottery courses and learned how to carve Eskimo-like carvings which were soon adorning our home. In short, mother was a fountain of creativity.

Renovating our basement, my parents built a little suite downstairs with a bar. They made a couple of couches and turned them into beds for visitors to sleep on. Soon it became my den of immorality where I would hold mixed parties. My grandparents visited us one year and my grandfather, who was always also a real workaholic, helped us finish the renovation to the downstairs suite. I was very interested in chemistry then, and to my utter joy, my granddad also built me a beautiful chemistry lab in the basement. There I occupied myself for days, especially before Halloween. Being the natural rebel kid, I always made a lot of bombs which I would detonate at night, while other kids just went trick-or-treating. As I grew older the basement served a different purpose, and I remember that I had big cardboard boxes set up under the ping-pong table to where, as far back as Grade Six, I would try to lure girls for some kissing and touching. I guess my male hormones had already kicked in by the time I was 12 or 13 and in grade six. Now, looking back on those frolics I realize these were mostly done because of my yearning to be accepted by the local kids, and this often came with outlandish stunts.

Summertime, from youth into my early teens, were spent at my Aunt Danuta's get-away cottage which was not far from Joliettte, Québec. While my mother and I would stay with my aunt at the cottage, my Uncle Franek ran a television repair business in Montréal. He would come out to the cottage on weekends and meticulously work on the garden and property around the small house. He always brought home some great Polish food like sausage and cold cuts from a real Polish deli in the city. Although my aunt and he never had kids, he loved children and often helped to organize games and other activities to entertain me and other kids from nearby cottages. Every year he bought a bunch of corn and threw a huge corn boil for all the kids and parents who would come by. Franek had a huge heart for all the kids and they often came by just to hear his stories.

My cousins John and Stephen Hayto spent their summers at a nearby cottage which belonged to their parents Marceli and Alina. John and Steve, being about five years older than I, had a small rock'n'roll band and they would hold parties with their friends from Montréal on weekends. They were in their late teens and were naturally a bit elitist, and didn't really want us younger kids hanging around. I fondly remember one Christmas when John gave me my first record album, Santana's Evil Ways – the black and white one with all the faces on it. Santana became one of my favourite bands and I think Carlos Santana is just an amazing musician. His music has passed through so many phases and he continues to innovate, producing a hit single in every decade since the sixties. That Latin beat mixed with his mesmerizing guitar solos had me a diehard Santana fan right from the start.

I have seen Santana play live twice: once as a high school student when I caught a bus ride with some older kids from the local University to a Santana concert at a high school in Moncton, New Brunswick of all places. Twenty years later and I saw Santana playing in Vancouver at the Orpheum theatre, and the music sounded just as good.

Years later I even tried to get the rights to use Santana's music in one of my films about Mount Robson, the mountain which would become such a big part of my life. The music had stayed in my head and I wanted to use what I thought was the perfect song, "She's Not There", for a section about when the mountain's north face was not ready to ski. I have always played certain songs in my head as I have skied those steep slopes and "She's Not There" was one. It was a great way to get psyched with its powerful lyrics like and till now the song has so much meaning to me in terms of women and mountains.

I wanted to use the song in my film, so through a North Face company contact, I met Santana's band manager from San Francisco and he gave me the okay to use the song. I even had breakfast with Carlos and the band when they played in Vancouver. We actually edited a version of the film synced to Santana music. We were so sure that we had the music rights. Unfortunately, wires must have got crossed somewhere, and record company lawyers in Los Angeles wanted $5,000 just to talk. We had nowhere near that sort of budget, so we had to change the soundtrack and have local musicians like Tad Campbell and Idle Eyes come onboard. They were able to "Santanitize" their own tunes beautifully to the picture.

Back to my fond memories of summers at the cottage. Every year in June when school ended, we would pack up the car and make the long ten-hour drive to Montréal and then on to Lac Cloutier near Joliette. There I spent many very happy summers surrounded by the Polish community of friends who gathered each year, bringing together a lot of kids of all ages. Letting our imaginations run wild, we played Batman and Robin and many other pirate games. It was a wonderful childhood, being surrounded by friends who came from all over Montréal and other places, and they were all children of Polish parents who had moved to Canada as we had. It was a nice break for me from Anglophone Fredericton. I was still Polish at heart and really enjoyed the company and being able to talk with my friends in Polish which was still easier than using English.

Most of the kids could speak Polish even though they had been born in Canada. I became the ringleader in building tree houses and doing other more dangerous things, so much so that many parents were a bit afraid of having their kids hang out with me, and complained to my mother. I guess in a way that was my real start at being so adventurous, which later came to be called extreme. I built what turned out to be rather dangerous tree forts, and as a result a couple of kids fell off, with one breaking his back and another cracked her arm. Ryszard had to wear a cast-like corset on his back for a while but luckily had no long-lasting effects. As I was the ringleader I was blamed for everything by their parents. We were maybe not the greatest builders, and the platforms sometimes just buckled under too much weight. Nobody ever pushed anyone off, the platforms just sort of "broke". So from then on we limited ourselves to less dangerous Batman and Robin games and let our young imagination wander into many interesting situations. The kids really took their new role models seriously and mimicked the characters so well from the Batman TV show. I remember one of the kids, Marysia Rytel, hissing just like the Cat Woman.

Scaring my aunt was another favourite pastime of mine as I climbed all the highest trees, regularly giving her heart attacks as I yelled at her from the treetops while she was sun-tanning on the beach. I am a bit ashamed to say I basically terrorized the whole lake shore, and soon the other parents had had enough and tried to stop their kids playing with me. Later, in my teens, I have so many pleasant memories of stealing my first kisses with girls at that lake. Sometimes I wish that I had pursued some of these girls more vigorously but as the summer ended, so did our puppy love affairs.

I still think Polish women are some of the greatest partners to have on earth. They are individualistic and well-educated, yet also have a nice traditional side and usually love to cook great food. I don't think I am much of a chauvinist, but I think some roles come more naturally to both women and men. Simple biology is the reason for this and that's all there is to it.

The Polish community at Lac Cloutier included some very liberal minded people. Every weekend the parents would get together and play volleyball behind Marceli's house. I remember many wild parties that the parents would attend, which would end up with everybody skinny-dipping in the lake together. God knows what else happened on such nights as the vodka flowed freely but partying was just one part of our good Polish heritage, and the liveliness of our community at the lake just proved that.

It's funny how communities that are so dear to you in your youth can drift apart later on in your life. As a child I thought the friendships from our lake would be forever, and I assumed the same was true for the friends I made there. Much later, when I was living in Vancouver, a few of those youngsters, now adults, had moved there as well. One whom I had been so close that he was almost like a younger brother to me, had moved from Montréal and now worked for a big ad agency. I tried staying in touch with him as our work could have crossed paths several times, but that bond from childhood and those cottage years was just not there anymore. We tried getting together a couple of times but it just was not the same. Tragically, Alex later died in a boating accident, drowning just offshore near Vancouver.

Another friend who built many tree forts with me was Ryszard (Richard). He ended up working in tech at Microsoft and then Facebook in Seattle. Richard and I were the original Batman and Robin team, and the our Cat Woman was Marysia Rytel. Although I often tried reaching out to Richard in Vancouver, there seemed to be a coldness between us. Perhaps this was because I had chosen such a different path from his in my life, or maybe he still held a grudge from our cottage days tree incident and his back injury. Richard had taken a very different route to mine in working for the high tech mega corporations, and so his outlook on life is different to mine.

Another friend from the Lac Cloutier days also moved to Vancouver and eventually became a lawyer working in the corporate world. Chris and I stay in touch as often as we can, as he is an avid outdoors-man himself. He is about 10 years younger than me and he and his wife recently had a baby. We still have fond memories from our times at the lake, and sometimes, I go to him for legal advice. His mother Olenka, who was always great friends with my mother, recently made the move to Vancouver. My mother says that whenever I have one of my accidents, she has often confided in Olenka, who just reassures her that I was always "just different."

There was a large Polish population in Montréal and Toronto in the '60s and '70s, and many of them have subsequently moved west to Vancouver. The city has a more moderate climate than those in the east with warmer winters and cooler, less humid summers. Those that love the outdoors will always enjoy Vancouver's location more than the east because the mountains are closer and much bigger. The skiing is world class and BC still has that "wild west" feel about it. Once you have driven past Whistler, you really touching true wilderness. Beyond Pemberton, there are only wild mountains, lakes and rivers snaking through uninhabited canyons and valleys.

Many Polish people moved here for just that, the overwhelming nature they had read about in books and what they had heard from others who had visited the province of British Columbia. Some, like my friend the Polish Himalayan climber Ryszard Szafirski, fell utterly in love with Canada's wilderness, and have bought land at Bralorne, which is an old deserted gold mining town which still has the charm of the old gold rush days.

So different than the safe cottage country around Montréal.

Those times at Lac Cloutier may also have been the start of my habit of always trying to rally friends together to go for some crazy expedition. Unfortunately, my screening system for getting people on-board was not always as good as it should have been, and I have sometimes chosen what turned out to be the wrong people for some of these trips. For some reason I have sometimes had a hard time saying no to people who on reflection, should never have been with me in the first place.

One of my cousins from the Lac Cloutier crowd, Steve Hayto, moved from Montréal to West Vancouver. West Vancouver has the most valuable real-estate in Vancouver, supposedly for its original British heritage. We always made fun of the area as being full of snobs who spoke in fake British accents – or so we thought. In over 30 years I've only been invited to Steve's house once, although we were still the closest family as far as blood ties went. Moreover, I never did get an invitation to the wedding of either of his two sons. This has always puzzled me. I didn't really know his kids and we would meet only once at Christmas dinner at my other cousin John's. Perhaps I should look inward in as much as I should have made more of an effort to befriend and get to know Steve better.

I just found it rather cold and distant behaviour, since our extended family really was so small. It consisted of John and Steve Hayto, the sons of Marcel, who was the brother of my father's mother. Stephen was always more reserved and we never really did get to know each other well. John on the other hand was very outgoing, loved to socialize and womanize in his youth as did I. On several occasions in Montréal, Whistler and even back home in our native Poland we would meet women, date them, and then pass their contact info to each other so we could both benefit from the sexual encounters later, taking our turns with girls. This went on until John settled down, got married and moved to Vancouver from Montréal and had three great sons. At that point our lives diverted and his frolicking ended. I assume I gravitated to John and Steve when I was younger, not having any brothers myself.

John has always been a true friend and also a great family man, often hosting fine dinners and somehow trying to bring the little of the family we had together back east at Christmas, and other occasions. He was really the only strong link, the glue holding our small clan together. Later in life he has battled successfully against cancer. I love him dearly and appreciate him for who he is, despite the fact he loves to shop at pricey Holt Renfrew and spends far too much money on what I think are ridiculously trivial things.

At one time John was a corporate man with a high end sales job selling fibre optic cable to some of the world's major telcos. On the other hand, I was always much more of a leftist rebel, and we have often clashed over this. He made sure his kids Matthew, Sebastian and Justin, went to the best schools like McGill in Montréal and Columbia in New York City. To my mind he has trained them to be corporate slaves, but that's just me. Sure they have money that enables them to fly around the world any weekend, but they really have too little time to spend this hard-earned cash. In my eyes they have joined the ranks of a meaningless consumer culture. But really who am I to say or to judge in the end? Everyone chooses their own bed that he makes for himself. His sons were deemed successful, making piles of money, travelling and partying during the little holidays they had and I think they kind of looked curiously on me with my unconventional lifestyle. The only chance they had for taking time off from work was between jobs, which sometimes could be terminated rapidly as there would be a transition period before they would find another one. John's boys are actually doing really well, and they are obviously good at their jobs because they do seem to manage to take time off and the companies they work for keep them employed.

I think John's three sons always thought of me as "crazy Uncle Peter who never grew up." John's wife Cindy also took a long time to warm to me. She is a very strong woman, a physiotherapist, and she is constantly practising sports like biking or sea kayaking. She has even entered triathlons, which are very modern events which really are designed for super athletes. John skied and biked, but also likes his lavish dinners and wine tasting evenings, for which I always made gentle fun of him. I often had radical remarks and always was quite controversial at the dinner table saying things like "jihad"? instead of "grace"? as my religious views were not as traditional as theirs. This was just my twisted sense of humour coming out in the open.

I have never been interested in having the latest and greatest skis. My attitude is the same with other consumer goods. I was happy with my old Kmart Lloyds stereo system, rather than the latest Sony or Pioneer hi-fi's which were considered the good shit back then. Many of my friends in Fredericton thought it important that they had bought their own cars, or their parents gave them hand-me-down vehicles. I on the other hand saved all my resources for travel and necessities like camping and mountaineering gear. I also came to realize that having time for adventure is the greatest resource that anyone can have.

I never grew out of childhood dreams of exploration to exotic lands. Old "Crazy Uncle Peter" would lay awake in bed at night with my thoughts carrying me away to those wild places which were still virgin lands for adventure and exploration.

One of these places in my dreams was Colombia's Sierra Nevada de Santa Marta, which I had discovered at age 12 in a 1970 edition of the National Geographic magazine, and also in a cherished book mine called "Secret Corners of The World". It seemed like such an untouched and mysterious place, with its jungles which came down to the sea on the northern Caribbean coast, all the way up to its towering 6,000 metre peaks perched only 30 km from the seashores.

The area was inhabited by the reclusive Kogi natives, who had avoided extinction at the hands of the Spanish and the Catholic Church. The customs and ways of their ancient culture had remained more or less intact. The area always presented itself as a Utopian place; a unique Shangri-La which might have come out of something like the movie Avatar, that at the time I could only dream of visiting. The inhabitants and the geography held a great allure to my young self and I knew would get there sometime in the future.

Such daydreams made me stray from activities which occupied most regular kids like playing too much pinball at the mall. The siren song of the jungles and mountains always seemingly called out to me instead.

These days people often ask me what makes me tick, what drives me? They also think that I should just relax, chill and give my mind a rest.

I cannot analyze too much about what I do or why I do it. I'm a project-driven guy, who has been undoubtedly influenced by my upbringing and education. Apparently I was somewhat hyperactive as a child from a young age, and being an immigrant made me stick out from the others. I was also forced to learn English at a later age which was not easy. These minor things alone probably have given me some complexes, but what the actual causes are is hard to discover.

I have had love all around me from my parents and grandparents from day one, so a lack of love and affection cannot be the source of my issues. To my surprise my mother still blames their divorce for the cause of me becoming an extreme freak.

Something I read which was crucial to my attitudes towards danger which I found fascinating came from some really interesting work from psychologist Dr Frank Farley. Dr Farley's research divided risk takers into two categories big T's and little T's. The Big T's were the risk takers, the entrepreneurs, the explorers etc.

I believe Big T's would probably find routine unbearable. If they can't push the envelope or try something new, they may end up frustrated and miserable. For them, fulfillment is about taking on the next big challenge and beating it. And each time their risk-taking is rewarded, they may seek out another opportunity to stretch the limits. Big T's aren't dissuaded by bad odds. She'll climb Mount Everest fully aware that many people have died making the ascent. Meanwhile, the Small T finds most risk unacceptably stressful. He may become anxious when the expected sequence of events is disturbed. He'll do his best to avoid change and look for situations where things are reliable and knowable.

Dr Frank Farley

I guess I was a Big T in Dr Farley's eyes. It is often said that the first ten years of a child's life are the most important. Through that filter my first ten years were just fine, a happy childhood. However, my parents divorced when I was 18 and my dad left home. This must have had an impact on me, although I was such a self-centred teenager at the time I kind of doubt it, because I don't remember feeling any of the mixed up emotions so many people say that had from their parents break-up.

In general, I think that I was just one of these project-driven people from the start. Maybe a bit of a feeling of guilt influences me as well. I always felt guilty to be just sitting around rather than doing something constructive. That may have come from my mother's side, the Catholic side that ruled the world by guilt, and with phrases like "idle hands are the devils work".

Later in life I found I could never just go on a holiday. To my mind it had to be a working "expedition", with a film being made or a festival or some sort of an event being attended or even created. This seems to give me a "raison d'etre" and gets me up to face each new day.

I don't think I could ever just exist by living a life of merely consuming. From early childhood I was the ringleader and therefore the chief troublemaker. I found I was always organizing kids into some kind of roles to play in a game rather than just going with the flow of the moment. Anyhow, this will be the extent of exploring my philosophy as to why I became the type of person that I am. Maybe just by writing these memoirs I will slowly reveal my true personality. To myself if no-one else.

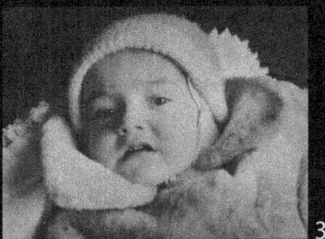

My family

1. Grandfather (1901 – 1978) Veteran of two world wars.
2. My parents, Adam and Maria (Nina) Chrzanowski. Zakopane, 1960's.
3. Peter as a baby.
4. First steps on skis surrounded by family, early 1960's.

My childhood in Poland

1. With my friend, to this day, Dominika, enjoying local folklore in Zakopane, early 1960's.
2. From a young age I wanted to fly.
3. My mother, showing off her technique. Crabbe Mtn. NB, Canada.

CHAPTER 1

MY PRE-EXTREME 1970's

I am inclined to think that the most important event in my life came in the summer of 1972, when my parents decided to visit South America for an entire year. I remember my father lining up lecturing jobs in both Brazil and Argentina.

The University granted sabbaticals to professors every eight years and they received a year's paid leave to do research or lecture in another country. But instead of doing what everyone else did, and fly direct to their chosen locations like most mere mortals would have done, my father cashed in the plane tickets and bought a Volkswagen camper van with the proceeds. He then informed us that we would be driving all the way down to the bottom of the continent!

It was a very brave decision to say the least. We went to Canadian Tire, the popular Canadian outdoor supply store, and bought all our camping supplies and outfitted the camper with whatever necessities we thought were needed. We said goodbye to all our friends and before we knew it, started driving through the length of the USA, Mexico and Central America towards Panama.

Once there we still had the problem of how to cross the dreaded Darien Gap, which is a notorious 66 mile section of the route between

Panama and Colombia. The Gap has no road – just treacherous mountainous jungle, and swamp and is really impassable. Overland travellers usually have to detour around it by ship, and this is what we did on board an Italian cruise liner, which would take us and our camper from Panama City. This way we would bypass Colombia and get directly to our next destination, which was Lima, the capital city of Peru.

We had kind of raced through Mexico and the rest of Central America, as we were trying to keep to a deadline to get to Dad's job in Brazil. The only problem then was that we had no knowledge of how long the wait for a ship in Panama would be.

I was 14 years old at this time. Being a teenager it was hard at first to leave all my friends behind even if it was only for a year. However, soon the spirit of adventure took over my worries and I became entranced by everything about the whole journey. I occupied myself by reading the South American Handbook and finding interesting places for us to stop along the way. In many ways my imagination from reading all these travel classics as a child finally had a chance to be expanded here by these exotic lands. I even managed to get an article published in the Fredericton Daily Gleaner, the local newspaper with a story covering the various culinary aspects of South America! So here I was, 14 years old and already a published author.

What an incredible adventure the whole trip turned out to be for me! I don't think my parents nor I fully realized what we were getting ourselves into. It was a timeless period in South America, before the modern era. In Peru much of the countryside didn't seem to have changed much over thousands of years.

To get on our way to Brazil we chose to drive Peru's central highway, which at the time was little more than a mule track on a one-lane muddy road. One had to honk the horn during the day as a warning to oncoming traffic, or flick the high beams on at night. Often the only places for converging vehicles to pass each other was on the wider curves that were carved into the steep slopes of the Andes.

The narrow track slowly wound its way through the Andes from Huaraz towards up to Cuzco. At this time, in the early '70's, people didn't do these long road trips and we would rarely meet other travellers doing a similar journey, and of course when we did meet they were in similar VW camper vans.

We arrived in Chile in late summer 1972 just as a revolution had happened. There had recently been a change of government, and Salvador Allende, the first democratically elected Marxist president had recently taken over.

Most of Chile's industries had been nationalized by Allende, so the US responded by applying economic sanctions. Unfortunately, while the revolution was initially successful, Allende's reforms had not been sustainable and this had led the country into an acute recession, with general chaos, runaway inflation and the flight of foreign investment. The situation reminded me a bit of growing up in Communist Poland – the black market, the line ups for daily necessities and the empty supermarket shelves.

Inevitably, I would see much of the same repeated later in Castro's Cuba.

However, my family was well versed in operating in such a broken system and we were able take advantage of its foibles. Specifically the black market exchange rate for our dollar was highly beneficial to us. My father clandestinely changed our American dollars in a Santiago hotel elevator, in order to get a better exchange rate. The 'elevator exchange' rate certainly turned out to be a much better deal. In the bank one only got 23 escudos for a dollar, but on the black market the rate was 800 for that same dollar. We felt like we had won the lottery.

To celebrate our financial victory we rewarded ourselves with a side-trip. We drove the long winding road up into the Andes all the way up to the base of Aconcagua, the highest mountain in the Western Hemisphere at 23,000 feet. It was home to South America's most famous ski resort, Portillo. We could never have afforded this vacation on the regular government exchange rate, but due to our black-market deal we had plenty of escudos to enjoy the comforts of a five star hotel. It made a nice change from camping. But here we were living it up at Portillo, while Chile was crumbling around us, and I think we felt a bit guilty about our good fortune.

In retrospect I am quite sorry about what eventually happened to Salvador Allende, the president of Chile at the time. It was the interests of Canadian and US mining companies, with the help of the CIA helped install the fascist Pinochet, the incoming dictator who attacked the presidential palace with Allende inside, eventually killing him.

Canada is viewed by many as a neutral power, rather like Sweden or Norway, but the big Canadian mining companies are as evil as any countries. I might add they are not really Canadian companies with Canadian owners, but are multinationals with offices in Canada, but who operate so ruthlessly in foreign lands.

Maybe Allende just did things too fast with his action of nationalizing all the foreign mining interests as soon as he was elected. This was not on and he was quickly ousted. Of course, what followed was much worse than the nationalization of a few companies: the economy did improve, but Pinochet murdered so many thousands of his opponents, who were students, and they were buried in mass graves in the Atacama Desert. Many years later I was in the area on a paragliding trip and the burial sites were pointed out to me around the town of Pisagua in Northern Chile. It's an eerie place full of evil, with so many thousands of unmarked graves lying there undisturbed.

Long lines at stores for common household goods were common, and the empty shelves were a chilling reminder to us of our life in post-Stalinist Poland, with memories of the scarcity still so vivid to me. A banana was a rare treat back then, and I remember with my grandfather slicing me sections with his pocketknife and giving me the last mouthfuls of the treat.

In contrast to the difficulties of the locals we lived in the height of luxury at the ski resort, with five fabulous meals each day and high-end ski rentals. For ten dollars a day, we enjoyed a warm outdoor swimming pool, surrounded by huge snowdrifts and lift tickets for our whole family. The skiing was also the best I had ever encountered being used to our eastern Canadian skiing up till then.

We were below the equator, so it was now winter in South America. The regular road and border crossing between Chile and our next destination Argentina, went over a high mountain pass that was closed in winter and thus was impassable. Being the crazy risk taker that he always was, my dad decided to drive straight through the 17 km railway tunnel, which at that time was the longest railway tunnel in the world.

This proved to be the only way to cross the border and we had to believe that we could rely on information from the military which allowed us to travel like that. It turned out that this was the regular drill in winter. First checking that no train was coming, we were waved through. It certainly was a crazy thing to do as we clunked over the railway ties that were engineered to take one way auto traffic. Somehow we reached the other side without disaster, and crossed the border into Argentina.

We had to hurry across Argentina because my father had a start date by which he had to be in Brazil. He had been invited to give lectures in the new Brasilia city, the country's capital. So we rushed across Argentina, and then Paraguay, which was probably the poorest and most desolate of the countries we visited. The craziest ferry I was ever on crossed the Asuncion River. It was a big wooden barge powered by a little outboard motor and attached to a cable. The cable drifted, the motor sputtered awkwardly with so little power that we barely made it across the river alive with our van.

Even though we were in a hurry, we still took the time for a side trip and visited the Iguazu Falls. They are spectacular, and although they look smaller than Niagra Falls in Canada, their cataracts numbered in the hundreds and actually looked a lot bigger. As we left Paraguay and crossed into southern Brazil we were charmed by some little blond haired kids selling strawberries by the roadside. When we stopped we were staggered to discover they spoke Polish. Surprisingly, this cooler more temperate part of the country had attracted a number of Polish and Ukrainian immigrants.

We breezed through São Paulo, the fastest growing metropolis in the world at that time with a new building completed every 8 minutes. Of course we also had to see Rio de Janeiro, heralded to be the most beautiful city in the world, or so it was described in the South American handbook that I was devouring every day and finding interesting landmarks to visit like Sugarloaf Mountain and the statue of Christ.

We finally made it to Brasilia which became the capital in 1960. To me it resembled a base on Mars. The Brazilian president at the time had decided to move the entire capital from Rio de Janeiro to the centre of the country, reckoning it would be a smart thing to do by giving the capital more geographical influence on the entire country. Few of the diplomats who were posted there enjoyed the move from vibrant Rio de Janeiro into this Martian-like desert. The barren landscape stretched for miles around in every direction. An ultra-modern city, had been designed and stuck right in the middle. The diplomats unfortunately had no choice in the matter, having been ordered by their governments to move to the new capital. I think they must have been sad to leave the fabulous beaches of Rio with its cosmopolitan ambience to move to this rather sterile city.

While my dad began to give his lectures at The University of Brasilia, my mother got busy preparing our apartment to be more liveable. Unwanted house guests presented an early challenge and we were attacked by an infestation of cockroaches which came up the garbage chute from the basement of the high rise. It really was like a horror movie with hundreds of cockroaches pouring out of the garbage into the kitchen like that.

From my cockroach infested home, I attended a diplomatic school full of spoiled little rich kids. We were taught in English, but I also managed to start learning Brazilian Portuguese there. It turned out to be a fun four month stay. A 14-year-old, horny teenage boy, meeting many beautiful young girls at school and going to extravagant diplomats' kids' parties. All in all, I ended up having a rather grand old time.

On weekends my parents would take me canyoning, only an hour drive away. Climbing up sheer cliffs, diving into swirling waterfalls and generally giving my parents a good scare, as usual.

I was now close to being able to speak Portuguese, but unfortunately our four-month stay was coming to an end. I figured I just needed a few more weeks to master the language, but we now had to move back to Argentina where my dad had further lectures planned.

Before leaving Brazil we had time for one last trip into the Amazon jungle. My dad had heard from his friends at the university about an incredible river. Situated between Brasilia and the Andes the Araguaya river flowed North into the Amazon. On further research, Dad had read about a fishing camp on the river, and his colleagues highly recommended it.

So, pulling off another one of his surprises, he loaded us up into the van again and we headed westward through deserts, plains and forests and after several days we arrived at a rustic camp.

We spent a week fishing by the side of the Araguaya. We watched the camp caretakers bring home a huge species of fish called Piraruku. They were massive at two meters long and weighing up to 100 kg. Sometimes they even managed to land a freshwater alligator. My exploring spirit seemed to really came alive there.

We heard a strange story there about a young child that had lived at the camp. At the age of eight he had gotten lost in the jungle and spent three months alone living off wild watermelons the whole time before he was found and brought back to the fishing camp. I had always felt so nourished and fulfilled after eating watermelons, and now here was proof that you could actually survive off them.

As we approached Brasilia on our return leg we had our one and only mishap of the entire trip. Climatically, when it gets windy the red clay soil around the city gets blown onto the highways. Then a little bit of rain can create a very slick road surface that is as slippery as ice. We had witnessed many crashes already but during the night our VW went into a four-wheel drift which took us off the road and plunged us sideways into a ditch. It turned out that there was not a lot of damage, but I remember being devastated by the crash. I thought the van could never be repaired properly and we would be unable to continue our trip further south to Tierra del Fuego. Luckily, my disappointment was short lived thanks to some great bodywork by a local garage which patched up the VW and make it roadworthy again.

After my father terminated his lectures and I finished my schooling, we piled into the micro-bus and headed south through Uruguay. It was here we spent a lavish 1973 New Year's Eve in the Punta del Estes beaches and the luxurious San Cristobal hotel.

Argentina is rightly famous for its meat, and I can say with certainty that the best steak I ever tasted was at the La Cabana restaurant in Buenos Aires.

Other memories from this time include the delight I experienced upon catching my first freshwater salmon in Lago Argentino, using a hook and line on a spool made from a tin can.

While in the mountain town of Bariloche we managed many great treks and hikes, including one to a dormant snowy volcano named Tronador. Here I donned some plastic skis and made a few brief turns.

Bariloche is better known as a ski destination, but we were here now in the summer.

Because of the mountainous terrain and other similarities, many Swiss and Germans moved there over the years as it reminded them so strongly of the Alps.

To complete the image, there are local chocolate factories, just like Switzerland, and there is even a whole sweater industry, which is highly profitable.

We continued south on our journey through Argentina and towards Patagonia, across the vast expanse of the Argentinian Pampas. The road was gravel all the way with only a few exceptions for tarmac. A rock managed to lodge itself between the windshield and the protective wire mesh and cracked the windshield. We therefore continued on to Patagonia with a handmade plastic and wooden windshield contraption, made by a local carpenter as it proved impossible to get a windshield for a 72 Volkswagen van, which was one of the modern one-piece design. All the VW vans that were in South America at that time still had the funky old divided windshields, so we were out of luck.

After crossing the Straits of Magellan by a short ferry ride we finally reached the town of Ushuaia. Nicknamed „The End of the World," Ushuaia is the southernmost city in the world, and also has become the gateway to Antarctica cruises.

After a couple of days spent contemplating our position in the world, we turned back: The only way from here was north.

The next place my dad had scheduled to lecture at was the university at Tucuman in Northwestern Argentina. Situated next to the Eastern foothills of the Andes, it was a very green place and an agricultural land with its fair share of cattle ranches and horses. It had the wildness of rain forests beginning to stretch up the ravines and valleys that were the beginnings of the „spine" of South America rising out of the flat expanse of the regular farm fields.

Here I was due to unroll in the junior high school for a short while. My parents did try to keep my formal education going while we were on this trip, but this high school turned out to be a joke. Out of the four months I was supposed to attend I actually was there for about three weeks. This was not because I was playing truant, but there was always somebody on strike. First it was the teachers, then the school bus drivers, then the regular transit system. Finally, to top it all off the students had one last strike of their own.

At that time strikes seemed to be almost a standard ritual of Argentinian life in which everyone participated. However, I was about to take part in an entirely different ritual of my own that was new to a horny but sex deprived teenage boy from New Brunswick. When a boy turns 15 in Argentina, his classmates chip in and take him to the local whore house so he can learn the true facts of life. It certainly was an exciting moment in my life, as up to that moment the closest I had gotten to sex was seeing my mother in the shower, or sneaking a look at my dad's collection of Playboy magazines. Prostitution was legal in Argentina and all the girls were regularly checked by doctors. It was an experience I remember to this very day, although I was extremely nervous at the time.

I have other very fond memories of Tucuman too. I spent a lot of time outdoors catching semi-wild horses which were left to graze on their own. I remember I would climb a tree and other kids would shoo the horse under my tree. I would drop down on to the horses bareback, only to be thrown off nine times out of ten. In hindsight, it is yet another miracle that I didn't get hurt seriously or break any bones.

Our nights in Tucuman were full of parties and we ate at Argentinian parilladas, which were the most amazing barbecues. Whole families attended and the food was never ending. It was so different in Tucuman to back home in Fredericton. In Canada teenagers tended to distance themselves from their parents and families, thinking it was not cool to have the latter attend their gatherings. In Argentina and most of Latin America everybody from toddlers to grandparents attends these frequent barbecue fiestas.

I had a chat with an older lady named Celia at a cafe in Tucuman. Later on, I was told by locals that Celia was Che Guevara's sister. I didn't know that much about Che's history as a 15 year old. All I knew was that his likeness was posted all along our marathon route though. I knew from the locals he was some sort of revolutionary who was highly respected here. I even wore a beret proudly imitating his style.

When I learned that his exploits around Latin America had turned him into a legend, I would of course also boast about the encounter to my friends.

This chance encounter with Che's sister turned out to be especially helpful years later on my visits to Cuba, when I would mention my meeting with Celia in order to impress the ladies. Her brother, so iconic for his exploits with Castro during the Cuban revolution, is now regarded by many as a complete psychopath but back then he was considered a hero by liberals around the world.

Although I had only gone to school for three weeks out of the four months, my teachers in Tucuman wrote me a nice letter saying I attended for the entire stay. I used this letter to help me skip grade 9 when I returned to Fredericton, and I went straight into grade 10. I did feel I deserved it, even though I had taken most of the year off „school." After all, I told myself, I had mastered the Spanish language, and effectively had earned a masters in geography because my travels, with 14 months on the road must have equalled a thousand field trips at a normal school!

We packed up the Volkswagen van in Tucuman and continued our journey north to Bolivia.

As we approached the Bolivian border at a river near Salta Argentina my dad asked me to jump on a passing bus and cross to the other side. He wanted me to film him driving the VW through the river for posterity on his Super 8 movie camera. I almost dropped the camera as my dad dived in to the channel without hesitation. Unfortunately he had chosen the deepest dip in the river, and I watched in shock as our van sank into the water right up to the windshield. Too shocked by events I had forgotten my cameraman role and failed as a filmmaker. I missed my dad's heroic struggles as he somehow managed to power the VW bus out of the deep current and onto the other side of the river.

The engine, which had been so reliable until now, did not entirely survive the sudden immersion in the glacial creek. The head gasket certainly did not like it, and failed shortly afterwards. With no way to fix it on the road, we were towed by a truck up the final kilometres of that windy road to the top of the Andes, only to be let loose to roll down the other side, coasting the whole way with very limited brakes.

We managed to get to a remote Bolivian village where our van was manhandled onto a train, on which we spent the next three days travelling all the way to La Paz. We spent the entire time in our van which made it a scary journey. The wires which kept the van held down on the open wagon would work loose, and we would have to crawl out regularly on to the platform even in the dark to tighten them again, all while the train was in motion. Now that was extreme!

The train finally came to a halt above the city of La Paz, the capital city of Bolivia. Here we unloaded the van amidst an unpleasant stench from what turned out to be the local garbage dump and public toilets. We were on the Altiplano high above the outskirts of city. We rumbled down the slope gently and the head gasket was eventually fixed in small garage in La Paz.

We continued our journey driving northwards through Peru. The engine gasket blew up again while we were on the coastal Pan-American highway, so our repair by the mechanic in La Paz hadn't lasted long. However, we managed to put the van up on the back of a larger truck and hitch a ride to a VW dealer and mechanic in Lima, where a factory gasket was installed. We weren't the only cargo, as a dump truck pulled up beside us and had poured masses of wrapped candies around our van. I got so sick eating all those candies while waiting.

Another problem with fixing our 1972 Volkswagen camper van in South America as a whole was that the 1972 model Volkswagens had an entirely updated engine and now had two carburetors. Mechanics in South America were only familiar with the older one-carburetor models, so even when we could find a mechanic to work on our engine they were not be familiar with it. Somewhat ironic given that Volkswagen had a factory producing cars in Brazil, but of course those were the one carb versions.

The Volkswagen office in Lima had the same problem. So the owner of the dealership, who was originally from Germany, took on the job himself. He seemed to enjoy the break from running the office as he rolled up his white shirt sleeves, to personally make sure that our engine was repaired properly. He worked long in to the night after the dealership had closed for the day, to make sure that our camper was ready for the long journey northward to Venezuela. "A good Nazi, isn't he?"

my dad would say, as my parents jokingly suggested that maybe the fellow was indeed an actual escaped soldier. In fact his work was very methodical but there were many stories of notorious Nazis escaping to South America after World War II.

Dad's comments came from the feeling held by all Poles about the brutal treatment of Poland historically by both Germany and Russia. Polish people have always had a chip on their shoulder about this. My grandfather's take on this was his story about how at least when the Nazis came to the house at five in the morning, they would always knock. In contrast, during their "liberation" of Poland the Russian brutes would just smash through the doors without any manners at all. Yes, he said, at least the Germans had some manners!

With the VW fixed again, we set out once more on the long drive home. I remember while we were in Ecuador we made a fascinating side trip to Banos, which is a popular hot springs resort and we spent a couple of days comfortably recovering from the excursions.

The next part of our trip was going to be the most dangerous part of our journey as we travelled up through Colombia, which was in the middle of a vicious civil war with the infamous FARC guerrillas. We had some really scary moments asking for directions from some real sketchy looking truck drivers along the switchbacks of Colombia's Cordilleras, which was so plush and green. So different from the desert dry coast of Peru.

After escaping Colombia safely, it was on to Venezuela and the city of Caracas, from where our van would be shipped to Norfolk Virginia. We carried on by air, stopping off briefly at Aruba. I entertained myself in Aruba by diving for conk shells and selling them to the tourists.

We went to meet the VW when it arrived at Norfolk, but bizarrely it could not be off-loaded, because it was totally surrounded by much more important cargo, which was a shipment of bananas. So we had to chase the boat overland to New York, where we were eventually re-united with the van and we finally drove north back home to Fredericton. As our epic trip neared its end many emotions went through my head. Mainly I was curious about my friends who I had left behind for 14 months. What were they up to now? Was I going to fit in OK after this trip?

I remember chuckling at the US border when the American customs discovered we had an exotic 26 bottle collection of alcohol on board the van. It was stashed in nooks and crannies all over the vehicle. They let us through anyway, saying "let Canadian Customs worry about it."

Thankfully, the Canadian customs boys didn't check us on our way through, and just said "Welcome Home!"

We had brought back a lot of souvenirs from our trip, as well as some very strange items to adorn our house in Fredericton. One of these was a huge chunk of quartz the size of a basketball, which my mother had found in Brazil and insisted on bringing back home as a decorative element.

Thanks to my mother's exotic shopping habits, I too would get a fixation for buying handicrafts and souvenirs to bring home from wherever I travelled. I thank her dearly for instilling in me the „collectors craft". She has always had incredible taste and is a self-made home decorator as well as an expert landscape artist working with embroidery.

Once I had got home, I suddenly realized what a great country we live in, after passing through and experiencing the corrupt, desperate poverty-ridden nations of Central and South America. I had come to love and respect the people and customs of South America, but it had to be admitted that Canada in comparison was very safe and rich. But all the emphasis on safety and all the insurance makes living here seem rather boring. I had left the bubble now and seen how the so-called Third World lived, and I was intrigued enough to want to go back for more.

Journey to South America (1972/73)

1. With my parents at the southern tip of South America, Tierra del Fuego.
2. In the Amazon with "Piraruku" fish, freshly caught by locals.

My teenage years

1. With the same VW bus in Alaska with parents, 1974.
2. During the Freestyle Skiing World Cup, Meribel, France 1977.
3. High School Graduation gala night, 1976. That's me crouching below.

CHAPTER 2

IN TROUBLE AGAIN; PERU, COLOMBIA TO FRANCE

By 1973, I was enrolled in Grade 10 in the first year of my high school. It proved hard to share my adventures with my teenage friends. For some reason which I didn't understand, people found it hard to relate to my exotic stories. My male friends were just interested in girls, beer and more parties, and then more girls and beer. They really seemed to care very little about my adventure.

This irked me and so I wrote a controversial article which was published in the local newspaper, complaining about how Fredericton teenagers had little motivation to do much beyond drinking beer in the woods. In my article I blamed this state of affairs on the societal realities of Fredericton where, I suggested, families distance themselves from their kids, which often caused them to take the wrong route in their lives. I tried to contrast the way Canadians brought up their kids to how I had seen it done in Argentina and the other countries of Latin America as a whole. There, entire families always celebrated together, but here in Canada it seemed to be taboo for teenagers to party with their parents. I continued on by commenting that the high school provided little beyond the school dance for entertainment, and the kids really had no other places to hang out and socialize beyond the local mall.

The article stirred a lot of controversy, and I had many letters for and against what I had written.

It turned out our trip to South America was not enough adventure for my father and he had further plans for our much travelled Volkswagen camper. On the agenda for the summer of 1974 would be for us to drive to Fairbanks in Alaska, and from there continue on all the way up to the Arctic Circle, to make it a full trip from Alaska to Tierra del Fuego, tagging both ends of the Western Hemisphere.

The trip went off without too many incidents, but on our way back from Fairbanks, we took a ferry from Haines to Juneau. I got to ride in a helicopter for the first time when we flew up to the Juneau ice field to stay in a temporary summer camp for several weeks. My father had been booked to give a series of lectures to the academic visitors.

The Juneau ice field is massive and one of the biggest ice fields situated outside of the two poles or Greenland. It is situated at around 8,000 feet, it covers some 800 square miles in area, and stretches from Atlin, British Columbia in the east, to Juneau, Alaska, the western edge.

I borrowed some skis and boots at the camp and got to do some hiking and skiing for the first time on real glaciers. At the end of my father's talks, he decided that instead of taking the helicopter back from the camp to civilization, we would make it a long hike from the 8000 foot ice field all the way down to the Pacific Ocean and our destination of Juneau. I remember it as being one of the most gruelling things my parents and I had ever done together, and my feet and knees were incredibly sore after the descent.

I was suffering at home from excessive boredom and monotony, so it was a stroke of luck that at the age of 17 my father came to my rescue. He took on a surveying job in Peru that was initiated by the University of Alberta. This allowed me to accompany him and to be employed in Peru – rather than be stuck in the provincial doldrums of summertime in Fredericton. The cottage community near Montréal that I had enjoyed as a child had since disintegrated, with many of the Polish families selling their cabins and moving on. I really felt I had no place left in Canada, as the lifestyle that my friends had chosen bored me.

I was now graduating from Fredericton High School, and I held what was probably the biggest party our town had ever seen to celebrate.

There were at least 300 people on our porch, which midway through festivities suddenly collapsed.

But the rock and roll band continued to play on. And the police? Well, they were just too scared to come near let alone come in. They stayed at the end of the block, snoozing in their cars.

My mother woke me up the next morning. There was an air of panic as I was to fly out to Montréal that day. But all flights out of Fredericton had been cancelled because of the weather. It was vital that I made that connecting flight from Montréal to Peru because I had to get to my first summer job. So we packed everything into our trusty VW camper van and we made the ten-hour drive to Montréal so I could catch my flight to Lima.

My job with my father was in the town of Huancayo, high in the Andes at 3259 m. Huancayo had a population of about 150,000 and is situated 300 km east of Lima. Being the largest city in the region, it is famous for its colourful Quechua market which is held every Sunday.

As bad luck would have it my ski boots and bindings for my skis were stolen while I was at the train station in Lima, so heartbreakingly skiing was out.

The railway from climbs from Lima to Huancayo is the highest railroad in the world reaching 4842 meters during its route. It is an engineering marvel with huge switchbacks that are big enough for a train to negotiate, and I heard that it was designed by Polish engineers. My country seems to have experts all over the world in the oddest places.

Above the town there was a very visible earthquake fault in the rock at around 4,000 meters that we would be measuring every summer. I became the research assistant and labourer, drilling holes in bedrock and carrying around the heavy surveying gear for my dad's graduate students.

The plan was first to drill holes in the bedrock around the fault, then set up theodolite equipment and distance-measuring devices on tripods over brass markers placed and epoxied in the holes. Measurements would be taken of the angles and distances between the points, and the data would be taken back to Canada and calibrated every year. It was a long-term, multi-year project to see how the ground was moving around the fault. The hope was to eventually be able to predict future earthquakes in the area.

It was from here that I started ski mountaineering. During time off from the labouring I began to climb and ski the glaciers that surrounded our base camp which was at 4,000 meters. My list of first ski descents in the Andes would start here, and this story was the subject of my first article, in what was known as "the Skier's Bible", even if its real name was Powder Magazine.

I liked being in a state of fear which the high Alpine generated for me. I found my body performed better in skiing precisely and technically when I was being terrorized and in awe of the terrain around me. Sure, the standard answer to climbing unconquered peaks or skiing ultra-steep lines is typically, "because it is there". In my case it was possibly in my childhood and always trying to impress my peers that had a lot to do with why I chose to climb and ski such seemingly impossible slopes. I felt the natural draw of the mountains, but really I could not articulate about their magnetism, and still can not do it justice to this day.

That first year in Peru I turned out to be a bit of a bad influence. One of the graduate students looking over me was Gary, a Mormon that my dad had hired to supervise the job. Soon I had turned Gary to smoking pot, drinking and even questioning his faith! On our days off Gary accompanied me on my trips up the glacier. Everything was a bit basic with our safety equipment comprising a length of old hemp rope, which was all that kept us safe as we navigated the crevasses.

By now I had become hooked on climbing the big mountains and glaciers of Peru. I guess the draw to big peaks had overcome me, just as it does to so many other climbers and ski mountaineers.

My work in Peru occupied me for just three weeks, and with the money I had made that left me almost two and a half months to travel to other parts of South America. Instead of making this just a skiing trip, I came up with what I thought was a brilliant idea. I would fly the length of the Amazon, stopping off at the major ports along the way, and then turn north towards Caracas in Venezuela, and from there return home.

I had been drawn to the jungle by the books I had read when I was younger and I got the first leg sorted. I was looking forward to seeing more of the Amazon having had a taste of it during a weekend bus trip from Huancayo – hurtling down the treacherous windy road to the bottom of the foothills and as far as the beginnings of the jungle.

I would start in Lima then fly over the Andes to Pucallpa and Iquitos.

While poring over maps, I had spied a sliver of land next to Peru that was owned by Colombia. It touched the Amazon port Leticia which happened to be one the most dangerous cities in South America. This was the place where all the illegal drugs were unloaded from airplanes and boats that had come from way up in the jungle, to be loaded onto barges and floated down the Amazon River to Belem for world distribution.

Being the silly 17 year old teenager that I was, I thought it would be fun to visit Leticia. Upon landing, I bought some marijuana and proceeded to look for my hotel room. On rounding a corner next to the hotel I was met by a policeman pointing a gun in my face.

I soon realized that I must have been framed, and probably by the people I bought the stuff from. After a strip search at the police station, where they also found two grams of cocaine hidden in my wallet left over from my time in Lima. I realized now how stupid I was with taking chances like that in South America, and especially in Colombia, of all places.

As it was, I was banged up in the local gaol, and I wondered whether this was to be the end to my free life? I wondered in despair. At least I was being fed some kind of gruel every day, which was thankfully accompanied by cups of great Colombian black coffee.

There was another foreigner in a cell next to me for a while. An American, he had been stuck there for a few years, but I only got a few moments to speak to him as he was moved somewhere else shortly after my arrival. I was sitting in my cell feeling extremely scared.

As it turned out, the police chief of Leticia gave me a three day sentence. In his spare time he took me for long walks from my cell, introducing me around town to all his friends.

Perhaps I was his gringo entertainment, and this was all fun until we met the Brazilian Consul on our rounds. On hearing my story from my gaoler, he immediately refused to give me a visa to get to Manaus. I would not be going on to Brazil.

The chief also took my passport and wrote in it in black marker ink that I was a drug trafficker from Canada. Everyone that read it was to be warned of my bad habits.

That was that. The end of my trip and I had to run from the jungle of Colombia.

My exit had a bit of a "Midnight Express" vibe about it, because when the police chief turned away from me, I was able to grab the passport from the folder on his desk and put it down my pants. Thinking he still had the document, the chief let me out to walk around town by myself as he got busy with some other matters, thinking he had me covered.

I quickly took the opportunity to make my escape. This was not as easy as it sounds because Leticia has no roads to other destinations. The only exit was by boat or plane, so I quickly took a cab to my hotel and grabbed my bags. Next I headed to a travel agency where I changed my plane ticket from the Brazilian destination to one going to Lima in Peru.

As I made my panicked trip to the airport, I managed to stop at a pharmacy, where I picked up some rubbing alcohol which I smeared over the page with the drug trafficker part. With my passport now a mess I just managed to make my flight, and looking out the window as my plane taxied to the end of the runway, I saw the police jeep arrive at the airport, but the plane took off and I was free. Or so I hoped.

Arriving in Lima I was still quite nervous about the events in Colombia, and I was wondering what the border patrol agents were going to do when they saw my mess of a passport, and asked the inevitable questions about it?

My story was that I told them that I had dropped the document on a busy muddy road in Colombia, and then a passing truck had run over it, making a mess of the page that they saw.

As I appeared to be an innocent but stupid 17-year-old, somehow they believed me and let me into the country.

When I got back to Lima I went straight to the Canadian Embassy crying for help because my funds were now non-existent. The embassy contacted my parents and asked them to wire money to pay for the balance of the airline ticket back home.

Once back home in Fredericton, I found I was sidetracked into many bad deeds by my teenage friends. But what else can one expect from a know-it-all teenager? My life reverted to chasing girls, attending wild parties, getting kids of drinking age to buy beer from the liquor store and playing pinball at the local shopping mall. I also stopped reading as much as I had earlier and that too I think was a direct impact from the crude camaraderie of the illiterate idiots who were my friends around me.

I started smoking pot at around 14 years old, and I remember being caught several times. It was the cause of a non-stop battle with my parents for many years. My mother would scold us when she caught us smoking with my big water pipe in the bathroom downstairs, under the ventilator fan which was a good place to disperse the smoke from the weed. Another time our scoutmaster caught us after sneaking up on us during a camping trip and caught us hot-knifing hashish off a tin foil plate around the campfire. This is of course resulted in yet another big lecture, which like all others had little effect.

As I grew into adolescence, I think my parents were terrified at the lifestyle I was being sucked into and with the company I was keeping in my teen years.

In 1976, as a solution to try and remedy the situation of my imminent downfall, they decided to send me to the University at Grenoble in France, to learn French and hopefully get away from the mischief back home.

That year in France turned out to be a definite epic. My time in Grenoble didn't last long, however, and I ended up leaving the university just a few months after arrival. I found the place to be so full of English speaking students from Britain, Canada and the United States that I was not learning any French at all. Everybody spoke English and there was no motivation to try and learn. However, I did make a lot of friends as the ski season started before I dropped out.

Every weekend we would be out in the mountains, and I made friends and useful contacts from France and elsewhere.

During this time I had an epic trip hitchhiking all the way from Grenoble to Nice on the French Riviera, and from there I took a ferry across the Mediterranean to the island of Corsica. I was travelling with a beautiful Swedish girl named Karin, but she was driving me nuts because she would not have sex with me, no matter how hard I tried. This was the only slight hiccup on what was an otherwise fabulous trip! I tried to console myself with the thought that it was not absolutely essential to sleep with every girl you meet. But sometimes such a refusal can be hard to take for a horny kid like me.

I felt bad that I did not last long as a student at the University of Grenoble, and I tried later to explain why to my parents. I told them the school was full of spoiled English and European kids who spoke English all the time. The purpose of going there: to learn French was not happening at all. Instead, I got a job in a local restaurant and bar called „L'Armour." The lady owner of the bar recognized my social organizing skills and made a nice stage near the bar so musicians could play. My role was to round up as many of the foreign students that I knew from the University, and bring them to L'Armour, which later turned into one of the most popular bars in Grenoble. To supplement that income from the bar, I got another job teaching freestyle skiing at Alpe d'Huez, one of the local ski resorts. This job came with a ski pass...

Before arriving in Grenoble, I did a trip by train all the way back to my native Poland, and then hitchhiked back to France. As a horny youth across the water, I had had no hesitation in seducing many young girls who I had known all my life. I was the bad boy and on this trip I had even bedded the fiance of one of my colleagues at a Polish mountain wedding, or Gorale as they are known. I barely made it out of what was then Communist Poland and through the Czech Republic, as my visa had run out, leaving me just minutes to cross to the Austrian border from what were then still communist countries.

I continued westward and stopped outside of Munich in Germany to visit some friends of my parents, the Dorers. Egon Dorer was a close friend of my father and, like him, was a professor in the Surveying Department at UNB. Bruni Dorer had become very close friend of my mother's, and they had even spent time with us in Tucuman, Argentina as well on that memorable trip. They had two young daughters who I had always picked on and made fun of from even when I was a child.

While I was in Munich, I grabbed the opportunity to buy something I lusted after: a pair of top-of-the-line Nordica ski boots. I might have been somewhat hung up about this due to the complex I had from never having owned such beautiful yellow boots when I had been a child back at tiny Crabbe Mountain. After visiting the Dorers, I continued hitchhiking on through Austria from Munich, and even went summer skiing on the Stubai Glacier on my way to France.

I had an amazing year in France, because I was no longer burdened with studies anymore I could concentrate on working at the restaurant, partying it up very heavily, and skiing with my university friends on the weekends. These activities were slotted in between my freestyle skiing teaching job, which was not that difficult to handle and did not take up a lot of time. I was sort of the token Canadian skier at the ski school run by Michel Vachez and consequently didn't get much work.

I took practicing my freestyle skills seriously though, and even managed to get an entry into the freestyle competition which was part of the World Cup when it was held in Meribel, one of the „Trois Valles" resorts in France. I came in about 60th place in combined aerials and moguls out of the pack of over 120 skiers. I was quite happy with this, as some real freestyle legends were competing, including such stars as Henri Authier from Switzerland and even Stephanie Sloan was there from Whistler.

I had always liked Pink Floyd's music, so when I heard that the band was playing in Paris during their Animals tour, I took the long train trip north from Grenoble to catch them there in concert. During the train ride, I met an interesting 'older' woman on the train. She was in her early thirties, while I was only 19. I found her very attractive and I felt she had this strange gypsy-like personality. In the spirit of the age we made love all night long in a compartment we had all to ourselves as the train covered the miles. Many years later she even came through Whistler and I saw her again. The concert was incredible of course, and one of the few times in my life when I have taken LSD because it seemed so appropriate in the moment. The drug was called pyramid acid and the purple tabs were shaped like little pyramids.

I fondly recall that weekend in Paris and from a small inexpensive hotel where I toured all around the City of Light, before returning to my life in Grenoble.

It was also here in France where my real mischievousness emerged once again. Since I did not have a lot of money from my various jobs, which were not that well paid, I had to devise ways to afford the cost of skiing and traveling around the ski resorts of France. My friends and I devised many ways to forge ski passes. For example we could erase and rewrite expiry dates on them, then putting the pass back in the plastic sheath, thus being able to use it for more than one ski trip.

One of my friends at that time was the son of a millionaire. Dan Sonis had bought a brand new golden Alfa Romeo 2000, a fabulously elegant Italian sports car. He had inherited some money from his father, but had left the Uni in Grenoble like me and invited me on a road trip around the Alps. Dan and I had a lot of good times on this trip including one crazy night of sex and the usual debauchery with two lesbians. One of the girls was a masculine dike from Belgium while the other was more feminine and French... I guess they were not really "pure" lesbians and had both liked to be with a man sometimes.

When we arrived in Val d'Isere I came up with another crazy idea of how we could ski for free. I made a side trip to Geneva, Switzerland where I purchased some LetraSet in order to make up some fake press passes. One of these declared I was a journalist for the "Penthouse Magazine guide to après-ski". I even faked the signature of Bob Guccione, the executive editor of the magazine at the time and I was quite pleased with the effort. I then made an appointment with the CEO of the ski resort, M. Jean Claude Trassens.

My grand plan to receive a free ski pass was to write an exciting account of the more outrageous après-skiing activities going on at the nightclubs there. I had also become quite active in speed skiing. So I needed Mr. Jean-Claude to give me the ski pass for two reasons. One was to genuinely write the guide book, and the other in order to train on a groomed run somewhere prepared for us by their snow cats, so we could practice our speed skiing exploits.

Mr. Jean-Claude listened intently to my well-rehearsed story, and seemed amused by it and had a rather curious grin on his face all the time. I think he knew very well this young Canadian kid was up to something but my story was so great and imaginative to him that he handed over the passes anyway, and instructed his groomers to even make a special run for us between Val d'Isere and Tignes.

My charm had worked and we were in. I spent the next three months enjoying for free as we bedded down in the condo of a friend who was also from Canada. We slept on the floor by night and skied all day.

I will take this opportunity to thank Gary Payne, the Canadian from Ontario for his hospitality back then. Gary now lives on Key West in Florida and visited me in Pemberton a few years ago when we managed to spend a happy day on the slopes of Whistler together.

Another time in Val d'Isere I skied with Jean-Claude Killy's brother Mick. Mick always skied fast like he had something to prove. He seemed to be always in the schussing position, but I guess you have to stand out if your brother is the famous Jean Claude Killy.

Another Canadian friend came up with another brilliant scheme. He also attended Grenoble University and found a crafty way to make free calls to Canada and the US from France. This consisted of using a bicycle spoke with a bend in the end of it. And inserting this into the small 50 centime slot. That would activate the mechanism in the phone into thinking it was going to receive money, and then we would insert the end of a spoon into the other one franc slot. As we would dial, we would use the spoon like a lever on a slot machine to fool the machine into thinking you had inserted coins. You would have to move the spoon faster and more often the further you wanted to call. For example, if you wanted to call Australia, you had to move that spoon up and down really fast. One time when I was on the payphone talking to a friend in Canada, some French gendarmes had sneaked up behind me, and caught me in the midst of my illegal act. I was terrified and thought I was going to go to jail in Grenoble. Once again I had a lucky escape, because one of the gendarmes turned out to be of Polish descent. After scolding me he just confiscated the bicycle spoke and told me to go home.

Once I used this ruse to call the K2 Ski Company on Vashon Island in Washington in order to try and get some speed skis couriered to us in France for free.

I guess the folks at K2 were impressed by all the long distance phone calls, because before the week was out we had two beautiful pairs of custom-made downhill skis with the name of the US Olympian, Phil Mahre, plastered all over them. Those were crazy times indeed, and being adventurous and creative with our stunts like this, we also seemed attracted many beautiful girls. I find the world is made up of two types of women. One type of woman plays safe and just goes for the money, while the other kind is more attracted by the guarantee of adventure. For some reason I always seem to attract the second type of girl. Can't think why.

I probably bedded more women in that one year in France than in the rest of my entire life. It was a very pleasurable year, making love to beautiful girls, skiing and generally partying it up with no responsibilities. It was a year of non-stop skiing and girls and girls and skiing. I am convinced that everyone should have at least one year like this in their life too. Of course it was really hard to leave it all when it was time to return home.

I made many new friends in Grenoble. One of them, Mark Bissel, was the scion of the Bissel vacuum empire, skied with us. There was also a beautiful Greek girl who was a government minister's daughter, who took us on several memorable ski adventures, like the time we went to a huge outdoor and ski trade-show in Milan, where we tried to find sponsors for our various skiing escapades.

There was another girl who was a great skier and I really fell for her, but would never agree to sleeping with me. There were rumours that she was the daughter of an a general who was demoted for some atrocity in Vietnam or Cambodia during the Vietnam War. Pam and I did some great ski touring trips in La Grave before they gondola, crossing over from the more conventional resort of Les Deux Alpes. We stayed in a beautifully cozy little hut in the park, which was a wonderful introduction to the joys of ski touring.

Another couple of Canadians from Whitehorse in the Yukon, The Hogan brothers had also come to study French in Grenoble. They were both keen skiers and we spent a lot of weekends together as well. Craig Hogan later moved to Vancouver and bought the outdoor shop Coast Mountain Sports which he ran for a while. Coast Mountain became a very popular outdoor camping and sports outlet in the trendy Kitsilano neighbourhood of Vancouver. It's funny, though, how we lost contact with each other after we left France. When he came back to Vancouver we hardly saw each other at all. Maybe my bad boy reputation from Whistler preceded me later in life, and has put off old friends from associating with me.

Another event occured that gave me a shock that year while I was away from home. My father wrote me a lengthy letter saying how he just could not get along with my mother any longer, and that he had packed up his bags and moved out of our family home to move in with Hannah, who was his graduate student.

They would soon get married and later produce a child, a pretty but frail-looking girl, Klara, and she later married a doctor. Although my father always took good care of me financially, I have always missed spending more time with him just talking about stuff. Hannah soon became his work partner as well, and he became very preoccupied with his new life.

I am not ashamed to say I missed not having a father around. I only saw him once or twice in the 30 years after I moved to the West Coast. Nowadays I find I don't hold anything against him anymore. He was a true workaholic who was a devoted scientist in his field and he just wanted some piece of mind in which to do his work. My mother, being the strong character that she was, just did not fit into his agenda. Hannah, on the other hand, became a partner that adored him both in work and in life.

I missed not having a father present during any of my life accomplishments, such as University graduation or, with my work in film, the many festivals, award ceremonies and premieres I later often attended. As a carefree teenager I admit I was so preoccupied with my own little world that I really did not miss my parents that much or give them much time. It was only later in life, when I saw other kids doing so much with their fathers, that it started to sadden me a bit. I know my dad really loved me a lot though, and he just got so overwhelmed by his work that it carried him away from being a regular family man, especially later in life.

He became well regarded in his field of surveying and mapping, receiving many honorary PhD's from universities around the world, including one from China. So my own life, which was based so far away on the West Coast, made it hard for us to stay in touch.

My father was also a real Polish patriot, and did his best to facilitate postgraduate studies to many university students from Poland in his field. He had a new family, a new life staying in Fredericton, NB and I was just so far away – certainly physically as well as in other ways. They accepted my adventurous lifestyle that had continued while he settled into a more mundane, regular family life. His new daughter Klara became quite a respected athlete as a figure skater, but we never really kept in touch either as our worlds were so different.

As I have said, I received nothing but love from my dad when I was younger. He always remembered to send me greetings and gifts for my birthday and my Polish name day, as well as at Christmas and the Easter holidays. When I was growing up he really did spend as much time with me as he could. He always managed to take my mother and me on great trips – from skiing in the winter to hiking and rock climbing in the summer. I have nothing but fond memories of those trips.

We used to play a favourite game of mine with my toy soldiers when I was young. We would both line up our armies of plastic soldiers across from each other in a room. Then with a cardboard tube we would roll marbles to see who would topple each other's armies first. It's funny the little things in life that the child remembers playing with his dad that gave him pleasure as a kid.

CHAPTER 3

THE DAWN OF MY RADICAL 20's

It was on the slopes of Huancayo and then Huaraz that I would really begin my life as an aspiring ski mountaineer and writer.

Upon returning from the French Alps as the summer of 1977 approached, I was charged and ready for another trip to Peru helping my father. On this trip I took great care not to have my skis or bindings stolen by not letting them out of my sight as I headed for my summer job. Getting my skis stolen would turn out to be the least of my worries.

We arrived in Lima only to find a highly volatile situation was developing and the police were on strike. As we arrived the Peruvian army were fighting the police, and had even rolled a tank through the Police barracks so I imagine the army won that round.

We didn't stick around Lima long enough to find out what was about to happen, because there were full scale riots breaking out everywhere, so it wasn't a safe place to waste time in.

As we arrived at Huancayo we found there was even a nightly curfew there, ending at 6am. Each morning we had to leave for our mountain surveying work at 6am as the curfew was lifted. One day, as we were trying to leave Huancayo for the mountains, crowds had spilled out on the streets at the same time as us right after lifting of curfew.

Because of the vehicle we had been given by the university, which had some government markings on it, a mob surrounded it and the crowd started rocking our cars. I crawled out through a window got up on top of our Land Cruiser and started yelling, pleading to the to the mob: 'We are from Canada, doing work to help protect you from earthquakes and predict them ahead of time' or something like that. Surprisingly my strategy worked and the crowd parted, letting us pass through. After that shock, we were soon once again in the high Andes above Huancayo for our second summer.

During that summer of Peruvian unrest and of my 20th year, I managed to climb and ski that first elusive virgin glacier I had been up the summer before with my Mormon friend Gary. This gave me enough material to write the story that became "Peruvian High", which was my first piece for Powder Magazine and it appeared the next year in 1978.

After my work duties finished in July, I boarded a plane from Lima to Santiago in Chile. I was heading for Portillo, which was then deemed the premiere ski resort in South America.

As it turned out disaster struck right off the bat. Arriving at Santiago airport, I learned that the Andes had received a huge dump of snow and all the roads up to Portillo were blocked. I met up with three other skiers who were also stuck at the airport, a Peruvian surfer, an Argentine guy and luckily, the nephew of Henry Purcell, who was the American co-owner of the Portillo Resort. Approaching a couple of cabdrivers, we found they absolutely would not take us up the dangerous avalanche-blocked road. Still, we persevered and, after almost having given up, we eventually found a driver who agreed to take us as far as the road would physically allow him.

So, after boarding the taxi with all our baggage and skis, we made our way up to the small town of La Guardia. Beyond that the road was blocked by a huge slide so we spent the night at a local hostel.

Undaunted by the apparent closure of the road, we got up at 5 am and sneaked around the Chilean army guard post, where the soldiers were actually making sure nobody tried walking through the dangerous road ahead. We walked the entire 15 km into Portillo with all our baggage. I recall being quite amused watching one of our group who was Peruvian, tie his suitcase on his back, just like the Quechua Indian women did with their loads. Unlike the rest of us he did not have a „proper" backpack, and did the local thing.

To our relief the resort was 100% operational and full of wealthy Brazilians as well as skiers from various national ski teams training for the Olympics. My three hiking companions were better off than me and got hotel rooms at the Hotel Portillo itself. I was a little poorer and took a room at the local train station below the hotel where a family rented out a few extra rooms for five dollars a night.

When the road was blocked the wealthy skiers had paid for a helicopter which flew them, as well as the ski teams who had the budget into the ski resort.

Besides great powder snow, Portillo also had some of the most gorgeous women I had ever seen. They were mainly from Brazil, coming not only to ski but also just to be around looking beautiful. One of these was a stunning Brazilian model named Claudia who really wanted to learn how to powder ski. I may have been just a poor ski bum, but I could definitely ski powder after the year of intensive training in France. Before I knew it, I received a sweet invitation. In exchange for daily powder lessons, Claudia offered to let me move into her private suite at the hotel for two weeks. Those were without doubt the best two weeks of my life. Need I say more? One night it snowed 9 feet or almost 3 meters. I skied on my 220 cm Phil Mahre K2 downhill skis the next day and they just floated through the deep powder. Soon enough Claudia was managing some fine powder turns herself.

One night we went out to look for a trailer that housed a favourite local restaurant, we found it totally covered by drifts of snow. We only found it by the lights shining through the drifts. We started digging down through the snow until we got down all the way to the door. We knocked and the family inside who ran the restaurant let us in for a wild night of partying.

We were staying in some excellent athletic company with whom we skied that year. They were the ski world's rock stars, Olympians on the US ski team like Andy Mills and Karl Anderson whom I had met in Grenoble several years back. Skiers came from all countries came to Portillo to train and ski during the Northern Hemisphere's summer. There were national ski team members, speed skiers, pro ski racers and freestyle skiers all skiing together. Friends of mine included Suzy Patterson, Scott Brooksbank, Kathy Breton and Otto Tschudi.

The summer of 1977 proved to be my last one working in Huancayo for my father on the earthquake fault study. The following year, we were told our jobs were being moved to the town of Huaraz, where another similar earthquake fault existed that we were to do measurements on.

I spent a terribly boring winter back home taking more psychology and sociology classes at the University of New Brunswick, during the semesters of 1977 and 78. I randomly chose Sociology and Psychology as I really didn't know what to do with myself.

I wrote a paper on the sociology of skiers as a different subculture to keep myself entertained and sane somehow while I looked forward to going back to my job in Peru.

While at UNB I met up once again with Peter Robson from Montréal whom I had briefly met for the first time in Grenoble the year before. Peter's father, John Robson, was also a scientist – of the nuclear kind. He had even won a Nobel prize in his field. His son Peter was another bad ass, and he and I dabbled in drugs and girls together. Peter always managed to have good black hash from Montréal on the side, which he generously shared with a few of us at UNB.

Peter was a good skier and our friendship prompted me to invite him to join me on what was my biggest expedition to Peru thus far, planned for the summer of 1978. I remember how concerned and thrilled his parents were for him. I vividly recall him proudly showing me the expensive back pack his dad had bought him for the trip. I think his parents were also happy to get him out of the house in Westmount, Quebec. They were probably aware that in that elite neighbourhood he was surrounded by a lot of badly spoiled rich kids who did little but party and sell hash so the possibility of him finding a new path was worth exploring.

I also met the world champion stunt and freestyle skier John Eaves during a trip to Montréal to visit Peter. He was famous for appearing in many of the James Bond films as a stunt double for 007.

At UNB around that time I also met a girl called Cauleen Bridges, who was from Montréal, and she would drift in and out of my life at various times over the next 43 years. I lusted after Cauleen, who was attracted to me by my skiing. Cauleen said she liked me as a great friend but teased me by allowing a few kisses. She usually had another regular boyfriend though, someone straighter than I was, perhaps someone who would make a more secure partner in a serious relationship, or so I guessed at the time.

Cauleen was one of the first of my friends who called me "Peter Peru" when we met again in Whistler after several years. Later, at a memorable party she threw in her Whistler cabin. I had managed to get more romantic with her.

Cauleen has always given me inspiration and claims to have left university for a life of ski bumming, due to my direct influence back at UNB! What a cross to bear! However, she stayed only briefly in Whistler and married a ski patroller named Patrick Combat, from Les Arcs in France, and moved to another of BC's ski resorts called Big White with him.

Over the decades ahead, we would only meet on occasion. One special night we hiked and camped above Whistler's Far West Bowl. We took fireworks up with us and hiked to Whistler Peak with them and all our camping gear after the ski lifts closed. That night we set them off, giving all of Whistler's Creekside a real good light show.

That summer of 1978 saw me working again once again at my surveying job at the new location of Huaraz, Peru, because of that big earthquake fault.

I had first visited Huaraz in 1972 with my parents on our VW voyage. It was then that I first laid my eyes on the impressive peak of Huascaran, and I started dreaming of being able to ski it one year. A good friend of my father, geologist Benjamin Morales, had shown us around the Ancash valley, which had been particularly devastated by a massive 1970 earthquake which killed 60,000 people. Huascaran itself had let loose a huge landslide which had smothered all life in Yungay, a town that had supported 30,000 people, and was located at the base of the massive peak. Only about 800 survived, mainly kids and young people, who could run to safety towards a statue of Christ on top of a hill. I guess to devout Catholic believers those who survived had proof that their strong faith had finally paid off for them.

The biggest mountains of the Andes around Huaraz became my spiritual place. I was 21 and I was ready to launch my most ambitious expedition to date with Peter Robson, alongside whom I had been a partner in crime too many times back home at UNB. I also brought my close friend David Clarke, a fine photographer – also from Fredericton. My father had consented to my two friends working with me on the surveying job in Huaraz so they were conveniently available for the expedition to climb and ski Huascaran, Peru's highest peak at 6,788 m (22,205 ft).

Indeed 1978 was a pivotal year for me. The word extreme, as it applied to sport entered my vocabulary for the first time. In the early seventies, a French skier called Patrick Vallencant adapted the word to describe his steep skiing feats in the European Alps, as well as descents in the Andes around Huaraz by calling his resulting book Ski Extreme. His meaning was that if you were risking your life in your sport, you were extreme.

Vallencant and I would later meet, climbing and skiing together on Huascaran, during my third trip to Peru. That year, instead of travelling far from Peru, I concentrated all my efforts on producing my first film, "Ski Peru," and also organizing a major Canadian extreme skiing expedition.

The word EXTREME would later evolve and be adapted by the media to describe too many facets of our lives. Now, while we still have extreme sports, the word's meaning has expanded and devalued so that it is now used to describe everything from 'extreme' food to 'extreme' real estate – and the list just keeps growing.

Much later in the early nineties, we joked about this around Whistler. Trevor Petersen, a genuinely extreme skier felt the word had become so devalued that he preferred to use the word "Severe" instead of Extreme when describing his own exploits. Another great admirer of Patrick Vallencant's descents, Trevor would start his career skiing in my smaller documentaries as he carved out his own legacy of extreme skiing descents in the Coast Range of BC and Europe with his partner in crime Eric Pehota.

Back in Canada I occupied myself all that winter by organizing my next expedition to Huascaran, while attending UNB. In trying to raise some sponsorship, I managed to pique the interest of the head of pr at Canadian Pacific Airways, Mike Dukelow. He believed in my dream and supplied the entire crew with 8 return airline tickets to Lima from Canada. Another friend who worked at FMH (Fisher, Marker, Dynafit), which was a big ski equipment distributor, kindly supplied Peter Robson and me with skis and boots. The skis were rather heavy Fisher 205 cm Racing Cuts with Marker touring bindings. We also got Munari ski boots and used these instead of the Dynafits as they were more comfortable.

For a 21-year-old guy, it was a crazy, even outrageous proposition. I had assembled a team of surveyors and rock climbers from New Brunswick. I had also enlisted a film crew, headed by my friends Jon Pedersen and Arthur Makosinski to film the entire trip. We even had an older gentleman named John Hooper who was a famous wood carver from New Brunswick, who came along as Executive Producer.

I still wonder what was going through my head. None of us had any alpine experience except for me, and my knowledge was minimal. It's has been said that fortune favours the brave – but was I being brave or naive, or both?

Luckily, Benjamin Morales in Huaraz came to our help with giving us crucial element by finding us good local porters, one of whom was his brother Cesar Morales, who was one of the top climbing guides in Peru.

Upon our arrival in Lima Peter Robson had bought rather foolishly 50 grams of cocaine for a bargain price, from a destitute tourist who had needed money to get home. So the partying and the womanizing had already begun – even though we still had a big mountain to climb and ski, and a major expedition to run.

After finishing our surveying work, we packed up the whole mule train with our gear, including some very heavy "Sherpa" aluminum snow shoes (showing just how inexperienced we were at the time) and headed towards Huascaran's base camp.

When we arrived at the base we encountered another team from Pittsburgh there. Their expedition had already ended in tragedy as two of their members had been killed on the north peak of the mountain. Unfazed by this ominous news, we made our way carefully though the hazardous ice fall of the glacier up to Camp One, which was located just above the icefall and out of harms way.

Little did we know that back in Huaraz, Patrick Vallencant and Dominique Andre, two guides from Chamonix, France had arrived and heard about some Canadians trying to ski the big mountain. They set out to catch up with us, and racing with them was another team made up of yet more French skiers, Jean Marc Boivin and his extreme ski partner Michel.

Imagine the shared surprise when we all finally met up at Camp One! It was probably my good luck that I only managed to accompany the seasoned French skiers as far as 6,200 meters elevation before I was forced to turn back. I was so impressed by how comfortable the French were climbing and walking on knife ridges, through the ice falls and over seracs, places where I would freeze up out of fright and virtually have to get down on all fours to navigate some of the terrain. My inexperience showed on such a big mountain in other ways. Too much of our supplies which I had brought were too heavy to be used for an alpine expedition.

I read Vallencant's journal many years later where he described meeting up with us on Huascaran at horspiste.com

"...I thought that Jean-Marc was ahead, it was 11 am, I gave the mule a prod and upped the pace. The road which seemed so long to us three weeks previously now seemed short, in the early afternoon we reached base camp at 4800 meters. From our tent we observed a group of three climbers walking down the moraine. They looked done in. They had been trying to climb Huascaran for the last five days. We were surprised; the group were part of a team including two Canadian skiers, which confirmed the rumours of the Indians. We asked them if their friends had already skied from the summit.

We chatted freely, one of the charms of climbing in distance countries is that it brings people of different nations close together and encourages dialogue. The group were extremely tired, they gulped down the tea we offered them. They had come to Peru, to this area shaken by earthquakes, to study the geology. They made marks and measurements and filmed everything. The two Canadians had piggy-backed onto the trip to make a ski film. The geologists were obviously not happy to accept the suffering that altitude brings and preferred to leave the skiers and their porters at the foot of the mountain.

The game wasn't up for us yet. We could maybe reach them in a day of hard climbing and who knows? Do the summit together? I spotted another face at the camp, Frédéric Labaye. What a coincidence, he told us „they are a bit overwhelmed by the task, if you try you can catch them, they are carrying a huge amount of gear". One can regret the element of competition amongst the high peaks but today I had to admit it was something that enchanted me.

The next day, at 10am, we crossed one of the Canadians, he had given up and was skiing down. He didn't seem to welcome our presence or maybe he was just tired? He skied really well. Our prey could not be far, at midday we spotted him and at 2pm we caught up with Peter Chrzanowski. He was suffering. His porters were loaded down with gear. We suggested resting the night where we were and continuing together the next day. The porters were happy to descend.

We had to take a look at Peter's gear. He had a diver's knife that weighed over a kilo; it said everything about his lack of experience. He was also carrying two cameras. One he could attach to his helmet, the other, incredulously, had a mount for ski shoes. We understood why we had caught him so quickly. On the plus side, an amazing amount of high altitude food and an isolated tent. In exchange for his help and food we agreed to carry a camera to the summit and to help Peter on the climb.

We had just finished supper when a couple of silhouettes appeared. Was it Peter's friend? Impossible. We then noticed they had skis fixed to their sacks. Peter thought they were a couple of Californians because he'd heard that an American team were also in the frame. Peter then pulled a whistle from his pocket and began to blow furiously. Nothing he could do would surprise us now.

„You are a real bastard" was how Jean-Marc Boivin greeted me. „What me a bastard? I thought you were in front so I had no reason to wait for you". It was Michel, normally taciturn, who calmed things down „We are not going to fight with our ice-axes, you two make up and we'll go to the summit together". Jean-Marc and I talked about the past, our lost friendship, I wasn't completely convinced by his explanations, there still seemed to be a grudge, it was better to remember the good times we had and look to the future.

We relaxed. „You must have climbed very quickly" I told them. I couldn't understand how they had caught up with us when we had walked so fast to catch Peter. In fact they had been hard on our heels since the first day.

The absurdity of the situation struck me. Here we were, on a summit that had never been skied and on the same day everyone was chasing after each other. Peter wanted to be first. We thought we were chasing our friends who were in fact chasing us. It should have been on television."

I skied down and met up with my other ski partner, Peter Robson, and our Fredericton photographer, David Clarke. Peter had managed to insult Vallencant by asking him if he was Sylvain Saudan when they had first met on the glacier. I still think that that was rather comical to this day.

Our New Brunswick film crew was not in great shape, all were suffering from altitude sickness, and were packing up to go down.

I managed to leave our trusty hand-wound Beaulieu 16mm camera with Patrick Vallencant, who used it to shoot the climactic footage we used later in Ski Peru. The film of the Frenchmen skiing from the summit was spectacular – even of lasting greatness, I would say. As it was, I would later judge an extreme ski contest in Chamonix, which was won by Jan Andre, the son of Dominique, but that was to be much later – in 1996. My film of this expedition, SKI PERU later won the prestigious first prize and the Golden Sheaf award at the Yorkton Documentary film festival in Canada.

Rarely daunted, at least we hadn't got stuck on the slopes of Huscaran without overnight gear. Unlike an earlier event on this trip.

Peter Robson, Dave Clarke and I took part in another memorable side trip during our survey before the Huascaran expedition. We wanted to get some skiing in before going up the big mountain.

While surveying our earthquake fault, we had always looked up to see above us Tsurup mountain and on its slopes was a formidable looking area that looked like it had recently been covered with fresh snow. So on a day off work we talked our driver to get us up as far up the approach as he possibly could, which he did amazingly well. By the top of the climb we had left the road and were navigating the Space Cruiser over the tundra that loomed over us.

We must have got to an elevation of about 5,000 meters until it was impossible to go further in the truck. From there we hiked up to the glacier which, to our pleasant surprise, had just received about two feet of fresh powder snow. The glacier was in the shadow of the huge rock face of Tsurup mountain above us, thus keeping the snow nicely light and dry. As David took pictures Peter Robson and I skied by him, and decided to ski down towards the lake. David was smart and took the same way back down to the waiting vehicle, which was a speck way down below, using the route we had hiked up.

Since we were so intoxicated by the powder run Peter and I made a bad decision and just kept on skiing down to Tsurup Lake. Upon arrival at the lake we realized that we were in a terrain trap. There were cliffs all around the lake and as it was getting dark so we couldn't make it out safely before night fell. We would be forced to spend the night here without sleeping bags or extra clothing.

The days are hot in the Andes but at night the temperature drops drastically due to the high altitude and the thin air. At least there were some bushes around which we used to make a bed from and we spent the entire time huddled together, not sleeping a wink, desperately awaiting only daylight and the warmth of the morning sun. I got to a pretty bad level of hypothermia that night and I experienced weird 'waking dreaming'.

The 'dreams' were about people I knew who I thought were there at the lake, to rescue us. These dreams are perhaps better described as hallucinations and are the result of cold and exhaustion. Later that day we made it back to our camp, exhausted but having learned another good lesson about the consequences of being unprepared.

Once more I spent the winter in New Brunswick, enduring another couple of semesters at the university. As before, I took courses I really had no interest in – sociology and psychology. I lived by dreaming: dreaming of returning to Peru and skiing more peaks there. We didn't have a plan but were confident we could reach some impressive mountains with our quest to ski some first descents.

And so I started organizing yet another expedition to my ultimate destination of Peru. I invited David Clarke again. Another friend who I invited to come, Jake Bekins was a less fortunate choice which I later regretted.

I once again approached CP Air, and managed to score three more airline tickets from them to get us to Peru.

I had known Jake from high school and we had skied together on the slopes of Crabbe Mountain. We also partied hard together and I should have known from the start that he was not the best partner for a serious expedition to the Andes. I was too gullible sometimes with people, and let them come into my world too often without much forethought. Jake never really did anything to prepare for or help the trip and I did all the legwork with the sponsors. I managed to enlist the support of Dynamic skis and Scott boots. These boots were the chosen brand of light ski equipment, which Vallencant had used on all his notable ski descents.

My first visit to Whistler was during that spring of '79 was for the cancelled Molson World Cup Downhill Ski Race. I was immediately awed by the place which later prompted me to go there in the fall of 1979. It was at Whistler that I actually met filmmaker Curtis Petersen, who was shooting "Pro Patrol" a film about the Whistler ski patrol. I tagged along and helped carry the heavy 16mm gear, but also got to ski some great powder in the "Gun Barrels" run in at the resort before the mountain officially opened, thanks to this gig. I was now fully hooked on Whistler. It was a ski town full of young people just living to ski and having fun. It was so exotic to me coming from boring Fredericton in New Brunswick. It was a place where people moved to ski. I wanted to come back and live there.

So my grand plans for an expedition to Peru that summer turned out to be a disaster. Jake, Dave and I tried unsuccessfully to reach some ski-able glaciers. Each attempt was stymied by the peaks being simply inaccessible or beyond our climbing abilities. While Dave and Jake gave up on the skiing, I stayed and looked for a way into the mountains while in Huaraz. My friends from Fredericton were not into attempting any more skiing and stayed and partied in Huaraz.

Then, I met someone who could help me get to the skiing.

I had met Americo Tordoya on Huascaran the previous summer. He was just 19 years old then, but we got on and I decided to take his advice and have him guide me to different peaks in the area. The peaks and/or the routes were Ranrapalca 6,162 m, (20,217 ft) and Ishinka,

5,530 m, (18,143 ft), which were approached by the Quebrada Cojup (Canyon) that led to both mountains' bases.

I felt I owed it to my sponsors to ski some Andean peak, even if I was to do it alone.

But I still needed someone to guide me. And so, leaving my friends from Fredericton behind, Americo and I hired a donkey to carry all of our ski and camping gear then set off for the base camp between the two mountains which was a full day trek from Huaraz.

While acclimatizing to the altitude for the Ranrapalca mission, Americo and I took turns at climbing and skiing nearby Ishinka, a nearby peak above our base camp. It was a fine peak and Americos feet fit into my ski boots enabling him to do some skiing while I remained at base camp.

It was an easier gentler peak and a nice introduction to skiing in the area. Americo was a hard core mixed rock and ice climber. He had no skiing ambitions in the Andes because there was no ski infrastructure like lifts.

He had learned to ski in Colorado, USA when he had been invited to train up and coming American climbing guides. Some American climbers had discovered the young man's climbing skills and wanted to train him for Outward Bound, a major guiding school in the USA. He was to be Outward Bound's man in Peru. He was certainly intrigued by my own plans to ski some impressive peaks while in the country, which prompted him to guide me.

The climb up Ranrapalca was intense. Americo led and I followed. This went on for 17 rope pitches each, a very long and very arduous climb. It was surreal to have the sun leave us in late afternoon, only to have the following full moon keep things as bright as by day.

I was intoxicated by the climb, the view, the light, and the entire ordeal. The face was severally fluted from previous avalanches. It was cold, about -20°C, which kept the ice and snow firm. Often times, we really had to kick in hard with the points of our crampons to get a much needed solid grip.

It was mainly a huge snow encrusted face – Americo placed snow pickets for fall protection. Occasionally, an ice screw would go in where it was boiler plate hard pack. There were some very icy patches which I certainly had hesitations having to ski through later.

Stretching day and moonlit night, it was a long climb. We settled into a good rhythm, placing one crampon boot relentlessly over the other.

Finally elated, we crested out onto the summit knife ridge. I straddled the ridge managing to get to the very summit itself. Like moving up an icy bareback saddle on a horse, helping with my arms.

I was clumsy and very tired but euphoric in making the summit of such a technically difficult mountain to climb. I stood silently on the top of the ridge, under the full moon – Ranrapalca, its name a Quechuan one meaning Peak of Dreams. We learned later that Americo was the first Peruvian and I the first Canadian to reach this dream peak.

It was time to prepare for the descent and put my skis on. High from the altitude, the moment, and the vastness of the Cordillera Blanca unfolding below us, I was unable to exercise good judgment. Americo warned me to climb down over the first icy bit. I ignored his advice though, drunk out of the sheer excitement of reaching the summit.

The whole scene had an unworldly and magical slow motion feeling to it. The snow sparkled from the deep moon rays that shone around me. I put on my skis and set off with my first turns on the 55 degree slope. I managed only about four of them before I lost an edge on the icy slope and went into cartwheel mode.

I kept falling for around 900 vertical meters (2,700 ft). As I tumbled – I just relaxed, let go, and thought – "Oh well, Peter, say goodbye to this world, this is it."

I finally came to rest, very lucky indeed having been lodged into a shallow crevasse. After losing my skis and boots in the fall, I opened my eyes from the land of the blue lights. Then somehow I managed to climb barefoot out of the icy hole. I waited three days until I was rescued.

I owe my life to the timely rescue efforts of Americo. As I waited, half dazed on the glacier he rappelled down to my predicament. Amazingly, I had fallen almost to base camp which was perched nearby, just below the giant face I had attempted to ski.

Americo swiftly went to the camp and procured a sleeping bag and tent to wrap me in. He also melted a big pot of snow and gave me water. It would be a three day wait for a rescue team to reach me. I ate some sleeping pills, probably a good idea as my metabolism went down and

I rested better. While still in a state of shock, I drifted in and out of consciousness or was it sleep?

Sometimes I would open my eyes to incredibly glaring light and strong sunshine reflecting from the snowy bowl I was in. At other times, I would awaken at night to the brittle cold around me. Most of the time the pills did their work and I would drift off. After having done his best to protect me from the elements, Americo then ran for 14 hours to the town of Huaraz, where he was able to secure a rescue team. Three days later, that team carried me down to the road and the waiting ambulance. Americo was an incredible climber known as Penique to his friends. Sadly, he died only a few years later in 1983 in an avalanche while he was on El Juncal, a peak which is situated north west of Santiago, Chile.

During my fall I had only suffered a concussion. My feet were badly frostbitten. Mimicking Patrick Vallencant by using the same light ski boots had been a big mistake as the buckles opened right away tearing ski, boots, and all off my feet. The Peruvian doctors wanted to amputate a few toes which were turning slightly black but I refused until actual gangrene visibly set in. Luckily it didn't, and my toes recovered.

I spent several months recuperating from this accident, first at the Huaraz hospital, then I was moved to the English American clinic in Lima, and finally, when I was okay to travel, back home in Fredericton. It was hard even trying to walk a straight line and I was often perceived as being drunk in public.

Life-threatening, near-death experiences certainly must have an impact on people. Mine definitely did for me. A few of my friends who have undergone near-death situations, as in the case of avalanche burial, have recounted effects similar to the thoughts and experiences that I had in my brain at the time. Many of them have travelled to a place they call the "land of blue lights" and I'm pretty sure that was my destination after my long fall off the mountain. It seemed to me that I was immersed in the very universe itself, that I was indeed a part of it somehow.

I felt souls around me but I could not be sure if they were from the present or the past. This land was indeed a pleasant place and to consider leaving it seemed most undesirable. However, being the anxious young man that I was, I rebelled against that place too. I felt it was just not my time yet and that I had so much more to do. It was in the midst of this realization of having more to do, that I opened my eyes and found myself surrounded by the blue icy walls of the crevasse – rather than the blue lights of the universe.

My friend Cheryl Condy once experienced a similar sensation. She had been buried in an avalanche and, upon feeling a sharp shovel hitting the back of her head, came back into the material world. Another skier, Troy Jungen, recounts a similar experience. He also had been buried in an avalanche but a second slide uncovered him, bringing him back into our material world.

In the end we can philosophize forever about these experiences. My own sense of them is that they contain no real evidence there is anything showing us the way to the other side. Maybe it is just our mind replicating what we have learned that we should expect. One thing is for sure: my near death experience certainly left an impact on me. And I don't just mean in the physical sense of leaving marks on my body for a few months. No, I refer to the change being more so in the way that I have come to perceive that some of us are on a long journey to an eventually better place. Some say that I have a death wish. Others have even called me a sociopath as I always continued in my risky ways after all the accidents which I have had.

Well, believe me, I have better things to do than lie in a hospital bed for a month staring at the ceiling. I like to think that every experience has just been a good lesson on how to do things better next time around. I am not afraid of dying. Why not? Because I truly believe that, if we do good in this world, we are only going to go to a better place. Be assured that I would love to live, ski and paraglide into old age! So, believe too, that with each accident I have been really trying to learn from the errors I have made – in order not to repeat them again.

My quest for seeking out rather perilous adventures has never really stemmed from any deep psychological convictions. These days, as extreme sports gain notoriety, many athletes may seek to find themselves through their risk-taking deeds. Some write self-help books or do lectures dissecting their experiences. I can't say that I ever used my experiences as a means of overcoming fear or to justify my quest for dangerous undertakings. In my case, I guess the fear that so many people write about was just never really there with me to feed off or even to contemplate. Sure, all exposure is scary but with practice – as with overcoming a general human fear of heights – it just becomes manageable. I have never felt that my motivations required a lot of explanation. I am, one might say, my own case. I think in general I do things technically better when I am scared or even terrified. I guess screwing up during those times is just not an option. So when I get stuck in a life threatening situation skiing or paragliding, the fear really makes me slow down and think things over as calmly as possible in order to overcome the predicament I am in.

Those of us that indulge in risky sports are sometimes referred to as adrenalin junkies as the body itself produces its own cocktail of drugs.

As for recreational drugs, although I smoke pot fairly regularly having started at a fairly young age, I have done magic mushrooms, and I have enjoyed a rare snort of Peruvian marching powder on the odd special occasion, I have stayed away from most other recreational drugs. Yes I will admit to some pretty crazy LSD trips in my younger years but these probably numbered less than five in total. Magic mushrooms were the craze of the times I remember, in the late 70s and early 80s. While in high school and still later at the University of New Brunswick, we would venture out to a provincial government experimental farm where we would pick magic mushrooms after the rains in the fall.

The farm's cows were fed corn. This diet supposedly produced the best mushrooms – which grew in their manure. I still remember a very interesting occasion when Peter Robson and I ate a good portion of mushrooms. Then we both focused and visualized that an alien spaceship was landing. As we both concentrated on seeing the ship land, it became very real to both of us. However, we did not continue concentrating on the spectacle, because we both got really scared. We certainly did not want to see the aliens themselves come out of the ship! I still cannot say if the experience was just a hallucination or whether there was some truth to the matter. I was always interested in the books of Eric Von Deniken, the Chariots of the Gods author. How Peter Robson was able to see the same thing I saw on one particularly strange night somewhere in the countryside outside of Fredericton New Brunswick will always be a mystery to me.

My mother had a good friend who was a mathematics professor at UNB. He also experimented with hashish and magic mushrooms. She even tried some mushrooms with him one day, but said that she only had a terrible experience as a result. The hallucinations had gotten out of control, she said. My mother was very progressive in many ways but hallucinations were just too much for her.

I did have one amazing experience with the San Pedro cactus which is a distant cousin of the Peyote cactus, another popular hallucinogenic substance, which grows in the mountains and deserts of Peru and other places in the world. This incident took place at our base camp while we were doing our surveying work in the Andes. It was a great place for a mind trip and the dreamlike diversions that ensued were spectacular. I remember seeing several goddesses, each playing a different instrument, as if they were wandering around with me in the upper tundra of the Altiplano that special afternoon.

Although I like to have a drink with my friends on social occasions, I never got into the habit of drinking a lot beyond that. I never became one of those "six pack of beer a day" guys like many friends did. I also saw a lot of lives ruined by alcoholism and certainly did not want to go there. At the same time, though, I do remember getting pretty drunk on several occasions at big parties – but never on a regular basis.

There is another interesting side story behind the tale of my skiing Ranrapalca. Although my fall was a horrendous accident, it may have saved me from a lifetime of jail in Peru. Jake Bekin had talked before we left about sending some cocaine back to Canada from Peru. In North America at the time it was the chic drug. The preferred technique was to put an ounce or so in between a collection of various postcards and send them out by mail.

Jake was always trying to work a scam. The son of a fireman he always had a kind of complex owing to his not being able to keep up with the boys from the more affluent Fredericton families – such as those of doctors and lawyers. As a result he was often trying to show them that he, too, could make some serious money.

Although he was an alright skier Jake was more interested in the coke and partying possibilities arising from being in Peru. Anyhow, the postcards somehow got intercepted probably because some didn't have enough postage on them for their weight. Jake was tracked down by Peruvian authorities and placed in jail in Lima. The RCMP (Royal Canadian Mounted Police) had an office in Lima, as they were monitoring the drug trafficking from Peru to Canada.

Jake was lucky because his mother worked for the RCMP back in Fredericton. She put pressure on the RCMP in Lima to ask for mercy for her son from the Peruvian officials. While this was going on, I had my horrendous accident up on the mountain and leaving the country earlier than expected, I slipped by the Peruvian officials who apparently had me on their radar.

After a terrifying week in a Peruvian jail, Jake was allowed to go back to Canada. Jail time in Peru would not have been fun having experienced a jail in Colombia. Jake said later that the prison guards had dunked his head in water to make him tell the full story. He had blamed me for organizing the whole cocaine scheme. I am sure the experience left an impact on him for the rest of his life. The accident was terrible but a lifetime spent in a Peruvian jail in Lima would have been much worse.

It was a hard lesson learned and from then on I stayed away from doing any business with drugs. I felt someone or something was teaching me a serious life lesson here. Perhaps my personal guardian angel was telling me, "Ok, you survived the accident and the drug squad but three strikes and you're out!" So I decided that, although I would dabble a bit in recreational drugs, with maybe a snort of coke on New Year's Eve, I would never get wrapped up with drug dealing and the people involved with it ever again.

Luckily I seem not to have an addictive personality. Furthermore, even though I might have snorted a bit of coke while on trips to Peru or Colombia, I have never had a real problem with it back home. So many people I have known though, have ruined their lives with the drug. Whistler especially had people whose abuse of the white substance turned into problematic addiction.

When I got back to Fredericton during that early summer of 1979, it turned out that I wasn't home free. The RCMP began to come to my house on a regular basis. They kept trying to get a feather in their small town caps by blaming and trying to convict me for the cocaine in postcards caper. During the whole predicament I realized just how nasty small-town cops can be, that they would do anything in order to obtain a conviction. That is when my lawyer told me the best thing I could do was to "get on the train out west, disappear for a while young man."

So after only two weeks at home I went to Lake Louise.

The Fredericton cops had used the carrot and the stick method on me. They warned me that, if I did not comply and admit that I had masterminded the whole cocaine episode, they would never let my friend out of jail in Peru. Here was the classic "good cop bad cop" routine at its finest. These cops watched too much TV. Their whole approach turned out to be a failure since once I had disappeared to Lake Louise, they let Jake out of jail within a week. I got to really distrust and dislike cops in general after that.

I shake my head when I recall those wild times in Peru. Each year when we arrived in Lima, we would book into a very conservative hotel called the 'Miramar' It was a rather elegant, colonial styled pension, run by an English madam. This lady was very strict and, although there was an in-house bar in the place, it was very properly run and closed early in the evening. I still find it hard to believe the ruckus we caused in that hotel. Once the bar had closed and the staff had gone to bed, it was then our real parties would begin. My mischievous friend David Clarke and I would meet all sorts of ladies around Lima, and then we would let them in through the back door of the hotel. We would then hold some pretty wild parties, full of cocaine and sex in the usually long-closed bar.

I remember this one time we met a set of rather gorgeous twins, named Letty and Charo. The scene that followed was definitely Libertine: David and I took them both back to the Pension, placed some nose candy up their beaks, and the next thing we knew we were swapping them between each other. I think I even got rug burn on my knees from the action on the floor of the bar. I can't believe the things we got away with to this day. In the mornings we would put on smug faces while we had breakfast with the staff and lady of the hotel.

During my stay in Lake Louise I lived in Touche town, the local trailer park for all the ski hill employees. It was truly a ghetto made up of decaying and delaminating trailers situated off the roadside near

Lake Louise. Although lousy as accommodation, it was a good location as a base to climb and explore the nearby Rocky Mountains and so much possible skiing terrain.

We were still young and eager and full of adrenaline and we yearned for adventure. I soon found eager more new friends to accompany me to try climbing and skiing some new chutes. I scoped them out above Peyto Lake off the Columbia Parkways between Lake Louise and Jasper and tried to continue my steep skiing exploits.

Unfortunately, this resulted in yet another frightening 500 metre (1,500 ft) fall in the Whymer Couloirs of Mt Temple in the Canadian Rockies.

I did the ascent with a local Banff climber named Peter Harvey, who had led and was quite far above me. I was carrying a lot heavier ski gear, while he was just free climbing. I think he heard me yell when I fell, and he was surprised to find that I was actually still alive, after cart-wheeling all the way down the couloir. A tourist at Maligne Lake, which lies below the chute, came across my battered body. He then kindly walked and drove me back to the local clinic in Banff. I was lucky again and only suffered 9 stitches on my head as my helmet had come off during the tumble. I also had a very hurt tailbone. My rear end was so battered from the fall that I had to take a laxative for several weeks in order just to be able to go to the bathroom. I met the tourist who took me to the Banff clinic in Whistler years later to my amazement.

Besides that misadventure I did manage to solo climb and ski a run called Andromeda, consisting of a steep bowl and face rising from above the Columbia Ice Fields that fall of '79. Many mountaineers have big respect for the climbing routes leading up Andromeda. It was a difficult climb and a steep ski. The visibility was not great due to patchy fog and I never recorded the feat. It's funny that I never really even mentioned that climb anywhere except now in my book. Maybe I blocked it out of my memory as I was quite scared during the ordeal and truly relieved when the worst of it was over as I skied and hiked out, returning to the Icefields parking lot that evening.

Back in Fredricton, Jake Bekins had never realized that I had nothing to do with him spending a week or so in jail in Peru. Now, thinking back on that event, maybe a little Peruvian jail time did him some good. Sometimes it takes harder lessons to learn, before starting something dumb again. I think my disappearing act of taking the train to Louise actually sped up his release from the Lima jail. The whole coke deal was now blamed on me as the mastermind. But, hey, if that helped Jake get out of jail in Peru earlier, that was fine by me. Jake later tracked me down and found me in Lake Louise and, out of vengeance, took a pair of my newly sponsored skis from my room in Touche town. I protested of course but was helpless to act as I was still recuperating from my battered tailbone from the Whymer fall. That is the last time I saw or heard from him. I was a bit sad: I had known Jake for so long and I regretted that he did not realize that by going out west that summer, I had most likely saved him from a longer time in a Peruvian prison.

The long range snow forecast was looking bleak for Lake Louise that autumn. So in November 1979, I packed my bags and boarded the Greyhound bus in Lake Louise heading for Whistler, British Columbia. I knew very few people there upon arrival, so I tried to look up old friends like Leigh "Ski Lee" Finck, who I knew from my childhood days back in Fredericton New Brunswick and skiing at Crabbe Mountain.

I found myself a job at the Ski Boot pub as a prep cook, but that did not last too long as I was never really much of a chef. Plus, I was always late for work after skiing powder till the lifts closed. So I was quite beat and rather useless in the kitchen, by the time my shift came up in the afternoons and I was fired.

Skiing Expedition, Huascaran, Peru, 1978

1. My ski descent of Huaytapallana (5,557m)
2. Members of expedition; From left – myself, David Clarke, John Hooper.
3. One of extreme skiing's pioneers – Patrick Vallençant
4. On the slopes of Huascaran with a visible mini-parachute intended to slow me down.

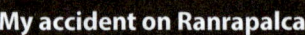

1

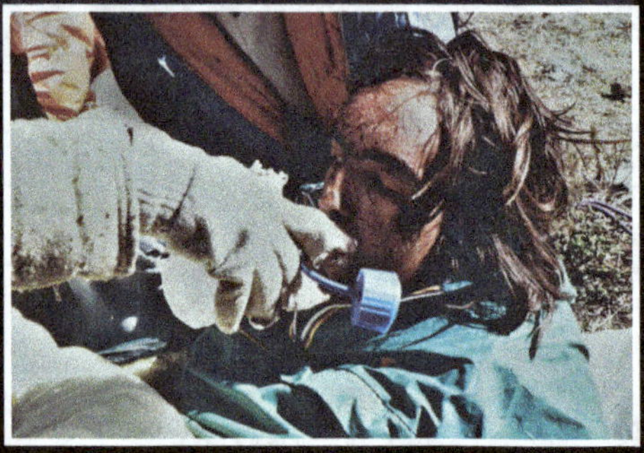

3

My accident on Ranrapalca

1. South West Face of Ranrapalca (6,162 m) where I had a 900 meter cartwheel fall.
2-3 Finally, after sleeping for nearly 3 days rescue arrives.
4. In Huaraz hospital, July 1979.

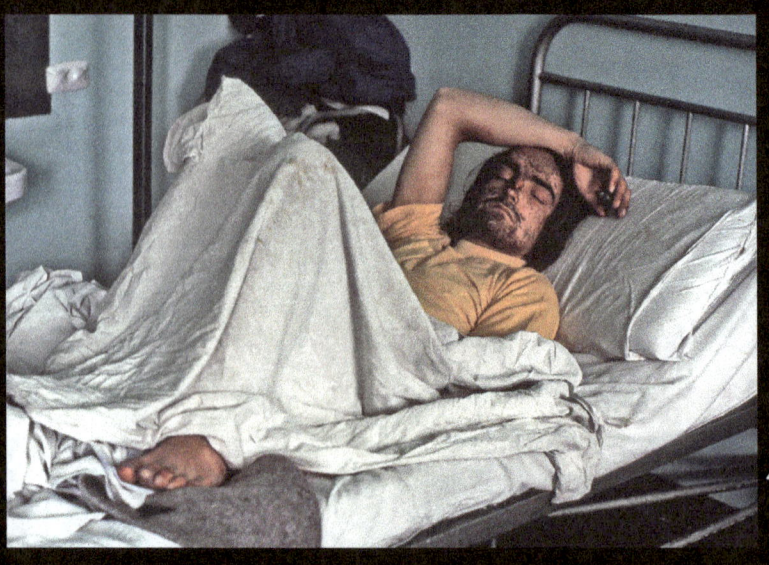

4

CHAPTER 4

MY TRULY EXTREME 80's

That same winter in Whistler I moved up in the ski world: I landed a job at McConkeys ski rental and repair shop at Creekside in Whistler. This was one of the hangouts for all the useless ski-bums and I still remember one particularly hilarious day, when all of us had been smoking hash in the repair part of the shop when ‚Diamond Jim' McConkey, as he was called, walked in. He smelled the hash right away and started to give us all shit. Dave Spears stepped in and saved the day by declaring, "Oh Jim – you wouldn't believe what just happened! These French-Canadian kids just came in here smoking a joint. I didn't notice at first but then I smelled the smoke and threw them out of here right away. The nerve kids have these days!" Dave Spears later became the head of Pemberton Search and Rescue and we had further encounters, hehe.

There was a lot of history there at McConkeys. Bob Dufour had taken over the ski school from Jim McConkey, and later Bob became Whistler's general manager. Tom Simister was a ski instructor back then, and thirty years later he built our house in Pemberton. For all of us working in the ski rentals and repairs business it was a bit of an upstairs/downstairs club. The boot fitters and retail people were upstairs, and they were a more polished crowd than us repair/rental monkeys.

It was from Whistler that I launched myself passionately into ski touring and mountaineering. I embarked on my quest to bring the Extreme word into our first ski descent exploits in the Coast Range of British Columbia. Once well settled into Whistler, I befriended a few other locals who were mostly squatters and other ski bums with whom I began undertaking various extreme skiing exploits. Not many people realized that the use of the word "Extreme" came from Vallencant's book 'Ski Extreme'. Then the word was adapted to describe everything from combat to yoga. I will smugly say that I was instrumental in bringing the word Extreme to North America and the English language by naming our new company 'EXTREME EXPLORATIONS' in 1982.

Another of my local expeditions was flying up to the top of Wedge Mountain by helicopter and skiing the infamous West Couloir. This is a steep 1,500 ft descent that starts at over 55 degrees, and then has a sustained slope of 45 degrees to the bottom. This expedition was to be the first ski descent of the couloir and there were four of us on this outing – Bart Ross, his cousin Chris, Gerhard Singler and me. Bart had also brought along his dog Spliff, which turned out not to be such a smart idea. After we got dropped off at the top we proceeded to ski to the top of the West Couloir entrance.

The icy chute was steep enough for us humans but definitely too steep for Spliff the dog to walk down. So Bart took the dog in his arms and started to ski down the couloir. Gerhard had the chute from another point, and had taken his camera out and proceeded to take pictures of mutt-carrying Bart when he slipped and lost his footing. He desperately tried to dig in to the surface to stop his fall but it was too late. I was already half-way down the chute when I saw Gerhard tumbling at a very high speed, cart-wheeling right by me into and an avalanche trough. He let out one choked scream as he hit the rocks at the bottom. It was a terrible sight as we skied down towards him. Gerhard had died instantly but his battered body was not a pretty sight.

The incident started a lot of ugly rumours around town, and many people in Whistler blamed me for the accident, saying that I should never have organized the trip in the first place. Others said chutes like that should not be skied – period. I had to endure becoming the obvious black sheep for the then-emerging destination ski resort. Various outlandish nicknames were tossed in my directions: besides "Peter Peru" and "Shouldnotski,"more outlandish monikers like "Chernobyl" started being used in referring to me, as my name now became linked to extreme disasters. One of the few people that stood by me was Ushi, Gerhard's widow. She knew her husband had always wanted to ski that chute, as they had a view of it from their house in Alpine Meadows, and he often talked about it. She remained in Whistler and after a while married another local ski patroller who eventually became Whistler's Mayor.

Despite the negative talk about me around Whistler, we continued our ski mountaineering exploits, hungrily climbing and skiing the many peaks and steep faces in the Whistler area. Most of the staff at McConky's ski shop had quit part way through that first winter in order to be able to ski more. I had also quit along with everyone else and I now had to devise another way to make some money if I wanted to ski all the time. So I came up with the idea of running a renegade ski guiding outfit in Whistler to show off its huge back country terrain. Since I could not run a guide service officially on Whistler Mountain because I had no qualifications, I dubbed my business a "photography ski business". I had business cards made up with a nice graphic of a skier, with the name FIRST TRACKS on it.

I would go around the bars after skiing and talk up likely-looking groups of skiers who seemed suitable. I would charge each client 25 bucks, plus my lift ticket split between them, so that I could still make about $150 a day – an okay rate for a ski bum back in the day. Private, one-on-one skiing and photography was optional and available at a negotiable price. After all, I was just being paid to ski my favourite places anyway. I had groups of lawyers and doctors, and all sorts of people whom I showed some great back country runs to. In order to camouflage the guiding part of my business, I would simply take a photo of everybody skiing and mail it to them after they got home. This way I could legitimately claim I was providing a photography service, rather than guiding. These were the days before mobile phones and few people carried cameras while they were skiing, so there was a market for this service.

I got away with this for a few months and had some fun with some great clients from all over the world. It was all going so well, and then one day I got a whole crew of Japanese tourists, which I recall numbered over eight people. I was really asking for trouble this time and furthermore the bus with the Japanese party arrived and parked right in front of the Whistler administration headquarters. So all the skiers clunked out of the bus, met me and then we went up the lift together. It was a weekday and consequently there weren't many skiers on the hill so we were a pretty obvious spectacle. Here I was, in front of a string of these Japanese skiers who were falling in the powder all over the mountain.

That afternoon, Whistler's resident general manager at the time, Bob Ainsworth, was really pissed at me. He called me into the office and gave me a huge scolding. Somehow, by responding in an extremely politically correct fashion, I was able to dissuade him from taking away my ski pass. But unfortunately I could not risk my FIRST TRACKS business venture any longer now. I fondly recall that incident with the Japanese, since the clients were organized for me by a local Japanese businessman Toshi Hamazaki. Toshi ran a clandestine helicopter skiing operation himself called Powder Mountain, helicopter skiing for years without ever being properly licensed. I guess he liked my spirit of adventure and for that reason had sent me the Japanese clients. Later he always carried copies of all my films on VHS. The films, for sale to the visiting Japanese, could always be found in his ski shop in Whistler Village. I have been told that my "In Search of the Ultimate Run" film became a bestseller in Japan. Toshi had helped me with some distribution there. It's funny because the film never did have the production value of my other films as it was shot in the amateur super eight format, but I guess it showed the right spirit which the Japanese had liked very much.

At one time we had enjoyed the freedom of using planes and helicopters to access the many peaks in the area around Whistler called Garibaldi Park, but this playground became off limits to us when Whistler became a bigger resort. Garibaldi Provincial Park stretches for nearly 100kms from Squamish in the south along the east side of the highway from that runs from Vancouver to Pemberton in the north and Whistler is in the middle. The Provincial Parks executive set up strict rules about using helicopter or snowmobile access into the Park. Years ago helicopter flights were easy and cheap to arrange, because British Columbia's economy of logging and mining relied on them so much.

So we had enjoyed many memorable excursions using helicopters to drop us off on the any of the hundreds of peaks in the range. Instead of a long slog into the interior of the range, we could grab our gear, fly in and set up a camp for a few days and bag some peaks. We could then ski out down the valley, or we'd get airlifted out. I remember one full moon excursion by helicopter to the top of Wedge Mountain, 2,895 m (9497 ft). Wedge was the highest peak in Garibaldi park. It was here where I had the misfortune to lose my friend skiing a year before. It is always an impressive mountain with the Wedgemont Glacier on it's north flank and beautiful 35 degree snowfields on the south side which were a skier's dream for 1,000 meters vertical. I had even taken along my cousin John Hayto, basically a resort skier, who had never experienced anything like that. We landed on top, set up camp and even did some skiing by the full moon on the Southwest side of Wedge. Next morning we did some skiing on the steeper north side, then packed up camp, skied out to the bottom and were picked up by a helicopter for our 5 minute ride back to Whistler. Wedge was one of those mountains clearly visible from the Whistler resort thus making it such a draw to the likes of us as we combed the Coast range for impressive ski descents.

On another occasion John Reed, Steve Smaridge, Nigel Protter and I took a float plane to access some summer skiing. John was a pilot and so we used his father's float-equipped Beaver aircraft to fly in to Garibaldi Lake, which is verboten now because it is within the park boundary. We left the plane tied up to some rocks, hiked up to the Sphinx Glacier and had some wonderful summer skiing. Then we flew back to Whistler's Alta Lake. We continued to use helicopters for access to the many peaks in the Coast Range to the west of Whistler as we could not use Garibaldi any longer. There were hundreds of peaks to explore on the west side of the highway, which was crown land and had less restrictive rules about heli access to the high alpine.

One early, short but memorable helicopter lift was one we had up to Whirlwind Mountain which is just east of Whistler and is now part of the Spearhead Traverse. Once we had landed, we skied down the north glacier of Overlord Mountain, then hiked up Fissile Mountain and skied down a chute called 'Fissile like a Missile.' Another of Fissile's chutes, the Banana chute, become one of our favourite runs after this trip. Scotty Paxton, another long time friend from Whistler was also with us on this trip.

Helicopters are still frequently used by ski mountaineers further out in the back country, but the enormous growth of recreational heli-skiing has meant a raft of regulations have been introduced. Only certified heli-ski companies can operate near Whistler and Pemberton. In the old days of my friend Chris Kettles and I getting flights from one "certified renegade" helicopter pilot who regularly took us on multiple hill ski runs from his base in Pemberton. However, I have to keep things hush-hush about that adventure. I will say we skied some fabulous runs on the glaciers which are just above both our houses.

Safety gear which is commonplace today had not arrived yet in those early days and avalanche beacons were brand new technology in our early years of ski touring around Whistler. In the early '80s, we were sponsored by a pioneer in the industry, Paul Ramer. We got to use his Alpine Research gear on a trip to we made to Colorado. This one I was accompanied by friend's Bart Ross, John Reed and Cheryl Condy, Bart's girlfriend. Paul Ramer was quite a character and a giant of the North American ski industry. He invented a whole lot of ski mountaineering gear, and he had also written a kind comment about my first ski article in a 1977 Powder Magazine story. Paul was a bit of a maverick entrepreneur, but he had actually managed to get a major military contract from the US Army to use his gear. We always joked that the Ramer gear under the name of Alpine Research was perfect for the Army. The ski touring bindings were actually made up of rather crude plates, were made adaptable using various nuts and bolts. "This way," we teased, "the army could take a particular binding," (as they did with their guns) "oil all the parts, and then put them all back together"– a great armed forces exercise for the wintertime.

We embarked on the long drive to Colorado in John's International truck, named Moby because it resembled a whale. We camped out on land at Ramer's beautiful ranch in Colorado where we were totally outfitted all the latest gear: Duret 8300 light honeycomb skis which were so-called because they had been used on Everest at that altitude by a French expedition. On our way back home from the trip to the Ramer ranch, we drove via the Columbia Icefields in the Canadian Rockies where we climbed and skied the north face of Mt Athabasca. It was here that we thanked whatever God was responsible because Bart had a fall on the ice while skiing and only managed to save his life by using his brand new Ramer ice-axe ski pole, which stopped him sliding further down the 2,000 ft, 55 degree face slope to almost certain death below. Paul had designed a handle for his ski sticks that incorporated an ice axe so it was always ready to use in emergencies. In this case, they had certainly been life-savers. Later we learned that our descent of Mt Athasbasca was actually the first ski descent and has gone down in the history books as such. I skied on Ramer bindings for many years, and even trusted them for my first ski descent of Mount Robson, mounted on my 207cm Dynastar Acryglass skis.

Another of my somewhat notorious episodes happened while we were skiing a run on Whistler called „Don't Miss". Whistler used to host an annual race called the "Pepsi Celebrity Ski Challenge". The spectacle involved some well-known Hollywood celebrities who were invited to Whistler for the event. The extravaganza was being held directly below Whistler's peak in Glacier Bowl. Don't Miss snaked down its steep face and ended in a narrow couloir. It was skied very occasionally and then only by very experienced locals, and the run was perfectly visible from Whistler's Roundhouse Restaurant, which was essential for any show-offs like us. This run is now closed to all, but back then the run was not even ruled out of bounds by the local ski patrol. Every young skier who wanted to be deemed worthy of skiing steep descents would eventually try to challenge 'Don't Miss', giving quite a spectacle to the Roundhouse Restaurant diners and to the skiers below.

Our plan, then was of course to ski the run to help celebrate the Pepsi Celebrity Ski Challenge. What ensued nearly turned into a full scale disaster. First to drop in was Shawn Hughes, a well-known local skier, nicknamed „So" and he triggered a major avalanche. Somehow he managed to ride it out, and I was up next. Thinking it was now safe, since Shawn's avalanche had surely taken out the majority of the loose snow leaving me with the scraped base, which I thought would be nice and safe. Scraping through the narrow rock entrance, I began my turns on the upper part of the run and I triggered what really is a very rare occurrence: the slope fractured again under my skis. Now we had a double fracture for the restaurant audience and I came careening down and over the rocks, luckily coming to a spectacular stop just above the Pepsi Celebrity Ski Challenge. The celebrities were a little shocked by the spectacle, and Whistler Mountain received a lot of complaints such as, "Why do they allow people to ski such dangerous slopes?!"

I got the blame again for that debacle from the more opinionated resident ski bums. From that moment on, 'Don't Miss' run was permanently closed. Of course, there will always be the game of 'Who dares?' among the local skiers who see it as a worthy challenge to try and descend it without getting caught. Years later I was the one who got caught skiing the run again. We had taken the Peak Chair to the top, where we hid behind a large wind drift on Whistler's summit, until the lift had closed and the ski patrol had done its sweep. With my friend Kent Rodler, we first skied the east face. Thinking we were the only people left on the mountain that late April afternoon, we decided to climb back up to the peak again, boot backing hard now to ski the real cherry on top, which was the actual north face of Don't Miss itself.

About halfway up the boot pack, we turned and were a bit surprised to discover a whole convoy of ski patrol snowmobiles parked below us in the bowl. It was truly like being the screen in a drive-in movie theatre. They were watching our every move, so there was little for us to do but continue climbing. And so we did until we reached the top of the upper north face itself. Then, as the ski patrollers watched impotently from below, we took a deep breath and just styled the run all the way to the bottom with nice thigh deep powder turns. The trick here was that we had to make a cunning escape by traversing to the left and stay out of the reach of the ski patrollers in the snowmobiles.

Kent managed to get away all right, but I took a wrong turn in the trees above the VD Chutes, and skied right into the arms of three awaiting ski patrollers who had been sent to look for us. I had to do a lot of ass licking and beer-buying to not have my ski pass revoked for good. Later, after the "Don't Miss" closure, many of our other favourite ski runs on Whistler and Blackcomb were also deemed permanently out of bounds. This included legends like "Friday the 13th," which was a real gem among local skiers, and is now closed forever.

This to me was the beginning of Whistler's true demise as a dirtbag ski town. From here on we had to play cat and mouse with Bernie, Roger and Brian, the three top patrollers, while skiing the out of bounds or on permanently closed terrain. It was definitely inspirational material for cartoonists in the local press and a cartoon series that followed the story of the "Peak Brothers" cartoon series was published in the Whistler Answer newspaper. These hide-and-seek episodes continued throughout my whole stay in Whistler as new patrol staff came and went.

I still laugh so hard when I recall what we dubbed the "Sneak Peak" episode. This occurred when I led a rather large group of individuals on a hike to the peak of Whistler while it was still closed for avalanche control. These were the days before the peak chair was in place and everybody would hike up to the top of Whistler peak to get the best powder snow. Each day, before the path up the peak was opened, the patrol had to do their avalanche blasting. We didn't realize this when we mounted our little expedition, and instead of hiking up the regular path to the peak, we traversed across the mountain and under the cornices to what was then called the „Safe Route". Here there was an entrance to a little ledge which was about 10 feet high between the cornices. From here one could hike up, continuing the route around the south side of Whistler and not be seen by the patrol or from the side where the restaurant was.

Our goal was to ski one of our favourite runs, Friday the 13th which had long been officially closed. To accomplish this goal, we traversed around the back of the peak and made our way towards West Bowl. Suddenly, we were being attacked by charges which had been fired from an avalanche cannon which was situated above Whistler's Shale slope on the other side of the peak. The bombs started exploding all around us. Nobody knew we were there and the patrol was still doing their bombing runs. Luckily none of us got hurt or killed by the explosives landing right around us. We still ended up skiing down our favourite run down into the Far West bowl and on down to the town, where we drank beer and kept quiet about the whole experience. If the authorities had ever found out what we had happened to us we would have surely been banned from the mountain forever. I can now say that our sneak peak crew included many Whistler locals including Sue Boyd and Scotty Paxton.

Sometimes I wonder how my life's events have a way of catching up to me as reminders of lessons in life. For example, I once had a great encounter with some climbers on one ski mountaineering outing to Wedge Mountain. It was sometime in the mid-80s, at least seven years after my accident in Peru. I came across some American climbers who had also summited Ranrapalca, the mountain of my 1979 horrendous accident outside of Huaraz. Once we started chatting, they told me they climbed this peak and, how on the way down, they had been very surprised to find one single ski. They said it was such a rare find that one of them took it home and now had it above his fireplace. They were even more surprised when I told them what kind of ski it was – A 207cm Dynamic VR 17. They certainly were shocked when I revealed to them that they had found one of my missing skis. It's amusing sometimes how reminders of the most memorable occasions from one's life's seem never to leave you totally.

I certainly had quite a few close calls with avalanches during my early days in Whistler. I remember 'swimming' with the snow several times as big sloughs engulfed me on a run. Luckily, every time I was somehow deposited on top of the snow at the bottom of the hill. One occasion I still visualize particularly well was when Trevor Petersen, Steve Smaridge, Beat Steiner and I had set out one spring day to ski Fissile Mtn, a good old favourite which is a three hour climb away from Whistler and its lifts. It was fairly late in the season and we had to climb a southern slope of the mountain to get up to the spot from where we could ski to one of our favourite runs, the northwest facing chute called The Banana Couloir which was on the other side of the peak. Our plan was then to traverse back to a nearby alpine cabin.

However something didn't seem right to me as we were boot packing up the face that day. I had this hunch, an uneasy feeling about the terrain we were on. So I decided to leave the rest of the party and picked a route along a ridge around some rock outcrops, rather than stay on the soft snow which lay on our route up. As Steve reached the top of the boot pack, a huge chunk of snow that he was standing on let go and dropped like a stone. It was terrifying to see him riding down on this huge chunk of snow which constituted an entire back portion of a large cornice. Below him were Trevor and Beat, climbing up the same path Steve had taken. They suddenly got taken out by Stevie with all the snow now sliding down on top of them. I remember looking on in horror as all three of my companions were soon cart-wheeling and star-fishing among the chunks of cornice slab careening downwards along with them. Trevor had just received a bright yellow North Face ski suit from his mom and he was the most visible of the three young men catapulting now down the slope. Amazingly all three were unhurt when they reached the bottom. We didn't know very much about avalanches at that time and were lucky to survive the lessons we learned from such predicaments. It is sobering to think that I have lost more friends to avalanches than from all other sport-based accidents combined while living in British Columbia.

We also started a summer ski touring business with Bart Ross and Nigel Protter, based on Ipsoot Mountain above Pemberton. We had a lot of fun flying a classic 'Jones Pioneer' like cabin-tent up to 8,300 feet, along with a wooden plywood platform to set it on. We had paid for the helicopter flights with Bart's earnings from logging, but we didn't have the funds to bring it back down in the fall, and it was in shreds the next summer when we hiked up there again. However, it certainly proved useful because we actually got stuck in it during a storm in late October one year. Running out of food, we had resorted to eating our potato peels. In fact, it was even a bit luxurious as we waited for the storm to pass, and even managed to pass the time by watching The Love Boat on a battery-powered TV which Bart had brought up!

One time the Whistler Search and Rescue gang took it upon themselves to try and rescue our motley crew during one major week-long storm. They never actually managed to get to us, however, as the storm was too strong, and they had to instead evacuate themselves, retreating soaked with their tails between their legs. They did send us an invoice for the rescue effort, however, which we laughed at. Why? Because you just don't pay an ambulance which gets a flat tire – do you? We had never called them or asked for their services in the first place, and they had taken it upon themselves to launch the 'Rescue Peter Peru and his crew" exercise." From then on I was also in the bad books with the Whistler Search and Rescue folks as well as the Whistler Ski Patrol.

Yes, those summer skiing escapades to Ipsoot in the eighties were sure fun. Sometimes, when we did not have enough money or clients to take a helicopter up, we made sure to fly up our girlfriends while we resorted to driving up the Rutherford Main logging road to the 7 mile marker. From there it was a 3½ hour bushwhack to just get to the Alpine and another couple of hours to the peak. In hindsight I can't believe the energy we had back then to bushwhack like we did.

Another funny incident I recall was when Nigel Protter and I rode our narrow-tired 10 speed touring bicycles up the Rutherford Road, complete with 60 pound packs, skis and all on our backs! Then we stashed the bikes in the woods, and made the arduous hike on up to our camp on the mountain. Sometimes, to make the hike go easier and smoother, we would take magic mushrooms before starting the trek. This medicinal approach certainly made the journey more interesting, and the time passed by rather differently. I swear the old growth forest spoke to us along the way!

The area where we set up summer skiing on Ipsoot was spectacular, and would have been a wonderful place for a small resort. This was a view shared by many experts, who dared not to say anything officially, because they then would have lost all their contracts with Whistler. Steve Smaridge and I spent two glorious weeks ski touring and exploring Ipsoot's many glaciers one August without ever leaving the alpine. All our food and fuel was flown up by helicopter. That was a glorious two weeks spent on the mountain with Stevie.

We all had so much energy back then. We invented many, many strange things to do in order to unleash it all in those days of our youth. One day, for example, we strapped skis on to our mountain bikes along with the ski poles, put a packed lunch and ski boots in our backpacks, and rode our bikes all the way up the 8km hiking trail from the Whistler resort up to Singing Pass. Then, as if that was not enough, from there we hiked our favourite Fissile mountain, and skied the respectably steep north face in the middle of summer. After a short rest, we would get back on our bikes, with our skis strapped on and ride the old mining trail all the way back to Whistler Village! Ah – Sweet Bird of Youth! Not a bad way to spend the day. Mountain bikes have long been banned from that trail now, so I only have memories of that one-time experience.

I also enjoyed a really memorable summertime visit from my father during those ski bumming years in Whistler. My dad and I rented a helicopter on one perfect bluebird July morning and flew up to the peak of Ipsoot. Here I showed him our cabin tent perched at 8,000 feet right below the summit. We had eaten our packed lunch, enjoyed the view, and my dad and I both had a most incredible summer ski run totalling almost 3,000 vertical feet to the base of the Miller Glacier, where the helicopter picked us up again and took us back to Pemberton. That was a long run considering it was in the height of summer at the end of July. I really relished those moments with my dad and only wish we could've spent more occasions together.

We got help from another Pembertonian, Herb Bluer to help move our base camp at Ipsoot. Bluer, a Swiss guide living in Pemberton, chose a great new location for us at a lower, wiser elevation at 6,500 ft which was significantly lower than where the cabin tent had originally been sited at 8,000 ft. Using the original base, we constructed a geodesic dome which Bart Ross had fashioned out of discarded aluminum conduit gleaned from building sites around Whistler. We then purchased a huge plastic tarp to cover the whole thing. The dome was placed down at a lower elevation among the rock outcrops, and by late-July and in to August the melting snow had caused little pools to form the size of hot tubs, which the sun would heat during the day and give us all natural spa tubs to splash around in.

I really discovered the natural beauty of BC during those times at Ipsoot. While our business never got a lot of clients, we sure had a lot of summer skiing fun. "Ipsoot Ventures" was the name that Bart had incorporated for the company. That summer was spent frolicking on Ipsoot Mountain but ended soon after. Bart and his wife Sue did several photograph shoots for Japanese companies there, using local ski talent as models and with Japanese film crews. I was told that the Japanese had used one portrait of me with my bushy dark beard at the time for many advertisements. People even told me of spotting a huge billboard of me in Tokyo. Fame at last! But I never got to Japan, so I can't verify the stories. Gradually our dream of setting up a permanent summer skiing operation at Ipsoot slowly came to an end over the years.

Skiing early Whistler and vicinity

1. Whistler and its upper lifts 1979.
2. Our crew on top of Wedge Mountain. From left: Jim Wharin, Me, Eric Wight, Shawn Hughes, Tom Simister, Bruce Hays, Rob Denim.
3. Summertime on skis near Black Tusk, Whistler.
4. Above Garibaldi Lake. From left: Nigel Protter, Myself, Steve Smaridge, John Reed.

Ski Bumming life, Whistler early 1980's

1. Summer skiing near Black Tusk, Whistler.
2. Rob Denim in Whistler's VD Chutes.
3. John Reed in his environment, in the back of his International truck, "Moby".
4. A typical squatters cabin in Whistler vicinity.

CHAPTER 5

SURVIVING MT ROBSON, SIMON FRASER UNIVERSITY AND EARLY DAYS OF FILMMAKING

In 1980 I started a love/hate affair with Mt Robson, which lasted at least seven years, and was later documented by my film "The North Face, Seven Years on Mt Robson". My first time on the mountain I was involved in what turned out to be a complete fiasco.

The whole affair was instigated by a certain Jacques Thibault, who had come to Whistler from Quebec and talked me into organizing an expedition to ski Mt Robson, at 3,954 m it was the so-called Monarch of The Rockies. The mountain certainly demands respect as a major peak. It was a seemingly impenetrable fortress, whether viewed from the tourist lookout off the Yellowhead Highway, or from any other direction for that matter. It rose out of the valley floor with huge outcrops on its flanks and it was crowned by impressive glaciers on all aspects which made all approaches extremely difficult. Mt Robson created it's own weather systems as the glaciers caused shifting micro-climates. Although it's elevation is dwarfed by the Himalayas, the mountain was known for it's fierce cold and technical climbing qualities. The Emperor and North faces were legendary routes with many scaring stories brought back by surviving climbers. Thibault was soon joined in his promotion of his crazy skiing idea by an American named Chuck Hammond – possibly not his real name. I now got suckered into joining the whole extreme affair as the nominal expert skier. I had by then acquired a reputation for skiing a number of first descents and I was starting to attract certain "wannabes" who wanted to emulate my exploits. I was still young and too gullible and I did not do enough to check out their credentials. Jacques claimed to be a certified mountain guide trained by the great Hans Gmoser, the inventor of heli-skiing, and who was himself a well-known heli-ski guide with experience on Mt Robson itself. When I tried to contact Herr Gmoser he was unfortunately out of the country. Luckily for Jaques, I couldn't check his credentials, and rather stupidly joined the venture.

The South West face of the mountain turned out to be unskiable at any time that season. Jacques turned out not to be a real mountain guide, or even the decent skier he claimed to be. And Chuck? Well, he was a crook playing at being a promoter. After the Mount Robson debacle Chuck, still needed some cash and managed to endear himself to "Sounds Fantastic", which was a well-known Vancouver stereo chain where he landed himself a job. Apparently while he was there he managed to write a lot of checks to himself, and left the store chain hanging with a lot of money owed to it. For a brief period he earned fame of a sort by being listed on the RCMP's 'Most Wanted' list for quite some time.

From hyping up our expedition when he actually appeared on the "That's Incredible" show in Hollywood during our Mount Robson fiasco, to absconding with funds and scamming "Sounds Fantastic," I must admit Chuck was pretty creative in his schemes. However, in the end, he was just a crook and I was left going back to Whistler with my tail between my legs. I was very embarrassed by the whole Robson ordeal and my reputation was forever tarnished.

The incident created a lot of media attention because Chuck was a great promoter. At one point during the event, he corralled 48 reporters and three helicopters on a high plateau below the South West face of Mt Robson, the staging area for the whole ordeal to document the start of this extreme ski descent.

It was October 1981 and I still remember being helicoptered up to the peak of Robson with Jacques. Mountain guides were up there already, and they had cordoned off the whole summit ridge with ropes, so at least the reporters would not fall off the mountain. Creativity was called for! I had to do something as all the cameras were on us. So, I began the motions of unravelling the short length of polypropylene rope which was all I had brought along at the last minute in order to make a good show of things for the gathered cameras and the reporters. With fitting flair I proceeded to lower Jacques, who was thrashing around at the other end of the rope, until I ran out of cord. Then, for the big finale, we all had to get together with the mountain guides and drag Jacques back up to the summit again. We all decided then it was game over for this time, and the South West face of Mount Robson was just not skiable at all.

At least that fiasco on Mt Robson did have its amusing moments. Chuck took great care of his talent: me and Jacques. He brought two French Canadian girls along for Jacques. Although Jacques never slept with them, they were sort of his entourage, one might say. I was getting horny myself during our week-long stay at the Valemount Motor Inn, while Chuck hyped the project to the media. I did end up sleeping with one of the French Canadian girls later but had to do it really discreetly, otherwise Jacques would have been jealous. It was one of those cases where he had the hots for her, but she just wanted to be 'friends'.

In a lot of ways Chuck really knew how to run an operation. He deferred all our hotel, helicopter and media bills. He charged each reporter for his own helicopter time, so he also got cash from that. Chuck made his play for media attention on the promise that a very popular television show out of LA at the time, "That's Incredible", was going to promote the whole event. Chuck knew well how to use the carrot around our Robson spectacle on the media and the town of Valemount. He often bragged how this was "his town now". Chuck put all his cards and sales expertise on "That's Incredible" which had good ratings.

One day Chuck came to me and said, "Peter if you want to get lucky, just go down to Jasper, pick up a girl and just tell her that if she comes back to Valemount with you she would get a free helicopter ride in the morning." And so that night I went to Jasper, went into the bar actually only 15 minutes before closing and met this really nice blonde German girl who was working in Jasper. We chatted for about 5 minutes, had the last dance together and then I popped the question "Hey – you want to come to Valemount and get a helicopter ride tomorrow?"

To my utter surprise she said yes to my rather sudden invitation. So I said the bus leaves in five minutes just down the block, let's go. She came back home with me to our motel, we had a great and wild night, and Chuck duly gave her the promised helicopter ride in the morning as promised, so it turned out to be a rare win-win situation for everyone. The funniest thing was that several years later that girl and her boyfriend ended up sharing a house with me in Burnaby, when we all went to Simon Fraser University. She was really embarrassed by the memory for some reason, and wanted to make sure that I would never tell her boyfriend about our incident back on Robson. The world is very small sometimes (and I didn't tell).

A torn ACL (Anterior Cruciate Ligament) in my left knee in April of 1982 took me away from skiing and back to studying Film and Communications at Simon Fraser University in Vancouver. The knee injury prompted a visit to my home town of Fredericton NB. My parents were very supportive and realized that I hated being back out East after all my adventures in the mountains. To ease the pain they sent me to the Rockford photography workshop in Maine, south of the border, which was a great experience. I took a course specializing in shooting 35mm slides, knowledge which would come in very handy later. I also took an English literature course during a summer semester course at the University of New Brunswick back in Fredericton which kept me busy as well.

At UNB, I also started once again to date old sweethearts from high school. But my return to old habits did not last long, because I met the first love of my life. Megan Hanson, a lawyer's daughter became my first steady girlfriend.

In fact, many relationships started for me when I was injured and thus slowed down in my life's adventures. It was only then that I slowed down enough to take serious notice of the women around me. It was wonderful meeting Megan, she was only 18 at the time while I was turning 24.

Megan and I headed back out west from Fredericton to shack up together and study at SFU. I loved Megan dearly but, as it turned out, my love for her was just not enough. At first she started skiing and even ski touring with me, but soon I realized that those passions were mine alone and not really hers. It never really works out when the girlfriend starts doing a sport to keep you company because you love the sport instead of doing it for herself.

Even so our relationship lasted for about two years. Megan was taking anthropology at SFU, while I stayed in film and communications. She was a bit confused, soon quit university and moved up to Whistler to share a condo with a girlfriend there instead. I was not an easy nut to crack as a boyfriend either. Although I tried to please Megan and take her on as many side trips as I could, her heart was really somewhere else all along.

My adventurous lifestyle usually carried with it a very messy nest. A home life "of sorts" back in Vancouver that was not that attractive to many women. I found that, although many of them claimed to desire adventure, society in the end would have its way. My girlfriends would be tamed into a more domestic form of life – one which was very different from mine. In fact, I was often embarrassed to take girls home to my impoverished, often ghetto–like accommodations, which were usually just a room in a shared house or dingy apartment in Vancouver's Chinatown.

Instead I would plan dates with girls around mountain trips. I was really good at that and masterminded some really romantic escapades in our great outdoors, where Mother Nature would provide the ideal setting for romance. One favourite place to take and get romantic with girls whom I met in Vancouver, was on the trek high above the Joffre Lakes near Pemberton. There was a welcoming mountain hut there, although I found it even nicer to take the woman up higher above the cabin, up on the ridge a bit, and just fuck like rabbits, among the wildflowers in the Alpine when the sun had set. This way I was somewhat able to keep my romantic dreams alive with the hope of eventually maybe – just maybe – meeting somebody compatible with my lifestyle. So far that person has never materialized. Mt Joffre and its lakes have since become overrun by tourists due to the number of people doing selfies for their Instagram pages.

Yes, I had some memorable moments in the great outdoors, including some which were a bit embarrassing. One occurred with one date as we were making love right next to a trail when, in the middle of our heated passions, a whole troop of boy scouts came walking by and caught us in the midst of our activity. I even managed to have one romantic encounter in the middle of winter on a cold day in December, while we were hiking up in the Joffre region. The temperature was well below zero Celsius as we made our way through the forest. Suddenly we both looked at each other and in the heat of the moment, took all our clothes off, threw them down on the snow covered ground below a big tree, then proceeded to make love on top of the pile of clothes which was all that shielded us from snow. I still recall that moment fondly.

Pemberton also had four different locations where hot springs can be found within a two hour drive from our house, and these hot springs were a great place to take a date. Given a little pot and wine, my partners would swiftly lose their inhibitions. I remember many memorable trips with various women to the springs for some incredibly amorous activity, and then relaxing into lovely deep sleeps in my van, or if it was warm enough, in a tent. I was certain to get lucky if my date agreed to take a trip to the hot springs or so it seemed with my most memorable companions.

Exhaustion via l'amour led to one bad road accident when I totalled the first of my white Delica vans. Coming back from the hot springs early one morning, my companion and I were quite exhausted from being in the springs most of the night. Because my friend had an appointment in Whistler, we were on the road pretty early, and the road in question is both gravel and tarmac and runs alongside Lilloet Lake and on to Pemberton, through the Lilwat Nations Reserve land. This road had long straight stretches, which were connected by sudden 90° turns. It was a hot summer that year but it had rained in some spots along our route back to Pemberton. Dust settling on the blacktop, followed by bits of rain, can make the surface of the road as slippery as winter black ice. It was a similar scenario to the one back in 1972 in Brazil when we slid off the road with my parents and our VW camper. The red clay in Brazil also dried up and as the wind blew the sand on to the highway it became very slippery when it was wet after a rainfall.

Although I was driving rather slowly, I was still a bit tired from the night before and I took one turn perhaps a little too fast and the next thing I knew we were sliding sideways on the highway. It seemed a very slow slide and I thought for a moment we were just going to stop and everything would be all right. But, unfortunately the Delica is rather top-heavy and when we hit the dry pavement, the van rolled twice with us in it. We were both shaken up but luckily had no serious lasting injuries – although my girlfriend missed her Whistler appointment and to take a few days off work. She had twisted her torso when she braced herself against the ceiling with her hand during the roll-over. However, a few physiotherapy treatments on ICBC fixed her up. As for my vehicle, luckily Delicas appreciate in value and in the end I got a good settlement from the car insurance company so, by adding a few thousand dollars of my own, bought a new one. So, things ended up even better in the end.

There were other relationships too. I tried my luck in romance with single mothers as well. There was one lady in particular I was very fond of. Her name was Melinda and she was an incredibly talented painter. She had a lovely little black daughter, whose father was a well-known Canadian sports celebrity. She lived on British Columbia's Sunshine Coast and I would often take the short ferry ride to visit her, or invite her up to Whistler when I was staying up there. But again that didn't work out too well after a while either, and we drifted apart.

Such drifting apart became the case with many women. Then, while living in Vancouver, I met another girl. Katherine Story was an only child – a very attractive, highly intelligent and spunky brunette. She worked for the Georgia Straight which was a popular Vancouver newspaper. Although she didn't do much in the outdoor sports world, she was in great shape from aerobics – indoors. I still vividly remember the snow mobile outing Katherine and I had with Nigel Protter one New Year's Eve near Pemberton.

The trip required an 18 km journey by snowmobile to where the ski touring would start. Unfortunately, snowmobiles are loud machines, and when Katherine fell, while being towed behind the machine, her screams went unheard. Nigel who was driving, was unaware that she was being dragged by the rope wrapped around her leg for a long way. Finally we noticed and called to Nigel to stop the machine. However, she was one brave cookie: she gritted her teeth, brushed off the snow and made the final ski tour trek to the cabin where we would spend New Year's Eve. I certainly admired her bravery as it must have been a horrendous experience for her. We made up for it that night as we ate chocolate along with magic mushrooms and had an amazing time all night long. Unfortunately Katherine did not last long either, like so many of my girlfriends. She paid me a visit one night after I had just come back from the annual Las Vegas ski show. Dressed all in black, including black lipstick and high heels, she clattered up to my residence in Vancouver and informed me that she had met somebody from New York, and was leaving me for him. She had always told me her dream was that she wanted to live in New York, so I guess her dream materialized for once. I was heartbroken again, as I always seemed to be for a short while, and I tried to give her flowers to mend whatever problems had been between us, but she really had her mind set and left within a couple of weeks.

No, I've never really had much luck at keeping women for very long. One woman who did learn to tolerate me was my good skiing buddy, Doris Spika. Although we tried dating upon first meeting, we found that something was just not right. Maybe we just lacked the right chemistry, or something like that. But we have ended up as lifelong friends and we have skied and traveled so much together. Doris is a successful interior designer based in Vancouver, with a very colorful past. She has been a World Cup level freestyle skier. Having shared many great times together, we have also remained best friends to the present. She often shows up to comfort my mother after my mother has received a phone call concerning my latest accident and subsequent hospitalization somewhere in the world.

In later years I would make a film, which "Paracinderella" touches on this romantic subject but as I now work my way through my life story, I thought this was a good place to talk a little more about the women in my life.

The truth is there have been only about five serious relationships that really stayed in my memory. Any others were just transients that I passed time with because, given the projects I always had going on, I usually never had time or the energy for a lasting relationship.

I hasten to add that I did love „my" women when I was with them: I was always true to them and never cheated on any of them. I always thought: why cheat on this person? Why should I have to look elsewhere when I finally chose a partner? In most cases I just knew deep inside that the relationship was only for a short time anyway. I wish the feeling of fidelity would have been mutual from the feminine side. I was cheated on and double timed by nearly all the women I've gone out with. Maybe that contributed to me being jaded a bit now and a bit suspicious of relationships in general. Or, I was just always somehow put in second place, with a better, more secure option always ahead of me on her list of demands.

But what could I really expect from most women? Certainly, I could survive living on somebody's porch in Vancouver while making a film, but not many other people could endure that, especially women – unless they were "head over heels" (and more!) in love with me, that is. I felt I somehow had missed letting love in to my life on several occasions. It was a feeling that I had, that some women in my life had reached out to me several times, hoping for a reaction from me, but from my side it really never materialized.

I guess I could never really maintain any of those past relationships. Most women left quickly as soon as they sensed that sex was really my main motivation to be with them in the first place, and after that initial sexual encounter they felt I just kind of pretended to be interested. Some women thought I was a bit of an animal in that respect and scorned me for it in a big way. But I really would have taken love – true love – if I had sensed it was really meant for me from someone. Then I would have probably even given in and let her have a child with me, although I was never driven biologically to do so. Neither did I nor do I have an urge to have children, like many people that I know have when they have reached a certain age. In short – I would have loved to have more opportunities to interact more with the intriguing female mind. Women really are such fascinating creatures. I wish more relationships would have taken me to explore their more intellectual side. I enjoy films made by female directors, always recognizing that edge and point of view from a woman. I really enjoyed "Innis", a book by Isabel Allende, a woman's perspective on the conquest of Peru and Chile.

I've had some nice things said to me by women though and some of these women were quite feminist. Indeed they were women who quickly sensed the wolf in the man, yet they gave me a break about. I still remember a rather nice comment from a meeting with a very strong woman's film group in Vancouver. A lady said a really kind thing to me at one of their seminars. "Women feel very comfortable around you somehow, Peter, they don't feel the machismo or aggression as they might from many men when they are around you." Those words still ring in my ears and mean a lot to me. Like I later would say, "I love women but I'm sure glad I never married any of them."

While studying at SFU, I continued my extreme dreams and, together with my old friends Nigel Protter, David Frazee, Beat Steiner and Alex Grzybowski, we formed a company named "Extreme Explorations" with the hook line "Uncommon Film and Video" attached, in 1982.

The SFU film department was geared towards more artsy experimental films and I had a hard time persuading them to let me make adventure documentaries. The department was then run by a group of rather hard-core art lesbians who really never did take a great liking to me or my adventure documentary ideas. I really do not think I am homophobic, but I wish they had been as diplomatic with me as they had were with the women's film group in Vancouver.

I planned to shoot a film I had dubbed "In Search of The Ultimate Run", despite the constant obstacles hurled in my way by the film dept. I remember borrowing the name from „Playboys Guide to Ultimate Skiing". One of Playboy's editors, James Peterson, was actually a speed-skier and had done a few runs on the track when Whistler Mountain had set up a speed track on the steep Shale Slope.

Ignoring the Film Department's political opposition, I once again went boldly to the top and approached Simon Fraser University's President Dr William Saywell with my crazy project. I had learned a lot about how University politics worked as our expedition up Huascaran had also been another University expedition, although that had been the University of New Brunswick. Having gained an appointment with Saywell himself, I hoped for the best, and somehow he became sympathetic to my quest as I outlined the plan to climb and ski Popocatepetl, the famous dormant volcano outside Mexico city. We would also proudly plant the SFU flag on top of the cone.

The President actually gave us our first $500 funding out of his personal contingency fund. Another $500 dollars came from Bob Moyer who was an executive producer in sport at the Canadian Broadcasting Corporation who I had badgered endlessly with phone calls prior to our departure. Our funding was secure, and that shut the lesbians up in the film department. We were off to the races!

I really did enjoy my time at SFU. I also got to make two other films while I was enrolled there. The Communications Department of the Uni was great because it was open to new ideas. By contrast the Film Department was a bit too artsy for my liking but I enjoyed the courses I took there nevertheless. I was swept up by watching a lot of German Cinema, and became a real fan of Werner Herzog, Fassbinder and those other German filmmakers.

There was a whole array of eccentric professors to learn from and deal with. Al Razutis was one, who was a famous experimental filmmaker, and his "Semiotics" film course was one that only a few of us would survive taking.

All that justified me being enrolled, although I didn't ski as much as I would have liked while I was there. SFU offered convenient studying, which I mixed with my passions and pleasures. Unlike UNB or UBC, it offered its students much more leeway in choosing their courses and the time allotted for them. The school's modern design was also much more centralized and this meant that one did not have to walk for miles, carrying all your books between classes.

The plan for the film was to load up two vehicles with our party of eight skiers, drive southwards from BC (skiing as many ski resorts as time would allow), and then continue down the Baja peninsula crossing in to Mexico. We would then take the ferry across to Puerto Vallarta and drive to Popocatepetl on a „mission" to climb and ski Mexico's second highest volcano which stood at 5393 metres altitude. Along with the team members of Extreme Explorations, we had two other friends with us, Clark Roberts and Rob Murray. Clark was a skier while Rob wasn't and had just came along for the experience. Rob role was crucial though because his was the second vehicle, and had borrowed the VW van for the journey from some friends in Vancouver. On reflection it was rather bold of them to lend their vehicle to a bunch of twenty somethings going on their ultimate road trip, but that sort of thing happens to you when you're in your twenties and slightly crazy

So in the end we had two vehicles, the 1972 Volkswagen camper van from our new friend Rob, and a Datsun pickup with a canopy, provided by friend and fellow skier John Reed, who also came along with us. Once again I had pulled all my marketing skills out of the bag, and we had brand new outfits in bright yellow provide by a Montréal ski wear company, Nat Lacen. We were on our way.

We managed to find all sorts of crazy stunts to film on our way down the Baja Peninsula. Our feats included being pulled on skis by dune buggies on Baja's beaches, and we found a gravel quarry where we decided to do some sand and gravel skiing. Here was John Reed's starring role in our film as he skied the sand, gravel and rocks for our cameras. Funnily enough, the bases of our skies got thrashed by the rock runs, but were later smoothed out nicely on the beach while being pulled by the dune buggies and they got a good stone grinding on the bases.

We also had some of the first mountain bikes to arrive in Canada for the trip. They were from the Japanese bike company Miyata. I developed a real liking for the new sport of mountain biking because it opened up yet more ways of accessing the back country.

Later, while attending SFU, we would often rip around the UBC endowment lands in Vancouver on our bikes. The sport has grown enormously since the early days, and Vancouver's North Shore and Whistler's bike trails would become world famous. I once met Gary Fisher who is considered to be the grandfather of mountain biking. Gary had developed the mountain bike concept in California in 1968 by basically turning a regular Schwinn bike into a trail bike by adding wider knobbly tires. Apparently they used the bikes to access their marijuana grow crops up in the California hills, because they were quiet and not as easy to track as the noisy dirt bikes they had been using.

I'm sure that not even Gary could have imagined how the sport would take off around the world after such a strange start.

Returning to our filming, while we were in Cabo San Lucas we heard a strange rumour that the Rolling Stones' Keith Richards was getting married that weekend. So we crashed the party, claiming to be photographers working for the UPI news agency. I even remember seeing Mick Jagger arriving in a glamorous white helicopter. We actually kept up the act for several hours enjoying the reception before the bouncers realized what was happening and threw us all out. Several of our crew ended up spending the night in a Mexican jail, but I managed to slip away undetected in to the night.

From the Baja's tip at Cabo San Lucas we took the ferry across the Sea of Cortez to Puerto Vallarta, where my mom was waiting to meet us for Christmas. It was really nice seeing her and we all had a nice rest but one night we almost got in a huge bar brawl. My good old mom diffused the situation, saving us from being beaten to a pulp by angry Mexicans who had wanted us to pay their overpriced bar bill. We had refused of course and things had got ugly, but my mom's calm words manage to sort everything out.

The next morning we packed up our vehicles again and left Puerto Vallarta, driving the 700 kms to the base of the Popocatepetl volcano, which stands 75 kms south-east of Mexico city.

Once there, we climbed and skied the mountain over the next two days without properly acclimatizing, and that proved really tiring. However, that oversight was remedied when someone pulled out a few lines of coke on the summit to celebrate and to make that ski down a little more aggressive.

And so, as we had promised UBC's President Saywell, we managed to climb and ski „Popo" by New Year's Eve, and we had also planted the SFU flag on top. Filming completed and photos taken, we turned north from Mexico City, travelling via a number of ski resorts northward through the USA and filming our exploits all the way home.

Nigel and his mechanical knowledge saved the day again near Durango, Colorado when the engine in the VW blew up. While he worked hard to replace it, we managed to make some turns in the nearby ski resort of Purgatory. Beat Steiner had a close call here when he caught an edge and fell careening down the steep slope just managing to stop himself right above a yawning crevasse.

We eventually got home two weeks late for classes. There was a lot of grumbling around the film department about our controversial journey and filming and whether it fitted in with their agenda of radical feminism. Luck was on my side again as I discovered that I didn't need to take a French credit course at SFU, because I had attended classes in Grenoble. That might have only lasted for a few weeks but I had been registered there officially, and the University sent me my diploma automatically. Since I had learnt French on my own while I was there, I felt it was perfectly right to use it for three University credits at SFU, and so I did just that.

I felt that University was 80% politics anyhow. One just had to know what your professor wanted to hear, and feed it to him, without him realizing what you were doing. I did work hard at the school while I was in the film department, but I guess I had made some foes there. The head of the department shunned me, and later she admitted that I had started to appear in her nightmares! I heard later that she had confided to friends that in one dream I now appeared as the Canadian Telefilm executive from whom she has sought all her funding.

We produced a half hour film from all our footage. It was extreme in every sense of the word, and called it the way things had turned out as we were truly 'In Search of the Ultimate Run'. Shot on super 8 film and then transferred to video, it never did aired on the national broadcaster CBC. Instead it got at least 10 showings on the new Discovery Network. I was very proud that my first film which was completely underfunded, had actually found an audience with Discovery.

As we had very little money for post-production on the film, I had to get really creative to make it all happen. I enlisted a friend who was also the local student radio announcer at UNB to narrate the script. Nancy Smith did a thoroughly professional job for a student DJ, with her smooth generic CBC voice which is eagerly sought after by television programmers and documentary film makers. I introduced Nancy to my skiing buddy Neil Price, and they later got married. I was always good at bringing people together.

By 1982 while I was at SFU I also realized that I had to choose between two different paths in life. The first was to go for a 'normal' life, with the struggles of buying a house, creating a family and having kids.

The second option was to take the cursed, wild side of underfunded and very time-consuming adventure documentary route, which would ensure a never ending life of travel, production and long hours editing to make the films. I chose the latter of course.

While we were at SFU, I made a return trip to the Baja Peninsula with my girlfriend Megan. She had been angry with me for not taking her along on our filming trip to Mexico, and so I wanted to make up for that. I thought I would plan a nice holiday together to make up for the last time. We had a roommate while at SFU, who was a Pakistani postgraduate student in geology. Crucially Imran had just bought a Toyota Land Cruiser and offered to take it on a trip to the Baja with us. We packed up the truck and proceeded down the West Coast during our Christmas holidays.

Setting off from Vancouver we took turns driving and camping on our way through the US and Mexico. About half way down the Baja Peninsula there is a massive metal structure, a statue of sorts which is the dividing line between the North and South parts of Baja California. It is also a government checkpoint not allowing fruits or vegetables grown above and below this point to be cross-mixed to avoid contamination.

The road is very straight but there is a huge 90 degree turn right below the statue. We had just awoken from camping that night and it was barely daylight just before 7am. As Imran sped along the highway at 70 mph, we all suddenly looked up, distracted by the gargantuan monument. Imran had taken his attention off the road for a moment just as he looked to the road again it did its sudden curve. As the Land Cruiser is top heavy, he could not compensate for the sudden swerve at such high speed. As a result, we rolled several times on the highway, then off into the ditch, and beyond to a flat spot, ending up on our wheels again. There was nothing left of the vehicle except the wheels and base and the roll bar which had miraculously saved us from certain death.

This had all occurred right in front of a small motel, which was across from the monument. There were a dozen people or so standing and staring at us in their pyjamas. They had all heard a sound like a huge tin can rolling down the highway and all had run out of the motel to see what happened. I still cannot believe none of us were hurt in the crash.

After our rather spectacular misadventure, the three of us gathered up our belongings and leaving the wreck we continued on south to Cabo San Lucas by bus. Imran chose to return early from our holiday selling what of value remained from the Toyota to a local Mexican scrap yard. Megan and I stayed longer, camping in our tent on the beach. I did manage to buy a nice pair of leather pants down there because at the time leather was in fashion. Maybe not a great idea as the purchase cut into our food budget, but we've all done something stupid like this.

Later, as we hitchhiked back to Vancouver, we had a strange encounter with a trucker that picked us up. He asked if I would allow him to have a go with my girlfriend in return for giving us a ride. In retrospect, such crazy occurrences no doubt contributed to Megan leaving after we returned home.

The Skiing Lifestyle 1980's

1. A crashed ultralight we were using in Tantalus mountains for reconnaissance and aerial photos.
2. First ski descents off Serratus Peak.
3. With Megan on Canadian beach.
4. Enjoying Meager Creek hot springs near Pemberton B.C.

The search of the ultimate run

1. Popocatepetl Volcano, the climax of our filming ski trip.
2. DVD cover of the film.
3. Our Canadian crew in Taos, New Mexico on our way back from Popo.
4. John Reed on top of Popocatepetl with the Canadian flag.

CHAPTER 6

MATURING WITH MOUNTAINS AND WOMEN

During the years after my first attempt at skiing down Robson, that unfinished project still lingered in my mind. In fact the 1981 fiasco haunted me! I had to make further attempts. Some of our "failures" had a somewhat macabre nature. For example, on one trip with Bart Ross and Nigel Protter we actually made it almost as far as "the Dome", a large hump below the Kain face. Unfortunately, that attempt ended when someone spilled scalding hot coffee over my chest before going to sleep in our tent. That very painful incident prompted an immediate evacuation of the mountain, as I had received 2nd degree burns on my chest from the cowboy coffee. To make my evacuation off the mountain less strenuous on everyone, Leigh Finck, alias "Ski Lee" who was also on the trip, decided to try to make things easier for me and our whole crew. He drove his truck illegally almost all the way up to Berg Lake on the narrow trail designed more for hikers and park utility vehicles. The rescue did not go smoothly as he got distracted somehow, and drove off the trail into the ravine below. At 3 o'clock in the morning, he ran back to the highway and somehow managed to talk a tow truck driver into also driving illegally up the trail and they were able to get the crashed truck out before dawn and before park officials got word on what had happened. The news got out anyhow, since gossip is a staple of small towns like Valemount and from then on I was not a welcome entity in Mount Robson Provincial Park, a status which had a lot to do with being refused filming permits and other things later on.

During the years at SFU Beat Steiner and I also attempted to ski Robson again the next year in the summer of '82. We did the brutal hike in with 90 pound backpacks as far as Berg Lake. We then made it partway up Robson Glacier before exhaustion did us in and we had to turn back.

I decided to return to Mt Robson yet again in August of 1983 with Megan Hanson, my girlfriend, and a kitten dubbed "Robson". I desperately wanted to clear my name. We hiked in again, me with my 90 pound pack filled with all the gear. Megan had a tough slog too with the heavy load during the two day hike to our base camp at Berg Lake. There Megan waited with the kitten for three days while I was on the mountain solo.

The whole Robson climb was a very special one for me. I had left my stove with Megan. I was counting on getting melt water from snow as it melted over the rocks to save weight having to carry a stove up.

I set out early in the morning, first having to ford the freezing river pouring out of Berg Lake. I was hoping to find a direct route from here up to the bottom of the north face, thus saving myself the more normal roundabout route up the Robson glacier. Robson is like a fortress and there are only a few routes up from the lake and finding the right one is not easy because the conditions change so frequently.

During the reconnaissance I had found a rock cairn at the bottom of a cliff face. As I looked up, there was another cairn left by climbers, then another one. I followed these rock piles which showed me the route through what seemed like an impenetrable vertical cliff. Within a couple of hours I had reached the top of the rock face climbing through a series of gullies. I returned happy to base camp and Megan as now I had my route dialed right to the bottom of the north face.

Mt Robson is the highest peak in The Canadian Rockies. It stands at 3,954 m (12,972 ft) in elevation and is highly glaciated with very prominent features and ice-falls surrounding it. These often create it's own weather, and the mountain is greatly respected by mountain guides who compare it to the Himalayas as it has similar climbing problems and proportions. It is often called "The Monarch of The Rockies." by the guide books.

On this solo summit attempt I followed the cairns with all my ski and camping gear. It was like a steep rock climb, and topping out on the glacier below the north face, I put on my skis and approached the North Face. The route here is over a crevassed glacier terminating at a col at the top. On the left is a 500 foot tall feature called "The Helmet." To the right is the North Face and above that is the towering peak of Robson.

By now it was late afternoon on August 22nd, 1983. I found an unoccupied tent and as I looked up the North Face I saw two specks reaching the summit. The tent must have belonged to those climbers. I must admit I spent the night in their tent instead of my less comfortable bivi sack as they didn't return that night. I heard later that the climbers descended the South West face of the mountain from the summit after a night spent in a cabin instead and came back around later to pick up their tent.

The next day I looked at the North Face more closely. Unfortunately there was a large sheet of ice which covered its mid-section, and there was no sense in trying to climb it as it was not ski-able. Instead I skied back down the mountain through The Dog to the Dome. There I met up with some climbers from Montana who would witness my climb up the face. They were camped on the Dome below the Cain face. I was so pumped I just said hi and kept on going, front pointing up the face on crampons and then putting my skins on and touring up for several hours, up the Fuhrer Ridge to the point where there was no more ridge to follow and the slope flattened out. I had reached the summit of Robson! A feeling of exceptional euphoria enveloped me, as it does to so many climbers after a seemingly endless ridge climb to the top. I savoured an orange that I had saved for the summit and took another look down the north face. Unfortunately, despite my greatest wishes, it was just not feasible to ski it due to the ice sheet in the middle. So I took off my skins and skied back down the Fuhrer Ridge and then on to the Kain face which brought me back to the Dome. Being psyched from my summit bid and the ski down, I continued passed the Americans in their camp and was intending to ski down a short cut and be back with Megan that night.

Unfortunately I had been overly optimistic. As I skied past the Dome, the slope which was like the top of a huge basketball, got steeper and steeper. Then suddenly, in the middle of one turn, a crack appeared and the hill avalanched. About 10 inches of snow had slid off the ice underneath. I dug in my ski edges with all my strength as I slid helplessly down the slope, and luckily managed to get control just before going over the cliff that was above the ice-fall.

Due to the euphoria of having just completed my first ski descent of Mt Robson, I had stupidly rushed and taken this bad route which ended above the cliff. I was paralyzed with fear clinging on with my ski edges to the sheet of water ice I was now left on.

I took a big breath, concentrating on the only option I was left with – to get back up the slope safely. Slowly, and very carefully I attempted a sidestep up, then another and another, using my skis and my poles in unison to always give myself at least three points anchored in the ice to avoid slipping. I eventually made my way upwards all the way back up to the American camp, arriving totally exhausted. The climbers from Montana were surprised to see me again and made me hot tea, and I spent the night in their tent.

Next day my new friends accompanied me as they down climbed to the Robson glacier and the traditional route down to Berg Lake while I skied and waited for them. They took a few pictures at the top with Mt Resplendent in the background. Then, I bid them goodbye, skied out and hiked back to Megan's campsite. Skiing is always a nice fast way out of long glacier approaches, and this was the case here with the Robson Glacier.

When I returned to the camp, Megan told me that the park rangers had come by and told her that they would "probably bring me down later in a body bag." Poor Megan – what a horrible thing to say to a frightened girl left at our base camp!

So that is how, in the end, I climbed and skied the first descent of the Kain Face and Fuhrer Ridge – finally settling my score with the mountain. I was severely dehydrated due to the little water I carried on my journey. I had lost about 10 pounds in the ordeal mainly due to dehydration. It was a hard lesson learned by not taking the stove along to make water.

I had managed to climb and ski the mountain solo despite a lot of hardships en route, and upon my return to Vancouver, I found I had made the cover of the Vancouver Sun newspaper and felt a pleasant feeling of smugness about all the publicity. My exploits made many papers and magazines, and for a while it was a good feeling – acquiring some celebrity status for a change. My friend from Whistler, Nigel Protter, had contacted Charles Campbell, a local writer, who got the scoop and wrote the story for the Sun on my ski descent. He later became the editor of The Georgia Straight and we often ran into each other at the Vancouver International Film Festival celebrations and galas.

Charles checked his facts with the Montana climbers who verified my ascent and descent. They had seen me skiing the Fuhrer Ridge and had even taken some pictures as well. A few mountain guides who landed by helicopter on the summit several days later also verified my descent, confirming that they had seen my ski tracks leading down from the summit of Robson.

Back in Vancouver I was beginning to rather enjoy my new found ski celebrity status, and I was even approached by a producer to make a feature film about all my Robson attempts. Chris Bruyere, a well-known Canadian scriptwriter who was a guest professor at some of my screen writing lectures at SFU, was hired to write the treatment. But I found the story they envisioned so corny that even the substantial money offered for the rights to my tale did not lure me. I declined to participate in the film which was perhaps a stupid move at the time since I was broke, and I could sure have used that money. But the story line was so dreadful I just could not do it. The producer had made me a half-breed Canadian-First Nations skier, with a famous Polish mountaineer father and gutsy native mom, and I ended up skiing Robson in the script. I thought my real mother would never forgive me if she was written out of the story. The funny thing is that it was an actual half native and half Swiss friend of mine, Troy Jungen who succeeded in skiing the actual North Face seven years later. It's very interesting how an idea drives events sometimes, how life follows art. Maybe it was fated that Troy Jungen was meant to be the guy!

Unfortunately the kitten, Robson got run over in front of my house on Cariboo Road in Burnaby after surviving the long hike and back from Berg Lake. I guess he must be in Kitty heaven by now. I had always liked cats and had a lot of respect for their solitary ways. I had a few great cats throughout my life. I just do not have the patience for dogs.

During those early years I wasn't the only one trying to ski Mount Robson. My main competition was a fellow named Doug Ward, a pro-skier from Edmonton. On one of his Robson ski attempts Doug and his crew got stuck in the high camp between the "Helmet" and the North face itself. A helicopter was called in during the first weather window of opportunity to rescue the crew and all their equipment but tragedy followed: one of the accompanying guides, Mark Sawyer, lifted his hand to keep his hat on when the helicopter was landing. As the 'copter touched down on the snow, it suddenly sank deeper and the rotor blade took off Mark's hand and scraped the top of his skull upon landing. Thus their expedition ended in disaster as well.

We actually showed up in Robson Park during Ward's ill-fated expedition to Robson. We had just skied Mt Athabasca at 3,491 m but it was not a good time for ski descents and the park rangers quickly shooed us away as tensions from the heli accident haunted everyone. From that point on Doug gave up on his own dream to ski the north face of Robson, but did appear in our ski film which documented all our attempts years later. I am grateful for all the footage he provided when we started to search for various attempts to ski Robson. I also have to thank another good friend of both Doug and me: Terry Gamble, who was instrumental in helping me get a good deal on the rights to other footage of Doug.

While Robson's north face always remained an objective for our Extreme Explorations crew, we also had our eyes on BC's Northwest Coast – an area which harboured a big mesmerizing mountain.

The next project on our Extreme Explorations agenda was to attempt to ski Mt Waddington, the highest peak in BC at 4,019 metres (13,185 ft). The "Wad", as we had called the mountain is an extreme undertaking just because of its remoteness alone. Its isolated location posed a great challenge to the pack of still young and rather inexperienced mountaineers that we were.

Mt Waddington is a serious mountain by any standards, Himalayan in it's scale but lacking in really high altitude. It towers 4,000 meters above the Pacific ocean, nestled between the Knight and Bute inlets. When looking for a peak that most resembled K2, it was chosen by a British film maker as the best look-alike peak to make a film about a climb on the Himalayan Giant. The lower altitude made it possible for the producers to fly the entire set and crews high up on the mountain without the hazards presented by an overly high altitude. It's hard to fathom the scale of Waddington and it's ranges rising out of the Pacific. It's size is equivalent to several Chamonix in the Alps but it is surrounded by total wilderness.

Nigel and I had always had ambitions to make our films more than just standard ski films with added music, which was what most of the other kids were making back then. We wanted to have a good story and not just something with simple voice-overs like Warren Miller's famous and popular versions which mostly consisted of a "Then we went to…" type of narration and that's about it.

We had both read Don Munday's book „Mystery Mountain" about Mt Waddington. Munday's work chronicled 30 years of attempts to climb the mountain by Don and his wife Phyllis.

We learned that Phyllis was still alive at 85 years of age and living in an old age home on Vancouver Island. Beat Steiner and myself made the trip to the Island and interviewed Phyllis about her adventures on the mountain. She told us that Don and she had never succeeded in ascending the taller rock spire of Waddington itself, but had climbed the slightly lower Northwest peak where we would have so many adventures later. Phyllis had first spotted the mountain – this giant peak towering above the others on the coast from across the Georgia Straight while visiting the north end of Vancouver island. The Mundays spent over thirty years trying to climb Waddington's summit. In those days they came in overland from the Cariboo interior of BC. They had also tried approaching the peak by boat from the Knight inlet side via the Franklin glacier.

The Whyte Museum in Banff had a good collection of old mountaineering films film and I obtained some great footage from the other early mountaineers who had also climbed in the Waddington area, including some by the climber Roger Neve. Our archive budget was so small that I had to negotiate with the Banff museum curator so as to be able to use their films in my production: we agreed to give the rights of our completed Waddington film to the museum in exchange for use of any footage we used in it. In hindsight it was not such a good deal, but film-makers can be so obsessed by their projects, that sometimes common sense goes out the window.

For our first trip into Waddington we flew in from Squamish with two planes, a Pilatus Porter and a small Cessna. It was a 100 km direct flight north to the Bute Inlet side of the mountain, with its many glaciers. There were various logistics to contend with. First we would fly to an abandoned logging camp nestled in Bute Inlet with both aircraft.

Here Alex Grzybowski, one of the initial founders of Extreme Explorations and a son of Polish doctors in Vancouver, found vehicles with keys and gas in them left by the logging company to await their return. The naughty boys who arrived earlier on the Cessna took the opportunity to rip around the logging roads in the area while the Pilatus arrived with the rest of our crew.

The plan was to ferry everyone with the ski equipped Pilatus from the logging camp up to the Combatant Col, which is a popular climber's advance base camp from which they would attack the peak itself.

Flying in involved another funny story: The Pilatus Porter aircraft, flown by an elderly pilot named Ron Banner, was owned by a family business called Air Alps. Ron was an eccentric older character in his 60's, and was quite the renegade pilot in those days, infamous for his various flying escapades.

Our initial plan was to land the Pilatus on the Combatant Col. But as we were approaching the col, a high glaciated mountain pass, Ron got rather transfixed by a fly on his plane's windshield. He started swatting the fly, which was driving him crazy. As a result he had taken his eyes off the plane's instruments and, before we knew it, we had lost the necessary altitude to land on the Col – leading us to land about 3,000 feet lower on the glacier. We lost three days out of our summit bid because of that fly.

We were all dirt poor then, being students. Except for John Reed and his wife Kirsten, we were all comparative paupers trying to carry off this complicated expedition. I went into high gear looking for sponsors, for anyone that might help with our expenses.

As far as food was concerned, I had managed to land one sponsor in the form of Vancouver's Venice Bakeries. I also persuaded the Idaho Potato Marketing Board, Magic Pantry Instant Dinners and Okanagan Fruit to become part of our list of supporters. All this hustling reminded me of many of the Polish Himalayan expeditions of the 70's and 80's, where they too were underfunded, having to drive across Europe and Asia and bring their own food along to save money. At least we had some food taken care of. We were also lucky to have a clothing sponsors in Taiga Works from Vancouver, and other ski and climbing companies offered gear.

I smile thinking of all this now. Polish alpinists have never had it easy, and Bernadette McDonald, the founder of the Banff Mountain film festival, describes the struggles of Polish Mountaineer Wanda Rutkiwicz in her book FREEDOM CLIMBERS:

Everything had to be assembled from scratch. At one place climbers would buy the fabric. At another the zippers. A mother and aunt would sew the items together. There was a shoemaker in Zakopane who handmade their boots and the ice-axes were forged in a local blacksmith shop. "We almost had to pluck the ducks and the geese ourselves to get down for the jackets".

Once we had set up our low base camp we made several ski touring attempts to climb the mountain via the Northwest Combatant Col, as well as a more direct route from the south. Impending storms quashed any attempts to ski from the summit on this trip but we knew that we would be back. This first attempt was during the summer of 1984, while I was still studying at SFU and we had wrangled the support of SFU's Kinesiology Department, which was the closest thing to a Phys Ed department, where we could justify funding a large mountaineering expedition. Waddington had managed to show us it's fury several times on this trip. Near the Northwest Col, where we were camped, we were woken one morning by the sound of a large rock fall which sounded as if it was coming ever closer. 'Avalanche!' someone shouted, and as I drowsily looked out of my tent I remember seeing Beat sprinting away from his tent and the incoming roar of the rock fall. Lucky for us none of the debris hit the tents, although there were several Volkswagen sized boulders now dotting the snowfield around us.

A day earlier we were buzzed by two Canadian C14 jets playing Top Gun with maneuvers up the valley as we toured the same route below them. They would have come across from The Comox air force base on Vancouver Island which was just southwest from us across the Straight. They must have seen our string of people ski touring, and pushed the throttle to deliver two sonic booms just above our heads below the Combatant Col. If only the pilots of the planes had realized how much danger the sonic boom created for avalanche in what were already dicey spring conditions.

How did this first expedition end? In failure…

The next year, 1985, we were more serious in our intent as we again returned to Mt Waddington with a party consisting of Trevor Petersen, and Steve Smaridge, Brett Bradley, Nigel Protter, Beat Steiner and Alex Grzybowski. This time we accessed the mountain via helicopter directly to the Combatant Col. Mike King, operating from Tatla Lake in the East, was our pilot. Steve Smaridge, Trevor Petersen, Beat Steiner and I managed to tour on skis up through the ice field towards Fury Ridge, then up the Angel Glacier right to the bottom of the last 300 ft tall knob which forms Waddington's Northwest Summit. From here we descended on skis back down to the Col. Although not from the very top of the icy Northwest Summit, it was the very first ski descent carried out on the mountain.

The entire run back to the icefall above the Col took only about 20 minutes and was filmed from the helicopter by a great camera man, Don Chaput, with old Betacam video camera. Film, which cost so much money per minute to shoot, was being replaced by the much cheaper video.

However, the day did not end up too smoothly. The weather window closed in on us as fog rolled in and we got stuck overnight in the ice fall as we tried to get back down to the Col. It was maybe not a good idea to be skiing through the icefall, hurtling our bodies over the big crevasses in the dark. We had no sleeping bags with us because the summit bid had been planned as a quick alpine ascent which was to be carried out during daylight hours. So we huddled together in a shallow crevasse with our teeth chattering uncontrollably until the morning light came and we could continue our route safely back down to the Col.

Our planned ending for this trip was rather naive as well. After making the descent from just below the Northwest Summit, our plan was to ski tour back up to the Fury Ridge, where we had left a food cache in a plastic milk crate, and from there we hoped to make our way all the way down the Franklin Glacier to sea-level and try to catch a passing logging barge on its way southward to Vancouver.

Unfortunately, when we set off next morning to climb up to Fury Ridge, we discovered our food cache had been totally destroyed and eaten by a wolverine. We were now in big trouble, with no food supplies for the long ski out, but luckily we heard the distant throb of a helicopter. Trevor Petersen quickly took hold of the situation. Grabbing the radio, he ran up to an icy knob above us and managed to contact the pilot. The pilot had been returning from a logging job on the other side of the mountain, and luckily caught our radio signal. He then managed to spot us from the air, made Avery neat landing on the glacier, picked all of us up and took us back to his base at Tatla Lake. We were indeed lucky that time because that was potentially a real problem. Wolverines may be small and look pretty, but no-one with a brain would want to get anywhere close to these little monsters. Bears and cougars show them all due respect.

This was one of our last excursions with my old friend Steve Smaridge as he died white water kayaking not too long afterwards. All of us missed him dearly.

Stevie was an exceptional skier and mountaineer. He also had a twisted and dry sense of humour, and gave us loads of laughs over the years in some very sketchy situations. He was Trevor Petersen's favourite ski partner in those early years. Stevie loved his black hash too, which he always had in his possession on most of our back country trips.

While editing the Mount Waddington film, and thinking somewhat laterally, I came up with the crazy idea that Pierre Trudeau (then the former prime minister) would be the ideal voice to narrate the film. Mr Trudeau had a great voice and was an avid skier. He had been a very popular Prime Minister who had brought the constitution home to

Canada from Great Britain. I thought his narration would bring some prestigious celebrity status to our film.

All of my friends laughed when I told them of my proposition. But I wrote him a nice letter explaining about our film and how I would be honoured to have him narrate. To my utter surprise I got a handwritten letter back in the mail from M. Trudeau himself. He said he was sorry to have to decline my invitation, although he would have loved to have done the narration. He revealed that unfortunately he had sold all the rights on the story of his life to the CBC, and the contract forbade him from doing any other media appearances. Whether his excuse was true or not, I was very honoured just to receive the letter back from Mr Trudeau at all. To me, it showed that people with class will always find the time to answer their correspondence. Unfortunately, hacks working in the new corporate world seldom show the same class. Other celebs who have taken the time to reply to my requests include Greenpeace founder and self-declared eco-terrorist Paul Watson, well-known scientist and activist David Suzuki and author Wade Davis. But these were individuals who also understood what it is like to be driven by a project – and not money alone. The corporate world finds it hard to understand such a perspective.

Although the Waddington film, once completed, was a bit of a mishmash of various formats, ranging from 70mm Expo aerials, through 35mm and 16mm film, to some super eight and three-quarter inch video, it was a great story. Indeed, I am very proud of it and was pleased that it was even screened on Air Canada as part of their in-flight programming. Several people told me they had seen the film during their flights. It also aired on the CBC, and later British Columbia's Knowledge Network.

In the meantime, Megan had gone back east to Chester in Nova Scotia, on the far east coast of Canada to stay with her father. Our Waddington film was finally out and we had garnered a lot of attention with it in the media. My world seemed so open for new adventures, and Megan was leaving me? My heart was broken. I even followed her to Chester and tearfully tried to win her back, but it was all to no avail.

It's funny how even those close to you tend to disappear as you move through life, and I got over the loss of Megan soon enough. This was such an exciting time. We were finally on a roll and managing to make the mountain films we always dreamed of.

As for Megan, I later heard that she eventually married an executive in telecoms. Maybe for her that was perfect, having someone who could give her the normal lifestyle she must have been looking for. It may have been that she correctly realized right from the beginning that I was just not going to provide such comforts for her. Some things were just never meant to be with many of my girlfriends and in my many short relationships with them.

After graduating from SFU in 1985 I continued on my path to make extreme adventure films.

One of my oldest friends, Nigel Protter moved back to work in Toronto to start a media company, got married to an artist called Karen Love. Karen is a talented artist who runs her art studio now in Pemberton, and they have two wonderful kids.

A new company called Adventure Scope Communications was formed by Jacques Russo, a newcomer from Montréal to Vancouver and Whistler. Jacques had a company called JR Productions that had designs on making snowboard videos.

He saw potential with all the content we had produced. He was instrumental in helping us post produce "Search for the Ultimate Run" and "Mount Waddington Now."

Later we made a film altogether from scratch called "The North Face, Seven Years on Mount Robson" Jacques later made his mark producing a series of extreme adventure films around with snowboarding icon Craig Kelly. Tragically the snowboard superstar died in an avalanche at the age of 36 in Revelstoke. He was one of 6 riders who died in one avalanche incident, which was a tragic accident and one of the worst disasters the heli industry in Canada has faced.

I felt a bit sad being abandoned in business by my two friends Beat and Jacques. When big money becomes involved partnerships often seem to fall apart. I guess in my case the film was perhaps an excuse to make the expedition happen.

It was also at that time that Beat Steiner and I set out from the base of Pemberton's Mount Currie with a plan to climb the North Face to make a first ski descent down that side from the its peak.

Known as Ts'zil by the local Lil'wat Nation, who were the original inhabitants of the valley, Mount Currie, the mountain, resembles the legendary Swiss Eiger peak, towering 7,500 feet straight up from the Pemberton valley floor and completely dominating the town's skyline.

Families from Switzerland were some of the first newcomers to the Pemberton Valley, originally drawn here by the similar geography to their old home.

We were still pretty inexperienced and so we decided to go straight up one of the three vast avalanche gullies which leading to the summit. However the couloirs are quite steep and stones whizzed past our heads as we started ascending the gully.

Given the number of falling rocks, we were pretty lucky that we were not killed by one of the falling rocks as we climbed. Once we reached where the first rock band we set up our tent, and we overnighted on a small ridge with a spectacular view of the Pemberton Valley below.

Next morning we took a wrong route initially, climbing a couloir directly above our tent. The chute ended suddenly in a dead end with an impassable rock band.

After skiing back down we found the entrance to what is now called the "Diagonal Chute" – an amazing run about thirty feet wide leading from the summit ridge.

The couloir was not as steep as it appears from the valley, but it was still a long tiring climb, post-holing in our boots through knee deep snow. Looming above us at the top was a sizeable cornice separating us from the summit ridge. It was a threatening sight as it could have broken off at any minute just from the vibrations of our climb. Luckily, as we neared the cornice we found we could climb around it on the left hand site without having to tunnel through it to reach the summit, which is the only option often presented to climbers. Topping out on the ridge it was another 45 minute further ski tour to the summit.

After reaching the peak we spent a half hour resting on the summit. Whistler Mountain was visible 30 km to the south. Looking north the mountain dropped away so steeply that the town of Pemberton seemed directly below us. It reminded me another stunning view, the one looking down on Chamonix from the Aguile du Midi on the North Face of Mont Blanc.

By now it was getting late and we had wasted several hours earlier in the day climbing up the wrong couloir, but fortunately we were climbing in mid-May and we still had lots of daylight hours.

To make our entry into the couloir we had to side-step in using our ice axes and inched down the icy and almost vertical top section. It was with a big sigh of relief that we got to the beginning of the actual run proper. The date was May 18th 1985 and the chute, which was in the shadows protected by a rock outcropping, still had thigh-deep light powder on it, which made for some memorable turns. We then retrieved the rest of our tent and gear, and skied, and then later hiked all the way back down to the base of the valley. We had made the first decent of Mount Currie, and without incident.

A few years later two of our local heroes, Trevor Petersen and Eric Pehota did the first descent of another steeper route known as the Y Couloir, which starts right near the peak of the mountain. From then on Mount Currie became one of our prime playgrounds to ski on. The local airport is located directly at the base of the mountain so flights were relatively affordable.

This new location of Mt Currie meant that we could either ski down one of the chutes or later to paraglide off the summit. On one memorable trip in April one year John Reed and I got a ride up to the summit with both our skis and our 'gliders. We skied the Diagonal Couloir to where the slope opened up, then set up our paragliders, took off and had a short, but spectacular flight all the way down to the Pemberton golf course, where we landed on a patch of snow with our skis. Yet another First Descent of mine (of sorts)!

Since then the mountain has shown it demands respect by claiming lives. One of those we lost was my neighbour on Reid Road, Jack. He had been skiing with a group down the Y couloir after a recent fall of snow. On the Y, you have to exit the original couloir half way down and climb into the Central Couloir to get to the bottom. He had skied too far down the Y, so he put his skins on and had begun the climb back up when he was hit by an enormous avalanche which had missed the others above. It was a tragic accident at the end of what should have been a normal day.

We had also begun venturing into the Tantalus Range for the first time. This small group of mountains provides a spectacular sight when seen from the Sea-to-Sky Highway which connects Whistler with Vancouver and the world. They resemble the Himalayas in grandeur and proportions, if not altitude. Like the Himalayas they are rough and heavily glaciated. What makes them so attractive to climbers is their proximity to Vancouver, which is a couple of hours drive, and their low elevation. At one time I even dreamt up a proposal to put an aerial tram like Chamonix's which was to rise from the Squamish River valley up to the top. I enlisted a top team of friends to support the project. I had Scott Flavell in charge of safety, ACMG's Alberto Alberti and Harry Measure in charge of development, and my Polish friend Andrew Rezmer was to lead the real estate sales. We had even got the local Squamish Native band on board.

Unfortunately the project never got off the ground. Whisler was planning its stunning Peak-to-Peak Gondola, and our project was competition. I have my suspicions that maybe the Whisler folks had made a deal with Squamish, because suddenly sacred burial sites were found along out gondola route, and that can put the kibosh on any developments in Canada. Just 10 years later another system called the Sea-to-Sky Gondola was actually built next to the monumental Squamish Chief, which sits across from Squamish. The new gondola is situated right beside the highway and is very popular with tourists and day trippers, but is not the 'climbers' lift that I had envisioned rising up to the Tantalus.

We spent a few days up in the alpine of the Tantalus, ski touring and bagging several first descents off the north face of Mt Serratus. Once I remember looking up in horror as one of the skiers who we had brought up, a local ski racer named Brett Bradley, was doing high-speed super G-style turns down the incredibly steep 55 degree face. Luckily he managed to slow down before hitting the crevasse-ridden glacier down below. I also managed to paraglide off the Tantalus range off the backside and toward the south, I landed on a safe spot then ski toured back up with my wing on my back. I also flew down towards the Squamish River and landed in a small parking lot there. To me those days were some of my greatest with our ongoing explorations of the Coast Range Mountains near Whistler. Not only that, but with the help of Jacque's new energy we also finished editing our

Waddington film. At the same time we started our next project, documenting a new series of adventures that became "The North Face, Seven Years on Mt Robson".

In August 1987 we did another return visit to try and ski Robson, this time with Eric Perlman, who I had met first in Peru in 1978. Eric brought another well-known skier, Scott Schmidt along. He had also brought sponsorship with him. The North Face Company would support us. This was the most prestigious company in the ski world and I had been trying to get help from them for years. It is hard to get your head around how broke we were doing these ski films. We would happily risk our lives for some new ski clothing and ski gear.

This time the rest of the party included Trevor Petersen, Steve Smaridge, Alex Grzybowski, Dan Savage and Dan Redford and also a small posse of keen helpers, including some straight out of Vancouver and who had absolutely no mountain sense whatsoever. We failed in our attempts to ski from the actual top because of the prevailing conditions that year, but we did get some great ski footage on the "Helmet" section of the mountain. We also shot an impressive ending with Eric Pehota and Trevor shredding it up on Blackcomb itself, with some of the best filming shot up to that time by anyone in the film world.

It was great seeing Eric Perlman again. We had first met in 1978 after I had skied Mt Huascaran. He was there in Huaraz, with Rick Sylvester. Rick was a genuine celebrity skier from Colorado. His main claim to fame had been making the spectacular base jump that was used in the opening of the James Bond film On her Majesty's Secret Service. He launched of a cliff in Baffin Island and opened up a Union Jack parachute. Friends of mine tell me this scene would get loud applause in British cinemas!

Eric and Rick had also come to ski on Huascaran that summer, and they had managed to climb and descend from the mountain's north, or lower peak. This mountain has twin summits, with the throat or "Garganta" separating them. I had read Eric's book "The Man Who Skied Down Everest", the incredible story of Yuichiro Miura, a Japanese kamikaze-like skier who had hurled himself off Everest's South Col in 1970, hoping that a parachute would slow his fall-line decent. It did, but only just, as documented by Budge Crawley, a Canadian who later won an Oscar with his film of the incident. Miura started his descent ok, and once he had some speed up, he released his chute. The thin air made the chute almost useless and completely ineffective, and after sliding for several thousands of feet, he managed to come to a halt just above a cliff which would certainly have killed him. Eric was from Truckee, California and was a great businessman. In addition to getting a load of gear from the North Face company, he also obtained a rare cash donation of $5,000 from them, which I can vouch personally was very hard to obtain from sponsors back in those days. The addition of Scot Schmidt, with his celebrity status as the star of so many Warren Miller films and commercials helped.

We produced the Waddington and Robson films in those years with the help of equipment and facilities contra deals with the CBC and the NFB (National Film Board of Canada) after a great deal of politics, involving the three CBC departments from CBC Calgary and CBC Vancouver – and Radio Canada, the French arm of the broadcasting corporation. The cameras came from CBC Calgary and the editing was in Vancouver.

When, despite all odds, we did get our film edited at CBC, the lady in charge just said "Well, you got your film done, did you not?" with a sour tone in her voice. Here again we ran up against mini politics: the woman in charge of scheduling our edit shifts seemed to have it in for us and she would mercilessly give us graveyard shifts which often started at 2 am.

I do find people who work within large institutions can be so cruel to entrepreneurs sometimes. It seemed like it was envy or spite that led to people blocking our projects and our dreams. Maybe they just hate their jobs so much.

'The North Face, Seven Years on Mt Robson' became my most successful and often-viewed film. It was aired on many networks internationally, including at least ten occasions on the Arts and Entertainment Channel or A&E as it is now known, was then a new cable network which would acquire works produced by independent film-makers like ourselves. The North Face film really did cover seven years of my adventures and misadventures on Mount Robson. We had made several trips to the mountain in between the first fiasco in 1980, my own successful solo descent in 1983, and finishing the Mount Robson film in 1987.

We had had to endure huge bureaucratic problems. One Friday afternoon in 1986 I received a phone call from the BC Provincial Parks telling me that I did not have a film permit for our planned ski expedition to Robson. As usual the government were causing me grief by stalling us earlier, and then waited until the very last moment to cancel my permit and stopping us in our tracks. We were planning to meet our helicopter early on Monday morning to transport gear into the Robson base camp and now everything was on hold.

Being the rebel that I was meant I never had much respect for authority. So I did my utmost to get around this ban. I got in a car and drove directly to the home of Elwood Veitch, who was the Provincial Secretary and thus the right hand man of the Premiere. With all my plans in hand I pleaded my case. I was also very lucky to have a good friend at the provincial Film Commission, Diane Neufeld, who phoned the Minister of Tourism on my behalf once she had listened to my hysterical phone call from the Provincial Parks office.

Because Tourism held much more clout financially than Parks, Lands and Housing, that Sunday night I received an interesting phone call from the Minister of Lands and Housing himself. „Peter," he said, „We cannot give you a permit, it would just not be right, but we have decided to look the other way, so just go ahead and do your trip."

The next day, on the Monday morning, when we arrived in Valemount, the base for our operations on Robson, we were still quite nervous because the RCMP was already there, waiting for us. We didn't have to worry though, as they had now changed their attitudes and wanted to assist us in making sure everything went smoothly. They even offered to serve us coffee while we loaded slings to carry our gear into the Robson base camp at Berg Lake.

The things one can accomplish with friends in the right places! From that moment on I have made a point of never giving into bureaucrats, as there was always a way I could find to defeat them.

So this time we managed to fly all our gear in to our Berg Lake base camp making this really quite like a commercial venture, and not like the true spirit of early ski alpinism as practiced by the pioneering

French extreme skiers. They, unlike us, would always climb in with all their gear. Being self-sufficient was part of the ethos and they shunned the use of helicopters.

But hey, we even brought some girls to accompany us. We were saying "no disrespect", but it was so nice to have some female company with us on what are so often entirely male trips, called sausage parties, for obvious reasons. This was to be an all-inclusive expedition.

With us were two feisty sisters, Thalassa Nicholls and her sister Maria from Burnaby. For many years I had had a big crush on Thalassa. She was an amazing dancer, and Jacques Russo, the other producer on the film, shot her dancing in front of the glacier at Berg Lake. It was a spectacular sequence to use with closing credits in the film. At first we all thought it was kind of tacky, but looking back at it now on I think it gave a little spunk and a greater ending to our film.

It was not till over 20 years later when we would finally get together again. Thalassa had moved to London, England where she was dancing at some exclusive British clubs. She later moved to dance on the Spanish island of Ibiza, which is probably the world centre of clubbing. She comes back to Whistler occasionally and we have even skied together a few times. We last met during the big party that Whistler threw for local Ross Rebagliati, who had won the gold medal for snowboarding for Canada. He had then had it taken away from him after testing positive for marijuana, but got it back again when the official ruling was that using dope had 'changed' his performance, rather than 'enhanced' it, and on this basis he was allowed to keep his medal. How very Canadian!

Thalassa still looked great after all these years. She had taken a massage therapy course in Whistler and gave that work a try for a year or so. However, I guess she just found Whistler too full of twenty-somethings and felt she no longer fitted in. She decided to go back to Ibiza, and we still stay in touch.

Another good friend, Dan Redford, was with us on our Robson trip. Dan was a celebrated climber and stunt man. He had doubled for one of the lead actors in the K2 feature film shot on Mt Waddington.

He had been stuck on the mountain once a few years previously when he was near the top of the North face. His climbing partner became very ill with altitude sickness and they had to be rescued by a team of mountain guides who landed on the summit by helicopter. They then lowered ropes down to the climbers and managed to drag Dan and his friend back up to the top where they evacuated them. Dan had a lot of respect for the mountain. We ended up having a lot of paragliding adventures together later on in life. He also married one of my ex-girlfriends, Heather, but sadly that only lasted for a year.

The 1997 release of the North Face Mt Robson film really was the peak of my career. Although we never actually got to ski the north face of Robson, the film was our biggest accomplishment to date. We had introduced new players in the ski world to the "extreme game" who would later go on to fame if not fortune. We featured Eric Pehota in his first film cameo, as well as Trevor Petersen and Doug Ward, The two US skiers Eric Perlman and Scot Schmidt brought their own celebrity status along with them.

We managed to shoot some great ski footage on slopes that had not been filmed before, and put together a captivating documentary film. For a while, we all felt like rock stars. We even arranged to have the film premiere in Vancouver's trendiest night club "Richard's on Richards."

I got lucky using my new film-maker status that night, and was taken home by Laurie, a very attractive lawyer friend of mine with whom I carried on a casual relationships in Vancouver for many years. Laurie usually dated 'Ginos', which was the name we gave to city slickers. I think she liked the more athletic outdoor types, as she would show up knocking on my window after the bars closed quite a few times afterwards. I guess success came with girls added, or so I concluded after the whole Robson film extravaganza.

There was another interesting saga which developed out of the making of "The North Face, Seven Years on Mt Robson". Putting a name to this, let me introduce you to Al Wagers (we never did find out if that was indeed his real name). Al was a character who showed up in Whistler one day throwing money around, buying rounds for the whole bar and looking for skiing friends. He skied on a classic monoski, which was suitably exotic, and claimed to come from Mt Alyeska in Alaska, where he said he had a restaurant. Al also claimed to have received several million dollars from a lawsuit. Apparently the lawsuit was one of the results of an accident, and another was the fact that he had a metal plate at the front of his skull, after he had suffered frontal lobe damage in the accident. We later learnt, as psychologists will tell you, that damage to the frontal lobe of the brain can result in a tendency for overindulgence by those affected. This meant when Al liked something, he REALLY liked it and sometimes things went haywire. For example, Al liked a t-shirt with a graphic that said 'No Work Team'. He liked the shirt so much that he bought all the shirts from the store and gave them away to friends along our trips, as a calling card of sorts.

The brain injury, if we'd known about it, well, that alone should have been a warning sign to us. On the other hand, Al was such a lovable guy and we were exceedingly poor ski bum filmmakers. Thus we slowly became entangled in Al's deceptive and confusing web of predicaments. We had actually first met Al, when he had gotten lost following locals' ski tracks into Whistler's 'Khyber Pass'. Back then the Pass was a little known but fantastic old school Whistler wooded ski run that is just outside the ski area proper. I was skiing down with Beat Steiner when we came across Al, who was lost, and showed him the way out of the woods and back to town. It was just after a fresh dump of snow, and Al enjoyed a great run with us. What happened then was a bizarre three month odyssey of travel, film making along with a wild spending spree, which was fueled by madness, and a lot of cocaine. After his rescue an immediate bond seemed to form between us in his mind. The day after our first encounter with Al in the Khyber, we were in a helicopter flying up to Ipsoot Mountain, shooting an intro to our still underfunded and unfinished Mt Robson film with Al's money.

Al loved to be in the spotlight and, in exchange for investing in Adventure Scope Communications he became the Executive Producer on The North Face Robson film. He supplied us with new 16mm movie cameras and paid for a lot of heli time. He made his filming debut with us in a sequence on his mono ski as well as one where he is drinking champagne in the opening credits. For a while it was amazing having funding readily available and being able to hire logging helicopters to carry us and our crew of shooters and talent to outlandish film locations.

Soon Al's crazy escapades became quite well known around Whistler. Sometimes he would rent a whole floor of a hotel to house his friends just to party wildly. He would invite women and give them champagne, which we later learned was often spiked with the coke to make things more interesting.

He also carried on with this pattern of partying while we were actually in the heli's, which was just too much for commercial operations, and before long the helicopter skiing companies refused to take him and his entourage on these flights anymore. I remember one day receiving a phone call from him. He had arrived back in Seattle from a trip to Alaska. He was on his way up to Whistler but was sounding anxious and wound up. He asked me to arrange a helicopter to take us skiing the next day, so I got on the phone and started making phone calls. Everyone turned me down when they heard who the client was, and just when I thought I was out of luck, I managed to contact a logging pilot who lived in Langley, which is a suburb of Vancouver, and he was between jobs.

He listened to my story and simply asked, "and how are you going to pay for all this?" I replied by explaining how the client was an American millionaire and that he would be paying in cash with American greenbacks. We love to be paid US dollars in Canada because 9 times out of 10 we do well on the exchange rate. That was enough for our new pilot and he asked me where and when he should meet us. I said we were ready to go, and that he should just meet us at a gravel parking lot by the Callahan Lake turnoff on the highway south of Whistler. So I quickly assembled a crew of my best ski bumming friends and 16 of us piled into vehicles and 45 minutes later we arrived at the pickup location.

Suddenly this enormous Bell Huey helicopter arrived. It was quite the sight. It was an ex-Vietnam helicopter, and had been renovated with rustproof paint but it still had gun mounts on it from its past service in Vietnam. We all piled in the chopper and headed towards Powder Mountain. This was the logging pilot's first ever heli-skiing flight and we just picked landing locations on the uncountable peaks in the area and he would deliver us there. It was one of the very best powder-skiing days of my life. It was the middle of February and we had two feet of the softest, lightest powder to enjoy. Should I say we were doing all this of course illegally – strictly speaking. We had none of the permits that official helicopter ski operations were required to have to fly in this government-designated tenure. So we were technically on somebody else's terrain and skiing totally illegally. We noticed a much smaller Bell Jet Ranger, which probably had the permit for the area, but he didn't seem keen on approaching our war machine for some reason.

Luckily our pilot proved to be an ace who was incredibly savvy about landing us in tricky landing spots. Somehow he could pick us up from really narrow gullies, and we watched in horror as would land with his blades just inches from the nearby trees. He could also hover just off a ledge on a ridgeline, letting us hop out on to the slopes that way. We were taking chances that no commercial heli ski operation would ever take, so I guess the amount of money I had offered to the pilot made it worthwhile.

Every run, every landing and every takeoff gave us new surprises to be reckoned with. We filmed the whole day, of course, but somehow we never got to use the footage in any of my films. At the end of the day Al paid the pilot in crisp American greenbacks, as had been promised, and the big Huey whomp-whomped home.

This turned out to be the high point of our experience with Al Wagers. There was a moral question we had to face about whether it was quite right to enjoy the hospitality of someone who is not quite all there? I have to admit we didn't think too long and hard about this. We rationalized it by thinking that if we didn't spend his money then somebody else surely would jump at the opportunity. At least we were keeping Al skiing, and in a way looking after him.

All this came at a price though, as we agreed to accompany him on an elaborate road-trip to the Mardi Gras in New Orleans, via The Flamingo in Las Vegas – and a side trip to ski Jackson Hole in Wyoming. Al's spending was spiralling way out of control, as we soon found out.

He bought a sports car, a lovely Saab Turbo 86 and a huge motor home, registering the ownership using our names, and we continued our drove around the US. It turned out that the vehicle registration ruse was because Al had some trouble with the IRS, so he preferred for us to become the owners of these newly-bought vehicles officially in the paperwork. I still remember the look of astonishment on Dave and Beat's faces one day in Vancouver when Al handed them a suitcase which was genuinely full of cash and said, "Go buy me a nice sporty car. You choose the style and make!"

So Beat and Dave walked into the MCL car dealership, which sold high end Land Rovers and Saabs in Vancouver and asked to test-drive the newest 1986 Saab Turbo. The car salesman at first did not treat them very seriously, as we were all punks still in our 20s. Then David opened up the suitcase and showed them the cash. Their attitude changed instantly and with much bowing and scraping, we were left in a brand-new Saab which we delivered to Al. And so we headed south led by Al in a crazy convoy comprised of the motor home and the Saab. Al was by now doing a lot of coke – so much that his nerves were a bit shot due to too many sleepless nights. In order to get some rest, he would often steal something from a shop or do some other petty crime, and get himself imprisoned overnight in the local jail. Being deprived of the coke for the night, he would emerge much fitter in the morning saying – „Ah, I finally got some rest". This actually happened on several occasions and was quite a creative solution that he found worked for him!

Often some sly character from Al's past would emerge at locations along our way with supplies of yet more coke and sometimes even the easy women that often came with it. After three months of this never ending debauchery we finally reached a point where we had to get out of this crazy situation and left Al in New Orleans. Unfortunately for him, he was later caught and jailed on a major cocaine charge later, or so we heard, and we could find sanity again.

It must be said that without his financial help at the start of our relationship the Robson film would never have been completed, but we paid a heavy price with our sanity! Twenty years later a cartoon strip in Mountain Culture magazine created by Stu Mackay Smith described the whole hilarious ordeal in a really accurate five page comic strip.

I still ventured out and skied a lot of different peaks, including a few volcanoes in the United States when a good opportunity came by. Leigh 'Ski Lee' Finck, from Whistler joined me in a first descent of the 'new' Mount Saint Helens when the park was reopened after the giant eruption of May, 1980. We also skied some of the other volcanoes of the Pacific Northwest, we skied Mount Baker and Mount Rainier. We also climbed Rainier, intending to paraglide from the summit. Unfortunately the winds were so strong at the summit that even after waiting for six hours for them to calm down, we had to hike all the way back down with our 40 lbs wings as well as everything else.

Our initial plan to fly off Mount Rainier was quite crazy in itself, as it is illegal to fly in national parks in the US. If we had been caught, we would have had our gear confiscated, been strip-searched and probably sent to jail for a couple nights to learn our lesson. That has happened to other paragliders and base jumpers in the popular Yosemite Park quite often. Our plan for Rainier was quite straightforward: we would fly off the mountain and land on a meadow down below. We would then take off our flight suits, stash them with our gliders, and then stroll out of the woods with cameras round our necks and looking like lost tourists. The next step was to return at night and pick up our gear. This plan was never put in to action, but it is the strategy that is used today by anyone who gets involved in these sketchy adventures, to avoid the fate of the Yosemite crowd.

In the summer of 1986, I took a short break from my mountain adventures. I had been going out with a rather attractive girl named Heather McDevitt. I had met Heather when I was at Simon Fraser University. She was working at the local student paper but was not enrolled as a student. We had had a huge argument when we first met: I wanted my article on Mount Waddington published in the paper and Heather refused to accept it. After a lot of internal politics and me making my usual phone calls I managed to get my way and the article was printed after all. Soon after, and despite all the odds, Heather and I started dating.

Heather and I had just come back from a wild adventure, crisscrossing the whole US of A. We had been involved in making a short film promoting the upcoming Expo '86 at American ski resorts. This had happened because Heather was a very pretty and feisty girl with perfect feminine public relations features, the kind which marketing men fall for in a big way. It turned out the marketing director of Expo '86, had taken quite a liking to her, and I had an idea on how we could capitalize on this situation. I asked Heather to put to him the following scheme: I would write a letter on his behalf, which stated that we were working for EXPO '86 to promote the Expo in ski resorts across the US. He bought the scheme, and put his name on the letters.

I then mailed out these letters to all the ski resorts and fancy hotels. We wrote to Aspen, Vail, Keystone, Arapahoe Basin, and Snowbird, and I guess they all liked my letters because we received invitations from all of them to visit for an all-expenses paid visit! It wasn't hard to get a crew together, and my old friend Beat Steiner, Brett Bradley, Heather, myself and a few others left as soon as we could. Brett had even fashioned a huge wooden box on top of his Ford Bronco to carry all our ski and camping gear on the roof, so we could take turns driving and had enough room to get some sleep in the back of the vehicle.

We also had the use of some incredible 70 mm footage that had been shot for Expo '86, so we used some of this and combined the footage with our own ski footage shot in Canada. It was funny watching these beautiful 70 mm aerials used in the intro of our Waddington film, since the rest of that film was shot on low budget, grainy 3/4 inch video footage and Super 8 film. It was a bit of overkill using the 70 mm stuff like that and using it with our mostly grainy documentary footage, but this is how many films are made.

My inexperience in the media still showed in these early films, but I made sure the Expo flag was in a lot of the ski footage, which made it much more official-looking. Unfortunately, being broke ski bums, even though we were often staying in five star hotel rooms and we had free lift tickets, we actually had very little money left for food. That's where my promotional tapes were useful, since we worked out a system where we were able to sell them to nightclubs along the way for our gas and food money. Our mountain bike sponsor from Calgary had actually paid for dubbing the tapes in Las Vegas, where we had stopped to try and pick up more sponsors on our never ending EXPO'86 trip. The 70mm Expo footage was edited into an hour long bar tape at the Vancouver National Film Board facility. It also featured skiing and clips of us waving the Expo 86 flag on various ski outings.

We returned to Vancouver exhausted but happy after the trip, which we had dubbed the 'Expo '86 Western Tour'. Shortly after this, Heather somehow got wind of an aircraft that was going to make a flight around the world in an old Air Canada DC-3 which had been newly refurbished, and they needed a film crew on board to document the entire trip!

I think Heather and I made a great team. We got all dressed up and went in for the interview for the job of filming the entire event. The organizers, Ken and Doreen Olson, liked us right off the bat and hired us for the job, but with only four days' notice before the plane left. And so we were off again! There were with nine others on the flight, including four pilots, a doctor, a lawyer, a photographer and a mechanic. Sponsored by Sheraton Hotels, the DC3 travelled through 28 countries and visited 50 cities.

At each of the destinations we were met by Canadian embassy staff and a reception would follow. In Manila, Philippines, we even got to shake hands with our Canadian Prime Minister, Joe Clark, who was on an official visit to the country.

After we returned from the trip, we only managed to produce a brief 15 minute version of the film because Ken Olson tragically died in an airplane crash. Along with his death, the enthusiasm from the rest of the crew for our project collapsed as well. I still have many boxes of the Super 8 footage in my basement from that very special vintage airplane trip. It was a unique opportunity to visit all those countries in such a short time, and was very different from our other road trips. The contrast between the different countries was hard to handle. One day we would be in poverty-stricken Bangladesh with its destitution and dirt, and the next day we would be swamped in luxury in the ultra-rich city of Riyadh, the capital of Saudi Arabia.

I had hopes that Heather and I would get to become a couple during this very special trip. Unfortunately, she became fixated with a Moroccan fellow who had played guitar for her back in Vancouver, and thought she was now in love with him instead of me. I have to say I was frustrated by the situation to say the very least. So, one night in the Philippines the two younger pilots, the mechanic and I picked up some beer and met some Filipino women. We all went back to our rooms at the Sheraton, where we had a night of debauchery, as they say. I don't think Heather ever found out about that night, but my hopes for being with her had gone by then.

The two young pilots, Bob and Bill, were single and in their 30s and shared the co-piloting duties. They were younger than the other pilots, and were also dedicated womanizers and they often got lucky during our trip. One time I caught Bill in bed with two pretty girls in Prague, the capital city of then Czechoslovakia.

In Manila I had an awkward situation: I had eaten a mango in the hotel room, and without thinking I had flushed the pit down the toilet, and went out to party. When we got back to the room we discovered there was nearly six inches of water flowing around our 16th floor of the Sheraton. Luckily nobody found out the source of the disaster before we had left the country.

Heather and I kept up a sporadic relationship of sorts for about five years, but then she was in a bad car accident, and she changed a lot after the crash. The accident happened just south of Whistler, at the "Welcome to Whistler" sign at Function Junction. The Sea to Sky highway had taken another toll. Over the years I have lost quite a few friends on that notoriously dangerous road. It was much improved for the 2010 Winter Olympics and is now as safe as any highway, But I think every Whistlerite knows somebody who has crashed on it.

Heather's was a serious crash, as she was thrown through the roof of a rag top TR6 and landed hard on the pavement. The result was a concussion, some frontal lobe damage and a 'floating' chip in her spine. This last injury was especially scary, as it could lead to paralysis. I tried to keep our relationship going and visited Heather many times while she was recuperating at her parents' house in White Rock. Heather became more mellow and seemed a little spaced out.

Slowly, we were drifting apart and I felt it keenly. She started to do things on impulse, yet she hadn't been like that before. Eventually she met one of my friends and married him on a whim. I had introduced Dan Redford to her, but the marriage only lasted only a year. Her parents had never liked me, and put pressure on her to be more mainstream like her two younger sisters. The latter were twins and both models, who ended up marrying men who worked in management for Intrawest, which was the company running Whistler/Blackcomb then.

After her car accident Heather also took up painting. She found she had a talent for it and becoming rather prolific. The Bank of Montréal has exhibited Heather's paintings in its branches all over Canada. It was really quite a change for her because before the accident Heather could hardly even draw. She later fell in love with a First Nations fellow and had a girl with whom she often travelled later. She visited me in Pemberton once, but the magic between Heather and I was just not there anymore.

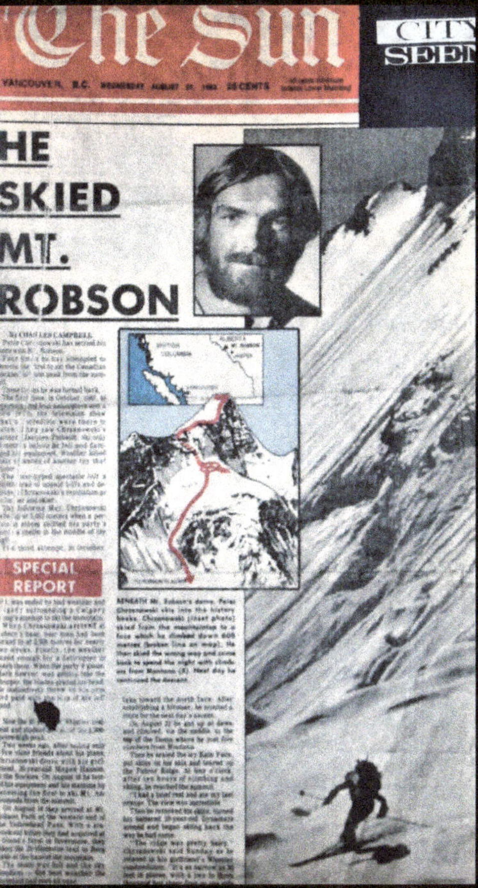
The Sun
CITY SEEN
HE SKIED MT. ROBSON
SPECIAL REPORT

1

2

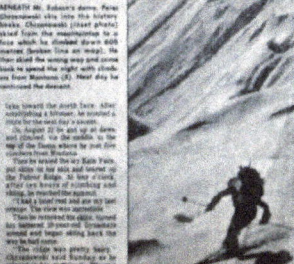

Mt Robson and Mt Waddington adventures

1. Article on the front page of the Vancouver Sun newspaper showing my route.
2. Alex Grzybowski on his way down from Mt Waddington and Combatant Col, 1985.
3. During my ski descent below "The Dome" on Mt Robson.

3

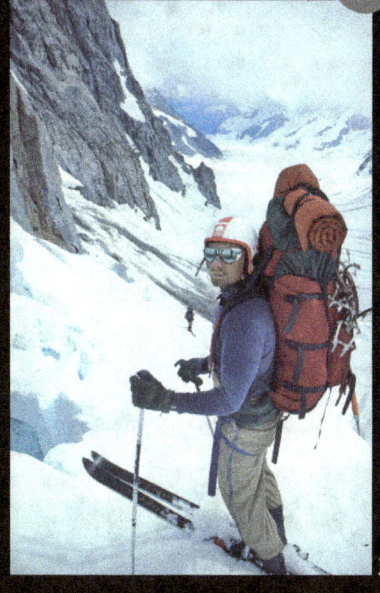

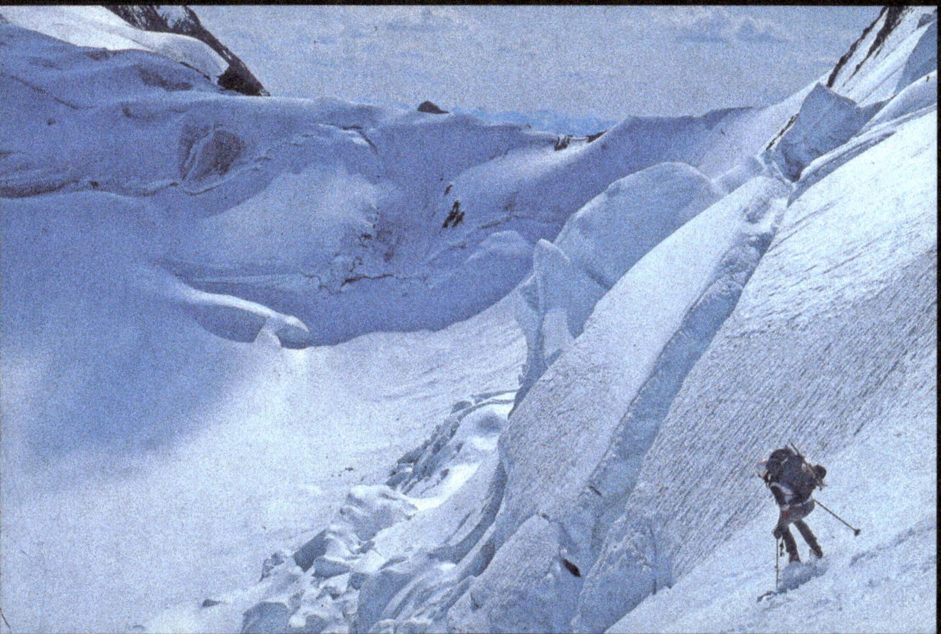

A comic strip made about our times as ski bums with a crazed US millionaire.

P6d

UNFORTUNATELY, THE NEXT MORNING WE HAD NO LUCK RENTING A HELICOPTER...

"SORRY AL, THEY'RE ALL BOOKED UP TODAY."

"I DON'T CARE WHO YOU CALL OR HOW MUCH IT COSTS! GET ME A HELICOPTER!"

"HEY!! I FOUND A GUY FROM LANGLEY WITH AN OLD LOGGING CHOPPER!"

"BUT IT'S GOING TO BE VERY EXPENSIVE TO GET HIM TO FLY UP HERE TODAY!"

"TELL HIM THAT HE COULD BE MAKING MONEY, RIGHT NOW! BIG MONEY!!"

"I NEED MORE POWDER!"

AND SO...

WUP WUP WUP WUP WUP CHUG WUP

"I GOT A BAD FEELING ABOUT THIS."

WUP WUP-WUP WUP WUP

"WHERE TO?"

"UP!"

WUP WUP WUP WUP WUP WUP WUP WUP WUP CHUG WUP WUP WUP WUP WUP WUP CHUG WUP WUP WUP

BUT EVEN THOUGH WE GOT OFF TO A SHAKY START...

...IT ENDED UP BEING ONE OF THE BEST DAYS OF OUR LIVES.

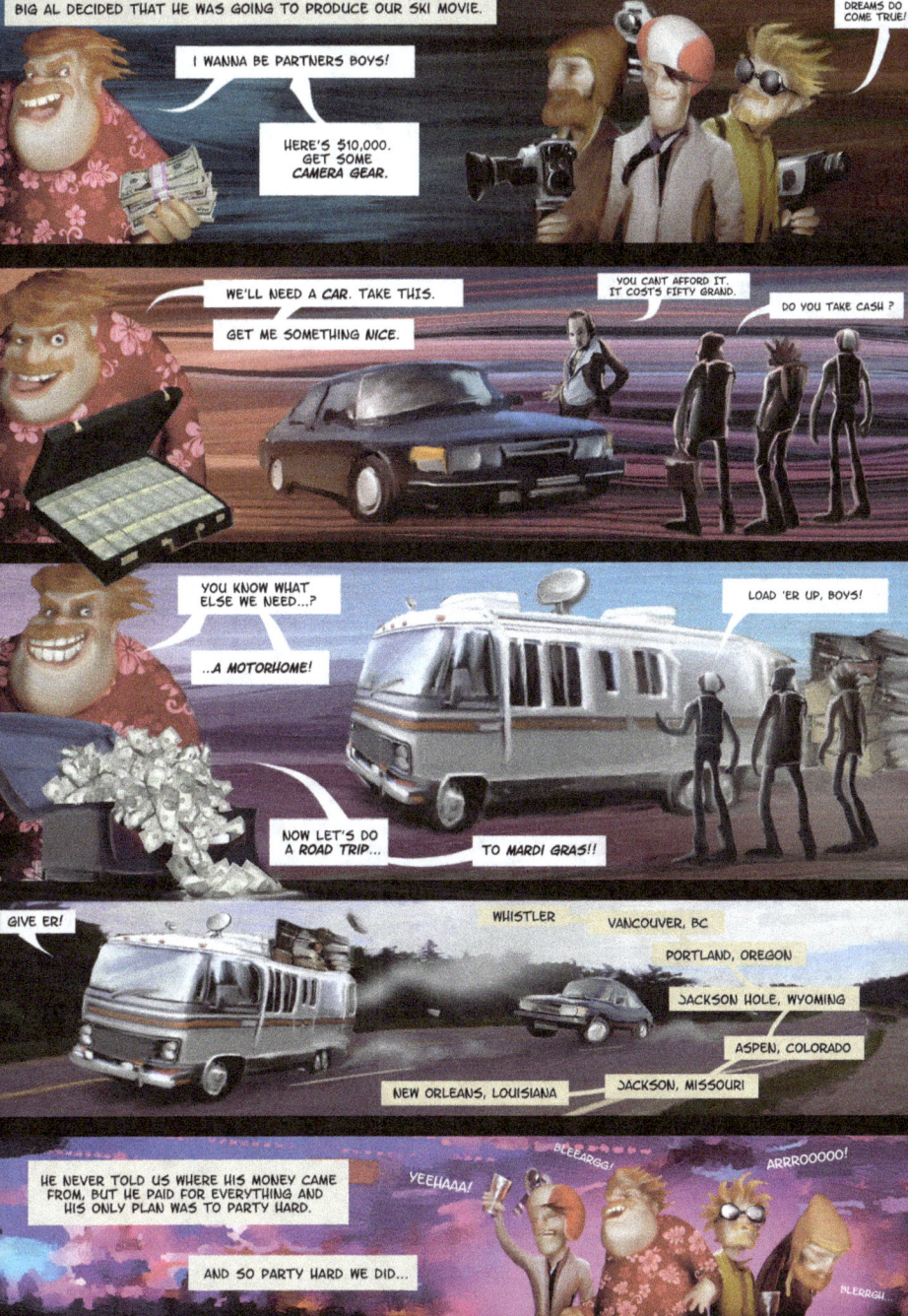

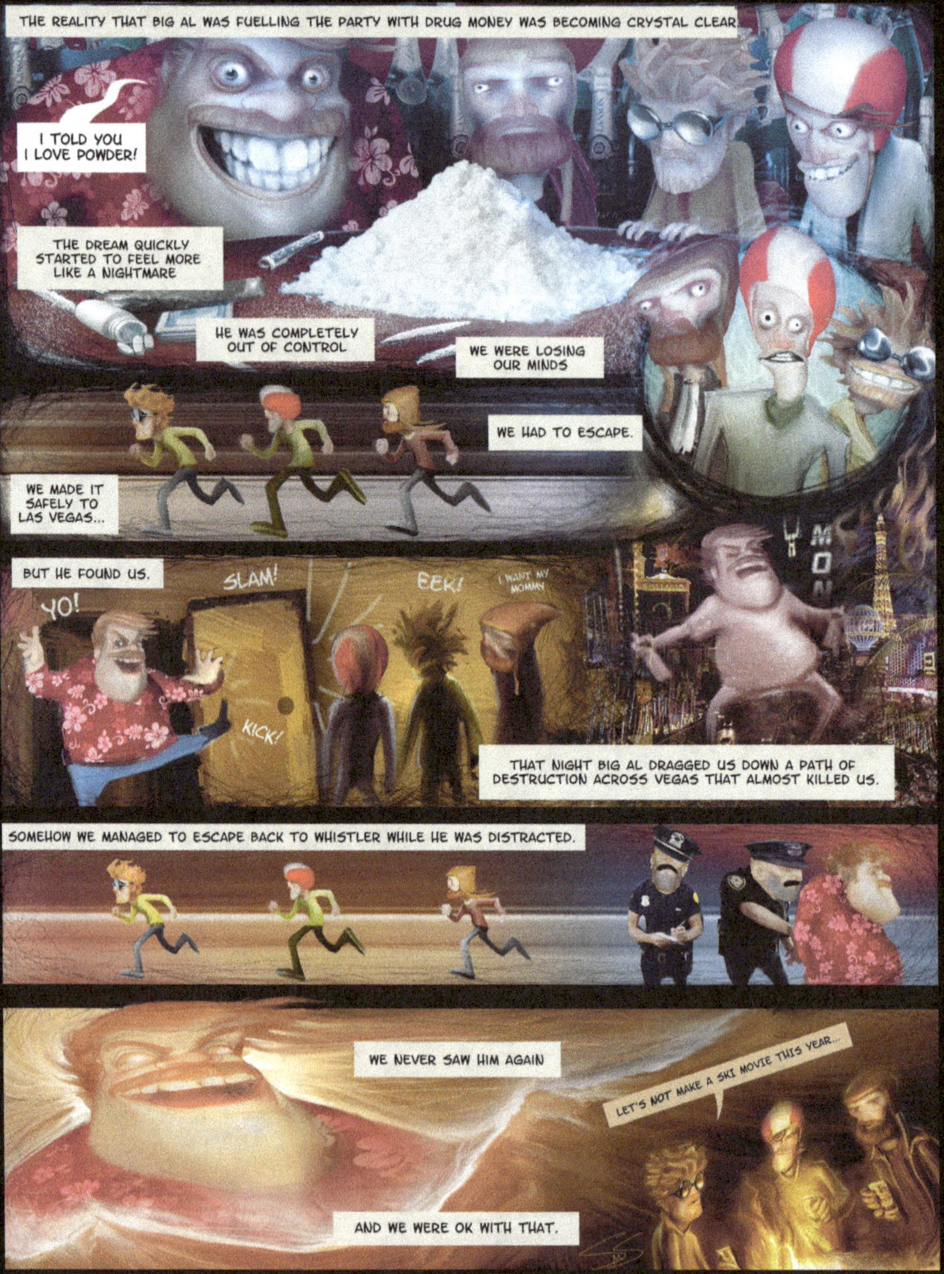

1. Alex Grzybowski in a crevasse field below Mt Waddington.
2. View of Mt Currie from Pemberton along with "Diagonal Couloir" and our approach up left avalanche gully from the valley bottom.

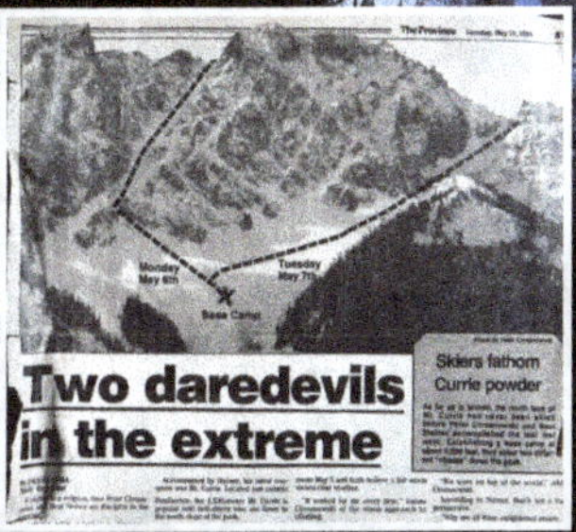

Two daredevils in the extreme

Skiers fathom Currie powder

The Dakota DC3 trip around the world

1. Our crew, on a round the world trip, a first by a DC3 airplane.
2. Heather in New Caledonia.
3. Colorful Rickshaws, Dhaka, Bangladesh.
4. Surrounded by local natives in Port Moresby, Papua New Guinea.

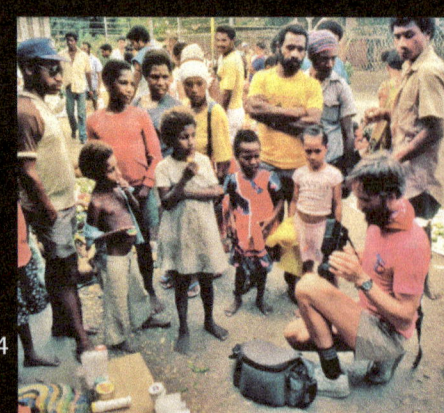

CHAPTER 7

FROM EASY LIVING TO FREE FLIGHT

I had always spent a lot of time in Whistler even while attending the SFU between 1982 and 1985. I managed to juggle my course load of 18 credit hours, cramming my schedule into three or four days at school. That usually gave me Thursday, Friday, Saturday and Sunday in Whistler, and then I would have a mad drive back down to the city early on Monday morning, to catch my first class at 8:30am. A few days at school, then it was back to Whistler again on Wednesday evening to ski Thursday. I managed to kill my beater Toyota Corolla with all those countless trips. My girlfriend Megan and I had an apartment in the city, and when we were in Whistler we took care of a friend's squatter cabin. It was a mad schedule but somehow we managed.

After graduating from SFU in 1985, I still had a place in Vancouver. However, I spent most of my time couch surfing with friends in Whistler, and doing ski descents, writing articles, making films and enjoying the ski bum lifestyle to the full. Those were magic, crazy times in Whistler which I will never forget. There were still about 30 squatters' cabins in the Valley filled with the early ski bums. The squatters had a special bond between themselves. They worked hard to give themselves all the time they could for free skiing.

There were all sorts of wheezes to achieve this. One friend, who shall remain nameless because he is a high-up in avalanche control here in Whistler, engineered a way to produce fake ski passes for all the squatters in Whistler. He then charged only $ 15 for a full season pass, which was just the cost of his materials, and was a big saving over hundreds of dollars charged for a real one.

The entire ski bumming concept must be relatively strange to Polish readers. Poland has always produced top athletes in skiing and mountaineering, but the idea of just living in order to be able to ski or climb full time was a foreign concept in a country under Communism until 1989.

The Polish Himalayan climbers had it best, as the socialist government embraced their sport as a sort of glorified extension of the Stalinist Spirit living on in it's people's mountain exploits. They got extensive government support on their lengthy climbs in the region. Support in cash was difficult as Polish currency had been devalued so much, so material support was forthcoming instead. Polish caravans were outfitted with trucks, carrying all the food and equipment needed for the entire trip, would drive overland across Asia to reach the Himalayan mountain destinations.

The climbers then returned home as national heroes to be lauded by the press and looked up to by the public as great ambassadors to the Communist cause. They would supply the requisite great tales of making the Communist system work for them.

Since dollars were scarce, black market dealings would abound. Polish climbing expeditions were full of stories such as that of the Polish ship that came to Peru with tons of pornography magazines aboard, along with the climbing expedition. The pornography magazines were to be sold in order to have extra cash on hand.

That one time the Poles were caught it became quite a diplomatic incident, as the Polish embassy in Lima got the full wrath from the Peruvian authorities as pornography was as highly illegal in the devout Catholic country then. It still is today.

Poland had no professional athletes who skied full time. Everyone, including the Himalayan heroes, had other official jobs. The police state would just not put up with bums in a strict society where everyone had a purpose and a job to advance the wellbeing of the entire collective.

Within Poland there lived the Goral people who actually did have some time to ski. They would herd sheep in the summer, and were so remote that they created their own local micro economy that was often forgotten by big brother back in Warsaw. They had a whole network of mountain folk that worked and supplied the mountaineering huts in Poland with food and supplies in the winter months by ski touring into these cabins and enjoying a great ski run upon their return. There were also professional "Goprowcy" or Polish high mountain rescue service personnel that managed to get some turns in while on call to their duty. A true ski bum though, would not have survived in those times without being flushed out by the junta and made either to work or go back to school in order to enrich the State and its ideology.

I still get raised eyebrows in Poland when I talk about our true ski bumming spirit. For instance Poland's dense population made it impossible to find a reclusive spot to build a rent free squatters cabin. There wasn't the vast expanses of forested wilderness offered in Canada or the USA. The cops would be informed right away and knocking on your door, unless of course you were the son of an important Communist party member and then the authorities could be made to look the other way. Alternately, if you came from a rich family you could bribe the local police to leave you alone.

Now, Poland has embraced Capitalism with such a vengeance that the entire concept of eating, sleeping and skiing as a lifestyle, and NOT making money has become foreign to my countrymen. Deprived for so long under Soviet rule they now seem drunk on making money and conversations around dinner tables are usually about business and making money.

Yet it is thanks to the bums of the skiing, climbing, surfing, and paragliding worlds with their vast experiences which has led to an intimate knowledge of terrain, avalanche, wind and weather to be passed to the younger generation to keep perfecting the art.

In Latin America, our attitude to 'ski bumming' was even more inconceivable. Leisure time in itself was so new in countries where economies were relatively basic and everyone just worked all the time. It is still like that in most places. Sure, the more privileged or an upper middle class was developing rapidly in Peru, Mexico or Colombia.

The Yuppie ideology was spreading south from North America and the developing world was keen to get involved in mountain biking the Andes, or climbing and skiing them. But these outings were still rare and seen as privileged by the vast majority of common population which survived by herding goats or farming potatoes in the highlands. There was no welfare system there, let alone unemployment insurance which we had access to back home. This feature alone meant we could obtain ski passes while living on next to nothing besides shelter and cheap food.

Ski bumming was a reflection of '60s culture, and the truest form of it is now a dying trend. It is found mainly in smaller outback smaller ski operations with low population nearby and more places for the ski bum to hide out and thus become less noticed.

So the costs of skiing in a high-end resort just keep on rising and with the advent of the latest smart technology, it is impossible to avoid becoming part of the system around us, and today it would be impossible to ski bum in Whistler. It costs $1,500 for a ski pass, and you can't fake them anymore.

You can't find anywhere to park your van to sleep in it. The squatting is long gone. So that's another grand or two for a month of accommodation. When you find something, you'll probably be sharing the house with 8 other people.

Add another $ 500 a month for bare necessities like food, which is of course more expensive in a tourist town, and another few hundred for bus fares or gas for your car. Then there is the cost of your ski clothes and equipment. So it all adds up to at least a $5,000 investment just to get your season started.

No, there is no more true ski bumming in Whistler. You have to work hard throughout the off-season and try to save enough money and if you're lucky you'll have enough to hold out all season. More than likely though you'll have to get a job somewhere, but its still not going to be easy to make ends meet. At least you'll be able to get a job, because there is always a permanent labour shortage at a world class ski resort.

The golden age of Ski Bumming flourished in the time before the rise of computers and cell phones, when you actually had to go to places to talk to people, like bars and cafes.

One of our annual rituals in Whistler each fall in the late seventies and early eighties was the creation of the fake ski pass for everyone. Somebody would know somebody who had actually bought a seasons pass and this would tell us the background colour that was being used for the ski passes that year.

We would then copy the background colour. Then everybody's picture was taken in front of it, all on the same night. Later, carefully using commercially available lettraset we would make a master pass. The original artwork would be the size of a regular 8 x 10 piece of paper, and then the ski pass maestro would photographically reduce the size of the pass accordingly.

Difficult times emerged one year for our forgery attempts, when Whistler Mountain changed everything and took everybody's pictures in front of curtains with their logo on it. The bastards! We solved that problem easily by enrolling the help of one of the cleaners working in Whistler administration borrowed a set of the curtains one night. We quickly took our pictures and the curtains were back up the next morning. I still can't believe the little things we got away with in Whistler in those early days.

There were other ways of skiing for free in Whistler in those early years. One could do a 45 minute hike to up to the first mid-station, above which there were no more tickets checkers. This route was nick-named The Ho Chi Minh trail in honour of the Vietnam era. Another option open to us was to buy just one ticket between four or five people, then drop it from the lift to the next skier in a glove, one after the other, until all of you made it up to the mid-station, and from then on skiing the whole day for a few dollars each. The only problem was that it took about twenty minutes to get all three of your buddies up that first lift, so if you were the first you could get a lap in while waiting. Another wheeze which could be used on Blackcomb was to drive up to the mid-station parking lot, where we would could join the other skiers who were already downloading. We would just stay on when it went around the big wheel at the base. Sometimes this confused the ticket checkers at the bottom, but they let us stay on and I guess they must have wondered why we never got off.

The early squatters in Whistler also had a big advantage over the regular ski bums who were just passing through. They had a tight community and the places in the woods that they created were relatively comfortable. Some squatters went to quite extravagant means to add hotel-like luxuries. In one, Nigel and Bart had installed an amazing sauna with a metal barrel wood stove that we could get the temperature up to 250°F. They also had put a lovely old-style bathtub in the creek, which filled with pristine water as it flowed through. It was quite something running from the sauna through the snow and jumping in to the freezing tub. Nowadays you have to pay a small fortune to get the same experience in the popular Scandinavia Spa, but we managed to enjoy it all for free!

Also, as squatters we could offer something really special to the girls we picked up at bars in the evening. Ladies would kind of melt as we would come up the trail late at night and see the cozy little cabin, candle lit and heated by a wood stove – like something out of a story book.

It seemed that a woman's maternal instincts would come to the fore in the squatter's cabin. On some occasions, they were often just too scared to return home at night, as we might have told them that there were bears in the trees and that of course it was much better for them to overnight with us instead. I must admit I took advantage of our squatter's cabin quite a few times for that purpose, and on one date I had brought home a girl and when we made love my friends could not help overhearing her rather high-pitched squeals of what I hoped was delight. She was nicknamed 'Squeaky' for ever after.

My friends Bart and Nigel had been some of the early squatters in Whistler. Bart had actually hitch-hiked up to Whistler when he was just 16 with a huge old kitchen propane stove.

One squatter in our camp in the forest north of Whistler's Emerald Estates even had a regular telephone installed in his cabin. He had placed an order in to the telephone company to install a phone post on the side of the road, and he then strung the cable for a good half kilometre through the woods to reach his little home.

Many cabins also had generators to occasionally provide electricity. Banks of batteries would be stacked up and charged. As most of the cabins were fairly deep in the forest, solar power didn't really work. I'm quite surprised that more of them didn't put turbines in the nearby creeks and streams to give us electricity. It's amazing how much power a small turbine can generate, as I have seen in Nepal. One whole village was able to get enough power from just a small contraption in a stream.

Another time John Reed, who was also ski bumming in Whistler back then, came across an abandoned freezer which was full of what seemed to be huge sirloin steaks. The freezer had been forgotten about and abandoned by the old Vale Inn which had just been torn down in Whistler. The freezer was covered in dirt and had somehow been neglected during the demolition. Luckily it was mid-winter and the meat was good, so John brought back all of these huge sirloin roasts, and the whole squatters community ate really well for several weeks.

I must also mention an incident that I'm still quite upset about. During my ski bumming years in Whistler, I became pretty good friends with many of the executives in the Whistler Mountain company. One of them was Bob Dufour, who was a good skier and friend. I think he appreciated what I was doing in with my ski films, unlike many of other more stuffy corporate people. He would occasionally lend me his season pass, as he appreciated I was a poor ski bum who was always looking for ways of getting up the mountain. One day my friend Kent Rodler and I planned to do some ski touring up beyond Singing Pass. Originally we had planned to buy one of the 'back country' tickets for Kent, which would give him one lift up the mountain, and I would use Bob's pass. That morning the line at the lift office was very long so I decided to hurry things up and drop the ski pass to Kent from a chairlift, as I described earlier.

Unfortunately I had not considered the consequences of getting caught, and this time it happened. As I dropped my pass out of the cabin window for Kent, I was spotted by one of the lifties. For whatever reason, he would not look the other way about the incident and shopped us. The result was almost disastrous for Bob, as he got in to some serious trouble and that the management even held a special meeting about this incident. I tried several times to apologize to Bob, but I think that episode rather ruined our relationship for good. Bob is a great guy and I am truly sorry for the shit I got him into. I appreciate the support he gave me with ski passes, which helped so much during my film productions days.

In the fall of 1986 as we were preparing for the ski season to come, which wasn't really necessary as we actually managed to ski every month that year, we had our introduction to paragliding. Beat Steiner, David Frazee, John Reed and I had been fascinated by the films of a French alpinist called Christophe Profit, who was using parachute-like canopies called "parapente" in the original French to fly off mountains that he had climbed.

After doing some research, we found that John Bouchard, who made climbing equipment under the name of "Wild Things,", had seen the same films and had produced a few parapente-like wings, copied from the original paragliders that were produced in Annecy, which seemed to be the birthplace of the sport. Mark Twight, another American Alpinist, turned up in Vancouver one fall weekend with four of the contraptions to try out. We drove from Vancouver two a large ridge that rose high above the Thompson River near the small town of Cache Creek.

The conditions were windy as hell, but we managed to give ourselves rides up the escarpment next to the river. We took turns attempting to fly these things in the unpredictably strong winds. We all somehow managed to survive the weekend, except Beat, who had to be admitted to the Kamloops hospital with a cracked vertebrae from a hard landing. We had our cameras with us and this pioneering video of early Canadian paragliding can be found on YouTube.

Thus started my obsession with paragliding. All of us were completely winging it and somehow teaching ourselves how to fly. From then on, I would take my parapente everywhere. I started carrying it when I went ski-touring in winter, and when I hiked into the high alpine meadows in the summers. I got to love the freedom that free flight gave me on the way back down. I did have several encounters with trees, of course, especially in some of the interior ski resorts of BC where I was attempting to fly off the narrow ski runs. The parapente had entered my life and, I guess like repeated doses of heroin, it became embedded as an addiction that I would both cherish and despise in my future adventures. Paragliding became an incredible source of pleasure and euphoria to me, but it has also nearly killed me on far too many occasions with serious accidents or near-death experiences.

Another friend in Whistler who supported our filming was Jack Evrensol. He owned the best restaurant in Whistler, Araxi's along with next-door bar called the „Savage Beagle". The skier Eric Pehota was working there as a bartender for a number of years, and Jack took a real liking to him and to all our ski filming escapades. He even paid for a paraglider to be made with the Savage Beagle name printed on it, which I got to fly above Whistler with.

In later years Jack did me another huge favour. His brother, Arthur Evrensol, was a successful lawyer in Montréal working for Heenan Blaikie, which was a big law firm with an office in Vancouver. One of Heenan Blaikie's clients was former Prime Minister Pierre Trudeau so they were a top firm. Jack called his brother, who wrote me a beautiful letter on this important company's letterhead, saying he was going to represent my company, Extreme Explorations, in Vancouver, when he moved there in the near future.

I have to say I used the letter on several occasions to get myself out of trouble, and it worked well every time. Later I would meet Arthur at many Vancouver International film Festival functions. One of these events was held each year at his trendy restaurant Cin-Cin, which served really good Mediterranean food. I always made sure that I would religiously attend flashing my press pass. The food was really exquisite and the restaurant was deemed among Vancouver's finest. It was shmoosing at its finest.

Sometimes the press office administration would start growling at some of us with press passes. Sure, I may have over-abused my privileges on occasion and eaten too many jumbo shrimps at functions, and I was often really only writing for my website, and not the national press. Nevertheless, I felt I had been there long enough to have earned the press benefits indefinitely.

Whistler had eclectic characters like Jack and a few other Whistler business owners who supported us and our dirtbag lifestyle. Others, I never managed to meet. For instance, there was a Polish man named Ed Pitoniak, who started the first cable television service in Whistler but surprisingly we never met. I can only guess my reputation had gone ahead of me. Many of the other new residents of Whistler did not even ski, and were just in town for the business opportunities.

I was by now becoming obsessed by paragliding. Unfortunately we couldn't use the most convenient location to fly from as we couldn't use the lifts of Whistler or Blackcomb. A couple named Janet and Jorice Moschard, had the special permit to run a paragliding school off Blackcomb's Seventh Heaven slope which faced towards the prevailing winds from the Southwest. They would launch their students on skis and guide them down to land in the bowl below. All other flying was prohibited on the mountain. However, many times I packed my paraglider into a mountaineering backpack and hope nobody would see what was inside. Then I would take the lifts to the top of the Horstman Glacier when lifts were open for summer skiing. From the top of Seventh Heaven, I would ski down the glacier, and then climb back up a short route called "The Chimney" and find a good takeoff spot above Crystal Ridge. Here I would usually find a patch of snow which had lasted through the summer and this would be a good place to take off from. I would launch myself and enjoy my illicit flight all the way down town, landing at Lost Lake on the beach near the nudist dock. I am still very good friends with the Moschards, and we often talk about those crazy early years of paragliding and my various antics always pop up. They have been flying for over 30 years now. without once having a major accident. Partly this is because they are really cautious about when they fly, and will only do so when the conditions are optimum. They still show up occasionally on perfect days in Pemberton, where we still fly together sometimes.

    I miss those early days of paragliding so much, the days of free flight. There was no HPAC (Hang Gliding and Paragliding Association of Canada) regulations, and no need for compulsory paragliding insurance. Those were the early days of paragliding exploration, when we would just climb any mountain searching out new launch sites around Pemberton, Vancouver and many other sites in BC. One of our favourite adventures was to drive up to the trailhead of the Tenquille Lake trail near Pemberton. From there we would hike up to the summit of Copper Dome mountain, which was only about an hour and a half hike. One typical trip involved hiking up on a beautiful August day with my friend Dan Redford and veteran Swiss pilot, Reto Marti. From there we found a beautiful alpine meadow full of the wildflowers that we could launch from. We flew back down to the valley in a setting sun. Later we had to retrace our path back up to the trailhead to retrieve our vehicles. This became a regular trip, and many similar such small adventures followed.

Business-wise, by 1988 we had things worked out pretty good. We were still not making any real money, but the perks were fun. The partners were all still single young men and we were surging ahead in all aspects of life – aah, the late 20's! Extreme Explorations had now officially changed its name to Adventure Scope Communications and we had made several films about ski mountaineering adventures and our various escapades. I kept the Extreme Explorations name for myself and still use it on my productions to this very day. In the late 80s and through the '90s, I juggled my time between Whistler and Vancouver, where I also had an apartment or rented a cheap room in a house while travelling and making my films.

Whistler was now growing into a serious destination ski resort, and the municipality was starting to come down hard on all the squatters' cabins peppered around the valley. Slowly eviction notices were sent out and the illicit cabins started disappearing one by one. Ours was one of the last to go. One day, as we arrived home after skiing, we found an official eviction notice nailed to our door. It was a really bad time to lose our accommodation, because I was in the middle of producing my film "Reel Radical." Bart had long since moved out of the cabin, marrying a doctor's daughter from Vancouver. Nigel, the cabin's co-owner, was in Toronto starting a media company. So I had sort of inherited it and was the caretaker by default.

Then, just as I thought all was lost, I remembered my friend, Diane Neufeld, who had helped us with obtaining the film permit on Mount Robson. So I phoned her up and explained how we were right in the middle of ski film production. Could she help us keep the cabin working somehow through the Film Commissioner's office again? I told her we were at an important part of our film shoot,

Diane listened for a while, and then unbelievably she said, 'Give me a little time and I'll call you back. I have a friend in the Land and Housing Ministry. I'll see what I can do'. She than called back within a half-hour and said, "You are in luck. My friend in the ministry found your file and pulled it – but then quite astonishingly he has now lost it. This means you should have quite some time at your cabin until the bureaucracy finds it again and catches up to you."

And so we got another full year out of our cabin before the law finally came down hard. We came home one evening and found they had taken all the doors and windows. It had been totally gutted inside too by the municipality-contracted goons who were sent out to finish off the last squatters' cabins in Whistler.

„Reel Radical" was the final film I made with Jacques, Beat, and David under the Adventure Scope Communications banner in 1990.

The film was the first to show off the talents of two of the best young local skiers Trevor Petersen and Eric Pehota. It set the stage for these two to become rock stars in the ski movie world. They soon became a hot commodity with various other independent filmmakers like RAP (Real Action Pictures) from Calgary. The film also had an appearance by Sylvain Saudan, the famous Swiss Extreme skier from Chamonix, France. I had invited him to come and ski with us on our Mt Waddington expedition. Manley Fredlund, the Chief Pilot from Okanagan Helicopters (now known as Canadian Helicopters), organized an incredible trip to Mt Waddington, a peak which was familiar to us from several past expeditions.

Manley Fredland was a true visionary. He had started a magazine called Sky Dancing, and his aim was to promote helicopter-driven activities in Western Canada. Using the prestigious name of Sylvain Saudan, he secured two Bell Jet Ranger helicopters for us to fly in to Waddington directly from Vancouver. We would make an overnight stay en route at April Point Lodge, which was a luxury fishing lodge docked along the way on Quadra Island. Sylvain was the true grandfather of extreme skiing and is still very much alive – unlike his compatriots Patrick Vallencant and Jean-Marc Boivin, who had both sadly perished in mountain incidents since our encounter in Peru in '78. This Waddington trip was certainly an interesting one, this time flying in by helicopter and with luxury camping along the way. We actually spent only two days filming on "The Wad" this time. Having two choppers gave us lots of vertical, and it gave us the ability to place cameramen along the way up the flanks of the mountain. We took Scott Fulmer along as second cameraman and we also had a photographer from the then-prestigious Super Natural British Columbia Magazine to give us some great coverage.

The segment on Waddington in Reel Radical turned out to be spectacular indeed. Sylvain, did some of those precise little ski turns he was so famous for from his celebrated ski descents and films. One of his ski descents was one of Pakistan's Hidden Peak. This descent got him into the Guinness Book of World Records as the holder of the record for longest run ever.

I also got to fly off Waddington from right below the northwest summit, in my paraglider which I had begun taking on many of my ski mountaineering trips. I managed to get two paraglide flights because of the convenience of helicopter support that particular day. Unfortunately, on my second flight that day I nearly died. As I came in to land on the col, a strong wind developed due and blew me sideways and I was being pulled towards one of a crevices that are everywhere on the mountain. The altitude and the geology combined with the cold, create vicious wind shifts called Venturis and I was caught by one of these. Some of those glaciers on the summit could easily swallow an entire building and as I landed the wind had really picked up and the next thing I knew I was being dragged at a very rapid rate straight towards a huge crevasse. Luckily after some moments of panic, I managed to pull hard on one of the brake lines and collapsed the wing. I had stopped just short of a huge hole in the ice, which could have easily swallowed me without a trace. It was on this trip that Eric Pehota made his famous ski descent right from the summit spire of Waddington's north west summit. This was heralded by some as 'the best ski filming shot ever taken'. Dave Frazee and Scott Fullmer shot the footage from a helicopter while Scott Fullmer filmed with another camera from an interesting angle below the summit knob itself.

Unwittingly, I managed to open up a whole can of worms by bringing Sylvain Saudan to Whistler Blackcomb after the Waddington shoot. As he was strolling around the centre of Whistler, Sylvain noticed that his name was plastered all over the mountain and resort. It was put on everything from coffee cups to posters advertising the 'Saudan Couloir Ski Race Extreme'. I think if the resort had just used his name quietly without commercializing it as much as they had, he would have not minded. But he saw big corporations like Air Canada, Solomon and Fujifilm were sponsors of the race, and they using his name prominently in the promotional material. He felt they were exploiting it for their own benefit, and he became quite annoyed because he wasn't benefiting in any way. I really didn't blame him for feeling this way.

The Saudan Couloir race, held on Blackcomb's steep north face, had become world-famous. This was all fine and dandy but Blackcomb had never contacted Mr. Saudan for permission to use his name. Somehow the technicalities of using a celebrity's name had never been questioned. The couloir had originally been named by some ski patrollers as an homage to Saudan, and for nine years the name had stayed.

So when Saudan saw his name everywhere, he approached Blackcomb to discuss some kind of reimbursement for using his name, Blackcomb's parent company, Intrawest put their collective heads in the sand, and ignored his request. They wouldn't even meet him to talk about it, so he launched a lawsuit to try to get some compensation, and Blackcomb just changed the name officially to Couloir Extreme, thinking that the problem would just go away. It didn't, and although the case took several years to sort itself out, Sylvain was awarded a significant amount of money by the courts to compensate him for his troubles.

This whole episode did not help me at all, with reference to my already not-so-good standing at the Whistler/Blackcomb organization. I still had the bad boy reputation which had resulted from some of my past antics in the skiing community but almost 30 years later I didn't help things by inviting Sylvain to Blackcomb where the famous couloir's namesake would eventually cost so much for Blackcomb.

My old friend Heather's sister married a marketing executive from Blackcomb around that time, and she told me that the atmosphere at the Christmas table was always rather glum when the family got together and my name came up. I always got a kick out of that story. I felt I was a bit like the Grinch that stole Christmas.

The Reel Radical film sold well, and was a huge hit in the mindless ski porn film industry. Ski porn was a genre of film making which was considered a bit shallow with its emphasis on spectacular ski sequences with loud rock music for the soundtrack, but other than that there was little storyline. Generally, I prefer to make more complex documentary films that contain a deeper story within them.

My beef with the film was that Jacques directed it and he had styled it more as a rock video rather than a documentary. That is probably the main reason I parted working with Jacques. We just had different ways of looking at things sometimes. This situation is often termed as having creative differences.

I did really like some of his ideas though, even if he had styled the film so as it became similar to a music video, editing the action to the music beats, rather than making the soundtrack serve the story line.

However, I have to chuckle at another one of his ideas, when he had our friend Thalassa do a dance in front of the glacier for our Mount Robson film. It was a great idea and made for a unique shot.

Reel Radical also had another first: we had one of the first ever bungee jumping sequences ever filmed. The shoot was necessarily a clandestine operation. After looking for a lot of bridges to hang our jumping apparatus from, we found an old logging span near Boston Bar, BC. We arrived surreptitiously in the morning, set up our cameras, then rigged all the bungee gear. We did as many jumps as we thought we could get away with, and then packed up everything and high-tailed it out of there, before the police arrived.

Wade Ferley, who was a producer from Circle Productions, one of Vancouver's bigger advertising production houses, volunteered to bring a camera crew. He offered to shoot the film just to have it in his archives for future use as possible stock footage, but gave us full use for it in our film. It turned out to be a great segment with four female jumpers, as well as all of us from the film crew.

Wade later married one of the girls, a Norwegian girl named Kareta. I had been very fond of her, and we dated for a while. I then turned my attention to Holly, another girl from the same film shoot, and we tried dating for a while as well. Wade probably offered to do the shoot because he liked Kareta.

Not too long after this I received an invitation I could not refuse. A good friend of mine, who is a very talented Polish filmmaker, Jacek Strek, who is also from Krakow, was with his wife and daughter on the Queen Charlotte Islands, working on a film for National Geographic, 'Charlotte Islands, Out of Time'. He called me via radio telephone. Jacek needed some help. He was a fairly new Polish immigrant in Canada and his English was not that good and so he was finding it very hard to fund-raise the money for finishing his film. He also needed money to be able to stay another winter in the Charlottes. (These islands, which used to be called the Queen Charlotte Islands, have been renamed back to their traditional First Nation name of Haida Gwai.)

Peter to the rescue! Rather than go looking for corporate sponsors, or look for funds by applying for government funding. Instead, I managed to find the money for Jacek from a sympathetic dope dealer I had known for a long time. The guy was just a nice guy and was always willing to help artists.

He was making good money selling dope on Vancouver's Wreck Beach, which is situated on the coast of Point Grey, next to the UBC campus and where getting cannabis had seemed to have always been easy. He said he didn't really care about credits or getting his investment back. We would do it as another footage swap. We would give him the footage once we finished the film. We had some nice landscape and ocean shots from the Queen Charlottes which were hard to beat. He could use it for a rock video, or a tree-hugger logging protest video.

When I told Jacek that we had the money he was almost in tears with happiness. He then invited me and Holly, for a two week trip to the Charlottes to join him in filming – moving around the islands on his inflatable Achilles craft.

Holly and I had an incredible trip, and I will cherish the experience forever. To get permission to visit the archipelago was extremely difficult, so this was a great honour.

The Islands are often called the "Galapagos of North America" and they certainly deserve the title. The huge old-growth trees, and the six-inch long moss alone make the place so unreal combined with the ocean, shoreline and ever changing weather.

As well, the sight of the old totem poles is quite startling. They have been left to decay among the elements generation upon generation over 14,000 years of human habitation.

I also managed to get a small local airline to sponsor what became 'Islands Out of Time'. This gave Jacek a few return tickets off the islands to be able to do some shopping on the mainland occasionally, and also it enabled him to deliver his 16mm film to the laboratory.

Jacek went on to make many other films, including one on the sport of falconry. He travelled the world for that production, rubbing shoulders with Arab princes who held huge falcon hunts in the Arabian deserts.

I guess he liked my look or something about my long hair at the time, because he gave me a role in his falconry film. In my scene, I was beating a drum in a ditch and yelling a call to bring falcons in, as a true barbarian. He also had me ride a horse, with one of the falcons sitting on my shoulder.

Jacek was also a really crazy driver, and a very anti-establishment person. He built a big wooden battering ram on the front of his Land Rover so that whenever his car was impounded, he could sneak into the impound yard at night. He would just get in his vehicle and ram his way out.

Since there was a view that because the impound yard actually took your vehicle without your consent in the first place, this was almost a legal loophole. The feeling was that if you drove it out yourself, the towing company could not really do too much about it.

Jacek taught me a lot about believing in faith and in a way gave me some real warnings about it. When he was in the Queen Charlottes he and his daughter would experiment with their faith. Jacek claimed that due to the abundant nature coupled with so little human energy and interference, spirituality was present everywhere around them.

He told me how they made little dolls out of wood to pass time and then would pray to them for good weather for their planned film shoots. Jacek claimed that because the remote Islands had such a sparse human population, it was easy to project their faith on to the dolls. Their wishes for good weather from the dolls seemed to materialize on many occasions.

I shuddered at the thought of such experiments since I sort of believed him. I also believe that faith could be used in a negative way as in witchcraft, devil worship, or even some of the voodoo or Macumba practices in the Caribbean and in Brazil. This was not a morally healthy way to live life and I thought Jacek was playing with fire in a way.

Jacek and I still stay in touch quite a bit. We share many professional contacts and he ended up using both my distributor Filmoption and a great video editor, Ron Ireland, a guy I had used on many of my films. As he is a great camera man and actually more of a director of photography, I have called on him a couple times to help me shoot a scene or an interview.

Just recently he had a feature film script written about a mystical cannibalistic witch living on an island in the Philippines that was based on stories that appeared in a lot of local legends. I told him if the project materialized, I would love to help them out in the filming in order to spend some time in the Philippines and even check out the paragliding potential there.

He has been married four times and has four beautiful daughters – one from each wife. The first two are Polish, the middle one was from Kazakhstan and the last from the Philippines.

I still chuckle on how he managed to handle his four relationships with his four kids.

He met each one of his wives while engulfed on a different film project and always had great plans to continue working together. However, since Jacek was project-minded, more than a regular family man, all his relationships had fallen apart just as mine had. Another thing that connected us was the he was also Polish and also came from my hometown of Krakow, so we bonded over film and our attitudes to life and anti-establishment sentiment.

A couple of my friends from past films managed to get into the film industry in Vancouver and the so-called Hollywood North. Dave Frazee, who started with us on the 1982 Search for the Ultimate Run film, actually became one of Canada's top directors and directors of photography. He worked on many hugely commercial and popular TV shows like 'Da Vinci's Inquest' for the CBC.

David enjoyed stepping back into the low paid adventure world. Thus he later on helped whenever he could on my films in between his professional productions. He also helped Jacek shoot some of his segments on the 'Charlottes' film, where they both had an incredible experience filming wild December storms on the Pacific coast of the Charlottes: both were thrown overboard of their vessel, and only survived because they were wearing dry suits.

Alex Grzybowski, another faithful partner in many of our old extreme adventures, also left. He got married in Victoria on Vancouver Island and later earned his Master's in Environmental Related Sciences

Alex, an incredible athlete, had been with us us on many of our adventures from the Tantalus Mountains trips to Mount Robson. He was a very strong partner to have on any expedition. Alex's strength and endurance shone through on many of our expeditions. He was another one who was of Polish descent, although he spoke very little of the language.

There came a time when all my past partners were no longer willing to follow my poverty-stricken road of making independent adventure documentaries. My old partners still shake their heads at me now and say, "Not much has changed, eh Peru?"

1989 was the year that my mother took a year-long sabbatical leave, and decided to come over and visit me from her home in New Brunswick. She wanted to see if one day she might move there to be closer to me. We really had no other family but each other, except for my cousin John with his family dinners. My aunt Danuta was also still living in Montréal.

I scouted out some property in Pemberton BC. When my mother arrived I showed her the place I had my eye on and insisted that, although I might not have been a good businessman, I knew there was real value here and that she should purchase the 5 acre lot. She was reluctant at first to spend her hard earned money but after doing a bit of research realized it really was a fantastic deal. One that would probably pay off well later.

I continued my crazy adventures but always with the guilty awareness that came from knowing that my mom was worrying about me back home. She cooked and took care of me, while I licked my wounds and recuperated after the many ski accidents and later paragliding crashes I was to have in the future. She was the only rock solid ground I really had to come home to. This probably really did save me from dying at an early age.

She is an incredibly strong woman, having trekked in Nepal during her late 70's, with her friend Tessa. She swam kilometers in laps at our local Mosquito Lake in Pemberton every summer. She also cross-country skis in the winter now – since she is unable do downhill now because of her plastic knee.

My good friend Jim Orava even took her for a paraglide tandem flight at the ripe age of 80, as she really had no fear of heights or trying new things. We had the Pemberton property until around 2006 before we subdivided it, selling half of it off at a good profit. This gave us the capital to build the beautiful mountain dream home she and I had always talked of having.

Jim Orava, a pilot who gave my mum that ride, had discovered the subdivision, which our property is part of, situated high above the beautiful Pemberton Valley. A bonus was that the paraglide launch was only 15 minutes drive up a nearby forestry road.

When I persuaded my mother to buy the property, I also told my father about the deal, knowing that he could never really move out here with his new family. But he was my dad, and I wanted to offer him part of the good investment as well. So he bought another 5 acre parcel in our subdivision shortly after my mother did.

I was a bit surprised when my mother was angry with me for doing that. However, I stuck to my guns, saying my dad had always helped me out financially over the years and I thought he deserved to profit from this good deal in property as well. Furthermore I said his work would never allow him to move out west anyway, since he and Hannah had just founded a surveying institute in New Brunswick. I was sure that that would keep them there for life, given his workaholic life.

Yikes: Local skier Tao Armengol gets a few long seconds of

Colorful 90's skiing Whistler

1. TJ Armengol takes decisive big air off Blackcomb backcountry.
2. TJ Armengol in trendy duds showing off to the camera during the filming of "Reel Radical".
3. Whistler's skiing rockstars, Eric Pehota (left) and Trevor Petersen.
4. With good friend Kristen Ulmer from several adventures and films together.

Return to Mt Waddington, 1989

A few shots as seen in Beautiful British Columbia Magazine from our Waddington trip with Sylvain Saudan.
1-2. Eric Pehota climbs the final top 100 meters to descend on skis from Waddington's north west summit.
3. Eric Pehota (left) with Sylvain Saudan enjoying catered lunch on Waddington from April Point lodge nearby the coast in BC.
4. My paraglide flight from just below Waddington's northwest summit knob.

CHAPTER 8

THE CONTINUING MOUNTAIN MADNESS OF THE 90's

In 1991 I was part of the first ski descent of the Siberian Couloir which rises above Squamish on the west side of the Atwell Peak on Mount Garibaldi. Our crew this time consisted of my long time partners Beat and Dave, as well as Peter „The Swede" Mattsson. Dave waited at the bottom of the chute, intending to film us skiing on our descent. To make things a little easier on the approach to the couloir, we took a helicopter up to the upper Brohm Ridge. From there we traversed below the rock bands across to the chute, and then climbed straight up 5,000 feet. The Siberian is only 30 ft wide at its narrowest, on a slope that is in excess of 50°.

I remember front-pointing up the entire face to the very top, and then, with my elbows resting over the snowy knife ridge, I was looking down on the glaciers of the Garibaldi Neve on the eastern side of the massif. After a short rest, Beat, Peter the Swede and I put our skis on, and made endless jump turns, in what was great chalky snow, all the way down the chute, past the point from where we had climbed up, and eventually reached the bottom. Our run went down in the history books as the first ski descent of the couloir. Years later the story was published in our local Mountain Culture magazine. Unfortunately,

David didn't get any footage of us, because just as we started our run, a cloud had come in between us. Nevertheless we did get some stills to later prove our claim. The ski-out from that day on a logging road, in the traditional pouring rain, was not the most comfortable ending to an otherwise epic project.

Later, Beat and Peter the Swede went on to start Bella Coola Helicopter Skiing, one of the world's finest helicopter skiing operations, in the spectacular Bella Cola valley in central BC. I have always hoped that one day they would invite me for some skiing up there, hint hint. Bella Coola is just 100 miles north Mount Waddington, and is the last stop on the remote highway that is the only land connection with the rest of Canada. It cuts through the Coast Mountain Range from the vast interior of BC's Cariboo-Chilcotin region.

Another old friend, Sylvain Saudan, had also started his own helicopter skiing operation in Kashmir, part of the Himalayas. This was the first commercial heli-ski operation in the Himalayas, where he was able to open up the incredible terrain to his clients. His operation ultimately came to a halt, as initially relations between India and Pakistan became increasingly hostile, making it difficult to operate. Eventually he had to give up entirely, following the arrival of Muslim terrorist groups affiliated with ISIS, and this was the final straw for him.

Sylvain had some incredible stories from his heli-skiing adventures. I recall being really entertained by one where he described crash landing a helicopter on an un-named Himalayan peak. He had to leave the pilot with the helicopter, because he was not a skier, and guide his clients down to safety as if nothing serious had happened. Then he organized a rescue mission to get the pilot back down to the valley the next day. The helicopter, on the other hand, is still on that lonely peak.

From 1989 through the early 90s, I based myself in the offices of Petersen Productions International (PPI), a film company based in Vancouver. Curtis Petersen was an old friend who was a kindred spirit. He was another ski film producer/director and ran his large outfit, including a film rental company, out of his offices in Vancouver. It was nice hanging out with Curtis again. Our friendship was rooted in working together on his Pro Patrol film in 1978. Curtis was the grandfather of independent film making in Vancouver. He was kept busy doing second unit photography on big Hollywood features, but he also did all he could to help support independent productions in Vancouver. I had office support and even some backing from him on some of my earlier films. A large number of emerging film makers in Vancouver got started thanks to filming gear supplied to them at greatly reduced rates by Curtis. He was also somewhat infamous for cursing out his on-set crew sometimes, although everyone seemed to love him all the more for it. He brought in the work though, and he often laughingly complained about "Everyone sucking on my tit!"

I had to incorporate my own company Extreme Explorations around this time, as it was necessary to be able to access funding from government grants. For some reason I only paid the fees for a few years, so the incorporation ran out after a while. Nevertheless, I kept using those original documents for years and nobody ever checked its authenticity. My bad boy habits towards bureaucracy in all forms have remained the same all my life – no respect and no prisoners taken! That has been my lifelong legacy in those matters.

While hanging out and working from of Curtis's offices, I often joined him on some of his own snowmobile filming projects. For one of them we came up with the idea of making our own snowboard film to be called Northern Rage. Marcus Rogers was another producer on this project and he also had his own small production company in Vancouver. Marcus had a passion for heavy metal, so our film ended up with a thrash-metal soundtrack.

Much of the footage featured the early beginnings of the snowboarding in terrain parks, which had its roots in the urban skateboard parks. I set up some spectacular shoots in the Squamish back-country, and the project ended up as a 'snowboard porn music' video. Ideally, if it had been my project, I would have liked to have seen a few documentary segments included, but there you go.

Another interesting adventure I had with Curtis involved a winter road trip through the United States for a new snowboard film. Some days we would be filming redneck snowmobiling events, and the next we would shoot our snowboarding stuff. The point of the story was to show how bad-ass snowboarders could connect with redneck snowmobilers, so we put the two cultures together and filmed the results.

It was a bit like cats and dogs fighting at times, but luckily no major fistfights broke out even with the obviously conflicting ideologies. Dope-smoking snowboarders meet Jack Daniels-drinking sledders!

I continued filming more sequences for our snowboard production in places that I knew, like Wedge Mountain and the Tantalus Range. Once again we had a close call when a snowboarder went off script and jumped right over my camera position. He hadn't checked what was below me and disappeared into a crevasse. Because I had my eye in the viewfinder of the camera, I did not see which hole he had fallen into and we spent a frantic hour searching around the crevasses. Because the snow was still partially frozen and sun capped, we couldn't find any tracks leading to the crevasse. Luckily a photographer called Ian Highlands, eventually heard a moan coming from one of the holes, and looking down, we saw Jeremy perched on an icy ledge not too far into the hole. He was all right, but had hit his head in the fall and had lost consciousness for a few minutes.

We dragged him out of the hole with a rope, and then called the local rescue in Squamish. The helicopter arrived quickly, but out stepped a team form the St. John Ambulance service. To our horror they were dressed in their normal street clothes, with slippery street shoes and wearing black pants and white shirts, instead of proper mountaineering gear. Now we were afraid we were going to lose those ambulance guys in the crevasses as well. It was a completely ridiculous scene, with our rescuers sliding all over the place and being of no use in helping us to get the injured snowboarder Jeff into the helicopter. Luckily we eventually managed to get everybody down safely back to Squamish.

I ran into Jeremy a while after the accident and he seemed not altogether. I heard that he seemed to be leading a chaotic lifestyle. The head injury had taken its toll. I have to say that attitudes to head injuries like concussions have changed completely since our day. Back then you took a couple of Advil and maybe you'd have a rest the next day, and we had no idea of the long term effects of these injuries.

Another of these trips was up Wedge Mountain in Whistler to film a local snowboarder. We all hiked up, Scotty Fullmer, my good friend, and cameraman John Griber and me, to film a local snowboarder named Wayne, who had his own brand of snowboards based in Whistler.

Here I have to introduce my good buddy Scott Fullmer. Scotty is a true friend who has worked with me as cameraman on so many projects. Scotty was originally from Calgary, and also had roots skiing in the Banff area. He's a great character who was a good friend of Doris Spika and had actually been the person who introduced us one day. Scotty was a freestyle skier and had travelled extensively, even spending time in Australia. While there he lived in a bus, and lived by giving events at shopping malls. He would build a ski jump from the roof of his bus and would thrill the spectators by executing freestyle maneuvers before landing on an airbag in the parking lot. He ran a gypsy type of spectacle for sure, but he claims he made a lot of money from this bizarre spectacle, doing it in the heat of Australia.

We had first met in Whistler in the late eighties where he also lived in his bus, hidden away in the woods. Sometimes we would take Scotty's bus on more distant road trips, when we would park it somewhere and it would become a comfortable base camp.

He had come from a Mormon upbringing, but you would never know it as he liberally indulged in alcohol as well as other things... Scotty and I did some great partying, and dragged many girls back to that bus...

Scotty had a company called Snowmotion, and we actually used that name later for a local weekly Whistler cable TV ski show that we produced. He was a very talented cameraman, but had problems maintaining his lenses and cameras while living in a bus.

One day, I hiked up Wedge Mountain with Scotty and a group of snowboarders all the way from the valley trailhead. It was an arduous thrash to the base of the West Couloir and took nearly four hours to get to the bottom of the couloir, and from there we cramponed, or front pointed, up the entire couloir with Scotty stopping half-way up to set up a filming position. To our horror, one of our snowboarders called Wayne lost an edge on a turn, and started sliding precipitously down the couloir, mirroring the death of my friend Gerhard Singler in the same couloir many years earlier. Luckily this time Wayne managed to get the snowboard below him, and by kicking into the still partially frozen snow to get some traction, he managed to ride the whole slope on his butt. He was a bit shaken up when we got down to him but otherwise totally fine from the ordeal. John Griber achieved first proper snowboard descent of the West Couloir that day, and we had it on film. Wayne achieved the award for first bum slide down the entire West Couloir, and that was not an insignificant feat either!

Another great project then appeared on my horizon. It all happened during a snowmobile shoot I was on with Curtis Petersen in Alaska, where he was doing a series of sledding videos. We were at Summit Lake where the hard core "Arctic Man" festival takes place. This is an annual event and snowmobile enthusiasts come from all over North America, driving their motor homes thousands of miles and where they set up camp for a week. The "Arctic Man" trophy is awarded to the winning two man team, comprised of a skier being towed by a snowmobiler. The course includes a climb up two big hills, from where the skier skis back down by himself, and then he grabs the rope from the snowmobiler as it swings by and does another lap. Snowmobiler and Skier in perfect harmony! It's an awesome redneck event for the whole family. Because the conditions are so severe this far north, there is a unique atmosphere as the sled-heads are extremely friendly and welcoming to newcomers like me.

Up here in the Thompson Pass, on the road north out of Valdez, Alaska, we came across the exact birthplace of now fashionable extreme skiing contests. A local businessman from Seattle, Michael Cozad, had a brilliant idea to cash in on the cleanup of the Exxon Valdez oil spill in March 1989, which had caused a tsunami of guilt money to roll into town. He was looking for ways of promoting winter tourism in Valdez. And so the first ever World Extreme Skiing Championships were held there in 1991. The Alyeska Pipeline Company was keen to help and offered its 300 employees a week off work on full pay if they volunteered. ERA Helicopters, who were the pipeline company's heli operators, were given the contract for all the uplifts needed for this new event.

Everyone in Valdez was excited by the opportunity to show off their incredible mountains which received such a huge yearly snowfall. Alaska was still relatively unexplored ski-wise, and it was just beginning to be covered by the ski media. It would take a big event to bring media as well as world-class skiers to publicize the area, and the World Extreme Skiing Championships became the ideal vehicle to get the story out.

What was great about Alaska and Valdez, was that it was still wild ski terrain, but was as yet untouched by the threats of litigation and the liability paranoia, which had managed to kill off extreme skiing in the traditional ski resorts down south. So Michael Cozad's forward thinking in 1991 was a really bold move.

The Chugach Mountains in Alaska are not as high as the ranges further south, but the snow covers everything down almost to sea level. They cap out at nearly 3,000 m, with Mount Diamond being one of the highest peaks in the Thompson pass area. The conditions tend to deliver ideal snow for backcountry skiing – the peaks look like ice-cream snow cones as they get covered by huge dumps of the white stuff. There is so much snow that all the rocks get covered. The snow that falls initially is fairly heavily, as the moisture laden storms roll in from the ocean. Later the colder air that inevitably follows blows through it and turns it into some of the lightest powder imaginable. Also, the threat of avalanches is diminished because the snow-pack really bonds to the slopes as it falls wet and then gradually dries out.

We could often ski slopes up to 50° without the constant fear of getting caught in a big slide, while only having to cope with smaller manageable surface sloughs. This combination of weather and geography supplied some of the best skiing conditions anywhere in the world. And so the WESC was born, and Michael Cozad invited a several of the world's top skiers including Scott Schmidt and Glenn Plake to come and do their stuff. He also invited me to be one of the judges. Perhaps it was because of my Peru notoriety and my Whistler extreme misadventures that I was asked to get involved alongside some of skiing's biggest personalities.

To begin establishing the areas for the events, we scouted the mountains around the Thompson Pass area, northwards of Valdez. It seemed such a crazy proposition, but how could we refuse all that free Heli time for reconnaissance sake and doing the trial ski runs? The plan was to find mountains that had suitable steep faces for the extravaganza to take place on.

Unfortunately for me, the Valdez locals had a small ski hill which used the switchbacks in the road up Thompson Pass. It was just a small run, but on that short descent I managed to fall in the crappy conditions, and snapped the other ACL on what had been, up to that point, my good knee.

For several years afterwards, until I got the knee fixed by arthroscopic surgery, I found it safer to snowboard. This way both my legs were on one plank, giving both of them less of a chance of the need to pop out or give away. I really got to love snowboarding on the lower angle glaciers but never really mastered the snowboard on steeper slopes.

I did manage one first snowboard descent, on the north side of Diamond peak, which was a short distance northeast of Valdez. I was with Bruce Griggs and Stephen Koch, and we were in an area dubbed 'The Dark Side' of Diamond. Surfing legend Laird Hamilton joined us on that run with his snowboard as there was an extra spot available in the chopper. Laird later told me what a special run that had been for him, and I made a new friend.

Those early years of WESC were really crazy. Skiers like Doug Coombs, Jim Conway and I would spend hours of heli and ski plane time with our eyes glued to the windows, as we flew up and down those amazing ridges looking for the perfect face for the contest. I still revel at the memories for the countless heli-skiing turns that I was given by the creation of this ground breaking event.

The whole thing worked like this – after determining which mountain would be used for the contest on a given day – firstly, us judges would first fly up to the top and do a trial run on the given face, checking out the conditions for later reference in the judging. Then we would make ourselves comfortable in lawn chairs below the run and watch the competitor's run with binoculars to be able to see the details of each skier's technique during the run.

Each rider was to be judged on the basis of the speed, fluidity, control and the air-time. The athleticism that each competitor displayed was quite something to watch. These were elite athletes pushing the boundaries of their sport, and taking it to another level. Sometimes I had to actually put my binoculars down, as the skiers dropped perilously close to rocks. I didn't want to have a close-up view of their possible demise. Miraculously they nearly always somehow seemed to recover, giving us much needed room to breathe.

Tragedy did strike one year when a skier fell off a cornice before his run had actually started as he was examining the entry point for his run, and very sadly he didn't survive the fall. On the whole though, during the 9 years that I judged the contest, there were relatively few injuries.

Gravity inevitably did take its toll and there were some big wipe outs. The most spectacular was the fall of skier Garret Bartel, who cartwheeled right past our camera positions ideally situated on the slope, and down out of sight. The clip of the fall ended with a momentum of its own, ending up being shown in many of those '90s TV disaster action shows which were so popular before the internet. That horrid spill down the side of a mountain in Alaska was beamed to millions of TV's around the world many years before anyone had ever heard the term 'going viral'.

While judging those WESC years, I saw many skiers, old friends who passed through Valdez during those years.

I met the skier Kristin Ulmer here again. I had first got to know her in her home town of Snowbird in Utah, during the filming of „The Search for the Ultimate Run", and then later when she visited Whistler. She was just 17 years old in that first film, and I think we were the first people to film her. Later she went to fame (if not fortune) in the US as a pioneer of filming extreme skiing, and was a frequent star in movies by Warren Miller, Real Action Pictures, and Teton Gravity Research.

WESC became a major event, with all the rock-stars of big mountain skiing showing up in Valdez. It followed that single women would naturally flock down from Fairbanks and Anchorage to make themselves available to the athletes. It was glorious chaos and we interviewed several of the ladies for our film. It was like the plot line of the classic movie 'Seven Brides for Seven Brothers', and I remember getting a piece of action there as well, but never found a bride.

The judges alternated every year. Among them we had Chris Kent from Whistler, as well as Kim Reichelm, the brothers Des Lauriers and the Egans, Jim Conway as well as others, and the list went on, with some of the best known extreme skiers from the US as well as Europe. Later as the sport evolved, the name gradually changed from 'extreme skiing' to 'free riding' which covers both skiing and snowboarding.

One helicopter pilot who became famous from appearing in our film was a local pilot named Chet Simmons. He was Vietnam vet, who carried a handgun on his hip most of the time. Chet regularly pushed the limits of his Bell Jet Ranger so much that the machine seemed to rev beyond control, sometimes apparently with a mind of its own. He would max it out – taking it to heights the helicopter should never have attempted. Sometimes he came in on ledges that were impossible to land on, and skiers would have taken a leap of faith, jumping out just before he had to dive the machine to a lower more manageable altitude to regain full control.

I got to know his roommate Lisa well, who was also an early paraglide pilot. She and I did some spectacular paraglide flights together from Mount Odyssey down below Thompson Pass, in the same area as the contest took place.

I had many memorable weeks during all those years. Every April I would spend the month scouting, judging, and filming in the incredible Chugach Mountains around Valdez, meeting great people for the first time and reconnecting with others. And every time, skiing in tit-deep powder.

Thanks to my Alaskan experience, I was invited to judge the American Extreme Skiing Competition that was held in Crested Bute, Colorado, which was a ski area that catered to extreme skiers, as well as advanced recreational skiers and had very challenging terrain. I had the honor to sit and judge the contest with the Frenchman Anselme Baud, who had been Patrick Vallencant's extreme skiing partner on many descents in the French and Swiss Alps, and the two were legends. Five years later I judged with Anselme again at a competition in Chamonix, and he kindly appeared in a cameo in my film honouring Trevor Petersen, called 'The Spirit'.

Of the 9 WESC events in Valdez, I filmed the first two of them. Then, a year later, we also covered the first ever extreme snowboarding championships that was held on the same mountains.

I partnered with producer Harvey Zlataritz from North Vancouver, my old friend and cameramen Scott Fullmer from Whistler, and Randy Renolds from Park City and we produced two films. 'Valdez Goes Extreme', documented the story of how the town and the local people came together to produce an extreme ski event. 'Sudden Exposure', was our film about the snowboarding competition and it had a similar theme.

The "Valdez Goes Extreme" film went on to win an award for creative excellence at the Chicago International Film Festival. I had since left Jacques and Beat at Adventure Scope Communications, which was now doing only snowboard videos. However, I kept the older Extreme Explorations name which I added to Harvey's Zinc productions company at the credits at the end of the film.

I had first met Harvey in 1988 through Vancouver film circles. He was producer and a sound- and picture-editor with 40 years experience, who was originally from Toronto. He seemed amused by our crude outdoor film antics and decided to see if he could help us out with some real work.

The first project from our collaboration was 'Snowmotion' which was to be a weekly television ski show, which we would produce in Whistler. Whistler Cable, the cable television provider in Whistler, gave us a half-hour slot each week to produce a ski show of our liking.

The CRTC (Canadian Radio Television Commission) had strict regulations in place about how community stations ran with strict rules about advertising.

Being a community TV station, the station could not not allow any ads with moving images! Only still images could be used in the commercials.

Little did Whistler Cable realize that they were not dealing with regular content providers, but rather we were a bunch of rebels who needed to make our shows no matter what.

Luckily, Whistler was out of range and well off the radar of regular CRTC monitoring. Soon we were putting up all sorts of broadcast tv ads which were provided by our sponsors. These ads were paid for by gear and services.

I remember we were so desperate one time that we took a couple sets of tires from Yokohama to sell so we could pay for producing the next weeks show. Soon the famous Yokohama tire ad, with the cat being chased around inside someone's house was being played several times a day in Whistler. They must have got their money's worth with the amount of exposure they had, even if the audience wasn't enormous.

The style of our shows were documentary, but we were always under pressure to make a new show every week, as the sponsors demanded.

We even resorted to making our own humorous fund raising moving ads. These were designed as comic relief in order to entice more local sponsors. One skit had an industrial dryer being loaded full of small cash bills by a lovely local girl – actually, Ross Rebagliati's younger sister. Amazingly, a local bar let us borrow all the cash needed for the one night shoot to make it look authentic!

Ross himself actually appeared in a snowboarding race segment of ours before his famous gold medal victory at the Nagano Japan Olympics, which he won, then lost and then regained it again during his famous marijuana scandal.

Other celebrities from the skiing world such as ski filmmaker Greg Stump, legendary producer of 'The Blizzard of Aaahs', also appeared on our show. We actually only managed to make eight episodes before we exhausted our supply of local sponsors, and it became impossible to get enough paying advertisers in Whistler's very limited market to keep our show running.

Later, in 1994 Harvey's Zinc Productions and I would co-produce a series of instructional programs on different ski styles. We covered how to powder ski in 'Into the Powder', telemark skiing in 'Whiteout', and snowboarding with 'Cruising Without Bruising'.

Barry Backus, who was a good friend of Harvey's, helped edit the Alaska and instructional films with us. Barry is an Oscar-winning picture editor, who had originally worked with Harvey in Toronto. I have turned to Barry for advice many times since then and we have often brainstormed successfully together.

As with all independent film productions, under-funding is a constant fact of life and politics plays its part. We had to beg and borrow to produce our series. We got some funding from the local BC broadcaster, the Knowledge Network. Unfortunately we made some enemies there right off the bat as Scotty unknowingly managed to 'rewire' their entire online facilities, while he was trying to make some video dubs.

We constantly had to negotiate our online editing time with the network in order to get our films completed. In the end I had virtually let go of the rights to my whole film library as a trade-off in exchange for all the post production time we had used at their facilities.

Harvey was the one who negotiated with the Knowledge Network, whose line- and production-managers thought we were all rather crazy. Harvey tried to keep us in line – but not always with success! I probably should admit that everything I know about film production came from Harvey.

He really helped add a sense of professionalism to my often chaotic and ad hock film protocol, teaching me about organization and cataloging – and how important it was not to get lost in it all. This was vitally important when one was dealing with hundreds of hours of footage, as was the case with so many of our productions. It was the little things that were so important – like marking all our tapes properly, and logging them on paper as well as having a data base. It really saved my ass on many future productions!

The „Whiteout" series which covered telemark skiing, ended up as a good looking production. Unfortunately, as things go with ski resorts, because it was not Whistler's idea in the first place, the mountain did not really get behind helping to distribute it. Both Blackcomb and Whistler could have really used this series to promote their ski schools, which were featured in the films. Once again, politics or my reputation got in the way and, as a result, they did not really get behind the distribution of our project.

We did manage to sell the series to German television, which helped contribute to the production costs. This sale boosted our spirits and convinced us we were on the right track, as German television standards were really high. Unfortunately in the late 90's rapid advances in ski technology, cameras, and styles of powder skiing meant our powder series was somewhat outdated.

In 2005 Harvey and I had a memorable trip to Poland and Slovakia. Our snowboard film 'Sudden Exposure' had been accepted to the Poprad Mountain Film Festival in Slovakia. We went first to Poland as I wanted to show Harvey the Old Country, the place of my birth and where I grew up.

We initially spent time in Krakow living at my aunt's place. Krakow is considered one of the most beautiful cities in Europe, and has often been called the 'Paris of Eastern Europe'. While the capital Warsaw was totally destroyed by Hitler and the Russians during World War II, Krakow somehow survived being obliterated, which was a miraculous blessing because it was so full of old Polish heritage. In fact Krakow is over 1,000 years old. During World War II, historians say, Hitler had planned to keep it intact as one of his architectural jewels in Eastern Europe and that is why he spared it from any Luftwaffe bombing.

Later, Harvey and I moved on to the Festival in Slovakia. When we got there, I noticed a beautiful girl who had been at Popad in Poland. She was absolutely gorgeous, a tall slinky blonde with exceptional features. I walked up to her and chatted her up – as I have such a weakness when I see a beautiful woman. She turned out to be a top fashion model who had worked for all the major agencies from Australia to Italy. Her name was Adriana Novicka. She had been plucked off the street by a modeling scout somewhere in Europe, and then whisked away to be trained as a top fashion model.

After the Mountain Film Festival, Harvey and I had some spare time so we arranged to take Adriana and her sister for a back-country outing in the beautiful Tatra Mountains. A Slovakian mountain guide I had also met at the festival came along as well. We managed to climb the highest peak in the area, which was Gerlach Mountain at 2,655 m. It turned out to be a really memorable trip, with both the girls summiting with us. The final pitch of the climb was especially challenging as it involved some metal clamps and ladders, which we all had to climb on during the last part of the summit ascent.

Although I had first met Adriana, who only 19, now it was nice getting to know her older sister Iveta, who was 25. She turned out to be a physical education instructor in Slovakia. She was fit and had a perfect figure, which always excites an older man. Since Polish and Slovakian are very similar Slavic languages we had no trouble communicating with each other.

I thought the best way of getting to know Iveta better was to do yet another trek through the Tatras, staying in cozy traditional mountain huts along the way.

After the festival in Slovakia, I had gone back to Poland by myself to the mountain town of Zakopane. There, I had arranged to meet the daughter of my good friend Ryszard Szafirski, who is a renowned Polish climber. Ryszard was best known for his participation in Poland's triumphant first winter climb of Mount Everest, on which he was a cameraman. I had invited Ryszard's daughter and her boyfriend to come along with Iveta and me on a few days trekking through the Tatras. I figured that having another couple along would make it more fun and less awkward for my new date.

The hike started at a beautiful alpine lake called Morskie Oko, and then the trail climbed over several scenic alpine ridges, and we would overnight at a mountain hut called Piec Stawow. I recall this excursion with Iveta as being one of the best romance-filled hikes of my life. Unfortunately, at the end I had to get back to Canada, and she had her life in Europe, but we still keep in touch.

A few years later I made a side trip to London, where she had emigrated to and got a job as a nanny, as so many girls from Eastern Europe did in those days. I felt a bit bad on arriving in London as I was picked up by a friend of Iveta's. The fellow was a really nice guy, and when he picked me up at the airport, I got the feeling that he really liked Iveta. I kind of felt guilty because here was this guy that really liked her, and she had arranged a cozy weekend for her and me! A cozy weekend to be spent together in London at a nice hotel she had found and rented for us. Anyhow life and love can be cruel sometimes. I really wanted to meet up with her again and reminisce about the first romantic encounter we had enjoyed in the Polish Tatra Mountains together. We spent a timeless weekend in and out of the hotel, going out to a few pubs and having dinners together.

Many years later I found out that my hunch was right about the guy who had picked me up at the airport. He really had been very much in love with Iveta. They later got married and had children together. Their marriage seems to have worked out really well. Iveta writes me on Facebook sometimes and I can see they are very happy together. I still think of her a lot. I often wish that maybe something more could have happened between us. What, for example, would have happened if I had followed through more with her earlier in our first encounter? But that seems to be the story with most of my women – my projects simply took me away from them.

1

2

3

From Alaska to Blackcomb the fun continues

1. Steep and deep powder in the Chugach Mountains.
2. The cover shot for the film Valdez Goes Extreme.
3. Ross Rebagliati in action on Blackcomb. Ross went on to win the controversial first ever gold medal in snowboarding at the Nagano Winter Olympics in 1998.
4. Randy Reynolds filming Dough Combs. Jim Conway in the midlle.

4

1

2

3

Powder frolics continues

1. I am enjoying a deep powder run here in the Chugach Mountains near Valdez, Alaska.
2. Jimmy Zell takes air during WESC, World Extreme Skiing Championships in Valdez, Alaska.
3. Eric Pehota takes air on "The Curl", a hidden gem on Blackcomb.
4. My bicycle trip for a day of summer skiing off Fissile Mountain, Whistler.

4

CHAPTER 9

THEN, THERE WAS FILM

People cannot imagine how difficult it was making adventure documentaries during the era when we were doing it. To get the best quality you had to shoot in 16mm film, which is a very costly medium. That footage would then be transferred to video, and that's what we edited with. We always looked for 'short ends' or left over, partly-used reels of unused 16mm film which we scrounged from bigger productions companies around town. Again Curtis Petersen helped out a great deal here and regularly managed to find film for us. We would use VHS for an off-line edit, during which the story would be constructed at a leisurely pace, and then we would move to an 'on-line' edit suite to put everything together with the picture, sound, and any graphics assembled in these high price edit suites. It cost hundreds of thousands of dollars to make an hour-long film at 'commercial' rates, unless one resorted to hustling as we often did. The problem with that approach was that you often had to give away the majority of the profits so for a producer like me there was really no money left in the end. Once in a while I would get some foreign sales but these were few and far between.

The process worked like this; usually you made your film in any way you could, doing anything to complete it, and then you would work the festival circuit. Entering all the suitable festivals, your appearances would hopefully deliver some TV sales. One could also do personal little 'premieres' on your own dime. In my experience distributors were often crooks and, for every 10 films of yours they sold, you only got paid for a couple of them. I have to say that I was rather lucky since I had a great relationship with my television distributor, and they even helped us with small advances sometimes. The accounting system was based on a sort of honour system, as you never really knew if your show was running on constant rotation somewhere in the world like Botswana. You could never really track which countries they sold the films to and where they had appeared.

Then came the seismic VHS revolution. We hoped that the new home video market would be an ideal market for our films. Unfortunately we ended up making a deal with a distributor from the American Midwest that claimed to be one of the biggest in the business. They chose three of our titles, packaged them very nicely and sent us quite a few examples of the packaging which was helpful. This way we could also sell the videos on our own to stores on a small scale to cover our local demand. But beyond the somewhat meager $5,000 advance, we never saw another penny from the deal. Meanwhile the distributor, probably made a small fortune from our material, as they were heavily promoted in Kmart and Walmart stores across North America. As is so often the case, we couldn't afford to hire the expensive entertainment lawyers who were specialists in this sort of caper, and we never took them to court.

Being what I would call an expert in this subject, given the fact that I was in this business for so long, I can say, choosing this route could never have given enough of an income to provide for a family. Somehow, whenever a new adventure loomed on the horizon, all the lessons I might have learned from previous experience went out the window, a new idea for a film would keep me moving forward and never looking back.

Times were tough indeed back then in Canada's independent film world. Making my films with their expenses was cleaning me out of resources, but I felt I had to go on, to carry the tradition forward. I still don't know what kept me doing it other than the films were a justification for keeping my lifestyle as it was and having something to show from it. Like every other film-maker, I lived with the hope that perhaps this time I would get that bigger distribution break and a good sale, and with that a budget for the next film.

I had to resort to apply for welfare payments in order not to starve and to somehow keep the film productions moving forward. Accessing social assistance is not something I am proud of, but otherwise the films would never have gotten made. Also I felt that, by using government money for my film projects, it could be seen as a grant. In some small way, each production stimulated the economy of the film industry. A great many salaries were still being paid to those government institutions which provided us with facilities deals. Their employees were on salary and we just provided the projects which they would work on and be paid from. This was how we justified our guerrilla film making practices.

I'm reminded of an episode in my constant battle back in Toronto: after our films had been processed, and we had paid the laboratory bills, we got home to find an envelope full of cash had been sent back to us. Somehow the receptionist, having received several thousand dollars from us to settle the bill, had made a huge error and instead of banking the money, she had mailed it back to us! And, no, we didn't send it back. Why not? Because, being as broke as we were, we used every penny of that cash 'refund' to pay yet more bills further down the road. In this case we sacrificed our karma and well-being for the benefit of the film – or that's how we justified it anyhow. The government funded organization never asked for it back anyway.

I really envy the young filmmakers and the new digital technology. Nowadays, a full broadcast quality film can be created with a $3,000 camera and a laptop. During my film-making days a Betacam camera cost $60,000, so we always had to make deals with cameramen or camera equipment suppliers in order to borrow gear and shoot our pictures. Technology has made film obsolete in the motion picture industry, which is also a huge saving. The revolution provided by wearable cameras like Go-Pros contributed further to the enormous changes in the style of adventure film making.

Some people say that along with these changes, the audience attention span has also diminished.

YouTube, Netflix and Facebook have taken over the way that films are made, shown and perceived. It is one creative choice to make a 15 second TikTok video or a four-minute sequence on YouTube, but that is a totally different process compared to making an hour-long documentary that tells a story and still keep the viewers' attention. I have many different formats since the late 70s. I started out shooting on 'standard 8' film, then moved to 'super 8'. Video tape then appeared, and I shot on 'three-quarter inch' video, which was surpassed by '8 mm' video, which was further improved to 'Hi 8'. These formats were analogue, but they were replaced by the digital revolution, which gave us 'mini-DV', then 'HDV' and we now in 4K, or 8K. We used all of these formats to shoot our documentaries. Sometimes we even mixed several formats in one film, which was acceptable in documentary filmmaking.

Getting a soundtrack done was another huge challenge. Because music rights are controlled by lawyers, they are prohibitively expensive. They seem to think everyone only makes big-budget productions but we didn't fit the mold. We would assemble our music track using music that was sent to us by lesser-known musicians who were happy to get exposure just to have their music played in our films. We made deals for music whenever we could, and so, for instance, the soundtrack for 'Search for the Ultimate Run' was provided by a popular ska band from Vancouver called 'The B-Sides'. We also managed to get them an appearance at one of our dances at SFU.

Sometimes we had to get really creative to get our hands on the music. We would let the bands use our spectacular footage in their mainstream videos so that we could use the track in our production. Such was the case with Tad Campbell and his band Idle Eyes. Tad was best known for his Canadian Grammy award-winning hit "Tokyo Rose", and in exchange for us using their song "Standing at The Edge" on our Mount Robson film, we gave them our footage in the rock video, and it became quite a hit.

I also have to thank Sony Music, for charging us only $500 for a great song called 'Miss You' by the Vancouver band '54–40' which we used in our homage to Trevor Petersen, 'The Spirit'. This was one of our better deals, but we did not have similar luck with many other labels who ignored our pleas to use their music on our low-budget productions.

The Traverse across the Pemberton ceﬁeld was something special for me. By 1995 I had been carefully monitoring the rise of various ski-mountaineering races being held in the European Alps every year. One event in particular, named the 'Grand Deﬁ' caught my attention. It consisted of race between ﬁve-person teams while attempting a crossing of a section of the Alps over several days and was an event of a kind then unheard of in North America.

So I thought we could create a similar event here in Whistler, which would be a race across the massive Pemberton Ice Cap, which is a vast high altitude plateau that is permanently covered in snow and ice situated to the north-west of the resort. The event was to be called 'The Traverse'.

Little did I know what I was getting myself into, and once more I committed to a project which was hugely under-funded from the start. From the start, I had to beg the relevant government authority, the Lands and Housing Ministry, to allow me to host the event without proper insurance coverage. They let me do it eventually, I still think we live in an over-insured, liability-ridden country and that's a shame!

As part of my fund raising efforts, I had contacted Isabelle Bombardier, who was the daughter of the founder of the Canadian industrial giant Bombardier. I had aggressively pursued her, trying to persuade Bombardier to help us with some sponsorship. Finally, after endless phone calls and faxes, Isabelle came through big-time with a significant $2,000 donation for fuel for the snowmobiles which we were using to patrol the event for safety. She had one curious stipulation which we had to abide by however. We would get the money, but the Bombardier name was not to appear anywhere, or to be associated in any way with the our Traverse race. It was the only case of reverse sponsorship that I ever encountered, where my sponsor did NOT want their name plastered everywhere.

Somehow the whole event materialized and, on May 8th 1994, seven teams, with each one including at least one skier, one snowboarder and one telemark skier, headed off from start at Brandywine Mountain, just south of Whistler. The finish line was 100kms away in a north-east direction across the ice field to the Meager Creek Hot Springs. I had managed to mobilize the local snowmobile club, and

I also had help from ski plane and helicopter operators, to help with looking out for the competitors and volunteers who were spread out along the route.

There were, of course, some unexpected problems and one of them was me! In the run-up to the race I had broken my leg while being towed behind a snowmobile. So I now had to organise the entire event with a cast on my leg.

Another issue which was beyond our control was the weather, as the storm named Hawaiian Express came in. The temperature rose to 28°C, which caused the snow to soften up and made the course treacherous in the extreme. The effort involved in travelling in those conditions was too much, and so the race was effectively abandoned. Later, seven of the original competitors got together and completed the course to the Hot Springs, Those seven who finished the course later proved it was do-able if one was experienced and fit enough for the challenge.

I had even been offered a broadcast from broadcaster TSN (The Sports Network), usually a hockey and baseball TV network and Canada's ESPN, to air our Traverse – as the race was to be called. The media later fried me on this one, and they were right on many counts. It was nearly a real disaster with all those athletes lost on the ice, and I had not been able to provide a good safety net. Unfortunately this is sometimes the case with under-funded events.

We ended up evacuating several people who we found by chance, spotting them from above in the airplane or the helicopter. Such was the case when we spotted one lost snowboarder who was a race volunteer. He was by himself on the glacier, and totally under-equipped with just a recreational quality sleeping bag for survival.

There is a great quote from local author Les Anthony on 'The Traverse':

We wandered the Callaghan Valley for another steamy day, images of a public Chrzanowski crucifixion spurring us onward, especially after we had to bivouac an extra night thinking we could get out in only a few hours. Meanwhile while we trundled along debating whether grizzlies could climb trees, the Traverse had truly "disintegrated."
– Les Anthony, POWDER MAGAZINE, ICECAPADES article, March 1996.

Despite the uproar of the media backlash, many of the reporters gave me some credit for actually doing something of this magnitude, the likes of which had never been attempted before in our Coastal Mountains of British Columbia. Nowadays, there is even a similar style event held each year called the Eco Challenge, so I don't think my idea was completely crazy.

However the "Curse of the Traverse" was now spinning all around me. Powder Magazine, the Bible of ski media, which had entered a team, was not impressed as they too had to be evacuated early (See Les Anthony's comments above). Paul Ramer, from Ramer equipment, and who had been my equipment sponsor for so long, was threatening to sue me for recklessness. And the list went on. TSN never did do the television broadcast, but that was no surprise. Another problem was that our mishmash of competitors, including several authentic dirt-bag skiers. did not really fit in with the Ken and Barbie demographic that TSN preferred. To cap it all, one of the volunteers, thinking he was never coming out alive off the ice, made a 'last testament' video addressed, to his family and friends. I have to say I used this video later as a sort of a black comedy intro at the front of the program itself.

My only video of the traverse still has the TSN logo burnt into it in the corner of the video. All of this hoopla and some bad publicity perhaps just add to the crazy courageousness of the whole event! 'The Curse of the Traverse' had me thinking – many years later – about what happened to the participants. Six of the people with fairly big roles in the project have since died from various causes, and surprisingly the majority were not related to any ski accidents, but it is a pretty high death rate for just a half hour film. The whole traverse race ended up being so crazy that Les Anthony, an editor of Powder Magazine back then, dedicated a whole chapter to it in his book about global ski culture, "White Planet."

Film "The Spirit" became one of my most important works.

On February 26, 1996, Whistler lost a great skier in an avalanche and, for all of us who knew him, a great friend. I had known Trevor Petersen for more than 10 years. He had become one of North America's strongest extreme skiers after moving to Whistler from the much smaller Big White resort at 19. As an eager young lad, he had read all the books about the legendary extreme skiers of France. He started skiing and filming with us soon after he arrived at Whistler in the early 80s. He went on to become one of the newer generation of rock stars.

The accident happened when Trevor had been making a last run in Chamonix France. He had just finished filming a well-paid Oakley eyewear commercial. He had gone up the Aiguille du Midi by himself, and then hiked and traversed in to the classic Cosmic Couloir. He was caught in a large avalanche which swept him down the chute and his body was found 250 m further down in the vast avalanche spill-off area on the Glacier Ronde.

Two young Swedish mountaineers later found his body. His eyes were still wide open and they said that he seemed to be staring out across the glacier, looking as energetic as if he was still alive.

When the news hit Whistler everyone was devastated. I just felt something inside of me telling me to make a film about his life, which I would call "The Spirit".

Although Trevor had made his mark in so many ski films shot by myself and other producers, I was surprised to find it hard to raise the funding to make a film about him. He was such a larger than life personality. Once again, I was so driven by this project that I decided to go ahead and do it anyway with outside funds or not. I did actually manage to get a $5,000 advance from my distributor in Montréal, but by this era that was really insufficient as far as making up a proper budget. To tell my story, I really had to go to France to retrace Trevor's steps. I needed to interview the two Swedes who had found Trevor, as well as shoot some background on his short stay in Chamonix, and then I would come back with enough material to create a good story.

I actually went over to Europe without a camera of my own. I took only tapes, and hoped to borrow cameras along the way. It seemed like Trevor's spirit was bringing me good vibes, and cameras materialised everywhere I went, and I was able to shoot all the material I needed. Along the way I even ran into a broadcast tv crew who kindly helped me shoot the important interviews which were so vital to the film.

Troy Jungen had his finger on the pulse of the ski bum network in France, so I was lucky enough to be able to kind of depend on him and his endless connections, and he found suitable accommodation in Chamonix and La Grave. In Chamonix, we got ski passes from the head of Chamonix Tourism himself, M. Prudhomme, who seemed to have taken a liking to us and our SPIRIT project and did what he could to help us.

Other pleasant coincidences occurred in Chamonix. I was invited to judge an extreme skiing contest, which was put on by Red Bull. Jan Andre, the son of skier Dominique Andre, won the event. I had first met Dominique when he was with Patrick Vallencant on Mt Huascaran in Peru. When I introduced myself to Jan, I told him that I had met his dad way back in 1978. I felt some sort of feeling that I had gone really full circle in my life here. Judging this event in Chamonix made up for the fact that by coming to Europe at this time, I had missed out on the opportunity to be a judge at the WESC event in Alaska. This was the only WESC contest that I missed in nine wonderful years.

There seemed to be something special about making this film about Trevor. I felt as if I was being driven me towards its completion, and as soon as I had returned to Canada I once again begged the CBC studios for a good facilities deal, so that I could finish the film. A CBC crew from Vancouver shot all our master footage with Trevor's wife Tanya, who graciously agreed to be interviewed. This footage became an integral part of the film.

Although the filming had been hard enough to shoot in Europe, the editing turned into a perfect nightmare. We had shot over 120 hours of video to review because we had been offered so much footage from other filmmakers around the world. To make everything just a little bit harder, we had somehow made an enemy in one of the senior CBC administration. The new woman in charge seemed to do everything she could to make it impossible to complete our project.

Our CBC nightmare of the past was happening again, because we had experienced similar treatment ten years earlier while making "The North Face". Once again we would be given graveyard editing shifts, often starting at 2 AM and ending at 6 AM. I did ask if there were any more convenient time slots, but the comeback was 'Well, you are getting your film done, are you not?' given with a sarcastically jovial tone in her voice. So, not much had changed at CBC for us.

Thankfully, we did have the very talented Ron Ireland, who was the CBC staff editor who had worked with me before so well on 'Mount Waddington Now'.

The next problem was that with so much material to view and choose from I needed more help. There was so much footage to catalogue that I could not cope. The script also needed another eye to try to fine tune it with the clips so that Ron could make to edit. For some reason I decided to put a 'help wanted' ad for the project in the Georgia Straight newspaper.

Chris Lockhart answered the ad. He was a Vancouverite who had grown up skiing on the North Shore Mountains and Whistler. He also had a background in corporate video production and making magazine style TV. He soon became my partner on The Spirit, as well as becoming my voice in the narration. He had done the "scratch" narration track for Ron to edit to and we all thought his voice worked well for the finished project. I don't like the sound of my own voice, and I felt awkward using my it for the narration. Perhaps I still had a complex from having a lisp as a child, and although my speech has improved I still felt awkward about it on a subconscious level.

Chris was a real trooper, and stuck with me on a number of my productions where everyone might have been slightly underpaid. He also later narrated "The Journey to the Heart of the World", which is a film shot in Colombia about a very unique expedition. More about that later. For some reason he would become a bit grumpy if the paycheck was lagging, but in hindsight I can't blame him.

We began to use celebrity athletes to add narration to our films. 'Seven Years on Mount Robson' had a commentary piece from Eric Perlman, who was a well-known author, climber and filmmaker from California. Ski legend Scott Schmidt,, helped out too. Vicki Gabereau, the CBC radio host, liked my script for the Mt Robson film, and narrated the entire one hour documentary for us for a small token fee. Later, I was really happy to be asked to appear on Vicky's own television show for CTV in Vancouver.

A lot of other interesting personalities ended up being part of "The Spririt" as well. Some music was donated by the brother of the great Jimi Hendrix, who lived in Seattle.

This offer of the use of a Hendrix track was very special to us because Trevor always loved Jimi's music, and we felt that he would have appreciated the soundtrack for sure.

I also managed to squeeze the Dalai Lama into the film as well! His Holiness was holding a lecture at the Pan Pacific Hotel in Vancouver. During the press reception after the talk, I cornered him and put this question to him: "What makes so many scholars, priests and holy men feel an attraction to mountains?" He was puzzled for a moment, pondering over my question, and got quite frustrated by it.

"I don't know," he replied, "I really don't know. Maybe it's because you can see the sun come up and go down from the same place but otherwise I really don't know." Not the most profound answer, but he later spotted me in the lobby afterwards and came up to me laughing, grabbing and pulling on my then-long hair. To be honest, that was the extent of my brief, if not profound meeting with the holy man himself. Still, it's an interlude I will remember forever.

While I had been in France, I had been lucky to get a revealing interview about extreme skiing with Anselme Baud, another of Vallencant's skiing partner, who was also an acclaimed Chamonix Mountain Guide. This was a man who Trevor had also really admired Anselm and looked up to. The film was really beginning to come together with his spirit, a reality the title hinted at.

There was another important segment in the film which I wanted to include. The story was about how two of my friends, Troy Jungen and Ptor Spricenieks, had recently made the first descent of what was beginning to be considered an un-skiable mountain, the North Face of Mount Robson. Trevor had wanted to ski that face as much as I had, and had been there with us during our previous unsuccessful attempts.

So I thought it would be appropriate to try include a piece celebrating their descent in the movie. The only problem for me was that my friends, being true dirt bag skiers, didn't have a video camera with them, and had only shot a few still photographs, so I had was very little material to support their story. I managed to get around that paucity of material by re-enacting the climbing and skiing segments with the two skiers in other parts of the world. Then I had the footage sent to me and we edited it into the film. People helped out from all over the world and sent in footage. A filmmaker in France shot Troy skiing steep spectacular slow motion turns on terrain above Chamonix which stood in for Robson's North Face, while Scotty Fullmer shot a sequence of Ptor doing similar steep jump turns here, at the foot of the iconic Black Tusk near Whistler in summertime.

I remember being very nervous at my first ever premiere of the finished picture in Whistler. We held the event in Whistler's popular Longhorn Bar. The bar which is usually obnoxiously loud was so silent that night that one could hear a pin drop. I smiled at Chris who was sitting next to me, and I then knew we had a great product. Our film went on to win several awards internationally, and got aired in Canada on both the CBC and Knowledge Network, as well as distribution abroad.

I'm sure Trevor got to see it too from wherever he is right now, as I swear his spirit was with us – making things happen all the way along our filming journey. We also got to show the Spirit again in Whistler during a mini-festival called 'The Best of Banff' held at the Whistler Conference Centre. I was extremely proud that we had a sell-out crowd.

The Spirit was a film full of rebellious ideas but never really got the backing of the Whistler establishment, although the kids really loved it. I was barraged with emails from kids writing to me and saying how they showed it to their parents. Others wrote and said how it inspired them to be a ski bum for a while. Letters like that certainly made me feel that all the effort I had invested to make the documentary was worth it, and I still feel proud about the result.

Ptor and Troy's first ski descent of Robson's North Face really was an outstanding accomplishment. I felt very honoured when the boys acknowledged that part of their motivation and inspiration to undertake the adventure was due to my own history on Robson. They took my advice and planned their trip around a full moon, as I had done in the mountains on many expeditions. It seemed that, either by fluke or luck, when I planned a major trip or expedition I would plan our departure at least a week before the full moon – with the main ski descent and filming taking place when the moon was full. This has worked for me so far, but do not ask me why. My full moon theory had worked for me on numerous occasions and I had used it to plan my trips to Robson, Waddington and many of other mountains. Who knows why this always worked for me. Obviously this couldn't ensure that the whole world would have clear skies when the new moon shone, but perhaps the effect of the moon's gravity, also has an impact on the alpine as it does with the ocean tides. Perhaps the clouds were drawn away from the mountains by the moon's gravity at that time. It's interesting how faith may work for us sometimes whether it's religion or just a belief one conjures up for oneself.

How Troy and Ptor managed to make that first descent of the North Face made for a good story. They drove over from Whistler to Robson and arrived just days before the full moon, in line with my recommendation. For once the conditions were perfect for the attempt, with the blue ice that normally covers the North Face was entirely covered by snow. This is a very rare occurrence, and unlike the conditions that prevailed during all my attempts most of the time. When the guys reached Robson's Berg Lake on their approach, they found to their utter joy that the North Face was caked in snow. Following my advice, they took a direct route up to the bottom of the face, and then climbed to The Helmet, where we had been on our 1987 attempt on Robson. They spent a rest day on The Helmet, and were then rewarded with the perfect weather window for the attempt.

They began climbing at 3am, a so-called 'alpine start' which ensured that the most critical parts of the climb could be completed before the sun could heat the face and increase the risk of avalanche. After so, after hours of methodically front pointing up the face, they finally reached the summit. The date was 1st September 1995. Ptor gave thanks to The Universe for allowing them to summit safely. Then, with their personal ceremonies done, they dropped back in, and onto one of the largest and longest mountain faces in the world. It is also one of the steepest. They had knocked off the first ever successful ski descent of the monster face. Robson is the tallest peak in the Canadian Rockies, and is certainly the most iconic. By any standards, this was a noteworthy achievement.

Indeed, it is such an intimidating face that another 22 years past before the conditions and fates aligned and their run was repeated by someone else, skier Dylan Cunningham, who did it in 2017. World renowned alpinists such as Patagonia's founder Yvon Chouinard and Barry Blanchard have told me of their admiration for what these two ski bums achieved without big money support.

Being Polish, and originally from Krakow, Poland, I decided to send a copy of 'The Spirit' to Pope John Paul II. After all, the Pope was another Pole who came from my home town, and he was famously an avid skier. Also, he was friends with the Dalai Lama, who made an appearance in the film. So, I crafted a nice letter in Polish and sent him the DVD. I knew he was also quite fond of helicopter skiing, because I had seen news reports of him accepting an invitation from the president of Italy to join him for a few turns. To my utter surprise and joy, a few months later a gold-trimmed envelope from the Vatican landed on my doormat. I opened it to see a letter signed by the Pope himself, Karol Jozef Wojtyla. He said he had enjoyed the film, and sent me his blessing. Unfortunately, a few years later I was moving out of my house, and threw out a load of boxes containing old documents. Somehow, this priceless correspondence became part of the junk.

Although I have never been much of a devout Catholic, as far as popes go Pope John Paul II really was a great pope who promoted world peace, and had a real part to play in bringing down the Berlin Wall. Maybe I should have had the letter framed instead of just keeping it in a box.

Completing „The Spirit" was part of a quest of mine to see what mountains really mean to other people, and this was why I had contacted the pope, as I did earlier with the Dalai Lama. „The Spirit" film was probably my most introspective film about my story in the mountains, and the friendships that resulted from sharing a common bond while being firmly in their presence.

I always enjoyed the feeling of quiet and the solitude of being in the mountains, although I would rarely elaborate on this during the films or in the articles I wrote. I certainly feel tied to the mountains in a unique way through these activities. At first I made this connection through skiing, but later I progressed on to paragliding, as both sports gave me what I was looking for.

The Polish climber Jerzy Kukuczka's words come to mind here. Jerzy climbed all fourteen 8000 meter peaks, many of them as new routes and in the winter. He was in a perpetual race with Reinhold Messner on this mission. Messner had all the resources of western capitalism behind him, and completed the list first, but acknowledged that Kukuczka's task was much harder without the financial help.

"After every safe return from a climbing/skiing or paragliding expedition there was always such a sense of euphoria and accomplishment as we always came back wiser from the experience".

From the journals of Jerzy Kukuczka, translated from Polish.

White craziness continues

1. Troy Jungen below the summit of The Lions between Whistler and Vancouver.
2. The approach to the direct route below Mt Robson's north face.
3. Troy Jungen on the first ski descent of the north face on Mt Robson, Sept. 1995.
4. "Matty Shred" trying out the ice-axe on his run.

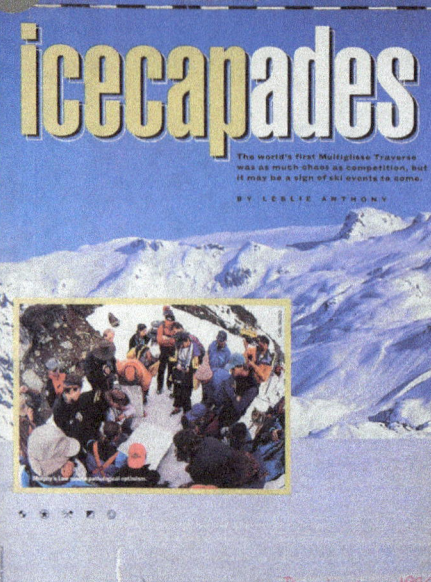

The Traverse race – A first of its kind, the ski mountaineering race in North America has still never been repeated in difficulty and length of course.

1. Feature story spread on the Traverse race in Powder Magazine.
2. It was hard to run the event with my broken leg.
3. The title to the story.

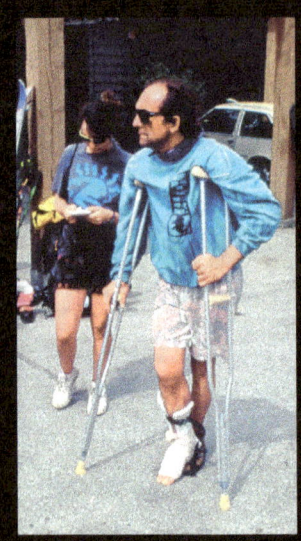

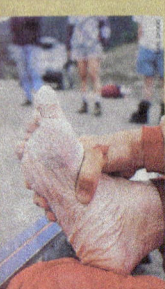

After breaking his leg, Chrzanowski became the first victim of a severe lack of safety contingency.

CHAPTER 10

DIRTBAGGING IT

In the annals of dirtbag climbers and skiers, a man called Fred Beckey held the crown as 'King of the Dirtbags'. He had tried living a corporate life after the War, but basically did nothing but climb from the age of 15 until his death at the age of 92. I first met him in Golden, BC when I was filming there, but more about that later.

The term 'dirtbag' originally surfaced with the climbers from California's Yosemite Valley in the 60s who did everything they could to survive while climbing full-time. This was the era of Ken Kesey and the Beat generation, and was a reaction to the events of WW2. This lifestyle was enthusiastically adapted by other outdoor evangelists such as Warren Miller and Dick Durance, who managed to craft a lifestyle by making ski-movies.

In Whistler our 'Team Dirt' was made up of various numbers ski bum afficionados. We were based out of a couple of notorious residences. One, the 'The Dog House', which was a Gothic-arched frame building on Balsam Way in Whistler. It was a safe house, a refuge and a sanctuary for all the wayward ski bums who needed a place to crash. The owner, Duncan was a kind soul who took in anyone who was bedless after the bars closed in Whistler. The couch was always there for us.

Several times I took advantage knowing the shelter was there for us. Sadly, the Dog House burnt down a few years ago leaving a huge void in our network.

Another infamous Team Dirt HQ was an A-frame house on West Side Road. Dirtbags occupied it for several years, and I remember a lot of amazing parties. We seemed to attract a lot of 'hippy chicks', who were welcomed and loved, or 'slayed' as local legend Johnny Trash would put it.

Johnny Trash was a classic dirt bag. He was famous for taking his clothes off at some memorable nights at various bars, and then showing off his climbing skills by crawling around the rafters in his birthday suit. He 'starred' in Johnny Zaritsky's famous film "Ski Bums" being towed in a Gyroscope while stark naked in the snow! This scene has a spot in The Skier's hall of fame for sure! During the filming of this extreme stunt, he was arrested by two female Whistler cops, and had to do some community service for it.

Johnny also played in a punk band called the Harpoons. Johnny was a hard-rock musician at heart, and believe me it was hard rock! Johnny certainly was an important founder member of Team Dirt during those glorious days at the A frame and the Doghouse.

One party which stands out occurred when a local punk band, the Day Glow Abortions, played 'till seven in the morning. There were several hundred ski bums there running around out of control as the band roared. The cops were powerless to stop the party because they were completely outnumbered. Whistler Muni finally ordered the local electricity company to come out and turn the power off. So the party sadly came to the 7am close.

The core members of Team Dirt were Troy, Ptor, Graydon Card, Johnny Trash and a number of other friends who would join us in our mountain escapades. One of the mysterious inhabitants of the A-Frame was a man called Lorenzo. He was virtually a snowboarding elder as far as dirt bagging went, since he was at least in his forties. We later met up in Chamonix again, and his snowboarding is featured in The Spirit.

Another honourable mention should go out to another local called Seppo, who was kind enough to open his home for so many years during the seventies and eighties to give a warm and dry welcome to wayward ski bums.

Seppo was an old Finnish logger from the old days who had cut many of Whistler's original runs, originally guided by where the best trees were. That is why to this day the mountain has so many unnecessary traverses. He is better remembered as the man who cut one of the best fall line runs on the mountain, which is now named after him.

Being a logger, he had built a monumental log house of incredible proportions for himself. He used the entire length of the trunks to make the structure, and had a hot tub hollowed out of the bedrock under the house. He threw legendary parties where the beer flowed and the hot tub was always full. There were rumours that in the early 70's, when loggers were making big cash, he would fly in hookers from Las Vegas for his parties. The ultimate logger's dream come true, if it ever happened.

Seppo's story ended sadly, when he died in his trailer, abandoned and forgotten by everyone. He had lost his beautiful log-house and everything in it through bad luck and local government politics. Originally, he felt he was treated unjustly when some of his land was expropriated for a widening project on the Sea-to-Ski highway. He became well-known for attending the legal hearings where he stared down the local politicians. Vengeance came from the municipality in the form of high property taxes. He wouldn't pay them, and so when his house caught fire the local fire department was slow in its response, and it was a total loss.

I took Seppo up on his hospitality a few times when I was stuck for a place in Whistler, as did so many other desperate ski bums. Seppo was always there for us with his kindness. After he was gone, we really felt a huge part of the 'Whistler Spirit' died with him. Once The Dog House, The A Frame and Seppo's were gone, little remained of sanctuary available in Whistler. The squatters in their backcountry cabins were pushed out first. After that, our whole dirt-bag network of available shelter and gathering places were lost forever.

John 'Rabbit' Hare was another ski bum who lived above the ski patrol maintenance building, which was next to the Roundhouse at the top of the original Creekside lifts. He was the sole caretaker for years, who later married and lived there with his hippy partner, and brought up his daughter Jessica and son Hess. He skied every possible day he could. Many stories are told of his escapades in Whistler, from his habit of dancing in ski boots, or schussing past onlookers on his skis. Rabbit sadly died of cancer at too young an age and we all miss him dearly. I personally recall skiing in the trees once with Rabbit. It was very cold and the trees were fairly tight as he maneuvered so well through them. I was not so smooth as him and caught a tip of my Dynastar MV2's on a tree stump, and it snapped right off on that cold December air. Rabbit stayed with me the whole way back as I struggled on one ski.

The deaths of Rabbit and Seppo marked an end to the old Whistler days.

I had first met Troy Jungen and Ptor Spricenieks in the late 80's, when they first came to Whistler, and they were among the keenest skiers I've ever known.

They were indulging in the time-honoured tradition of grazing for their lunch at the Roundhouse, Whistler's huge cafeteria which sits at the mid-station area of the lifts. Grazing was a dirt bag tradition, passed on from 60's climbers, where in order to get a free meal, you just sampled the leftover lunches from tourist folks who perhaps weren't used to the altitude, and now didn't have an appetite.

Troy is part Beaver First Nations from his mother's side and part Swiss from his dad. With a family line like that it was no wonder that he had such zeal for skiing and being in nature.

His brother, Brian Jungen, is a wellknown First Nation artist. His works combine native and western art, using modern consumer goods from companies like Nike to create new versions of ceremonial masks and Totem poles out of rucksacks and sneakers. His work is exhibited in Whistler's Audain Museum and other galleries including the Vancouver Art Gallery and The Louvre in Paris.

I guess it was his Swiss genes that kept Troy religiously skiing and touring. We have had so many numerous adventures together, and I still consider both these guys as two of my best friends.

Another dirt bag friend, often part of our adventures when we filmed the Spirit, was Graydon Card who was one of the skiers in our powder skiing television series several years earlier. Grady back then had some particularly amazing dreadlocks, which made him such a great character in my films. He also had a memorably twisted sense of humour, which made everybody laugh – adding a great element of entertainment to any motion picture.

Troy Jungen and Graydon Card were the true inspiration for today's dirt bags of Whistler. As well as achieving true ski bum notoriety by working as little as possible, they also starred in 'Ski Bums' the documentary by John Zaritsky, who was an Oscar winning documentary film director. Many of my closest friends had now appeared in John's film, making me proud of the dirt bag entourage in my own projects.

Troy also helped me a great deal in producing my Spirit film about Trevor Petersen. During the shooting in Europe he really helped by knowing who to talk to and this helped keep my costs down. We had so little money that his help was vital in keeping us fed and housed in La Grave and Chamonix, which came about through his extensive ski bum network. We later enjoyed some memorable road trips.

I still laugh about the time when we went to Seattle and Troy's van brakes gave out. At one point as they failed we veered off the highway, trying desperately to slow the van. We came to a halt by actually crashing into the side of a gas station. We heard the clatter of everything falling off the shelves inside, and a group of black guys came running out screaming at us. Troy slammed the van into reverse and we got the hell of out of there before the cops came, or indeed even before we were caught by the vigilantes, laughing all the way.

Another memory with Troy that's seared into my brain took place during a trip to Banff on my big 40th Birthday in the fall of 1997. This happened just after he had skied Robson's North Face with Ptor.

We were driving over the Rogers Pass, when Troy carelessly fell asleep at the wheel. We careened off the road, traveling sideways on the other side of the concrete barrier, until the van stopped before a culvert. We were just teetering there – held from death only by the roadside willows, which prevented us from crashing down the mountainside and dying in tandem.

It took two tow trucks to haul Troy's van out of there. One stabilized the van from toppling over and rolling down the mountainside, while the other truck pulled them both out horizontally. Yes, the towing bill was kind of large but, considering we had survived the crash and we still had working transport, it was nothing to worry about. We patched up the one broken window in the van with cardboard and duct tape, took several deep breaths and continued on our way to Banff.

Once we arrived, we met up with and interviewed well-known ski mountaineer Doug Scott and Yvon Chouinard about Troy's descent of The North Face of Mt Robson.

On our return trip to Whistler from Banff we managed to include a side trip on the Icefields Parkway. We climbed and skied the notoriously steep "Sky Ladder" run which towers above the Columbia Ice fields. Troy, who was equally talented on his snowboard as well as on telemark and downhill skis, claimed the first snowboard descent off the face, while I made one of the few early ski descents of the „Sky Ladder." I remembered my ego being bolstered by an encounter we had as we hurried off the bottom of the glacier, trying to avoid being caught in total darkness. At this point we met another party of younger skiers, who greeted us as rock stars for skiing and boarding the run. They had been watching our descent. We were truly a little humbled by their words, and wished them the best of luck on their own upcoming mission. My ego had received a very nice boost!

I returned yet again with Troy to the Banff Mountain Film Festival in 2000 for the 25th Anniversary edition, which was a definite signature event, and one where a significant number of the world's most famous mountaineers had converged. After we had safely arrived without any more "sleep-driving" incidents, we rubbed shoulders with stars like Yvon Chouinard, the writer Joe Simpson, climber Reinhold Messner, and many more. Troy and I still laugh about one particular incident. The two of us were sharing a taxi with Chouinard and Joe Simpson. The millionaire philanthropist turned to the Pulitzer winning author of „Touching the Void" and asked, "So, Joe, are you here to tell us about another one of your mountaineering fuck-ups?"

Joe's second book, "This Game of Ghosts" was actually one of my main motivations to write this book. I have never possessed anywhere near the academic writing credentials that Joe had. He has a Masters in English Literature from Oxford, after all. But I loved the way Simpson had described his youth and travelling the world with his British parents. I found his attention to detail masterful, and although I could not relate personally, his description of the sibling rivalry that existed between him and his sister was especially entertaining.

Another author who was at the 25th anniversary Festival in Banff was Wade Davis. He had also inspired me with his book "One River", about the Indigenous peoples of South America and was an illustration of their culture from an ethnobiologist's viewpoint. He was committed enough to document their ceremonial use of hallucinogenic drugs through his own participation in the ceremonies. He wrote very engagingly about his encounters. One tribe from Colombia, the Kogi, are notoriously reclusive and have kept their culture largely intact during the 400 years since first contact. They live high in the Sierra Nevada in the Santa Marta range which had been one of my dream destinations since I was 12 years old.

Troy and I had recently come back from the our own expedition to the Sierra and we met Wade for the first time in Banff. Wade wrote a page in the book which was produced to commemorate the Festival's 25th anniversary, called "Voices from the Summit", about our own ski expedition to the Sierra. He really was very articulate about our visit with the Kogis, and was surprised how the Indians had let us into their Sierra home.

"I recently met a group of young Canadians who had travelled to the same mountains intent on becoming the first to descend the high glaciers on snowboards. Finding their way blocked by the Kogi, they instead sought permission to visit for a few days. Welcomed formally by the elders, they entered a world beyond their imaginings, guests of people whose societal ideal is to abstain from sex, eating, and sleeping, while staying awake through the night, chanting the names of the ancestors. After a month these gentle adventurers had lost all interest in becoming the first to snowboard the Sierra Nevada. Indeed they had forgotten altogether the purpose that had initially propelled them to Colombia. And they had no regrets."

Wade Davis from NGS/Banff Centre book ; "Voices from the Summit."

Wade, who is an incredible writer, speaker and academic, was also very opposed to the drug war the US has waged in South America. He had even been summoned to speak to the American Congress about it, where he was insistent in his opinion that prohibition never worked with alcohol in the past, and there is a strong likelihood that it will never work with drugs.

Whistler's own Johnny Trash accompanied us to the BMFF several times, and of course took his clothes off and climbed around the rafters at one of the closing parties to everyone's amusement. He was always great for a few laughs at the wrong moment.

Bernadette McDonald, who was the author of the book Freedom Climbers, about Polish Himalayan climbers, ran the festival, and was kind enough to give us dirtbags a handful of press passes which got us in to all the screenings. I always managed to keep her happy and return the favour by publishing glowing articles about the Festival which appeared in both Whistler and Vancouver publications.

It was in Banff at the Festivals where I made so many important contacts in the climbing and outdoor world. I met the likes of Reinhold Messner, the author Conrad Anker and many of the Polish Himalayan rock star climbers including Krzysztof Wielicki, Piotr Pustelnik, Woytek Kurtyka, Leszek Cichy, and Zbigniew Piotrowicz who made good livings as professional climbers with sponsorship from the Polish communist state.

Later I would get together with some of the Polish crew at the Vancouver Mountain Film Festival, and got to take them skiing at Whistler. Zbigniew Piotrowicz invited me over to Poland to be a judge at the Ladek Zdroj Film Festival in south-western Poland. He was deputy mayor of Ladek Zdroj and I stayed with him and his partner Natalia at his comfortable house.

I was always impressed by Polish climbers Himalayan achievements. They were now older men who are mostly in their sixties. Many of them have divorced but they are always seen in the company of beautiful outdoorsy women. I call them "rockstars" because they had always been as famous in Poland as the elite hockey players are in Canada.

When talking about rockstars, one friend comes to mind and that is Ptor Spricenieks. One of the founding members of our „Team Dirt",

Ptor had come to Whistler around the same time as Troy did. They would be considered a the second generation of notable skiers in Whistler, coming a few years after Trevor Petersen and Eric Pehota. Ptor was Latvian by descent, and in his early life had studied engineering. He was soon taken over by the mountains and decided to pursue ski mountaineering instead. He did this with a vengeance, initially skiing the backcountry slopes of BC, and then later avidly following in Patrick Vallencant's footsteps, and skiing on the big high faces of the Andes peaks.

He adopted the name Ptor, instead of his real name of Peter. He wanted to reflect a certain viking-like image, and prided himself with his brute strength, often by letting out a primal roar when he was with friends. I will always be very grateful for his help and participation in our films.

Our encounters were not always happy ones, though. I remember once how I didn't get out of the way in time, and he buried me in an avalanche up to my waist out in the Blackcomb backcountry. As usual, he was skiing a little too quickly and too enthusiastically – and I could not get out of the way in time. Such mishaps become part of friendship in the mountains.

Another problematic situation occurred with Ptor when we made a memorable April trip to ski the West Couloir of Wedge Mountain. We had skied down the Spearhead Glacier from Blackcomb, crossed over Wedge Creek, and ski toured up the south-west face of Wedge Mountain to enter the couloir. After skiing the couloir, we descended through some incredible powder in an area of old-growth trees. This route is not used nowadays, and by the time I had got down to the logging slash level, I was exhausted and was suffering from some knee problems, but Ptor didn't want to have to negotiate the woods too late in the dark. I felt I was just slowing him down, so I said, "Listen, you go ahead and continue walking out. I'm just gonna dig a hole here in the snow among the slide alder and rest till morning."

I must admit I didn't think he would ever abandon me, but in fact Ptor did leave me alone that night. It became too cold to spend the whole night there, so I made it out later to the highway. Although I was living in Whistler I got the first ride that turned up and hitchhiked to Pemberton. It was 11pm and there was no traffic going to Whistler, so I caught the first ride that turned up, which was going in the other direction towards Pemberton. However, I knew my friend Nigel Protter had a guest room made out of a chicken coop at his place, so I spent the night there.

If you understand ski-touring you would have understood Ptor's actions a little more. Although his leaving me might seem harsh to the average recreational skier, Ptor knew that I was totally capable of making it out of there safely at my own pace, even if it was as grueling as it turned out. We had been through so much together that we knew each other's limits, and Ptor had come to the conclusion that I would manage fine, and he wasn't wrong.

He is now happily married with two kids and lives in the small village of La Grave in France, where he built his house with his own hands.

Interestingly, he made a film in recent years exploring how his attitude to taking risks in ski mountaineering has changed over time.

He was on an expedition in Pakistan, when several other climbers and skiers from another party were caught and died in a series of avalanches which happened nearby. Ptor came to a whole new realization with these accidents. Now that he has two children he has decided to refrain from taking risks and getting into situations like the ones he used to on a regular basis. Having a family and two young boys at his home in France has changed Ptor.

On the other hand, similar family circumstances never seemed to bother other extreme athletes. Shane McConkey, another legend who perished while base-jumping on skis from a cliff in the Italian Dolomites. Shane kept on pushing the limits higher and higher with each adventure, but he sadly left a wife and daughter behind.

It is always sad to consider lost friends, so I guess now is as good a time as any to change the subject and move on to our expedition to Colombia and the Sierra Nevada de Santa Marta, and the film we made there called "Journey Into The Heart of The World". I wrote earlier how I had always dreamed of going to this exotic place. It is surrounded by tropical rain-forest, and its peaks reach 6,000 m but they are only 30 kilometers from the Caribbean. When Columbus landed in Santa Marta in 1525, it became the oldest Spanish city in Colombia, the natives who were descendants of the Tairona Culture, packed their bags and moved into the mountains. The terrain was too hard for the Spanish to follow, and so their descendants have lived in isolation ever since.

In 1995 the Colombian government made the entire area around Santa Marta into a park especially for the natives' benefit. The park would be administered by the natives themselves, allowing them to let in only the people they wanted into their reclusive settlements. As a result they have managed to keep their own culture and language alive and relevant, unlike the majority other indigenous tribes in both Americas, which were either killed off or ruined forever by the colonial powers or the Catholic Church.

The Kogis and Arhuacos had even managed to burn down the Jesuit Mission when the Church tried to colonize the Sierra. I commissioned a painting of this historic act of resistance from an artist in Calgary, and I took a photograph of this with us and used it to show the tribal members and used it in my documentary.

By December '98, we had managed to scrape together the budget to finally travel to the Sierra. I was quite nervous about returning to Colombia after my daring escape from the jail back in 1976. Luckily, there were no computers then, and any records of my crime had been long-lost. Also I assumed that any of the policemen in Leticia from whom I had made my crazy escape were probably long dead.

Our crew comprised some very well-known American skiers, including Kristen Ulmer, as well as snowboarder John Griber, who brought along photographer Greg Van Doersten with him.

RAP, or Real Action Pictures was another ski film company from Calgary, wanted to film a segment with the American skiers and snowboarders for a tv ski show that they were producing, and so helped us with expenses. I still have to thank James Angrove for helping out there.

As so often seemed to happen with my adventures, the trip started with a disaster. American Airlines lost all Kristen's skiing gear. In fact, it had probably been stolen, as the airline had a bit of a reputation then for having this happen to flights in Colombia. We managed to salvage the situation for Kristen for the moment by suggesting that she used Troy's gear. But first we had to reach the snows, and this was proving really difficult to arrange.

We tried approaching the mountains firstly from the direction of the town of Valledupar, on the south side of the Sierra Nevada mountain range. We rented two Land Cruisers in the town and made it up to the next town, Nabusimake. Once we had passed Nabusimaki, the track became more and more difficult. We eventually managed to find a local Arhuaco guide who had a mule that could carry some of our gear. We also had to make friends with the Arhuaco natives who were living on the lower slopes of the mountains, so that they would give us permission to go further.

After three days of hiking we made it up to a village at 3,000 metres called Mamacana. Here the terrain was all tundra and savannah-type vegetation which was much drier and completely different from the lush rain-forest on the northern Caribbean side. Here we spent an incredible Christmas Eve, with our Arhuaco hosts in a little stone hut.

Both the Kogis and the Arhuacos believe that anyone from anywhere else is the 'younger brother': we are all pretty bad and they call us the "Little Brother." They see themselves as the wiser, more ecologically sensitive elder brother in the relationship. After all, from their perspective it is us that have produced all the wars and the pollution, which they see and can sense from the top of their mountains. They truly believe that they are the real guardians of the universe and are higher beings on the food chain. They guard the Sierra absolutely from intruders and they call their habitat "The Heart of The World". I think we cannot blame the Kogis for thinking the way they do. After all from their viewpoint we are the ones that cause all the wars, pollution, and devastation on our planet, while the Kogis live within their means on what they grow and produce. They even make their own clothing, and use only the essentials of our technology. They are generally against all the rest of our innovations.

Another unique aspect of their way of life is that if a Kogi youth is born and is deemed special and is chosen to become a priest, or "Mama", he is placed in a cave or dark place to live for nine years, meditating and hoping to elevate his telepathic powers. Sometimes, he will even return to the cave for another nine years, in order to really get his powers working.

Both the Kogis and the Arhuacos habitually chew coca leaves to cope with the altitude. The leaves are mixed with lime from ground-up sea shells and chewed until the action is complete. The spittle in turn is deposited on a Poporro, or stick that they always carry with them and which is a big part of their spiritual belief.

As we ascended up through the chain of villages, we found that our arrival was anticipated somehow. This was strange, since there was no telephones or telegraph, yet nobody would pass us to let the elders know that we were coming. The tales of Kogi Mamos having telepathic abilities were actually coming true here for us. In each village we would stop and rest, while the elders of the village would meditate at some length before giving us their permission to continue.

It turned out that having Troy in our party helped a lot. As a First Nations skier from Canada, he looked just like them, yet didn't speak much Spanish or their language, and this made them very intrigued by him for sure. In a way he seemed related to them and this brought all of us closer to each other.

When we finally did make it up to within striking distance of the snow covered slopes, we finally got turned back by the natives as they believed the snows were sacred, and only they could touch them. So far, it had been quite the life changing experience, and we weren't about to give up now. So we turned around and went back down to Nabusimake, where we found drivers and vehicles, and then following the Rio Magdalena, went all the way around the entire Sierra Nevada range to the north side of the mountains so that we could approach the snows from the north side.

Once we had got back to the Caribbean coast and the town of Palomino, we hired more porters and set out on an eight day trek into the Sierra. The American skiers and snowboarders had already left after the first part of our trip to the Valledupar south side.

In their place, we were now joined by two of my good Polish-Canadian friends – Pawel Boryniec and Maciek Siwocha, who arrived with Derek Lynn from Vancouver. The temperature on the trek up from the Caribbean side was an overwhelming 42 degrees with an unbearable 80% humidity. The climate was definitely not as pleasant as it had been on the dry south side of the mountains which we had experienced on our previous attempt via the southern flanks of the Sierra. Somehow we persevered, and were rewarded by a scene that could have come straight out of a science fiction movie.

The trek itself had been beyond our wildest expectations. The Sierra is famous for harbouring the most diverse flora and fauna in the world, because its climate zones vary from the sea-level 43°C heat on the beaches of the Caribbean, all the way to sub-alpine and glaciated zone in just 30 km. As we went upwards there were different layers of fruits and vegetables that changed according to the elevation. Along the entire path there were groves filled with either mandarins, cocoa, yuca, or maranga.

This time we had brought gifts of machetes, flashlights, and dried fish to ease our passage, as we had been told these were items that would be most welcomed. Mules carried our heavier gear through the day and we slept in hammocks covered by mosquito screening at night. There were established rest spots with thatch-covered roofs on posts with places to sling our hammocks along the way. Our mule driver, Monuno had also brought along his two young sons in order to help out.

Occasionally through the rain forest foliage, we would catch a glimpse of the snowy peaks of Cristobal Colon, at 5,960 m, and Pico Bolivar at 4,976 m, which are the highest peaks in Colombia and names that I remembered from a treasured 1970 National Geographic magazine that I had read as a child.

Instead of being rushed through villages on our climb as we expected, we were sometimes allowed to spend a few days with the Indians, and were welcomed into their homes along the way. So we slowly progressed up to the next village, where we would have to stop while the Indian Mamas, or priests, meditated to get a feel for our spirituality and whether we would be allowed to continue, just as they had on the other side.

Eventually they would let us through, and just as on the other side of the range that's how it went village by village, until we got to the highest point of our route on this northern side of the Sierra at 2,000 meters elevation.

Troy had been giving demonstrations to the locals en route. He would get into his ski boots and put on his skis for the curious Indians as we passed through each jungle village. The demonstrations were all part of our plan in seeking permission to keep going higher each time. It was quite a comical sight as we strapped on our gear and adopted the downhill skiing position for the Kogis, so they could watch and laugh at the little brother!

When we reached the last high village of Taminaca inhabited by the Kogis, it looked like a scene straight out of a classic Star Trek episode. The landscape was dotted with little round huts that seemed as if they had come from another planetary existence. Once again this was as far as we could get and we were prevented from going higher up to the sacred snows. However, we were invited to spend a wonderful week in the village, where we enjoyed the Kogis' company, spending our days swimming and washing our clothes in the river.

To our delight, we discovered the Kogis produced some of the best coffee we had ever tasted. A type of java bean that just couldn't get any more organic if it tried. The beans grow in a perfect environment at an elevation of 2,000 metres. The beans were then ground in a timeless contraption called a Donkey Mill. It was a giant stone grinder which was connected to a mule and this beast of burden would spend its time walking in a big circle while it was attached to a large beam of wood that turned the grindstone. It was like something out of the ancient times, but grinding coffee beans instead of grain.

We had also brought along with us a large bag of marijuana, which had kept us happy during the trek. The locals of this region do not usually smoke pot, but we did meet a Kogi local in Taminaca who did, and he would sneak into our tent in the evenings to have a puff from our joints. However, he made it clear that he didn't want his compatriots to know, a deception which we found rather curious considering their enthusiasm for cocaine.

On our final night in Taminaca, Mama Filho, who was the resident Mama, hosted a celebration for us with many dishes and featuring a local liquor made from rice. We danced and drank around the campfire all night long, and then packed up, said goodbye to our kind hosts, and began our long journey back down to the Caribbean.

I had had a strange relationship with Mama Filho. As I was the nominal leader of our group, he always seemed to be on my case, testing me in one way or another.

I found that on many of my expeditions I have had a similar power struggle with local authorities like the Mamas here. Perhaps they see me as a threat to their power in the valley, in that I am the chief of our crew here, and so I am always the one to be tested.

I have found this with many other authoritative figures I have had the misfortune to meet in my life, even here with the Kogis. Human nature is the same around the world!

We arrived back at sea-level after a pleasant three days walking downhill. We had an unsuspecting little pig accompanying us on a leash, which we later barbecued at Monuno's house on the coast in Palomino.

The beaches of the Tairona National Park are some of the best beaches I have seen anywhere in the world. There is only one lodge on the peninsula, and with no camping officially permitted, we ventured far away from the park entrance and slung our hammocks among the palm trees for a few days. We lived the life of marooned sailors, as we picked coconuts, and became quite good at cracking them open using rocks.

We felt like prehistoric men here, and a little of the Neanderthal came out in all of us, and especially in Ptor, who turned into the Viking of the South. What made it even better was when we met some really funny young hippy chicks to keep us company during our stay in Tairona National Park. The partying was full on.

When we got back to Vancouver, I put together a great film called "Journey into the Heart of the World." Using the RAP footage, with more video from Frederic Jacobi, stills from photographer Derek Lynn, and a narration by Chris Lockhart. It was screened in Whistler and went on to several adventure film festivals in Europe.

It had been a very special experience with not only the Kogis, but also with some great friends. It had been a true dirtbag trip, and in many ways because of our dirtbag ways, the Kogis had let us further into their paradise than others who tried. The adventure was momentously successful to me personally, since I had always wanted to go into that area on the north coast of South America, ever since I had been 12 years old, and now a dream had come true.

Another pivotal moment happened in Santa Marta when we met Natali Vasquez. Ptor was so smitten that he went back to Colombia and Medellin to get together with Natali. She came back to Canada with him, then later when he moved to Chamonix, she followed, and she learned to ski, climb, and paraglide there. Although Ptor eventually went on to marry someone else later, Natali has remained a close friend. She has also come back to visit me in Pemberton and we are in touch often. Natali is an artist, who paints unique portraits of nature. She really is an amazing gal, and has taken up sky-diving and flying with wing suits. She says she won't get into proximity squirrel suit flying though, as she has lost too many friends to the sport's inherent danger. For money, she crews on yachts and keeps moving between Europe and The Americas. Natali is truly one of the freest spirits that I know.

Another story from the Colombia trip involved snowboarder and photographer Derek Lynn. He brought along his girlfriend, which I have always found to be a bad idea. The reason is they often lure their man away from the task at hand, and this can cause friction amongst the team. Such distractions and diversions can often cause trouble later. This time his girlfriend insisted on coming, and somehow we all agreed. Unfortunately, or fortunately, she found she had misplaced her passport when they arrived in Bogota. Unable to find it, she was placed in detention overnight by Colombian Customs, and then sent back to Canada the next day, and thus sparing us from her presence on the expedition. She was a stubborn and strong willed woman and I think she would have been nothing but trouble on the trip. I still thank the Universe for that occurrence with her passport.

It is a general truth that it is always fun getting free services while on our trips. One time I remember we arrived at Salt Lake City to attend the annual giant outdoor show called Interski. It was a full-on dirtbag trip, which involved using every freeby possible. We parked our van for free near a motel in Seattle and used the free shuttle to the airport. Once we arrived in Salt Lake City, we used the free shuttle again to the Marriott, where we left our luggage with the hotel staff. They thought we were customers, while we went to the outdoor show on our press passes in the name of Extreme Explorations. Free! Free! Free! After cruising the show, we went back to the hotel and picked up our bags. We thanked the bell boys and carried on to stay with our dirtbag friends who lived nearby in Sandy. Once again Free! Free! Free!

It was a few years before the Colombia trip that I met Pawel Boryniec, who came to be a significant part of so many of my adventures. Pawel and his wife had immigrated to Canada from Poland with a stint in Germany along the way. By the time I met them, they had three young children.

Coincidentally, they lived in the same house as my friendly local dope dealer resided, and so we started hanging out. This was just at the beginning of the dotcom era and everyone had schemes for somehow riding the internet wave to million dollar bonanzas. I helped him get into snowboarding and back country skiing, and we did a few memorable trips together. Pawel was always laughing at something, and his happy demeanor made me glad to have him around as he always radiated such positive vibes.

Pawel dove into many crazy projects with me. Some of them turned out to be unworkable, but finding that out was a lot of fun nevertheless. One such project we got involved in was to film, and attempt to stream on the internet, a ski descent from the summit of Mount Everest down the north side into Tibet.

One of America's first steep skiers, Craig Calonica, had seen some of my films. He had originally made his mark in speed skiing of all things. He lived in Squaw Valley and was a good friend of another speed skier called Steve McKinney. They had been to Everest on the first hang-gliding expedition in 1986. During that trip Steve piloted the first hang-glider to take off from Everest's Northwest Col. Sadly, Steve was later killed by a drunk driver while he was sleeping in his car by the side of the road.

I had always been an admirer of Steve Mckinney. Steve was a six foot four "Viking on skis" who had broken many speed skiing records. He was also a well-known mountaineer, and his Everest achievement was certainly impressive.

He was an incredibly strong athlete and I remember reading an article in the old Powder Magazine about how Steve put his skis on and skated part of the way up the side of Popocatepetl Volcano in Mexico. Skating is a ski technique used in cross-country skiing on mostly flat surfaces, but he was so strong that he could do that instead of hiking or ski touring up on skins. So when I was contacted by Craig and he was professing to be one of McKinney's closest friends, I thought myself lucky to be in such great mountaineering company.

Pawel and I first visited Craig in Squaw Valley prior to our departure to Nepal in 1997. Meeting Craig for the first time, Pawel and I were surprised to be met by what appeared to be a fairly overweight, pudgy guy, who nevertheless claimed to be in shape to ski Mount Everest. "I get like this every time before I go on a Himalayan expedition," he boasted to us as we strolled around Squaw Valley together, "I may look overweight now but I'll look like Gandhi when I come back, hahahaha."

I helped Craig out with a few of my sponsor contacts for his production, and eventually we arrived in India. On arrival we acclimatized by doing some easy treks in the Jomsom region in Eastern Nepal. Then the plan was that we were to hike over the Thorong-La Pass to Manang, and from there we would climb to Tilicho Lake which sits at 5,000 m, making it one of the highest altitude lakes in the world. To make things a bit more eventful, we would then head back to Jomsom for a flight back to Kathmandu, where we would regroup for the main expedition. We would then head off from Katmandu overland to Tibet and on to the Everest base camp on the north side of the mountain. I was to work alongside legendary filmmaker and climber Jim Bridwell, who was also on the trip.

The first part of the expedition went smoothly, and we had an incredibly beautiful acclimatizing trek. It helped that we had yaks to carry our camping gear and food. I had come straight from sea level and it took me a while to get acclimatized.

Back in Kathmandu though, things were going downhill with both Pawel's and my relationship with Craig. Pawel was a bit of a joker at heart, and Craig was a bit oversensitive regarding what was released to the media in our press releases about the trip. So, one day Pawel referred to "combustibles" in his blog, meaning hashish, Craig went ballistic with us in response. It was just meant as one small joke among our many other reports but he would just not have it. "My corporate sponsors will leave us all because of this" he screamed at us. He had a point, I suppose, because it was his expedition, but it was only a joke.

Later he sacked us from the expedition, and left us stranded in Kathmandu with only our ski and snowboard gear, but nothing else. No tents, no sleeping bags, nothing. We were unable to do any side trips of our own. Ironically, the sleeping bags which he kept had been part of my sponsorship contribution from friends at Moonstone Equipment in the USA. I liked Craig though, and in many ways he was a great guy. But sometimes two strong minded individuals just cannot be on the same expedition.

It had always been a big dream of mine to ski in the Himalayas. Since we were already there, we felt we had to make the best of it. So we rented replacement sleeping-bags and a tent and jumped on a small plane to the town of Lukla. It has a tiny airstrip, and has been called „the most dangerous in the world." Perched on the side of the mountain the runway is short and steep. Lukla is the gateway to the trek to Everest base camp, and also is the start of treks up to the nearby higher glaciers.

Arriving at the airport, we met two keen Nepalese porters, Pasang and his friend, whom we hired to carry our ski and snowboard gear, as we had a plan to ski whatever we could find during our trek. The failed Everest trip had instead morphed into a charming adventure in our usual dirtbag style.

The first section of our long trek was from Lukla to Gokyo and took 11 days. Miraculously we avoided falling into any crevasses on the two glaciers we crossed, by doing the right thing and roping ourselves together. We even managed to get a few ski and snowboard turns on these two glaciers. These first turns weren't spectacular but they were our first in the Himalayas, and they represented the culmination of a life-long dream of skiing the mountain range.

As one of our porters was wearing flip-flops on the snowy part of the trek, we had him use Pavel's oversize snowboard boots to give his feet some protection from the cold. Our dirtbag attitude was confirmed by all four of us squeezing into a three-man tent. Even so we had a great many laughs along the way, probably helped by the big chunk of yummy Nepalese black hash we had brought along.

Somewhere on our trip we also made two new friends, one was from Iceland and the other from England. Unfortunately, one of them got a bad case of altitude sickness during the night, and had wandered away from the campsite. Luckily we managed to find him before he died, but Pawel had to escort him down to a village that sat at a lower altitude.

As we made our way to the end of our odyssey, we crossed the Chola Pass which topped out at 6,200 m. This was the highest altitude we reached, as well as the climax of this unforgettable skiing and snowboarding adventure in the Himalayas.

We had to celebrate once we arrived back in Kathmandu. Pawel found a bar which had the Polish flag draped across the ceiling. The flag had been left by a Polish mountain climbing expedition and Pawel is such a patriot! The Nepali bar owner also turned out to be the mayor of Kathmandu. Pawel and I told him we wanted to hold a rave party at his bar all night long. This was unheard of in a town where everything usually closed down by 9 pm.

During the few days before the night of the rave we had gone to a printer and made up some nice coloured fliers for our event. Then we painted our faces, and invited some nice climber ladies to do the same and we all set out to do some flyer distribution.

For two days we gave them out to every foreigner we met, and the bar soon filled with tourists and locals alike. Once started, the party did indeed go on all night long, and the mayor had to replenish the bar's beer supply several times. In the end the owner was begging Pawel to stay on and become his social director.

I ended up bankrolling the "Peter & Pawel's Himalayan Ski Trip" on my mother's credit card, because at that time both her son and Pawel were basically poor vagrants, but we did manage to pay her back eventually.

Skiing the Himalayas had always been on my bucket list, and in the end we both considered the trip a great success. Our ex-employer Craig never did manage to ski Everest, although he tried several times, always blaming something else for his lack of success. We totally lost touch afterwards. I guess my life story's constant lesson repeated itself again: don't get involved with the wrong people. It seemed to be a recurring story in my life where I let strangers and their projects into my orbit.

In the end, the chance to go on a good ski trip with my good friend Pawel meant a lot more than supporting some egomaniac trying to ski off the top of Everest.

Before leaving Kathmandu, we had another very interesting encounter: Diana was a glamorous Russian lady, and Gary was her much younger boyfriend. She had moved into an apartment in town and claimed to be a shaman and a kind of good, or white witch.

There certainly was something special about her right from Day One. We were in her apartment and she showed us several plants left there by the previous owners. Although they had been totally dried out when she had moved in, she claimed that they had all blossomed with new flowers. She also had broken a bunch of bottles and made a bed of glass asking us to trust her to protect us while we walked on it. I was very hesitant at first, since (unsurprisingly) I didn't feel like having my feet cut up. But soon I decided to give it a try – as did Pawel. Before I knew it I was actually walking on, and even jumping up and down on, the broken glass without having any cuts or injuries. In fact it felt more like paper crunching under my feet.

From that point on I decided to sit down and listen to more of what Diana had to say. For example, she claimed she could recount our past lives or where we were reincarnated from. She claimed Pawel and his wife had actually been brother and sister in their past lives.

As for me, her story was that I had been a famous French airplane pilot and inventor. Supposedly, I had been famous in the aviation industry, along with a brother who made an even bigger contribution to aviation history. I listened carefully but, truthfully, I did not really believe in the things she was saying and was just being polite. It was a very interesting evening anyway.

A year or more passed and I kind of forgot about the encounter, then one day I was surfing the net and came upon an aviation history museum in Paris.

This reminded me of Diana's story of my previous life. I wrote to the museum and even phoned the curator to see if there were any famous brothers that contributed to aviation history during the time that I was supposed to have lived. I mentioned that one brother was supposed to have died in an aviation accident.

To my utter surprise I received the name of two Parisian brothers, Rene and Gaston Caudron, who had lived during the time in question. There is even a street in Paris named Caudron. Gaston was famous for inventing the first bomber aircraft ever made and he had died in an aviation accident. René, who I was supposed to be, worked with him on many inventions and accompanied him on various adventures involving aircraft.

This left me all very puzzled. I must admit that I feel very comfortable around French people and was told several times that, although I had learned my French in the Grenoble area, I had a Parisian accent. One thing didn't make sense however as I did further research. The reality was that René had died about three years after I was born making everything Diana had said utter nonsense. I had thought the soul had to pass soon after its host death into an infant for it to continue in that infant.

When I called to query her about this, she asked me if I was quite sick as a child and put under anesthesia. To that I replied that, yes, I had been very sick several times – had my tonsils out, my appendix removed, and had suffered some other ailments which had put me in the hospital.

She explained that the soul can enter another body up to about three years of age, especially when one is under anesthesia, and such was the case with René's soul. According to Diana, Rene's soul had entered my body later, while I was sick.

Even now, I can't really say whether I believe Diana. However, keep in mind that she never took any money from me or Pawel, so why would she make all this up? Sure, she could have just adopted famous people and told their stories to travellers she had met along the way, but that would have been really strange. All that detail and the whole convoluted story: it just seemed like too much trouble for anyone to go to and make up.

Even now I really don't know how much truth lies behind my life history and what Diana had said. Don't forget I speak with a Parisian accent, although I learned my French in Grenoble. Maybe this was another test of my faith as a whole. Maybe I should have fully believed Diana but that would have meant accepting full reincarnation as a possibility in the universe, something I perhaps was not ready to do. I think there may be close parallels to faith and superstition and it would be easy to get sucked into a whole belief system on the basis of a few seemingly magical occurrences. In general, apart from my full moon good weather theory, I always tried to remain outside and neutral to belief systems inside and out of organized religion. This was all part of the lesson I had learned earlier when I wrote about my friends Jacek's dabbling with praying to his dolls in the Queen Charlotte Islands.

Around that time I also tried my own luck at working in the film industry, officially in Hollywood North, that is. I have always loved fictional films in general and the excitement of being around the sets when they are being made. I have worked on a couple features with my friends at Petersen Productions. These had been minor roles, but I did get screen credit as a 35 mm camera operator on the film "Ski School". This was a terrible film in reality and went straight to video. It was a lot of fun to work on though, and is now much sought after for its kitsch.

I was quite good with finding sponsors and helping friends get good facility deals, as I had done for myself on many occasions. I helped another friend make a science fiction film in Nelson BC, with an unlikely Willie Nelson of all people as the star. Ray Don Chong, Billy Wirth and a few other celebrity actors also appeared. That film turned out to be a bit of a turkey. It was so bad the cinematographer wanted to take his name off the credits. We kept Willie happy, though, and delivered a good bag of dope to him every day during the shoot.

By now I had been getting pressure from my mother to get a real job for a long time, so I finally succumbed to her admonitions and managed to satisfy her by joining the Directors Guild of Canada. This normally means you have worked your way up through the ranks from coffee boy up to second assistant, and then first assistant director, and eventually direct your first feature. Then, after receiving your first directing credit, you needed to show you'd worked a further 150 days of directing on other films, before you were then invited to join the prestigious Guild.

I managed to circumvent all of these processes by getting letters from television broadcasters, distributors, other directors and producers who all attested that I had logged hundreds of days of directing, but operating as an independent on my own films. Somehow this tactic worked, as I was a specialist in doing things the unorthodox way. And astonishingly, I was finally accepted into the Guild.

However, it was an expensive proposition for me because the annual dues were very high, being such a prestigious body. I stayed by my phone, hoping for a call for work from my membership of The Guild but I never got the expected work. Instead, I do get to enjoy a grand lunch every year, and with it the pleasure of hobnobbing with a few of the really important people in the industry.

In Vancouver's Hollywood North only a few Canadian directors get much work from the mainly American productions. I did manage to make a fun short film called "The Good Life" which was a parable about cultivating marijuana under the guise of growing potatoes. It all took place in medieval times, and starred many of my friends. We shot the short film for a contest called the Crazy 8's held by the Guild. Many of my friends helped me shoot the film. We had eight days for the entire production, and a budget of $800 given to us by the Guild. On top of the cash, we also received the use of cameras and the post-film facilities from sponsors in the Vancouver film industry.

It was a great challenge being given such a short time for production. I chose Pemberton as the location to shoot the film, and again I seemed to have a lot of luck with me on this little production. For instance, the script called for a big medieval party, and I was scratching my head on how we were going to do it since our budget was almost all gone, and we had hardly any costumes. Then, by sheer luck I heard that a neighbour of mine called Bruce was actually a fanatic about the medieval era. Even better for us, he was going to hold his annual party in full costume just down the street from my house on the Saturday that fell perfectly in the middle of our production. I quickly asked Bruce if we could put our actors in front of his friends, who were dressed in medieval costumes and shoot our dinner party scene. We couldn't have planned for this coincidence in a hundred years, but everything turned out amazingly well and it looked like we'd spent a million bucks!

I really did appreciate Ptor's help and patience on the film. He was a hands-on ski guy, and the shoot was probably driving him crazy. But he was a true friend and endured the entire four days of production and camera work with great patience. He never complained when we made him do his stunts over and over again. Chris Lockhart came along as the Director of Photography and did an excellent job shooting aaaaand he was never grumpy about doing the unpaid gig.

Eventually, I stopped paying my dues at the Directors Guild because in the end I was not getting my money's worth, and went back again into the underfunded world of adventure film making. In the end I don't regret the decision at all. I had a lot more fun on our productions than the boredom of standing around a set all day. I still use the Director's Guild initials after my name on my business cards as I have paid a couple of thousand dollars really for nothing over the years except my one annual complimentary lunch and the honour of making the Crazy 8 film. If anybody asks and gets anal about it, I just tell them that it's an old business card from when I was actually in the Guild. I have found this a useful defense as the film industry does get very formal and protective at times.

Over the years I have had a lot of fun pretending to be the big film guy while attending the Vancouver International Film Festival, with its formal galas and other glitzy celebrations. Yet I never really found any support in the established industry for my own productions. I did enjoy using my forging talents to get many of my dirtbag friends into the lavish ceremonies at the VIFF. I would procure an invitation to a fancy event for myself plus one through my Guild contacts. Then I would go to a good graphics shop who had the right range of card stock, and I would make copies of the invitations. What followed was the pleasure of having at least a dozen of my friends join me as everybody partied it up and pigged out on the great food. Telefilm Canada and other organizations have to hold these parties for the PR. And free drinks – a lot of free drinks. Many of these events were a bit stuffy anyway that without my friends there they would have been really boring parties.

As I was often broke from producing my films and expeditions, I learned how to use my press credentials to the full when attending these big events to avoid paying the costly entrance fees. I managed to attend countless film festivals, workshops and industry trade shows for free. Industry events like the Banff Television Festival as well as the Banff Mountain Film Festival, the Las Vegas ski show, the annual NATPE (National Association of Television Program Executives) show in Vegas or New Orleans. It was the same for the Vancouver International Film Festival and many other seminars and gatherings. I partied heavily at many of the shows with my good friend James Angrove of

Real Action Pictures as we would often meet up on the circuit. James was always full of hilarious stories. But of course we had a healthy sense of rivalry between us.

I had to play the game in order to get my films made. As well as sponsors for travel and production, I also needed the latest climbing and skiing equipment. Every year there was an enormous ski trade show in Las Vegas, and this was a must. Luckily there were many cheap flight deals from Vancouver with all-inclusive hotel facilities included, which made it a no-brainer for me to drop in because I would come home with thousands of dollars' worth of gear to use in my film productions. Frequently we could not pay our talent or our camera people in cash, and so we could keep everybody happy with free ski lift tickets, clothing or ski gear from our sponsors.

I am still very much indebted to my many friends, associates and supporters for believing in me along the way. I was often criticized and looked down upon by so many others for working things the way I did during all those years. However, without being as creative as I was, I would have never finished many of those productions, as I rarely had the cash in hand to pay for gear and everybody's expenses. I knew of so many "one film wonders" or producers who managed to make their one dream film but did it by burning people and permanently tarnishing their reputation in the industry as a result.

I still chuckle at one of my festival memories: I was at the Banff Television Festival where I picked up a very attractive children's tv producer from Toronto at the gala dinner. Instead of going back to her hotel, I helped her climb over a fence in her ballgown as we made our way back to my tent where I was camping in a friend's backyard. This didn't put her off me as she came to visit me a few times in Whistler. So she must have been a little thrilled with the whole fence-climbing ordeal, and hopefully she remembered it (and me) fondly for many years.

I did manage to get quite far up the ladder of success in our world of adventure film-making. I was invited to judge at various film festivals around the world including Peru, the Czech Republic and Slovakia, as well as my native Poland. These events were a lot more fun than the sometimes stuffy crowd and parties that was the Hollywood world of big feature films.

Later I founded my own film and expedition school for making adventure films. I held a couple of workshops in Golden, BC as well as one-on-one lessons out of my house in Pemberton. I found I really enjoy teaching film and have approached a few film schools with my bio over the years working at GIFS, Galliano Island Film School, where a fellow named George started an ingenious program for youngsters wishing to learn film-making.

He set up a small logging camp-like operation and trailers where the kids stayed and went through the whole film making process with them. He invited me to be a guest teacher for a full week. Later I hosted the whole crew of his students on Blackcomb Mountain where I designed an adventure course for them. It was kind of nice to feel young again among the youth of this program and leaving some of my knowledge behind.

During the dotcom years of the late-90's I met another interesting character who was in and out of my life for many years. William Mutual was a fanatical skier, nicknamed "Wild Willie" on Cypress Mountain, where he had a knack of getting himself in trouble in the back-country. He rode out a few nice slides and lost a few skis in the process. Outside of his love for skiing William was a genius in many ways – although his near-constant flaunting of his high IQ sometimes was a little much.

William was trying to launch a new venture called ITV.net, which was one of the first companies ever to get involved in video on the Internet. Well, I can't really say video as it actually was more like a slideshow at the time, but William was always so great at hyping the next step that he actually managed to get some serious sponsors interested in him web-casting their events live over the Internet. He started out in a shared offices crammed in with filmmakers and other creative types. Once he had some corporate money behind him he rented an office in Vancouver's trendy Gastown district. By chance, it was conveniently situated next door to the infamous "BC Hemp Co", and we often shared joints with their employees at lunchtime. The notorious activist Mark Emery had founded Hemp BC in Vancouver, but later he would controversially spend several years in a US federal prison for distributing marijuana seeds illegally in America.

ITV.net was made up of a motley crew comprising a combination of computer programmers, graphic designers, media people and others all somehow trying to make it work for William.

William Mutual was a true visionary. He dreamed up all sorts of projects, but got married to the love of his life who was a high-ranking Apple executive at the time, and surged forward with his new webcasting company. I liked William a lot and even settled down to work with a real office job for nearly two years because I just loved what he was doing. On one project he gave me the task of arranging press passes and media accreditation so we could go and make a presence at the Cannes Film Festival, which is the grand-daddy of all festivals. I really don't know how William did it, but he would always just laugh and say, "Peter, you know I am always going to be on the verge of making billions or declaring bankruptcy!"

The Cannes trip was unforgettable as William pulled many rabbits out of his hat to make that webcast actually happen. He must've had a huge budget as we stayed in a penthouse apartment just across the street from the Palais, where all the film Festival celebrations took place. We interviewed celebrities and producers, as well as other various interesting characters attending the Cannes spectacle. It was a great trip. To show how incestuous these do's are, I met a TV film crew who were from Poland. Once they heard about some of my own extreme film adventures, they featured me in a TV show they were making the Festival and we had a lot of fun doing comical extreme stunts for my segment.

On the way home from Cannes I made a detour to Chamonix, where I managed to paraglide off the north face of the Aguille du Midi as well as ski the infamous Glacier Ronde run with Troy Jungen. We almost summited Mont Blanc that trip but were turned back by the conditions and reached just short of the peak on Mont Blanc du Tacuil, due to deteriorating weather. I had dropped in on M. Prudhomme from the Chamonix Tourist Office, who I had met while making "The Spirit" when his help had been really appreciated. Very nicely, he once again gave us passes so we could do some climbing, skiing, and paragliding.

I also helped William put on a webcast from the World Extreme Skiing Championships in Valdez, Alaska. This was sponsored by Microsoft, and was an opportunity for them to show off their technology.

Our webcast was watched live on the Microsoft stand at the NAB Computer Show in Las Vegas. Their guests watched us as we skied powder, filmed live from helicopters, from their booth at the show. I still don't know how he pulled off that one, but it all worked apparently!

I decided to be a real "fish out of water" and spend two weeks manning William's office on Hollywood Boulevard in Los Angeles. It was a draw for me, a usually devout outdoor bumpkin to really experience the big city and bright lights thing. William had opened a new office in LA in a penthouse on top of an old bank building, surrounded by gargoyles. We spent an amusing couple weeks partying and schmoozing with the Hollywood crowd looking at other webcasting opportunities. Making a splash in Hollywood is important, by any means, and William had bought a Cadillac limousine which had been converted from its former life as an ambulance. This didn't stop it crashing on the freeway in the crazy LA traffic, but luckily my ITV.net colleague Alan, who was driving, nor me was hurt, but our exotic ride was totalled.

We also visited the (now famous) Burning Man Festival in Nevada, and webcast that spectacle when it was still a relatively small happening, with about 25,000 souls attending. William had arranged to upload the footage with a satellite truck that he rented with a driver in Las Vegas. I still giggle as I remember the driver who manned that big truck. He was the kind of a guy that you would see at an NFL game. He was a true redneck, and was therefore very much like a fish out of water at Burning Man with all its attendant naked hippies. In fact, he stayed safely within the confines of his truck for the entire week as all the freaks partied around him. Burning Man was a lot of fun any way you looked at it, and I couldn't understand why he wouldn't partake.

My old ski friend Kent Rodler was with us on the trip. We were living in luxury as we had a huge motor-home to work from in the official camp premises. We all also had press passes of course, which got us in to all the most exquisite private parties and gatherings that Burning Man is famous for. It really is a worthwhile festival to attend at least once in your life, because it is a mix of the latest technology with music and art. It also features some of humanity's best thinkers and creators so it is interesting to hear what they have to offer for mankind's future. The festival revolves around an interesting barter system in which only ice can be bought for money – otherwise everything is traded using a barter system. I bought a cup of coffee with a can of tuna once. Burning Man has its origins in a small gathering that originally was held in San Francisco. It outgrew that location and moved to the desert. Each year the festival ends with the burning of a huge wooden statue of an upright man as people dance around it.

Unfortunately William's involvement with ITV ended with a paragliding accident in Pemberton. He had sky-dived before, and decided to get into paragliding as I has said it was fantastic. He had got hold of a new para wing from a company called ITV Paragliders because of the similarity of the names and he thought it would look good. He had also arranged for an instructor to give him some lessons, but the instructor failed to show up, so William insisted I do the job. Although I protested that I was not qualified, William was my boss as well as a friend, and was persistent in having things his way. So after two aborted tries, I finally let him take off and watched him fly down towards the Valley. Apparently William panicked high above the landing field and while heading towards some trees, he pulled both of his break toggles down to his ankles trying to make a turn. This made him plummet to the ground, breaking his back and giving him internal injuries as well.

Because he had skydived before, he had used the sky-diving technique of pulling on both toggles to descend with control. Unfortunately paragliders work very differently. And according to witnesses, when he pulled on the toggles he was about 150 feet up. Considering the height that he fell from, he was really lucky just to be alive. While in the hospital bed dealing with his injuries, William was dealt another blow, and this time one involving his business. The man he had hired to be CEO of his company, stabbed him in the back by using the situation with his accident to take over his webcasting company. The business world can be brutal. To show there are no hard feelings between us, William and I still meet up quite often and go skiing together on Whistler.

I felt really bad about how the paragliding accident had destroyed William's business. That crash definitely ruined his life, and it should have been a warning to me as well in my paragliding forays. On the other hand, that's what happens to risk takers sometimes. They are a kind of people who will often risk it all in business as well as recreationally. I did some reading on risk and found some really interesting articles about it written by psychologist Frank Farley. Dr Farley claimed that there were various personality traits inherent in risk-takers, and my friend William was a prime example. Farley said risk-takers are more creative, and more likely to be entrepreneurs. People who are not so attracted to risk will take safer options in life, and they are the ones who land steady jobs in corporations or banks. William operated on whims: he would do a back-flip without scouting the landing on skis as unthinkingly as he would make an investment. Incidentally, non-risk takers also were less likely to practice extreme sports. I was keen to do a whole television series about the psychology and history of risk, but I could never find the backing.

Years later, another near-disaster story: during one back-country outing with William, we decided to take a helicopter from Pemberton up into the nearby Cayoosh Range. There was a sea of clouds which filled the valley entirely and rose to the tree line level, which is at about 2,500 m on the surrounding mountains. Because of these clouds, few peaks stood out in the sunshine above them, and the pilot let us down on what I thought was the peak of Cayoosh Mountain.

The plan was for the four of us to spend the day ski touring up high and then ski out to the Duffy Lake Road, which should be about 1,000 m below us to the west. So, as the helicopter landed, we enjoyed a fine day of touring and getting some fine powder lines. Then after eating our packed lunch, it was time to ski out as it was getting late in the day.

Below us we could see a lake, from which I was sure there was a trail back to the Duffy Lake Road. So we skied down to the lake, toured over to the far end of it, and began working our way down the ravine expecting to find the trail head I had used 12 years earlier. After descending for some time we gradually came to the realization that we must be in the wrong valley, which had an identical looking lake at the top. All of us, including the helicopter pilot, had been confused by the cloud cover and we had landed on Saxifrage Mountain instead of the neighbouring Cayoosh by mistake. It was not the pilot's fault that it had been the only peak that had been sticking out into the sunshine out of the clouds that morning.

By now it was 4:30 pm on December 28th which is one of the shortest days of the year. It was getting dark, and the skiing was getting steeper and steeper. There was no way of going back up and so we made our way down clinging to slide alders and frozen willows, and eventually we found a flat spot in the ravine where we spent the night. It turned out to be a very cold night, getting down to -15°C. As well as we could, we made a bed of boughs and huddled together for warmth. We had enough wood to make a fire which burnt for about two hours, and after that we just huddled together until the daylight came. After many hours of a cold and sleepless night, we continued on our way down the gully. At times we were jumping from one snow-covered rock to another underneath frozen waterfalls. It was a really difficult staying upright, more like a tightrope walk, wearing our plastic ski boots and jumping from frozen rock to rock. It was crazy, dangerously crazy! Eventually we knew we would make it back safely because we came across the strangest site of civilization, a rusty mountain bike frame which had been stripped of all its components, which had probably been left by some thieves.

Shortly afterwards, as we worked our way down we heard a barking dog, and knew we were near civilization. I had been in too much of a hurry to make sandwiches before the trip, and had just grabbed a huge piece of turkey left over from our Christmas Day dinner. That large piece of turkey probably saved us, since it had a lot of energy and we chewed on the carcass all night long, feeling less pain from the piercing cold around us. The helicopter had dropped us in a neighbouring valley from the one we intended to use, and instead of skiing down to the Duffy Lake Road, we had ended up 3,000 feet lower in the First Nations settlement of Mount Currie. We now had an opportunity to cancel the search and rescue operation which had been called to look for us after we had not arrived back the night before. Luckily it all ended well. But William's wife never really forgave me for that one either. Since then William's ski trips with me have been much tamer, and we have stayed in the back-country of Whistler, straying not too far from the lifts.

This mountain fiasco was now my third incident of this sort. The first had been at Tsurup Lake in Peru in 1978. The second was a night spent out on Waddington in 1985. No one had been hurt in any of these adventures but I hoped this latest experience in Pemberton would be my last.

The Sierra Nevada de Santa Marta and domain of the Kogi natives

1. The view as we exit the rainforest at 2,000 m elevation and get a view of the 5,000+ meter peaks of the Sierra.
2. Taminaca, a typical Kogi village in the Sierra.
3. A Kogi family in front of their mud hut.
4. Our adventurous team in January 1998.

Burning Man Festival

1. Huge sand and wood structures are typical sights at the festival.
2. The majority of the 50,000 strong in attendance leave their clothing behind.
3–4. Interesting art, science and architecture make for a unique event.
5. At the end of the festival, a massive wooden effigy of a man is burnt as a finale to the festival.

1

2

3

4

5

CHAPTER 11

SURVIVING THE MILLENIUM AND BEYOND, THE 2000'S

Not too long after William's paragliding accident, I suffered my own incident. By then I had been flying for about 13 years and they all had just been "sled rides" – which was simply climbing up mountains for the simple thrill of flying back down them again, without any gain in altitude while air born.

By 1999 though, I had started to somewhat discover the skill of thermaling upwards in a paraglider by riding within invisible bubbles of rising hot air called thermals. Circling inside them enabled you to gain altitude as birds do. I had actually gone up a few times before, but had not really understood the finer points of the atmospheric mechanics of air currents. At the time most of the local paragliders in Pemberton were self-taught, and I was no exception.

In search of the elusive thermal, I carried my paraglider all the way up to the top of the iconic Black Tusk near Whistler. The mountain's cone is made up of black volcanic rock which was very grippy, making it relatively easy to climb since is has a lot of hand and footholds. Once on top of the rock, and after some difficulty I finally managed to put my lines out.

When I launched, I was immediately immersed in a thermal wind forming from the heat given off by the black rock, and quickly started gaining altitude. I had never been in these conditions and didn't know how to ride inside thermals, and I rapidly lost altitude as I left the thermal and crashed on my butt on the Helm Glacier as I landed downwind when I rapidly lost altitude in downdrafts. Luckily I wasn't hurt but my behind dug a big rut in the glacier as I was dragged along it. It looked sort of like a bobsled run. Luckily, I had landed on the steep slope of the upper glacier, and the gradient reduced the impact of my fall.

Another one of my incidents happened when I decided to fly off the backside of Whistler Mountain, and have an easy flight down to Cheakamus Lake 2,000 m below. I launched safely on my skis, and was flying without thermaling, and simply planned to land in the logging slash, which is an area that has had all the trees felled, on the other side of the Cheakamus River. Suddenly and for no reason, one of my brake lines suddenly snapped. The loss of one of the brake lines is not catastrophic, but one has to steer the glider with the rear risers instead.

This tends to work alright, but one loses a lot of altitude fast. So before I knew it, I was skimming over the tops of giant 50 m tall cedar trees until my luck ran out and I finally hit one. I began to fall backwards down the tree with my back breaking the branches of the cedar, one by one, which helped break my fall.

I didn't like falling on my back, so I leaned forward and managed to get my skis under me so they were now breaking the branches. As in the most unlikely movie, I miraculously landed on the ground completely unhurt. Thankfully, it was at that point that my binding came undone, and not before!

I looked around to survey my situation. I had sheared the branches off the entire side of the tree, and luckily my paraglider had followed me down without getting snagged, and was sitting right next to me in a heap.

Nobody had witnessed my ordeal, and I was bruised but otherwise okay, so I packed up my stuff, and with my glider on my back, I skied all the way out to the traffic lights in Function Junction at the south end of Whistler. From there I hitchhiked home, too embarrassed to really tell anybody about what had happened.

There were other smaller mishaps along the way with my „Wild Things" glider, (the first glider brand out of the USA), including a few more tree landings with skis on at various ski hills. But somehow, I never had any bigger mishaps for about 17 years flying with that old eight-cell vintage glider. Most of my bigger accidents came in the later years when I started thermaling regularly which led to bigger flights.

One accident I had was in Pemberton, in the summer of 1999. I had set off my glider from our launch above the Pemberton Valley and was to flying towards a field where we usually landed. However, I experienced what para-gliders call "sudden sink", which are caused by the downdrafts that occur next to thermal up lifts. I knew immediately that I was in trouble and was not going to make the landing. What ensued was a real disaster. I kind of panicked, because my options for a safe landing were fast becoming scarce. Suddenly as I thought I was in real trouble, a house came into vision on my right and it had a big corral in front of it – perhaps it was my last chance? So I turned sharply, thinking I would make it to the corral. Instead, I clipped the roof of the house with my legs, which sent me crashing heavily to the ground from a height of about 30 feet.

Writhing in pain, I did not realize that I had actually crashed into a friend's house. As I looked up through my tears of pain, I saw my old pal George McConkey standing over me. Alongside him was his three-year-old daughter, and at this point he gave her the cell phone and said, "This, my dear, is going to be your very first 911 call," which I still remember to this very day, as she carried it off without a hitch.

I had two broken legs, a broken arm, I had lost a couple of teeth, and had a very hurt ego. I spent the rest of that summer in a wheelchair and unable to walk, which was not that surprising given my myriad of injuries. I managed to keep myself busy however, working with an editor to finish the "Journey To The Heart of the World" film about the Kogi people in Colombia.

That fall, in order to speed up my recuperation, I decided to take a relaxing trip to Baja California. Accompanying me were my old friend, Doris, and another good friend, Ryszard Szafirski. We set off southwards just before Christmas in Ryszard's big GMC van, intent on zig-zagging back and forth across the Baja so that we could check out the beaches that lie on both the Cortez and Pacific side of the peninsula.

During our journey to what I was sure would be a kind of Paradise, I was laid low by the worst case of flu I have ever had in my life. The virus was so bad that I was convinced I was going to die. I was sweating buckets and soaking T-shirts every few minutes. Finally, after a nightmare journey to the Baja, I began to think I might live again, and started gorging myself on bags of oranges. The vitamin C finally killed the virus, I guess.

That Baja trip remains one of the most memorable journeys I have ever had. I love it there so much more than on the mainland of Mexico. Sure, I have some great memories of the latter from my first film back in the 80's, when I was still a student at SFU, and also the time I had hitchhiked once with my girlfriend Megan all the way from Vancouver.

But this trip was different: we had much more time and for once we did not feel rushed or harried in any way. We went on side trips into little coves and peninsulas, camping in places that were so remote that the three of us were probably the only people for tens of kilometers in any direction.

One night Ryszard found a great campsite for us. Since he had moved to Canada he became enamoured with the Canadian wilderness and was now a real outdoorsman. Ryszard was quite a famous Polish Himalayan climber, and he had been the cameraman on the first successful Polish winter Everest expedition, a noteworthy feat in itself.

He was a real charmer with the ladies and I loved him for it. Perhaps in some way, we were birds of a feather. We got along so well in many other ways, as well with our shared interests. He was a true rebel, and that was perhaps the most obvious attraction between us.

If truth be told, Ryszard had a bit of a drinking problem, which upset Doris and left her feeling more than a little scared throughout the whole trip. As he drove, Ryszard sipped constantly from a glass, which at first she had thought was water. Later she realized it was pure vodka. I personally think alcoholics somehow get used to being in that state and so he probably drove as well as anyone on the deserted roads with his vodka, rather than going through withdrawal symptoms without it.

All in all, and apart from that minor hiccup, we had an amazing time.

Ryszard had brought a sea-kayak with him, as well as some snorkeling gear, and we discovered many amazing sites that were really off-road. My favourite beach was at a beautiful and desolate spot called Agua Verde on the Cortez coast. It had sparkling green water, which explained the name of the town, and an incredible beach yet it was almost deserted.

To get there we had to cross a high mountain pass which was about halfway down the Baja, and make our way down towards the other side. At first we passed a little fishing village that seemed deserted and then hit what seemed like endless stretches of beaches, without a soul on them. By now it was the dawning of the new millennium and we sat on the beach in Agua Verde on New Year's Eve looking up at the heavens, which glowed in the dark unpolluted sky. We pointed our lawn chairs northward, in expectation of the Apocalypse that was about to ravage civilization. Everyone was panicked by the Y2K computer bug, thinking it would result in the end of the world. Planes were due to fall out of the sky.

Well, in the end the „End" never came. Eventually we had to leave, and we made it back home safely. Well, almost safely. As it happened, a wheel fell off our van right near Seattle, but we managed to control the van and bring it to a stop before it went rolling off into a ditch.

Earlier, at the other end of the States, as we were drove through California, Ryszard said he had a good friend living in LA who we should visit. His friend had a lovely 22-year-old daughter, and Ryszard insisted that she had always listened keenly to his stories, and so he thought she was sort of enamoured with him. When we got to LA, Ryszard and the girl went shopping in the van, while Doris and I stayed at his friend's place.

When they returned from shopping, Ryszard was blushing and had a red face. He took me aside for the story: the young girl had jumped and seduced him in the van! He said he would love to have a romantic romp with her, but if his friend ever found out, it would ruin their friendship. After all they were best friends, and there was a four decade age difference.

He seemed to be seeking my advice. So I said to my friend something like „Ryszard, you only live once, so take it while you can. When we get back home I'll arrange for a ski weekend – saying we are all going to a ski resort with a bunch of friends. Then it won't look like just you and her on a date. But just make sure you don't fall in love, as you're such a romantic. So remember that you should know that relationships like that just do not work out beyond being, effectively, just a dirty weekend".

So when we got back to Canada, I did the ski trip with Ryszard. He must have felt relieved that the girl's father, his old friend in LA, never did find out. Of course it didn't last, and he was devastated for a long time, even though he should have known it would be just a short fling. Later he happily married a lady who was closer to him in age.

As for myself I was always curious about potentially promiscuous women. So I decided to visit Ryszard's girl, who was by this time studying medicine in Poland. We did have a quick romantic evening but the magic was never between us. She later got married and moved to England.

Sadly, my friend Ryszard died a few years ago. He was not much older than me, in his seventies and I will miss him dearly.

It was around that time, I started regularly visiting the town of Golden in the Rockies. Troy had married a beautiful Swedish girl named Tove and had moved there for the great back-country skiing.

There was a small local ski resort, if you could call it that, in Golden. It was named Whitetooth and like many local hills around N America, had only one chairlift that had been built in 1986. This one lift however gave skiers incredible access to the spectacular Dog Tooth mountain range situated above the town. The locals had this hidden gem of a ski lift that gave perfect access for ski touring from the top with long runs back to the valley. The area is famous for its abundant "champagne" powder, which is generally thought to be lighter and better than we had in Whistler, with it's heavy wet coastal snow.

We were touring one day from the chairlift when Troy informed me that a huge gondola was coming during the next year. A large ski resort was being planned and built, and the idea gelled that I should come out and document the change that was about to happen to the town. It was a memorable day skiing, and we were even joined by the climbing legend, Fred Beckey, as he was a good friend of Troy's, and with whom

I was just starting to get acquainted. It turned out that he often showed up in town and crashed on Troy's couch.

Fred was already well into his 80s, but he had acquired some ski touring gear and Troy often took him out for short tours. A group of Colorado filmmakers were making a documentary about Fred called Dirtbag. I shot some footage later with Fred climbing around Squamish as my contribution to the project.

Fred was a funny old cat and it was hard getting his acceptance as a friend. I have found this with other climbing and skiing celebrities as well. Perhaps they have heard of my apparent notoriety in our world. I found it true that most extreme athletes like Fred was in the climbing world, have rather big egos.

This seems to be a complementary part of their personalities which is necessary for them to have achieved the things they had done. Fred tolerated me but he never became as close to me as he had been with Troy. We ran into each other quite a few times over the years, and I still remember meeting him for the first time in Las Vegas, when he was manning the booth of the Coleman Company, which was one of his sponsors back then. As I recall he was 62 years old then, so it must've been during one of my early visits in the early 80's.

Back in Golden I was following up with Troy's idea for a documentary about the coming of the destination ski resort called Goldenrush.

Golden is the eastern gateway to Rogers Pass, and is now a centre for helicopter and snow cat skiing, and Alpine touring. Originally a logging and railroad town, the place has a true mountain heritage.

It was the birthplace of mountain guiding in Canada and the home of the original Swiss guides which the Canadian Pacific Railroad brought over in 1899. They were employed to safely guide the hotel guests through the mountains as a means to help promote "Alpine" tourism. An added benefit to the CPR was that they also trained the railway workers in managing avalanche hazards.

I interviewed some real classic Swiss old school mountain guides that came from that line, as well as mountaineering personalities during the filming of Goldenrush. One was Bruno Engler, a Swiss guide who originally had plied his trade out of Golden and was, at the time, also famous around his home town of Banff.

I also interviewed Chic Scott, an author who wrote the book on the history of Canadian mountaineering, and was very knowledgeable on the Golden area.

I also interviewed other experts who worked in the industry from Banff who spoke on the sustainability of building new ski resorts.

The film had a very interesting outlook on ski resorts in general, featuring commentary from such names such as Hal Clifford, author of "Downhill Slide" – a book on how greed and real estate development was the real driver behind many ski developments. I also had an appearance by Wade Davis commenting on what happens to a town when the old logging industry dies and a ski resort takes its place as the driver of the local economy.

Golden's ski resort was being built by a big Dutch company named Ballast Nedham, which supposedly had a big tax break due from the Canadian government after building the Confederation Bridge between Prince Edward Island and New Brunswick many years back. The architect hired to design the project was an Italian-Canadian living in Vancouver who was an avid skier himself and rather fanatical about the projects he got involved in. Oberto Oberti, while trying to build the resort of Jumbo, his dream project south of Golden near Invermere, had come across a little gem of a ski hill called Whitetooth, in Golden, which he planned to turn into a major destination ski resort. Since Jumbo was being endlessly stalled by environmental protests, he put his energy into designing what became known as the Kicking Horse Mountain Resort. Little did I realize that the smell of powder snow had me starting on yet another huge documentary project, one which would once again virtually bankrupt me and take up four years of my life.

Golden also had some of the best paragliding in Canada during the summer, which made the community even more attractive for me to hang out in. A few years later I would actually make my longest ever cross-country flight, from Golden to Invermere which was a distance 112 km. The ride wasn't totally comfortable though: halfway through the flight to Invermere over the little town of Brisco when I had to pee. I did not want to cut my flight short, so I kind of stuck my little guy out and put the paraglider into a bit of the spiral, so as I peed it would spray away from me instead of soaking me in my own urine. Since then,

I have used that technique several times and it has always seemed to work quite well.

It has been the story of my life that I have been attracted to projects by the idea, not the possibility of upfront cash, unlike most producers. Because I felt this was such a good story, I moved to Golden for as long as it took. It was in December 2000, the month of the official opening of the new gondola to the top of the mountain and the birth of the new Kicking Horse Ski resort. In exchange for promoting the bar in my film, I got a free hotel room above the biggest, loudest redneck bar in Golden, named Packers. I earned that sponsorship in sleepless nights.

I managed to ski my butt off that winter with Troy, his wife Tove, and many other friends that visited from Whistler, Vancouver, and elsewhere while filming all the time. I am proud to say that Goldenrush turned out to be my most thoughtful film, as well as my most provocative and contraversial undertaking. I told the story of what happens when a big corporation moves into a small Canadian logging town, and takes it over. They seemed to have the attitude that it was elitist and filled with European scorn.

I spent two ski seasons filming in Golden, documenting many of the local outdoor operations that ranged from ski touring to snow cat skiing. I also told the story of birth of the town of Golden, as well as that of the newcomers who were there to build the new resort.

Opinion was divided when the film was released. The people of Golden loved my film and later bought many of the DVDs. On the other hand, the resort hated me, but they could not really do anything about it as I had just documented the reality of how removed they were from the everyday life of the locals, and had been careful to not cross any legal boundaries in my commentary.

As is often the case, I seemed to spend far more time chasing the funding that I needed to edit the film than I spent actually skiing the sweet powder lines of the Kicking Horse ski area. Once again, I have to thank good friends such as Troy Jungen, Derek Lynn and Chris Lockhart who helped me so much in filming and in the post-production of the documentary.

I remember I was almost driven to tears because all my funding leads were producing nothing. I was beginning to lose all hope, but

I was driving my mother's car in Vancouver when I got an unexpected phone call. I had to pull over to hear the good news: the call was from the Canadian Studies program. Speaking at the other end of the line was a Quebecois-accented guy from the Ministry of Canadian Heritage telling me that I would receive the $42,000 grant which I had applied for a year before, and had given up on. Yelling to myself inside the car out of joy and happiness, I almost managed to crash the car on West 4th Avenue on my way home. What a huge relief it was, as up to that point I had been paying people with promises rather than with actual cash. I had so many debts that I resorted to a technique that many producers will admit to; I was paying for the production by using my credit cards, and had got to the stage of paying off one credit card with another. That, as we all know, is just a downhill spiral to debtor's hell.

Later I managed to negotiate several production facility deals and managed to save enough cash to pay some long-overdue wages to the rest of the crew, such as my partner Chris Lockhart and editor Ron Ireland, both of whom had worked on so many of my films before. I managed to get a national television broadcast from Learning Television and Access Alberta, which in turn triggered the granting of the fund from Heritage Canada and Canadian Studies. My best deal was that I managed to get the online edit done at the Banff Centre for the Arts, which had state-of-the-art facilities at the time. The Centre also agreed to put Ron Ireland and me up at its exclusive and rather posh artists' accommodations. We were really styling now!

Another dear friend I do have to thank for his essential help was Ian Waddell, who was my Executive Producer on Goldenrush. He helped me in so many ways! Sadly, Ian has since passed away.

The soundtrack in the Golden film was also a killer, and the product of very talented friends at Vancouver's best sound studio, Pinewood Studios. Their top technician was a snowboarder who put a lot of his heart and soul into the sound production. I had imagined the soundtrack and narration as a fairy tale kind of story about a small town and how it was changing without having a say in the process.

Sadly the film only received one broadcast on the national Learning Television channel, but that's the way it is with so many Canadian documentaries and this one was quite local in its appeal.

In the film I compared the new Golden resort to the small ski resort of La Grave in France. The tiny ski station had gotten deeply into my spirit while I was making "The Spirit" about Trevor Petersen. Both ski resorts have a lot of similarities. They were both old mining towns and they both had a single gondola which accessed endless high back-country terrain, one in France and one in British Columbia, Canada. My neighbour and good friend Chris Kettles helped me by letting me use some great footage from La Grave when he visited Ptor Spricenieks there.

I have to admit that I still feel very lucky at not getting sued by the Dutch corporation after I used some of their footage given to me by their architects, and I used it without permission. But I guess it was small potatoes to them and my film was never a big commercial venture. The architect Oberto became a close friend through this and later I helped him film some promotional clips for his Jumbo project which has, as yet, still not materialized. In his gratitude for my help he designed my beautiful home in Pemberton for free, a generous act which I feel forever in his debt.

I swear I have enjoyed some of the best powder skiing in my life at this new Kicking Horse resort. Some days were even better than helicopter skiing. The Dog Tooth mountain range stretches both north and south of the top of the Kicking Horse lifts, making it very easily accessible for ski touring and mountaineering. With just a few short hikes in either direction one would come across a new virgin chute or bowl with very few tracks on it. We got so spoiled that sometimes we would come to a small bowl with one ski track down it and Troy would say, "Aahh it's all skied out, let's go to the next one!" And, so, on we would go – enjoying waist deep powder run after run in the dry Golden powder. At this time there were no tourists, as the Dutch company had no idea on how to market the area. So, instead, all these ski bums moved into Golden, and we ended up with about 50 of them from around the world.

One Sunday morning we drove up to the large base parking lot. It had just snowed 55 cm the previous night and there were a total of six other cars in that parking lot. On days like that we would do lap after lap on the gondola, hooting, hollering and racking up at least 20 runs in the deep powder, before crawling to the pub exhausted at the end of the day. Golden was still a redneck logging town and had a charm all its own, but when all the ski bums moved into town, they seemed to bring a new energy with them, which the old town people embraced, and welcomed them. One local bar, for instance, had a very special Monday welcome called "Fresh Meat Mondays." On that evening the welcoming began with a strip show, then the band would come on and half pint beers were sold for a dollar.

I think I even got to ski even more powder than I did in Alaska. The new gondola made it just so fast and accessible to get that many runs in during a day. Then, once the regular groomed runs were all skied out, we needed only to hike for a few minutes to get to another huge line which ran all the way to the bottom. Once you got to the base of the valley, there was a simple ten minutes traverse to get back to the lift bases and do it all again. Troy and his wife were in such amazing shape that they kicked my ass too during our many skiing escapades, particularly some of the longer trips from the famous Rogers Pass.

2004 was the year that I really got into paragliding and tried to launch a documentary about the sport. It was to be called Airhead Diaries. I had made a great 15 minute trailer, edited by my good friend Barry Backus, to try to attract sponsors for the long form version. It introduced some of the more colourful characters from the Pemberton paragliding community, otherwise known as the Pemberton Flying Monkeys. It was around this time that I met a Russian couple, Tanya and Dennis who became firm friends. I helped Tanya get into paragliding by supplying her with a sponsored wing from a Ukrainian company, Sky Country, for my "Airheads Diaries" film. She really took to the sport eventually becoming a full instructor and tandem pilot. We enjoyed many memorable paragliding outings together in Hedley, Pemberton, and from her home flying site at Woodside, in the Fraser Valley as well as in La Malinche in central Mexico.

Producing the "Airhead Diaries" project ended up taking me to Europe, once again with my good friend Pawel Boryniec, where I was trying to secure a paraglide sponsor. Before we did that I had a special presentation planned in Pawel's hometown, Lodz, Poland, where they were holding an Explorers Festival which also featured a small mountain film festival. I gave an hour-long power point presentation which summarized many of our mountain adventures over the years. I was happy that I had managed to keep an audience entertained as it was my first presentation of this kind.

On a side note, Lodz is also home to a famous film school which Roman Polanski attended. He even made his film debut there with his short film Two Men and a Wardrobe. Today the school attracts top film directors like Quentin Tarantino, who are given residencies to conduct workshops.

We then travelled on to Ostrava in the Czech Republic, which is a medium sized town near the Polish border and is the home of Sky Paragliders headquarters and factory. Sky had liked my proposal for a documentary about the characters who paraglided in Canada.

The management at Sky called in their test pilot Thomas Lednik to vet us. They wanted him to talk with Pawel and I so as to determine how genuine we were. Luckily Thomas liked us and our ideas, and gave the go-ahead to the marketing people. And so we obtained our fist big company sponsor for Airhead Diaries. It was a hard shock when I heard that Lednik had died in an accident while flying a tandem in Kenya in 2018.

Soon after our return to Canada several big boxes arrived at the Vancouver airport. They were all our paraglide gear and were being held for us at Canadian Customs. Being that we were in our usual state and broke again, I remember feeling really worried about how much import duty we would have to pay on all the gear. So we decided strategically to send in our best ambassador, who was Pawel.

Luckily, the customs officers turned out to be an all women crew. Pawel did his job very well, charming the ladies by looking into their eyes and telling them how beautiful they were. His flattery must have worked, because they handed over $15,000 worth of gear and charged us only $100 in customs fees. The shipment included three wings, designated for Pawel, me, and a woman we knew named Asia, who was the wife of another Polish friend, Maciek Siwocha. I was hoping Asia would be one of the stars in the upcoming Airhead Diaries film, as she was a keen pilot and had a genuine interest in the sport and was beautiful too.

My obsession with paragliding took full flight now. I started flying more and more, discovering sites all over British Columbia in places like Kelowna, Revelstoke and Golden. Soon, even my favourite sport, skiing, began to take second place, so taken was I by flying. In the winters I discovered that all my paragliding friends migrated down south to places like Mexico or Colombia, and I started doing the same.

My first paragliding trip to Mexico was to Yelapa, a small coastal community with a fantastic beach that could only be reached by water taxi from Puerto Vallarta. Yelapa had two beautiful paragliding sites. In the morning if there was an ATV ride available we would go up to Tapa, a site in the hills above Yelapa. From hear we could actually thermal for about an hour or so before landing on the beach below. Then, in the afternoons, we hiked up from the beach to a soaring site riding the ocean wind that flowed up the bluffs.

Always travelling so much, I usually had very little time to actually meet single women in Canada. I always found it easier to charm the ladies abroad during my travels. Then I would invite them back to Canada for a visit. For example, I had met a beautiful girl named Klaudia Mroz on the previous trip to Poland. She was only 21 years old, but somehow I was naïve enough to think that there might be some chemistry between us. It seems clear in retrospect that I was kidding myself, after all, I was 48 years old. Anyhow I invited Klaudia to visit me in Pemberton for a summer. When she arrived she immediately became a real hit with my many single friends.

She was really a gorgeous girl, with a very feminine and well contoured body like a slim pear. Very friendly and outgoing, she soon started flirting and dating other guys including several of my younger friends. It's only natural that youth attracts youth, but I was upset because I was, after all, the one who paid for her plane ticket from Poland. However, Klaudia was a great graphic designer and artist, and I had an idea how she could help me in another way. She redesigned all the covers to my videos, and the value of doing this was certainly more than the cost of the plane ticket. So in the end, everything turned out all right. We are still great friends and when I visited Poland later, she even gave me a beautiful painting that she had made of Mount Robson and its north face, a gift that I later I gave to Ptor as a beautiful wedding present.

My next paragliding trip to Mexica was to Valle de Bravo – the capital of hang gliding and paragliding in Mexico and a step up in complexity of flying from Yelapa. Situated two hours Southwest of Mexico City its topography featured the potential for cross country flights. It was the place where the sport had really started to boom in the country. I went there a couple of times and had some really memorable flights, ending up in the trees on only one or two occasions, and unhurt. I took these tree landings as just being part of the sport as sooner or later everyone had had an encounter with a tree on landing when flying over wooded areas.

During one of those visits to Valle de Bravo, I was lucky to meet Ewa Wisnierska, who was another flyer of Polish origin.

Ewa was an elite pilot. She was a paragliding champion who had flown all over Europe. We made an hour side trip from Valle de Bravo with a few other pilot friends; our aim was to fly off the perfect cone of the Toluca volcano which was nearby. The first time we tried we waited for a few hours on its flanks but we decided that it was too windy to fly, so we went back down. But it looked so nice that we didn't stop trying, and on another trip a few days later we again found it was too windy. However, being flying fanatics, we had climbed to the summit and managed to get some short flights into the crater of the volcano itself, which would be shielded from the wind, or so we thought. The outside wind pushed down into the crater and this created rotors which can be dangerous as the air is turbulent and can collapse a glider. So although these flights were short, they were actually relatively dangerous.

Later I interviewed Ewa in Polish at the Penon paraglide launch back at Valle de Bravo, and these clips came in handy in my Paracinderella film when I was talking about female flyers.

Ewa would later become famous after her own horrendous experience in Australia, after being sucked up into a huge thunder storm cloud at 10,000 meters, an elevation higher than Everest. Having passed out due to a lack of oxygen, she flew unconscious for up to an hour covered in ice, whilst being battered by hailstones.

Her glider collapsed under the weight of the ice that covered it as well. She then free felled some 2,000 metres and then miraculously her glider reinflated. The jolt must have waken her up and she regained consciousness in the lower altitude.

She managed to land her paraglider safely, bruised by the hailstones and slightly hypothermic, but otherwise OK. Her experience was widely reported on in the press and was made into a film called „Miracle" that can be viewed on YouTube.

In 2006 and back in Pemberton, I came up with the novel idea of hosting what would be the world's first Paraplegic Paragliding Fly-In. The location was going to be the small south Okanagan community of Hedley. Since we could only find three paraplegic pilots, and we wanted the event to have some stature, we included an FIA sanctioned event, which was to be a cross-country contest.

I had discovered the area while shooting a promotional film about a gold mine dating back to the turn of the 20th century. The mine which was no longer operating had been turned into a tourism opportunity by the local First Nations people, the Upper Similkameen Band. The entrance to the mine was perched up like a bird's nest, 3,000 feet above the valley floor, on the side of a cliff at the head of the box canyon that Hedley sat in. The tribe received a government grant to build an information center in Hedley which could promote local tourism, including tours up to the mine. The 15-minute film historical film featured archival footage and interviews with former miners from Hedley. It was shown in a small theatre that was in the local indigenous centre to encourage tourists to take a look at the mine.

By chance, there was an ideal paragliding launch on the way to the mine, and I got this crazy idea that our film really needed an aerial shot of the mine. We had no budget for a powered flight, so I enlisted my good friend Jim Orava to tandem launch with me from above the mine, and then fly over it, while I got some excellent aerial shots. This was a few years before the use of drones became common in filming, and gave us a unique view.

And that is how the sport of paragliding started in Hedley BC. We had enlisted the support of the First Nations by giving the chief, his family, and many other band members free tandem rides, which they all truly enjoyed. We then showed the aerial footage to our friends, and a group of paragliders from Pemberton made a road trip over to Hedley and checked out the great flying there.

The feedback was so positive that plans for my event were soon well underway, and the three paraplegic paraglide pilots, along with several hundred other recreational pilots, arrived for our inaugural Cross Country event and Fly In. We have tried to make this an annual event and hold the Fly-In during the Canadian Thanksgiving weekend, as Hedley offers the last best place to thermal during the Canadian autumn. At that time of the year Hedley is often one of the warmest places on record in British Columbia.

The Thanksgiving Fly-Ins produced many memorable weekends in Hedley, a community that in a way is a very peculiar place. With a population of around 500 – half of which were natives with the other half being a strange combination of individuals seemingly settled there in order to escape from something or perhaps, someone. It really was different from most other places in Canada, and was full of these elderly people and artists resembling characters straight out of a Quentin Tarantino movie. Indeed, the director could have easily shot one of his twisted films in the town, getting inspiration for instance, from Hedley's own reclusive Buddhist monk. He lived up in the mountains above the town, in a cave he had converted into his own dwelling, and the rest of the town left him to his own devices.

During each of our events the town kindly provided us with a spot to stay. Sometimes we chose to camp outside a local pub whose owners greeted us with open arms. Another fellow we became great friends with was Rod Collins Moncrief, the local historical junk collector. Married to a much younger wife who had a daughter, Rod and his family had moved to Hedley long before any paragliders arrived. He showed us great hospitality, and also often hosted us during our paragliding trips there. His birthday coincided with our Fly-Ins and to celebrate it he would always have a great big dinner ready for us.

After all our tandem rides, we also quickly became friends with the First Nations. In fact, the Upper Simikameen Band became one of the sponsors for our paragliding events. There Their contribution was providing the shuttle for us up to the launch, using the same buses that they used when they were taking tourists up to the gold mine. One unforgettable night we were on the summit under a full moon, intending to attempt a flight down to the valley. Most of us thought twice about it and didn't launch, but several people did the flight and landed safely with the landing field lit up by the headlights of our cars.

Hedley really opened my eyes as to the wonder of paraplegic flying. I helped Polish pilot Andy Rosen to get to Hedley for the Fly-In all the way from Poland by persuading the Polish National Airline LOT to come through with a ticket for him. Unfortunately Andy had broken his back while coastal soaring next to the Baltic Sea in Poland in 1995. He could not give up on flying, and soon had his friends in adapt a wheelchair for flight. It wasn't long before he changed his launch technique and gave up using a wheelchair altogether, preferring to use his regular paraglide harness. He would sit on the ground and at the right time he would raise the glider to the appropriate position above his head. At that moment, two friends who were on either side of him, would lift him up and run with him as he launched. Andy really was an incredible pilot just to be able to take off in this way, and once he was in the air he was as good as any pilot.

The two other paraplegic pilots that joined the Fly-In at Hedley were both equally impressive pilots. One was an ex-British Special Forces guy who had broken his back rock climbing. He flew on a specially made little trike he had designed for himself, and launched on wheels. The third and final pilot was another Okanagan local, from Vernon. Lars was a former Olympic cross-country skier, but he had broken his spine in a mountain biking accident, and now he flew in his wheelchair.

Later on we had another local paraplegic flyer who often paraglided with us at home in Pemberton. Sam was really quite an athlete. He had won a medal in the world renowned extreme games in the dual slalom sit-ski competition. Sam was one very gutsy flyer, often doing long cross-country flights. I remember one particular incident when he went for a long flight from Pemberton but was forced to land near the highway in the middle of nowhere on the notorious Duffy Lake Road. He managed to flag down a very surprised truck driver, who loaded up his gear and returned him to Pemberton that evening. The balls that this takes, when you are guaranteed a to have a wilderness landing in your wheelchair, and then you have to cope with the difficulties of getting to a road, where you have to wait patiently for someone to show up, is extraordinary.

Later, after the Hedley adventure, another paraplegic pilot, Andy, joined us in Peru and Mexico. We would help him launch and off he would fly, often making record breaking flights. Once aloft, he would start looking for a soccer field or a landing place with people nearby. Once he made the decision to land, he would spot the field, land his paraglider. Then he had to crawl around, and ask for help folding his glider. He always managed to get a taxi back to the hotel, because everyone wanted to help once they understood his predicament. In Europe he says the same tactic works and he always made a habit of landing near a road, and then flagging down astonished drivers to pick him up.

1

2

Charm of Mexico and paragliding

1. Flying in Yelapa, Mexico.
These were pleasant beach landings.
2. The Baja peninsula also has impressive mountains besides it's fabulous beaches.
3. Good friend, Natali Vasquez from Medellin Colombia lands her paraglider in Pemberton, BC.
4. Ryszard Szafirski, Polish Himalayan legend, in Baja California on our road trip.
5. Tonya Solaris at La Malinche flight park in Tenancingo, Mexico.

3

4

5

Into the Paragliding world

1. Flying over one of my favorite places – Lillooet Lake near Pemberton.
2. The Hedley valley became a site for annual paragliding events.
3. The first ever paraplegic paragliding contest. In wheelchairs from left; Lars Taylor, Andy Campbell and Jedrzej Jaxa-Rozen.
4. Fred Beckey, the eternal "dirtbag" climber, still climbing at 92 near Squamish BC.
5. At a meeting discussing a new ski resort in Valemount. From left: Myself, Tomasso Oberti, Troy Jungen and Oberto Oberti.

CHAPTER 12

BACK TO PERU

In 2007, I received an invitation out of the blue to judge a film festival in Peru. The festival was named "Inkafest" and was being put on by an entrepreneur named Ivan Canturin from Lima. He had somehow found out about my ancient adventures in Peru, and there was even a climbing foundation named after Americo Tordoya, the man who had rescued me after my fall on Ranrapalca in 1979. I was thrilled to return to Peru because I had not been there since, so I accepted the invitation gladly.

Unfortunately, as so often has happened in my life, I had a 'small' accident just before my departure to Peru. I broke my fibula while top landing in Pemberton on our lower launch. The grass was about two feet tall where I had intended to land so it was hard to predict where the ground was beneath the tall grass. I had a not-too-hard landing, and I remember standing up and not even realizing I had done any damage. I was packing up my paraglider when I first noticed that I sprained my ankle through a full 180°! It is funny, as well as convenient, how shock sometimes prevents one from feeling pain. I got into the vehicle which we had parked up at the launch, and somehow drove myself down to the town clinic, where they informed me that my leg was indeed broken. Unfortunately the break was fairly high up my fibula so they had to totally immobilize my leg with a full cast. I was devastated by this setback, but feeling that it was too late to cancel my trip, I decided to go anyway, even with a full cast on my leg.

Initially I was a bit hesitant about going back to Peru after my 1979 fiasco and the stupid cocaine episode with Jake. It was a similar situation to the one I had experienced in Colombia as a teen in 1976, although when I went back there in 1998 nothing had actually happened. Luckily though the situation in Peru was also a similar bureaucratic mess, and I was in the clear because my "crimes" had occurred at a time before computers. So I felt my chances of getting caught for my past naughty deeds were very low. Hence, I chose to take the risk and go.

As things turned out there was no reason to be worried and I had an amazing time in Peru during the festival. I was wined and dined like a celebrity, and transported free of charge from Lima to Huaraz where the festival was taking place. This was the moment when I met one of the loves of my life, a girl named Jenny Altamirano, and she was so beautiful I could not take my eyes off her.

Jenny was really talented as a journalist, and I would work on several projects with her in the future. Unfortunately, I later tried to invite Jenny to Canada for a visit, but her Peruvian nationality meant that Canadian Immigration refused her a tourist visa. Jenny was a very proud woman, and the whole episode at the Canadian Embassy proved very embarrassing for her. Quite angry, I also felt that the whole episode with Canadian Immigration contributed towards me losing her in the end.

The initial year of Inkafest turned out to be a real success. It was well attended and had many great adventure films to show, and became the first of a continuing event.

While I was in Peru with my broken leg, I managed to enjoy two tandem flights even if the landings were a bit worrying. One was in Miraflores on the Pacific coast, and the other was high in the Andes above Cuzco and its Sacred Valley.

The Cuzco flight with my friend Jose Infantas above the Sacred Valley was the most special of them all. The flying was epic and we rose at a rate of 12 meters a second in the huge thermals. When it was time to land in the thin air, José had me lift my leg up as high as I could as he slid both of us in for the landing. Tandem flyers in Cusco and at the other higher altitudes zones had their own method for landing their passengers safely and had adapted the gear for the thinner air landings. Some of them riveted plastic crazy carpet-like skid devices to the bottom of the harnesses to help their passengers slide in gently at the landings. This techniques mandatory as due to the thin air the gliders came in rather fast, and getting the clients to run fast enough on landing would have led to too many accidents and broken legs as it was just too fast.

The tandem pilots in Miraflores, Lima down near the coast were in general intimidated by flying in the Andes. There were a few good mountain pilots there, such as my good friends Hubert and Lucho, but most of them were content with staying and soaring on the coast. Also, the pilots were making good money from the tandems, and maybe the money became as addictive as any drug.

Miraflores probably has one of the busiest commercial tandem operations in the world. Ideally situated in the popular "Parque del Amor" next to a boulevard filled with visitors from both abroad and Peru, all strolling above the cliffs along the ocean. The tandem operations were so busy that 10 pilots alternated each week. They would take turns flying their many clients. There was a little commercial tandem booth set up and it usually had a lineup of people waiting for their chance to soar on every flyable day.

From 2007 on I began regularly visiting Peru to see Jenny, as well as being involved with setting up a major project to be called X-Andes. This was inspired by the infamous Red Bull X-Alps race, which is held in the European Alps every two years. I wanted to do a smaller version of the European event and holding it in the awesome terrain of Peru. Starting in the north in the Ancash Valley, working southwards to finish in Huaraz. I considered maybe then having the pilots continue on all the way down to the coast, but this proved impractical. Jenny was involved in completing her masters in ecotourism at Lima university at the time, but helped me a great deal as we started to put a proposal for the project together.

She was improving as a paraglider, and one day we went to the sand dunes south of Lima, and Lucho just let her go for it and fly away from the nest as it were. She made her first maiden flight that day after some rudimentary instructions. I was proud of her bravery that day, and it was an impressive sight to see her take off successfully over the golden dunes.

While working on the X-Andes project I got yet another invitation that I could not refuse. A man, claiming to be a shaman from the Dominican Republic, and was now living in the US, needed a guide to take him into the Kogi lands of the Sierra Nevada de Santa Marta. He had somehow heard about my adventure with the Kogis 10 years before, and e-mailed me while I was in Peru.

Of course I instantly agreed to the task and said yes. This time, I came up with the craziest idea of all. I would bring my paraglider along, because I wanted to see if the Kogi would allow me to fly over their sacred lands. After all, this time I was not going to touch their sacred snows with skis on, which had been the problem on the last trip. This time it would be different, I felt, as I would be admiring the mountains of the spectacular Kogi territory from above, with a wing on.

The shaman had a Russian wife. They offered to pay for my airline ticket to Colombia, and cover some of my expenses for guiding them. We were to meet in Santa Marta in January 2008, where we would organize porters and mules and begin our eight-day trek into the Sierra.

Surprisingly, if you've read this far, this trip actually came to fruition. I was excited because I had a brand-new paraglider from a top Swiss company called Advance. I also had an assignment to write an article for Cross Country Magazine, which was the biggest magazine in the paragliding industry, and virtually the Bible for the sport, so I felt it was quite a big deal.

Upon arrival in Santa Marta I was freaked out that my wing was nowhere to be seen. It should have arrived by now from the US distributers and so I anxiously sat it out in Santa Marta. I was extremely worried that it might not come at all.

American Airlines, or at least their office in Colombia had a bad reputation for thefts on flights. Indeed, that had been the case 10 years earlier on my first trip when Kristen Ulmer had lost all her ski equipment which was never to been recovered.

I decided to go on the warpath against the airline. After getting the 1-800 number for the baggage claim department, I emailed about 20 of my friends and asked them to phone the number every 10 minutes or so, to enquire about the whereabouts of my wayward paraglider. My strategy worked, because we tied up their phone lines so much about the subject of my missing wing that it magically showed up in Barranquilla. I was incredibly relieved when I got a phone call to pick it up.

I was fortunate enough to be put in touch with a woman from Bogotá. Andrea Molina was a veterinarian, and she had already been in the Sierra on a Colombian Government project, counting the Condor population that resided in the mountains. Even better, she was also a Himalayan climber, with an ascent of Shisha Pangma in Tibet under her belt. I invited her to join us in our little expedition to guide the shaman and his Russian wife, and luckily she accepted the offer.

Back in Vancouver I had another couple who wanted to accompany us on the trek as well. Dominik Bac was a Polish photographer for that country's arm of the National Geographic. He had just completed the Northwest Passage on a small yacht, sailing south from the Arctic around Alaska all the way to Vancouver, which was an unprecedented feat. His wife had always wanted to go into the Sierra so they were keen to join us.

Another person on our team was a young Polish lady Kaja Kosiuk, who I had met in Pemberton while camping with Polish friends. She was working in IT in Panama, and since she was so close to Colombia I invited her to join us as well.

So a varied crew assembled for my second journey into the Sierra or, as the Kogi call it "The Heart of the World." As the situation unfolded however, the American shaman and his wife became rather unbearable. It turned out they were on this trip to see if they could bring tours into "The Heart of the World." They wanted to exploit the Kogi, rather than be of any help to them.

So we left them in the lower village to practice their magic with the Arhuaco tribe who were already habituated to contact with little brother. Unlike the Kogi, the Arhuacos are a tribal group who are more influenced by and comfortable with modern civilization. Although they wore clothing similar to the Kogis, their members would often make the long walk from the Sierra into the heavily populated city of Santa Marta. Our guide, Argemiro, who was an Arhuaho, even had a regular modern-day clothing which he would switch to upon reaching the city.

This suited them because they were sufficiently enamoured with the exotic nature of the Arhuaco and didn't need to travel further.

It actually took some doing for us to go any higher. I had to do a ground-handling demonstration with my paraglider to the natives in the lower village, to try and explain what I wanted to do. This was necessary because I needed to get their permission to carry on further on our journey.

As I had hoped, the natives were impressed by my paraglider and my plans to fly without touching their sacred snows. As well, they were curious to watch me flying from below. They gave me the thumbs up.

We proceeded higher with our guide Argemiro, who helped carry my paraglider up to an elevation of about 2,000 meters. After a five hour hike I found a ridge that I thought would be a good place to launch.

I have crystal clear recollection of being very sick with a stomach flu as we reached the summit ridge and I planned for takeoff. Even though I felt exhausted from the stomach virus I decided that having come such a long way, I was going to fly despite all odds. The ridge launch spot had an obstacle – 3 feet of long native grass growing on it. Our faithful guide came to the rescue. Argemiro took out his machete and in short order had cleared a suitable area for take-off.

My original plan was to gain enough altitude and actually fly back to the beaches of the Caribbean near the city of Santa Marta. If that actually happened the crew had agreed to hike down and meet me on the coast.

Since I had hadn't flown the glider yet I was anxious as I waited for the perfect thermal and forgot about the stomach ailment. The thermals formed around 10am, hidden bubbles of hot air rising above the Heart of the World. I could see the evidence of them in the way they brushed the grasses and how the breeze felt on my face. The wing came up perfectly on my first try and I managed to launch without a problem and rapidly gain altitude above the vast Sierra Nevada de Santa Marta.

I looked towards the Caribbean side to see that there was an ocean of clouds between me and the beaches. Since I didn't have a GPS with me, I wouldn't have known how to successfully navigate through the cloud layer in order to land on the beach instead of the ocean. Instead

I turned away from the ocean, flew around for about an hour, and then decided to land in the village of Taminaca where we had been 10 years before with our motley crew of skiers. I had told our current group to meet me in Taminaca if they saw me headed that way.

As I approached the grass field I had chosen for my landing zone I was fortunate to miss a large granite boulder. Upon touchdown, I seriously spooked two Kogi women that were walking and carrying firewood nearby. After witnessing a man drop out of the sky, they instantly turned and ran in the other direction.

All in one piece, I brushed off the dust off my flight suit, packed up my glider, and proceeded to walk into the town. To my surprise it was totally deserted. Only one guy from Santa Marta lived there in one of the empty huts. He gave me some coca tea and took care of me while I rested for the day, while my other friends from the expedition hiked all the way down from the ridge to meet me. It was strange to see the once so vibrant village deserted like that. I wondered why.

Throughout our expedition we had been following the Colombian army, which had been cleaning out the jungle of remnants of the FARC guerrillas who had been known to take up refuge in the Sierra. Ten years earlier, during our unsuccessful ski expedition here, we had heard of a group of eight tourists which were captured on the more popular trek in the lower Sierra. One of them, a British fellow, had managed to escape by jumping into a river and swimming out of his captors' range.

I was actually very impressed with the way the Colombian army Colonel had been directing his battalion's operation in the Sierra. He always had the army camp sited on the outskirts of a Kogi village, never wanting to be overly intrusive on their native habitat. Another fact with our group was that it was made up of five women and only three men, and I think that helped us both with the Kogis, as well as with the Army. Women are universally thought to be less aggressive and intrusive than men, and that probably worked in our favour.

We also had photographs from my ski expedition 10 years earlier with us, which we showed to them to prove we had already visited the area. My photos included shots of several Mamos who had died in various accidents in the Sierra. It was sad to see that they were now gone, but we realized the Kogi population was unfortunately shrinking abruptly.

After so many generations of healthy separation, Colombian rebels had encroached on their land with illicit coca plantations and labs in the jungle. There had also been an influx of adventure tourists, although not all of them were as misguided as our shaman, but this too had taken a toll on the Kogi.

The fate of the Kogi is so troubling because according to anthropologists they are said to be the last surviving members of the civilizations that were once active throughout both Americas. It is also said that they are the true descendants of the Tairona culture, which once had thrived on the Caribbean coast.

By civilization, it is given that the Tairona, like the great civilizations of the Aztecs, Maya and Inca, left behind big monuments, roads and structures. This was unlike other indigenous cultures which were more typically hunter and gatherers and did not make permanent structures out of stone.

Back in Taminaca and now fully rested, I was still really sick to my stomach.

By the late afternoon, the others had managed to hike down to meet me as planned.

Now we all had to hike back up to the ridge where I had launched from, getting there by dark. Kaja was waiting there for us, as she was also really sick. A kind Kogi family let her rest in their little mud hut.

We put up our tents and spent the night in the village. The next morning we packed up our bags, said our goodbyes, and started the long journey out to the Caribbean. I was still feeling under the weather, so I rented a mule from a nearby village on our way down in order to make things a little easier on me. The ride down on the mule was rather terrifying because these incredible animals go down very steep slopes, not stopping for anything and several times I was nearly thrown off.

We spent the last day relaxing in Santa Marta, before we all flew back home. We had parted earlier from the Russian lady and her shaman husband, and I never kept in touch after that. It had been a good decision in the end to not take them further up than the Arhuacos and into the Kogi lands. I think they would have only tarnished the innocent Kogis with their bizarre ideas.

In the end, everyone got what they wanted from the trip. The shaman and his wife got to meet some natives in the Sierra. When we left them they seemed quite content, and they had definitely got their money's worth, and the innocence of the Kogis was left untouched. Kaja, Andrea, Dominik and his wife all experienced the adventure of their lives. As for me, I got a plane ticket, and some expenses to visit the most special place I have ever visited.

I spent much of the next year editing the film about the expedition, which was called "Sacred Flight", with the help of a new partner, Ivan Hughes who did an amazing job co-directing and editing the finished picture with me. It ended up being one of my best productions, and I was really pleased when it was accepted into the big Vancouver International Film Festival. This was a big step up from the smaller mountain film festivals that my earlier films had been shown at. All told, the trip had been a huge success for me and being back in the Sierra for the second time was a pleasure despite the sickness and my weird sponsoring couple.

In the summer of 2008, I was invited to judge several film festivals in Poland and the Czech Republic, and thus I returned to Europe. My good old friend, Arthur Makosinski, had given me a great idea for yet another film, which was to be called Paracinderella. "Peter", he said, "The best way for you to find a partner or a soul mate in what you love to do is probably just to make a film about it."

Indeed, my dream has always been to find a partner in life who was also a paraglide pilot. I had watched the cult classic American film "Sherman's March", about a documentary filmmaker who was supposedly following the Civil War, but instead was really looking for a female to make documentary films with and be a life partner. This film became an inspiration for my latest effort.

Years later, I actually met a real film buff, who recognized elements of "Sherman's March" in my film, and I was happy to see that somebody else had recognized what I was trying to do with „Paracinderella."

As I left for Europe, my plan was to meet up with as many paragliding women as I could in Poland, Slovakia, the Czech Republic and France. I would also look for new paragliding friends in any places where I was attending or judging film festivals.

My filming odyssey resumed in August 2008 when I arrived in Poland. For the first part of my trip to my homeland I was based in Krakow at my cousin's place and while I was there I found out about a great flying site not too far away, at ZAR Mountain. The place was also a popular glider plane airport. With its local paragliding school, it made a great home base for me. I thought it was a good place to start with, as I would meet various paragliding women who were learning to fly. It was awkward at first, approaching all these women but I was honest and upfront with them. I told them that it was indeed my intention to find a partner to fly with for life. I explained to them that the romantic segments in my film were also meant to be humorous. Sometimes the women would understand the idea and really flirt and play along with the Paracinderella story, making it really fun.

When I first arrived in Krakow I met my initial test case – a brunette in her 20's that was a beginner paraglide pilot. At first it felt really awkward to proposition women to be in my documentary. I was lucky though because the first girl had a great sense of humour and totally caught the drift of what I was trying to do. She helped to build my confidence in continuing with the idea.

To add some drama. I had a separate mission to complete. I was carrying the ashes of my favourite aunt Danuta, from Montréal with me to Poland for her service there. I even filmed the funeral as a segment in the Paracinderella film which was now becoming my autobiography, of sorts, on film.

I continued my paraholic ways – a word contrived with my friend Jim Orava.

I had become one of the "Pemberton Flying Monkeys", as I had passed the most difficult period, what many call the "Intermediate Flying Syndrome" or a stage in ones paragliding life which was considered the most dangerous. This is when pilots begin to gain a bit of confidence and they feel they are now experts after learning to thermal, and get to think they are invincible. That stage for me had resulted in a few close calls, and a few broken bones.

All in all though, after 12 years of serious flying, I thought I was doing great. The essence of paragliding is finding lift in the atmosphere so one can maximize the time aloft.

I had achieved this in a big way flying cross country during my own record flight from Golden BC south along the Columbia River valley to Invermere. The flight was aided by being pushed down wind and took four and a half hours, and I covered 112 km.

I actually hadn't even planned to land in Invermere as I wanted to keep going. My plan was to fly as far as I could that day as the conditions were so perfect, but it was the end of the day. As luck would have it I came down on the beach on Lake Windermere.

I wanted to do more cross country flights, it intrigued me because it was the most challenging as you have to calculate the risks of crossing terrain which had no landing spots until finding lift again and continuing on. The XC record then was over 300 km set in South Africa. That mark has since been broken in Brazil where three paraglide pilots managed an incredible 560km. They were able to go so far by flying close together and helping each other with finding lift along the way. It had been a team effort.

A lot goes into a good XC flight including being lucky with the winds that day and having enough daylight to fly for over 8 hours. The record flight in Brazil had thermals starting as early as 6 am thus allowing close to 12 hours in flying time.

Continuing the story of my little romantic paragliding epic, one highlight happened in the Sudety Mountains of South Western Poland, where I managed to have a few laughs with Anna Czerwinska, who is a respected Polish climber and author. A household name in Poland, she is best known for being the second Polish women to summit Everest and for her exploits on K2. She is also the first Polish woman to climb the Seven Summits.

I took Anna to a local ski hill near Ladek Zdroj, which is a hot springs resort that has welcomed European royalty since the Middle Ages. I had been invited to judge the film festival held at the resort that has since become the biggest mountain festival in Poland.

Anna was intrigued by paragliding, and I had my wing with me so I thought this would be a great time to let her practice some takeoffs on a gentle grassy slope at the ski resort. We had a lot of laughs as we hurled our carcasses forward trying a few hilarious launches and landings. An afternoon I'll never forget. I even found out about

Anna's publisher, Annapurna, the one I am using for the Polish version of this book.

May she rest in peace, as she sadly passed away on January 31st 2023.

I had always wanted to fly off another particular ski hill, Poland's Kasprowy Wierch. It is a popular ski resort in the winter and a favourite sightseeing destination by summer. The peak is in the national Park and so paragliding is not allowed. It is serviced by an aerial tram which replaced an older one built in pre-World War II days.

A couple weeks after introducing Anna to paragliding in early October, another paraglide friend of mine from Warsaw, Jerzy Kraus and I took the tram up to the peak which was engulfed in a small dark cloud. It had also snowed about a meter and we were in a total white out when the gondola reached the top station. Anticipating the conditions, I had memorized and knew which direction the valley lay. I then commandeered the six tourists who were up there, to hold up my glider as there was no wind. I pulled up the wing, screamed at my helpers to let go, and ran frantically through the knee-high snow. Somehow I managed to launch safely, and emerged from the cloud above the middle of the valley a few minutes later and then landed safely in Zakopane about 15 minutes later.

It was a short but memorable flight which I had always wanted to do. Jerzy followed me a half hour later when conditions allowed him to launch.

On this trip I also managed to fly in the Jasna ski resort which is in the Lower Tatra Mountains of Slovakia, which I had last visited as a 12 year old with my parents.

Another welcome respite from sitting in dark theatres judging films was a chance to make a flight taking off from Czarna Gora in the Czech Republic, which was close to the festival in Teplice. Upon landing it was a pleasant coincidence to run into a paragliding friend all the way from Pemberton. Peter Bronfman had moved back to the Czech Republic from Pemberton, and meeting him was a complete surprise.

On the way to the festival in Teplice I stopped in Wroclaw and spent some time with Jedrzej (Andy) Jaxa-Rozen, the paraplegic paraglide pilot who I had become good friends with flying in Hedley, Peru, and

Mexico. As it was getting late in the season, the flights were shorter but it was such a joy to fly with friends.

I then packed my bags and joined a commercial Polish paragliding tour to France. I was intending to fly at Annecy and Chamonix, and also I hoped to witness the famous air sports Festival in St Hilaire, France.

I also took the opportunity to make a side trip to La Grave to attend the wedding of my good friend Ptor Spricenieks. Ptor and I even managed a short paraglide flight from his lodge up above the village of La Grave on his wedding day! It made quite the nice entrance. Quite often the valley is too windy to fly but we were lucky that day. The wedding turned out to be an interesting mix of Ptor's many hippie friends, as well as a very straight contingent from Belgium who seemed to be mostly bankers – friends of the family of the woman he had married.

Paragliding had now entered my life with a vengeance. I had thought nothing would compare with powder skiing, but I now realized flying was even better. All other sports went out the window, only to be practiced when the weather kept us grounded. It didn't matter were you were the world if the weather allowed for flight the high of simply being like a bird in a foreign land trumped all else.

For sure, Europe was the paragliding mecca, with so many varied locations to fly from and so many great pilots to learn from.

This may be a good time to explain the different styles or disciplines of paragliding out there these days:

There is Cross Country competition flying, where pilots follow a pre-planned course of GPS co-ordinates, and is like a big slalom course in the air. The first to reach the end wins.

Then there are the Accuracy flying competitions with spot landings. This involves having to land as close to the centre of a target which is placed on the landing zone. This competition originated in Slovenia and is now an official competition. I organized a small demonstration Accuracy competition in Huaraz one year, along with the Inkafest Film Festival.

The next style is called Acrobatic flying and does what it says. The pilot spins and stalls the glider, which enables him or her to do manoeuvres such as one called the Infinity, where the pilot goes over his wing spinning as many times as possible, which leads to getting some incredible G forces and is spectacular to watch.

Finally (as of today) there is Speed Flying, pilots use smaller wings, and often fly on skis to make the landing as safe as possible, Reaching over 80km per hour, often skimming the terrain, these flights resemble the skydiving Squirrel Suit flyers with their "proximity flying". These are the most dangerous flights of all. Pilots skim ridge tops and drop down through gullies and ravines in these stunts, and at these high speeds a tiny error is sure death.

Although I am not saying that normal paragliding is totally safe, landing a speed-flight with skis on or without in summer is much more dangerous than normal flying.

Another type of gliding is known as Proximity Flying. which is derived from the ultra-dangerous BASE jumping from stationary objects such as towers, buildings and mountain tops is probably the craziest of all. Somebody said professional base jumpers have a 6 year life span at the most. Base jumpers, such as my friends Bridget and Natali, have lost so many friends in this sport. I am worried about Natali, my Colombian friend who has just started base jumping after years of skydiving, and she is also starting to fly with a wing-suit so she can do Proximity flying.

As far as my own goals in paragliding I would be happy to continue flying for fun and have no interest in competing in XC comps, but rather flying long distances for fun and being safe. I have no interest in Acrobatics, as the idea of deliberately making my wing not fly just terrifies me. I have never skydived, but I am intrigued by the idea of making a relatively controlled BASE jump off a Fjord in Norway, just once, to see how it feels. Jim Orava did a flight once on the French island of Reunion and told me he loved it. Speed flying using skis for the take-off and landing intrigues me due to my long ski history. When I started paragliding all those years ago I used a small canopy which was effectively very similar to a skydiving wing. We never did the speeds of speed gliders today but it was still relatively fast flying, probably reaching 60 kph.

Returning to the summer of 2008. Troy, who had been with us at Ptor's wedding in La Grave, came and joined me while I was in Poland and he did some rock climbing while I was paragliding and filming.

It was so nice to have him there and to show him around the old country as he had made a real effort to join me, even renting a car which made our travels around Poland a lot easier.

At my side was my trusty JVC HDV camera, which was a palm sized camera and used the smallest broadcast compatible format of the time called mini-DV tape. Cheap and disposable, this camera was really useful during the Paracinderella shoot and everything went really well.

I met a lot of interesting female pilots while filming along the way. However, one of them, after agreeing to be in the film, got upset when her clip was put up on YouTube. It turned out her new boyfriend had got jealous when he saw her starring in the 12 minute segment, and had it removed from YouTube.

As soon as I had got back to Canada, my friend Pawel managed to talk me into accompanying him to Peru and Chile again.

A few days later, and we were on the plane to Lima to meet the marketing director of the biggest luxurious hotel chain in South America, a company called Casa Andina. Pawel was an amazing salesman, and in a very positive and upbeat manner, he pitched our scheme to the marketing director of the hotel chain, who was named Inigo Maneiro. The proposition was the familiar one, we were making a documentary movie about meeting girls while paragliding, and could we please have some hotel rooms for free while we filmed.

Our crew consisted of Maciek Siwocha, who had been on our first journey to Colombia and had also started to paraglide with us. Along also were other good friends: Peyman Imani, a relatively new pilot who had just starting acrobatic flying with Pawel, Tyler Armstrong, an old friend and memorable character, was with us as well as Pawel's son Philip, he too was just learning how to paraglide. Another one of "Pawel's Family Posse" with us was Kamil, Pawels cousin. He had his first flights on the coast near Lima.

Pawel's sales-pitch had worked and Inigo gave us free accommodation at three of their hotels in Miraflores, Lima and Cuzco, as well as in the town of Arequipa. It was very entertaining to watch our motley crew of dirtbag paraglider suddenly being teleported into such luxury accommodations. The hotels were unlike anything we had experienced on our earlier travels. Most of the other guests at these high-end hotels were not very friendly to us and, in general, the other ultra-rich clientele around us did not seem like a very happy lot – it seemed they rarely smiled while we just had a grand old time. Each morning the hotel would provide a huge complementary brunch buffet, from which we would fill up our doggy bags. There was free food for the rest of the day, during our filming and paragliding, just like on a big movie set.

We think we got about $6,000 worth of hotel rooms from our new friend Inigo. I guess he must've really liked us. At the same time though he was also leaving the company, so his gift of free accommodation to us could be seen as his last going away hurrah with the Casa Andina hotel chain. We even befriended the hotel manager at the Cuzco location, a beautiful woman Sandra, and got her flying with us on tandems. Although the other guests just grumpily scurried around the hotels, usually giving us the dirty eye look, we partied it up every night and probably left quite a reputation behind us. The Casa Andina hotel chain was really quite incredible. Every hotel was unique and fitted its environment. While the hotel in Lima was a very modern skyscraper, the one in Cusco, for example, was an old monastery on the outside but had been totally renovated with modern fittings inside. The one in Arequipa was also incredible and one of the finest I've ever been in. These establishments set a new benchmark in luxury for me, and certainly out-did the Sheraton hotels that had sponsored us on the DC-3 flight back in 1986. We were all dumbfounded at times by the level of luxury we were suddenly living in.

After our stint of 5-star luxury in Peru, we got on a bus and headed south from Lima for the Aticama desert and the city of Iquique in Chile, which was known to have some of the best paragliding conditions in the world. Apparently you could start kiting your glider right at sea level here. Then before you knew it you were about 20 feet higher on the dune, then you flew back a bit, and made your way higher and higher as the dunes increased in height. Suddenly you were way, way high up over the Andes, taking advantage of the thermals pushed in by the warm sea breeze from the Pacific.

I really hadn't experienced anything like this paragliding anywhere else in the world. The area receives virtually no rainfall, when we arrived, word was that it hadn't rained in 14 years. We established our base camp in Iquique at the Altazar flight school, which was run by a Swiss pilot called Philippe, who had been there for quite some time and had married a Chilean wife. His flight school and accommodation consisted of a courtyard surrounded by stacked shipping containers, which he had converted into hostel type accommodation.

Pilots from all over the world would converge on the place for the amazing flying the area had to offer. We spent several memorable weeks there flying our brains out, and filming with various women from Brazil and elsewhere that arrived to do some flying.

One such flier was Danuza. She was average height, and looked as if she had a Portuguese or a European background. She was an Iquique regular and a good pilot and we quickly made friends. I told her about "Paracinderella." And asked if she would appear in it and she agreed to play along and gave me a great on-camera interview. We both laughed because up to now, both of us hadn't found a partner as our wings were more important to us than another human. Danuza joined our crew for the rest of the trip, but unfortunately for me, she took a liking to Maciek and my hopes faded again.

There was one hilarious incident when after a wild night of Polish-style vodka drinking, Pawel and Maciek took Philippe's Unimog four-wheel drive beast of a machine for a joyride around his property. Somehow the vehicle got stuck in drive and they couldn't bring it to a halt. They eventually managed to control it by driving it into a concrete wall where it lodged itself with all its wheels churning the dust until it ran out of fuel and the engine finally died.

We next headed 250 km north to Pisagua. Here we were briefly given a dose of the brutal reality of living under the Pinochet regime. It was in this barren wind-swept desert where Pinochet's goons murdered and buried an unknown number of his left-wing opponents. A local showed us the grave sites, which lie silently in the ground. We will never know the exact number of people that are buried here, but it is in the thousands.

Our return home was made by retracing our steps the long way back up to Lima.

Once in Lima, we had time to make another detour up to Huaraz. However, the rainy season had arrived high up in the Peruvian Andes and the paragliding was rather poor. We were able to do some shorter flights at a couple of locations in the Ancash Valley, which is on the way to Huaraz. Of course, not everything went according to plan and while I was flying in the Pachacamak area near Lima one day, I had a very scary and unforgettable experience. Pawel and Jose Infantas had set out on a cross-country flight, which took them from the launch over very barren desert site and back again. I followed their route later in my paraglider. Everything was hunky-dory until I got to the most remote part of the route over the desert. I found myself in a huge sink, and realized I had no choice but to land. The only question was where to come down?

The landscape was totally barren and featureless and I knew I was in real trouble. Landing would have meant hiking out a distance of some 25 km across the sand dunes and in the heat of the day, to get to the nearest road.

Thankfully I got lucky! Again.

I spotted a vehicle and managed to land near the car. It was parked near what had once been an entrance to a mine, and the Peruvians who were sitting in the car were quite surprised at my sudden appearance. Once they had got over their shock, they kindly drove me back to the highway, and I was able to catch a bus back to our base. With that close encounter with trouble behind me, my friends and I managed to get some wonderful soaring over the cost at Miraflores, where it was sunny that time of the year. Using the constant breeze that blew in off the Pacific, which then mixed with the thermals that grew over Lima itself, we were able to go high and then back over the city for a short distance. However we were always careful to be able to fly back to the cliffs above the seashore. Some pilots have started a flight from the coast and flying over the city of Lima itself, and got as far as the foothills of the Andes. But crossing over Lima, with its population of 12 million people, was a very risky proposition. I was amazed that we were allowed to fly over part of the city as it was filled with a lot of air traffic, mostly helicopters. It is totally banned in Vancouver, although several rebel pilot friends I know might have soared over all of Vancouver's beaches, and the skyline of the West End of the city.

Back in Canada by spring, I continued working on the " Paracinderella" production. I managed to take a side trip to Oceanside in Oregon for a beautiful soaring session, once again filming with Pawel and Tyler Armstrong.

Once I was back in Pemberton, I met a girl one day at our landing zone which is on the local soccer pitch. Bridgit Liss was a single mother and she was riding her bike with her eight year old son, Shaefer. She got to make an appearance in my movie. She was a base jumper, who had spent two years in Utah's Zion National Park, climbing and jumping off things with her girlfriend. She was now in Pemberton and had been watching us paragliding and wanted to take up the sport herself, but she needed some equipment.

As often happens, Bridgit's equipment arrived in the luggage of a girl I had met earlier in Peru. A change in romance played a part, because the girl had just quit paragliding, because her new boyfriend was a mountain biker. Thus a new boyfriend meant she took up a new sport, and she was selling her gear, the glider, harness, reserve 'chute, helmet, and even a radio, for a mere $2,500 Canadian dollars. I told Bridget it was the deal of the century and she shouldn't pass it up. She took my advice and had her a wing. I then tried to teach Bridget how to fly, and she scared a lot of my friends because her launches were terrifying. She would run off the mountain fearlessly because she was a base jumper. She would head to the edge without any doubts at all, giving everybody else the jitters on launch.

I decided that it would be best for me to take Bridget to Hedley to learn. The gentle takeoff and big landing field were perfect to learn on. There were few other paraglide pilots around to feel uncomfortable while Bridget ran off the mountain, and she did a few great flights there, considering she was a beginner. They were good enough to be used the Paracinderella film.

Although we never did get it together as a couple, she has turned out to be a great friend. She had a second child, Everest, with a Brazilian lover, but with two young boys in tow, she came to realize she couldn't afford to paraglide anymore. So she sold her gear and moved to a hippie commune on Vancouver Island, and we still stay in touch on social media.

By 2006 my mother and I had managed to sell half of our property in Pemberton to an old friend from my early skiing days in Whistler,

Chris Kettles. This enabled us to finally build our own house at last. Chris is a great friend from our ski bumming years and I am so happy to have him now as a neighbour. He is also a good buddy of Troy and Ptor, he made an appearance in the highly acclaimed documentary "Ski Bums", made by my friend and Oscar-winning filmmaker, John Zaritzky.

Chris grooms the slopes as a snow cat driver on Blackcomb in the winter and is also an avid backcountry skier who, during the summers, swaps a groomer for a boat as a fishing guide.

He was able to build his own dream house and marry his long-time Whistler sweetheart, Margo, and they have a wonderful boy named Jack. Both Margo and Chris were former paraglide pilots but, after they had a child, they decided the risks were too great and both stopped flying. Perhaps waiting till Jack was older before beginning again.

A devoted dad, Chris regularly takes his son skiing and fishing. In addition Chris and Margo took Jack along on exotic holidays to the Philippines, Nicaragua, El Salvador and Mexico, in order to let their son experience the world outside of Canada at a young age.

I admire them for that, recalling my own life-changing experience of seeing South American during those early adventures with my parents. There is really little else, beyond exotic travel, that teaches us to really appreciate the way our world goes around.

In Canada, we live in such a safe and protective environment that it is important for our kids to see how the vast majority of the rest of the world really lives in order to appreciate what we have. I do think that if more people could do this or had the means to do it, especially in the United States, the world would be a much better place.

My Mom and I used the proceeds from selling half our acreage to build our own dream home in the mountains. The original plans included a rental suite, so that we could have some extra income, and sometimes I rent the main portion of the house out as a luxury vacation rental, which gives me some income to travel and work on my projects.

Since the house was finished I have been lucky to welcome many of the friends who I have met on my adventures around the world, offering cheaper accommodation in the upper loft which I made big and open, dormitory style. It has about eight beds available for friends to just throw their sleeping bags on for more affordable lodging – a very rare commodity in the Pemberton-Whistler area.

It took three years to build our house. Our first contractor, who laid the foundations, started well but the bills kept climbing, and we had to rethink our project.

I got in touch with another old friend, Tom Simister, and luckily he was able to take over the whole job using his own people and his team of contracted carpenters. Tom was a ski instructor turned snowboarder and master carpenter. He had started out at Jim McConkey's ski school, and we had actually worked together when I first arrived in Whistler and found a job in the ski rental department.

Tom got help for some of the bigger jobs like putting up the main beams and subcontracted out other specialized tasks like the roof. Tom was such a good builder.

We were also very lucky to have the plans drawn for free by Oberto Oberti. Oberto has designed the ski resort at Kicking Horse, and took a liking to me after I got to know him while making the GOLDENRUSH film.

I love my home on Reid Road above Pemberton. We have fantastic views of Mt Currie to the South, and of the mountains surrounding Lilloett Lake to the South East. It is situated just a short 15 minute climb by four-wheel-drive to the lower paraglide launch and a few of my friends have also bought property and built houses on the same road. At one time we had 15 paraglide pilots living on it, which was probably the biggest concentration of flyers living on one street in Canada, and perhaps all of North America.

We actually thought about making a reality TV series with my good friend and editor Barry Backus. It was to be called „Reid Road Flyers", but was another one of those projects that we just couldn't get off the ground. Now, thinking back, it may well have been quite the invasion of privacy. Since our plan was to keep the cameras rolling on the private lives and families, of individual pilots and couples on Reid Road in between the times they would be actually flying. Reality shows usually like to document real people in their natural home environment.

The Pemberton community was full of these eclectic pilots so we certainly had a good cast of characters for our show. There was Peyman

Imani of Iranian descent on Reid Road. A good friend of Pawel's, Peyman built a beautiful villa like place right on Ivy Lake after he also discovered how great the flying was above us off Mount McKenzie.

Visiting pilot friends such as Norwegian prankster Stein Myhrstad are often holed up here clowning about and playing guitar. Peyman has a great sauna in the yard close to the lake. In winter when the snow is deep and ice covers the lake, we have chopped a hole in the ice and jumped in during some memorable sauna sessions.

There was also a Russian contingent. Dennis and Tanya Rumyantsev, had just immigrated to Vancouver from Moscow. They had two young boys who also started paragliding as tandem passengers in Pemberton with us. I had gotten Tanya started in paragliding by arranging a sponsorship for her from SKY COUNTRY paragliders, a Ukrainian manufacturer. She has also played a role in my „Airhead Diaries" film.

The couple took up the sport with a passion. Tanya has since passed all her tandem and instructor exams along with Denis and they were able to build a lucrative business in the Fraser Valley, giving people both a first taste of flying and instructions on how to do it.

Dennis is a gifted Cross Country flyer. He managed to complete a fearless first flight from Pemberton all the way to the Fraser Valley. A very impressive undertaking that took him 8 hours to fly the 168 km route. Crossing over a remote no man's land and Grizzly country with few places to land except on the shores of two massive lakes, Harrison and Lillooet, for a road landing or perhaps coming down on some knarly logging slashes or ducking under the Hydro lines to find a spot.

The Russians seem to take well to the sport of paragliding. There were several other Russian pilots that lived in Vancouver including Igor Tolsky who flew some amazing record breaking triangles around the mountains here. Flying cross country triangles is done in one day with the idea being you come back to where you started from. Flying triangles is tricky because to take advantage of thermals one has to fly eastern sun facing slopes in the morning, and fly back over western facing slopes in the afternoon. Igor especially amazed us with the risks he took flying in no man's land as did Dennis. Yes, the Russians like to push the envelope in this sport.

I have owned two Delicas, which are a superior four-wheel-drive vehicle very useful in the Pemberton Valley, both on and off the highway and popular among outdoor adventurers such as paragliders. BC has about 2,000 of them in circulation in the province. They tend to sit in the garage in Tokyo, hardly used at all since 4x4 travel possibilities in Japan are rather rare.

I managed to write-off my first Delica while coming back from the hot springs one morning with a young lady friend. It was early morning and I must have been distracted looking over to my friend.

It hadn't rained for a month but on that late June morning there had been some sporadic showers. A month of dust blown on to the road and a month of oil spots leaking from cars combined to form a very slick road – like black ice in winter.

I was travelling 30 km per hour as I rounded a curve and all of a sudden we were gliding sideways on the highway. It became one of those slow motion experiences, we just sat silently in our seats then slowed down to nearly a crawl. Then the Delica hit dry pavement, and voila, being top heavy we rolled twice then ended up sitting right side up, on the wheels, with our seat belts on, which was better than the alternatives. The beloved van was totalled though.

Due to high demand Delicas appreciate in value, especially in BC, so the insurance paid me it's true worth. I went and I bought a second Delica, which I have to this very day, no more highway rolls! I adore my new 1998 turbo diesel 4x4 Delica, which I bought with 111,000 km on the clock and the tire jack never even used. I wish I had the money to convert my diesel-burning Delica into an electric vehicle one day but, for now, it has great gas mileage on the highway. It also has the torque in its low gears so one can walk faster than the car can travel downhill – and with hardly even touching the brakes.

It's funny but the incident reminded me of the time we went off the road, also on slick red dust, in Brazil back in 1972 in the trusty VW camper.

Unfortunately, over the years tragedy has struck our cast of pilots. We lost four good friends who had flown with us for many years, and two of them were in paragliding incidents. Marty was a forestry park ranger, who died from cancer and for whom his best friend Oni still holds an annual Summer Solstice party at the lower paraglide launch. It always turns out to be a great all night rave party. One night I counted nine other Delicas parked at the lower launch for the Marty Party. Basically everybody goes up, takes anything from mushrooms to ecstasy, and dances all night for Marty's spirit.

We also lost Rudy Rozsypalek, a dear friend and paraglide pilot who ran the local glider school. Rudy came from the Czech Republic and tragically died when his glider plane hit a Cessna in a midair collision above our valley. Rudy was a generous guy and had a heart of gold. He had worked hard on preparing our paraglide launches. He even helped us get some great aerial footage for „The Good Life" using his motorized glider to take up cameraman Chris Lockhart.

Then of course, there was Judd, a real character who drove our shuttle to launch for many years. He was a self-taught flyer, as many of us had been and never really took much care to learn the sport properly. On one outing Judd was going to fly to meet a bunch of friends camping overnight and top land on Copper Dome Mountain, something we did often in Pemberton. But then, he just disappeared, never arriving at his destination.

The next day we called in Search and Rescue. They found he had been blown back several ridges, threw his reserve parachute, but was too low and he crashed, cutting his femoral artery and bleeding to death. The story goes on to say that, when the search and rescue guys found him, he had a joint in one hand and a beer in the other. It takes about 20 minutes usually to die from severed artery like that so he had time to have a sip of beer and a puff before he left us for good.

Judd was always a carefree flyer but he learned better habits quickly from the Pemberton flying monkey community. He had spent the last seven months before his death flying and bumming around Valle de Bravo, Mexico, often camping at launch at the Penon which is a pillar of rock at least two thousand feet high. In fact, he left quite a reputation behind. In his early flying career, to the surprise of everybody who witnessed it, he accidentally had to do a forced landing on the old community centre roof. He was such a great soul and everybody will miss him dearly. After Judd's death a few people in Pemberton quit paragliding for good.

Finally there was Lucas or "Grampa Dave," who spent summers flying in Pemberton and winters doing the same in South Africa, where his daughter and granddaughter resided. He perished flying over a beach in Iceland. We never learned the whole story of how it happened, but he spiralled right into the black beach and died on impact in front of 400 people.

Such losses of dear and memorable characters hit our small community very hard. Yet the rewards offered by paragliding and soaring over the countryside make up for those inherent dangers in the sport.

I for one respect the sport very much as it can be such a fine line between flying and crashing. You are a pilot of an aircraft and should never forget that. There is a preflight checklist and an intimate knowledge of the weather and winds is required so that on the day you know they are okay for your flight.

You can't just huck your body off as if you are on a bungee cord or a zip-line or even as a tandem passenger. There is so much to learn about meteorology, instrument and GPS use, as well as learning the myriad of other skills such as watching the habits of birds as they, of course, are the champions of free flight. But on the other hand, they can sometimes trick you as well in that they go to where the thermals are but the birds are far ahead of us in finding the lift we also are constantly seeking. The problem is that not all thermals are created equally and some work best only for birds.

1

2

3

4

In the Sierra again with the Kogis and Arhuacos

1. A young Arhuaco boy with our trekking poles.
2. The launch for my "Sacred" paraglide flight.
3. A group of Indigenous women we met on our trail in the Sierra.
4. Our faithful Arhuaco guide, Argemiro (on the left) of the Kogi family and hut.
5. In the company of Kogis and Arhuacos.
6. Our guide crosses a creek with my paraglider.
7. An Arhuaco boy dressed in our clothing.

5

7

1

2

Paragliding and my house

1. Glider over the Andes.
2. Jenny, my dear friend in Peru.
3. Mountain bike madness in Pemberton.
4. Jim Orava taking filmmaker Geoff Browne on a tandem.
5. My mother at an art show with her tapestry work during the World Ski & Snowboard festival in Whistler.
6. My house above Pemberton BC on Reid Road.
7. My Peruvian styled bedroom at home.

3

4

5

6

7

CHAPTER 13

AIR HEADS TO X-ANDES

I had kept working on the X-Andes project with Jenny. I was hoping this might bring us closer together after Canadian Immigration had ruined my romantic plans when we had first met. Unfortunately, things never did materialize with her and, in the end, she pursued other men younger than me. There was some consolation that at least we had produced a very professional looking draft proposal together for my X-Andes vision which helped generate interest in the event.

The Red Bull X-Alps in the European Alps is deemed the hardest adventure race in the world. Only about 37 invited athletes, closely screened by Red Bull before the race, are allowed to participate in the gruelling event. The course itself takes place over a 1,000 km distance, starting in Salzburg, Austria and ending in Monaco, Monte Carlo on the Caribbean sea shore. Each athlete must run and fly the course in the time limit of under two weeks or be disqualified. Often big peaks in the Alps like the Matterhorn and Mt Blanc are included as GPS points the pilots have to fly over during the race. Often, only a few people ever finish, out of the whole starting field. I planned my Andes version of the race to be only about 250 km long and I thought of giving athletes about five days to fly, run and fly the course. I had to be careful about making this event possible for all visiting athletes, especially in its first year. Word got around, and soon top Red Bull XALPS athletes were emailing me about their interest in participating in an X-Andes version.

By 2011 I had assembled a team of eight paraglide pilots and friends from Colombia, Canada, New Zealand, Peru, Poland, The USA, and France to recon the area and develop a route.

The founder of PWC, the renowned Paragliding World Cup Competitions, Xavier Murillo came along. Xavier lived in St Hilaire, a town in France which is famous for its annual paragliding spectacle and festival that takes place every September and is called the Coupe Icare. We had originally met in Pemberton, where we flew together and where he stayed in my house. Xavier loved my X-Andes idea and even got Cross-Country Magazine interested in commissioning him to write a story and take photographs.

Once in Peru we were also joined by James 'Oroc' Johnston, alias "Kiwi", a seasoned paraglide pilot and storyteller, who was quite famous for his books on hallucinogenic drugs. Travelling with James was another old friend from the United States, Jeff Crystol. Jeff was from Telluride, Colorado and a veteran of flying in the Huaraz Valley. The two had been flying and travelling around Peru together and they joined our reconnaissance team for X-Andes in Huaraz. With us also was a good friend, Glenn Bitterman, a pilot from Grand Prairie Alberta. Rounding out the crew was Jedrzej or Andy, the paraplegic pilot from Poland who had flown with us in Hedley and Yamid „Mauro" Sierra from Bogota, Colombia, who would become my flying partner on many adventures.

Benquelo, or Benca Morales, my good friend and the son of Benjamin Morales, had been organizing a major mountain sport festival, FESTIVAL DEL ANDINISMO CORDILLERA BLANCA. He welcomed our paragliding crew and even scheduled a media day so the press visiting his event could take some spectacular pictures of paragliders launching off a new site above the town north of Huaraz. Readers will recall I had a long history with Benjamin from trips to Peru going back in 1972, and it was nice to come full circle years later and be working with his son.

With the help of Benca's contacts, our X-Andes recon crew started scouting various roads down to the ocean with the help of local guides who knew the area well. We searched hard to set that perfect course for our X-Andes event. Testing the winds and the landscape, we flew in some really crazy and windy areas and, luckily, nobody got hurt. We also found some ideal new soaring spots in the sandy desert north of Lima near the town of Huarmay, where the conditions were just like in Iquique, Chile in the Atacama desert.

After looking at all these possible routes for our race, we arrived at the Caraz paraglide launch north of Huaraz for Benca's media day. Benquello proceeded to make a good show for the reporters, as we launched one by one, high above the Ancash Valley. Jedrzej (Andy) the Polish paraplegic paraglide pilot, surprised everyone, flying a record of 87 km all the way south of Huaraz.

Andy never ceased to amaze us. Being unable to walk he usually found a football field or somewhere with people around in order to land. One can imagine the surprise the local Quechua Indians had when they saw a paraglider for the first time and on top of that the pilot could not walk. Jedrzej would quickly make friends, ask the locals to fold his glider and call him a taxi. Then, someone would piggy back him to the cab and he would make it back to our hotel that night. He did this repeatedly on several occasions.

However disaster struck us again. Xavier, who had launched earlier, was nowhere to be seen. We had all taken off from the Caraz launch. Some of us took it easy and flew around for an hour, and landed safely outside the town near Caraz. A few pilots flew south to Yungay with Andy doing the record flight. Next day we started to mount searches for Xavier. This included climbing some of the lower peaks across the valley in the Cordillera Negra and trying to get him on the radio and on the cell phone – to no avail.

Shortly afterwards this fellow seemed to come out of nowhere. He was from Canada, was living in Santiago, Chile and was fairly well known in the competitive paraglide community. He took it upon himself to trick me as I thought we would be working together.

In the end however, he pushed me out of the whole rescue mission. We had already started aerial surveys looking for Xavier's body and this guy just came in and took over the whole situation. It was quite clear that he wanted to be the big man in charge.

Again I was naive and let a bad person into my world and my life too quickly. So often my downfall comes from getting involved with the wrong people. But on the other hand I want to stay open and positive to new ideas, not become a sort of paranoid reclusive hermit.

After a desperate week of flights back and forth along the Andes using a slow flying Pilatus Porter aircraft, Xavier's body was finally found at the base of a glacier, below the north peak of Huascaran. He had thrown his reserve but he was too low for that manoeuvre to have had any effect. His body was found with a professional camera in his hands. This meant that he must have had the big camera out, trying to take pictures as he was hit by a rotor, which is a dangerous funnel of air, or fell out of a thermal. Trying to evade a crash landing, he threw his reserve parachute, but by that time he was already too low and crashed. This was a real tragedy and put a complete stop on our X-Andes project.

Some people were of the opinion that flying comps should not be held in the Huaraz valley because of the dangerous wind conditions. I disagreed with that view and felt it could be held safely. I later proved my detractors wrong by hosting another event called the "Aerothlon" in the same area several years later.

All mountain ranges have their particular personalities when it comes to flying in them. The Andes are high but have many commonalities with any other mountain area, when one is paragliding. Flying in such circumstances, a pilot should expect sudden changes in wind and weather, and should be prepared for such exigencies.

Like in Mexico, in the Andes it is safest to launch between 10 AM and not much later than 11 AM. By noon the wind usually starts getting very strong and, in general, it picks up. It is therefore best in mountainous dry areas like the Andes to get out and up in your paraglider early. Once aloft, stay aloft and then do some cross-country, and land in the late afternoon when things cool down.

Given that in the past I had found myself getting involved with the wrong people, I should have recognized his unsuitability for the task at hand. Why did I ever allow a guy like this into my world – a guy who most inappropriately made himself the King of Xavier's rescue mission? But I guess, in many ways, I was still naïve about how ruthless and deceiving people could be. The guy was a perfect example who not to associate with! In fact, he had never really been invited to our town in Peru.

To explain further, I had been coming to Huaraz for nearly 50 years and had had friends in that community since 1972. Beto, Anthula, La Luly and Monkey Wazi were all longtime associates who ran guiding and hospitality businesses in Huaraz. We did not need this interloper and were quite capable of organizing the rescue ourselves. After all, we knew all the local resources and could have access to his rescue fund as well.

I realized a long time ago that while I have made numerous dear friends over the years, I have also managed to make a few enemies along the way, and this was the situation centred around Huaraz and Xavier's rescue. As of writing this, because of the tensions we still have not managed to hold an Aerthlon in this area. Not yet! But stay tuned!

Once I had got back home for our Canadian summer and flying again in Pemberton, I continued to contemplate what to do with X-Andes. I also nurtured some ambitious ideas for a similar X-Aztecas project in Mexico.

I also had to contend with a few critics who were trying to pin Xavier's death on me and another one of my crazy projects. I kept my head low as some people continued to stick their nose into my life but eventually the truth came out and the majority of pilots stood by me. They knew it was Xavier's choice alone to accompany us on the X-Andes trip. I had an already tarnished reputation among some locals after years of ski antics, and now it was translating to my misadventures in paragliding as well.

I had developed a travel pattern of alternating North and South American summers. In any case, I returned to Peru again the following year to attend Benca's festival. With me this time was my good friend Doris.

Benca demonstrated great competence in running his event, which featured various sports like mountain biking, cross-country running and even a ski and snowboard race at the high 5,000 metre elevation Postoruri glacier, to where all the participants were bussed. A lot of work went into making the situation safe. For example, ladders were put up for everybody to climb up over an ice fall onto a snowfield above on which the race would take place. It was a really unique event and drew quite a lot of competitors. These were mainly foreign Spanish language students from Lima, who came from many European countries and gave the event a real international flavour.

Prior to the Andean festival in Huaraz, I was invited on a side trip to another fabulous happening. A music festival was being held in Andahuaylas, Peru, near Cuzco and a day's drive from Lima where we were staying. Seventeen of us Lima-located paraglide pilots were invited on an all-expenses-paid trip by bus and with our hotel accommodations all covered! We were to fly above the big music festival being held at the incredible Inca ruins. As the famous Peruvian band Alborada played, the organizers freed two trained condors, who would accompany us paraglide pilots as we flew over the concert. There were 6,000 or so folks, a mainly Peruvian audience, attending and it was really quite an incredible experience. What made it even nicer was that there were very few foreigners in attendance making it primarily a real Peruvian festival, without the trimmings for the tourists.

The main attraction was when entertainers re-enacted a war that the Incas had won centuries back against a tribe that had tried to invade and conquer the Inca Empire from the Amazon. Besides our flying, there were dances, mock battles, great food and many activities that kept us busy for several days at the event. Then, we were all herded back into our buses to make the long ride back to Lima.

A few days later I was again on another bus to Huaraz, and Benca's festival there. with the usual sporting events happening, as well as a paragliding free day – and another show for the media in which the paragliders once again took off from the Caraz launch. I had a nice flight, flew around and then landed at the designated LZ outside of the town of Caraz.

After the festival in Huaraz, Doris went on to Cuzco to sight-see and visit Machu Picchu, while I stayed on to do some free flying myself. We planned to meet in Lima later on.

One day I hired a taxi driver to drive me up to a paraglide launch at the Barig mine, high above the Ancash Valley. I often did this when

I went flying alone. I would first secure a good driver who would accompany me, and help me at the launch, making sure I got off okay and I followed the routine again this time.

With this driver's help, I launched and he watched me fly off as I headed for the centre of the valley. Just before my event at the Barig Mine, I had flown off the Caraz launch above the city of Caraz, north of Huaraz. The purpose of my trip was to install a plaque which was in honour of our friend Xavier, who had disappeared flying from that launch the year before. After finding the perfect rock appropriate for bolting the plaque to, I did my flight with the taxi driver assisting me at takeoff. Unfortunately this story is how the plaque never got put up.

I had left it with the tourism department in Caraz, with specific instructions where it should go but the tourism people there just did not follow through. The tourism department in the town of Caraz had seemed very keen to have more events in the town such as our paragliding media day. Yet when it came to putting up the plaque, the will just was not there. Maybe the guys were just working for the government and collecting their pay cheques. Anyway, unless that plaque was part of a designated task schedule, I was out of luck. This is unfortunately a lesson I have learned in my years of working with many government entities in Latin America and Mexico.

I planned to do my same launching technique: going to the takeoff spot with the taxi driver above the Barig Mine, and flying from there. This was a really high launch, at around 4,000 meters elevation but I had flown here before several times without incident. As the taxi driver looked on, I managed to get off launching all right and caught a great thermal which took me soaring fairly high up over 5.000 meters. I then headed for the centre of the valley.

I had been given the wing by a sponsor. Actually I had always thought it was a little big for me. It was a size 29 and I was usually flying only a 26. But the manufacturer had assured me that I would be all right, that I would just have to be more active on my break controls. As I made my way towards the centre of the valley, I happened to be just over these huge double power lines, when I got hit by something. I am still not sure whether it was a rotor, or just me falling out of a thermal. Suddenly I was in washing machine mode, trying everything to get my glider flying again, but being afraid to throw my reserve parachute – because of the aforementioned power lines crossing the landscape directly below me. This continued for several minutes and it was terrifying right to the moment when I crashed into the ground. The impact knocked me out and I lost consciousness. Someone must have called the local Search and Rescue people as they watched my out-of-control paraglider spiralling towards the ground. When I opened my eyes the ambulance guys were already there, taking me out of my harness. I felt a huge pain in my right leg as well as in my torso in general. What followed was a week of recuperating in a hospital in Huaraz, then being transferred by a special ambulance plane to a private clinic in Lima. Somewhat ironically, it was the same plane we had used in searching for Xavier's body the year before.

I had broken my femur as well as having received several cracks in my pelvis. After my femur operation, I had to spend a month lying on my back recuperating in a small private clinic in Lima. Luckily at that time I had great travel insurance, which covered the $60,000 bill. While I was in the clinic I had at least some good luck because my old heart throb, Jenny, came to visit me every day. It was a two hour bus trip each way for her as she lived in a northern suburb of Lima, and I realized even more deeply what a great person I had lost. How I wished things would have worked out better between us but it was wonderful to see her anyway. Somewhat bizarrely an old friend, Richard Leiptag from Whistler, who on his way to Machu Picchu, dropped by just briefly to take some photographs of my broken body in the hospital bed. I found that rather strange, because he did not stay long enough to even have a chat and had to get going. The two of us had experienced some pretty wild times together in the past when Richard managed the Whistler Vale condominiums on Whistler's Southside. He was a famous womanizer back in those days, so he often had many worthy and somewhat wayward ski bum girls staying with him. Of course I didn't hesitate to join in and benefit from some of the fringe romantic benefits. Since those mis-spent days he had moved back to Hamilton Ontario which must have changed him from the laid back lifestyle out-west into his now seeming harried ways. Sometimes that hospital made me feel like an animal on exhibit in a zoo.

Eventually I got back to British Columbia and Pemberton where I spent another few months recuperating and so was unable to fly that summer. However, at the same time, I made plans to start my travels again. Cuba came to the top of my list. Some interesting ideas about "Fidel's Island" materialized in quite a funny way. When I had my accident in Peru the insurance company insisted on sending a male nurse down to accompany me back up to Canada on the airplane and to make sure I would get home safely. We were scheduled to take an Air Canada flight home on a new plane which was equipped with bed-like pods in it. This would have allowed me to lie down and rest my still-cracked pelvis. Unfortunately, at the last minute the airline had had to change the plane. So, even though we were in business class, there was no way to lie down in the replacement and my cracked pelvis had to suffer on Tylenols all the way back home. As a result of his patient's inconvenience, my nurse complained magnificently to the airline about the sudden change in aircraft, and in the end I received a nice travel voucher from Air Canada, which I would later use for this first-ever trip to Cuba. Throughout all my adventures up to that point, I had been continuing to film my Paracinderella documentary and it had become an autobiography of sorts, with its humorous romantic twists and turns. I even managed to film while I was in flight on the ambulance airplane as well as some of the hospital scenes and made them all part of the Paracinderella story. I thought the airplane ride footage back to Lima in the ambulance plane came out especially well on video.

Throughout the summer, I had effectively been a cripple and had to use a walker while recovering, but finally I started walking by myself in the fall. I thought this was the right time to go somewhere warm and heal my broken body some more. Many people recommended Cuba to me, so I thought I would give it a go. Looking through the Air Canada promotional packages I found a nice all-inclusive resort in Varadero for my first visit to Cuba. This was really the first holiday or trip that I had taken where I had no film or festival to organize: it was pure pleasure in itself. That didn't last long though as I got bored after only a short time resting on the beach. Soon I had many ideas on how I would start organizing future outdoor film festivals in Cuba. At that time, for me Cuba was a fascinating place.

I was originally from communist Poland, and I could not help seeing a lot of similarities between Cuba and my old homeland. In many ways it was like stepping back in time to the Poland of the 1970's. However, I found it very depressing that the tourism industry was the preserve of an elitist clique of rich Cubans, while the rest of the country was caught in a cycle of disarray and poverty. Basically, once one leaves Havana or the major beach resorts and ventures into the countryside, one sees quite deep poverty everywhere. People literally have barely enough food to eat. I was told the military elite here are heavily involved in all the major seaside resorts. Most tourists never see this actuality as they are kept in their little bubbles at all-inclusive resorts, and may be doing one or two side trips to Havana but experience little of the real Cuba that lies beyond.

As I returned to Canada in April 2013 I had good reason to be quite excited. Why? Because I had a guest coming to stay in Pemberton, a girl from Poland who I had previously corresponded with at length on Facebook. It was going to be a nice change having a visitor to hang out with for the summer. Ania had a two-year work permit in Canada and she was going to stay with me for the whole summer. She turned out to be an attractive brunette and quite a good skier – aaaand she was interested in learning how to paraglide! I actually filmed a whole session with her learning how to ground handle a glider and it is in my Paracinderella film. The film was coming along quite well, yet the ending kept on changing, as I kept on meeting different women who wanted to fly. Finally the version that seemed most natural was that the story up to now was that my paraglider has remained my most reliable partner, and that is how the film ends. My plan was always to continue filming and have the end change if I met new partners along the way. The Paracinderella project ended up being shot and edited over 10 years of my life, but is something I can be proud of.

Although Ania loved being in Canada, she had learnt very little English because we spoke in Polish too much. She had always wanted to go to Australia. She had a hairdressing diploma from Poland and so, at summer's end, she managed to get a working visa there, and arranged to take an English course in Australia. They were short of hairdressers "Down Under" so it was a good opportunity for her. I was sad to see her leave as she was really good company, although I felt she might be trouble in the end. She did help to motivate me to start flying again after my horrendous accident in Peru and for that I'm very grateful to her.

It's amazing how a the attention of a younger woman can do wonders towards restoring an older guy's ego and self-confidence! Although I was flying again the accident had really set me back – probably at least 10 years as to how much confidence I had in my flying. This arose from a lot of demons in my head, and this really affected my launches, which had seemed to have been deteriorating even before my accident. People had always given me a hard time for only being able to use the forward launch technique. I did understand that in high winds the other option, the reverse method, was much better. But I carried on with my usual take-off because I suspected that what had caused my 1979 concussion in Peru was using the "turning around" method. It just disorientated me, and thus I have stuck to the forward method: it's safer for me.

Paragliding in the Peruvian Andes

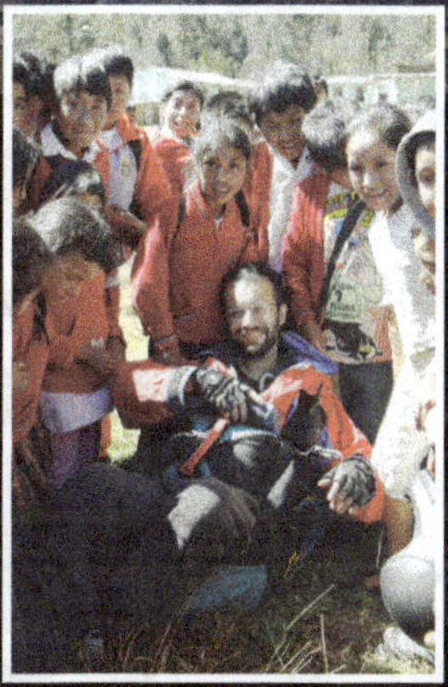

1. A Quechua woman looks out for paragliders.
2. Xavier Murillo before his final flight.
4. Jedrzej flying high over the Andes.
4. Gliders flying over the Andahuaylas Festival in Peru.
5. Jedrzej on approach to landing at a school near Huaraz.
6. Locals look on as Jedrzej lands.
7. Jedrzej surrounded by kids after landing outside Huaraz.
8. Some of our crew with new friends in Lima, Peru, upon arrival.

The charm of beautiful British Columbia, Canada

1. View of Fissile Mountain and the "Banana Chute".
2. The raw beauty of Lillooet lake near Pemberton.
3. With my good friend, Natali Vasquez from Medellin Colombia on a chairlift in Whistler.
4. A painting by Natali Vasquez in her unique style.

CHAPTER 14

CUBA AND BEYOND

In the fall of 2013, I went back to Cuba to organize a small adventure film festival at the Hotel Tropicoco, which was about 10km out of Havana and on the way to Varadero at the "Playas del Este." Having my paraglider with me, I did a side trip to Vinales – the rock climbing capital of Cuba, located near the extreme western end of Cuba. About a 150 km west of Havana, the community is a major stopping point for those tourists willing to venture out of the world of all-inclusive resorts. Here I made a great new friend, Yaroscal, and we were also joined by Mauro, another friend who was visiting from Bogotá, Colombia. I had met Mauro on the X-Andes project in Peru a few years back. I had also met some local pilots from Havana who joined us as well. We learned from them of a nearby paraglide launch, which was reached by walking or horseback. I never managed to do any bigger flights than these but it was just nice to even have small ones in such a beautiful area.

At first Cuba was really a lot of fun, with all the salsa music and, for me, all the available women. Unlike most of Central America, it is not a Catholic country, so sex was pretty easy and open, but one always had to pay something for it in the end, because the people are so poor. To my surprise I discovered almost all women would quite openly have sex with you if they could make a little money from the deal. It is a very ugly side of what is touted as a successful country by some fools. At least Mauro and I had a really good time in Cuba together. The Havana Film Festival was also taking place in December so we both made sure to attend as much as we could, taking in some great parties and many excellent films. The festival headquarters was in the old and elegant Hotel Nacional in downtown Havana. Curiously there was even a whole week of Polish films at the festival, sponsored by the Polish Embassy, so it was really nice to see some of those films from the old country. Our nights were starting to get especially wild with Mauro and I bringing home various women on many occasions to our rented apartment in Havana during the film festival. I tried to justify what we were doing as being almost like what counted for social work in Cuba. Yet I guess it was a sort of prostitution, but what is prostitution? You pay for a personal service for an hour or night, or you marry and pay till the end of your life – so what's the difference?!

I remember one of these nights in particular. Mauro and I had been to the disco and brought two women home. He had met a beautiful black girl and I had found an older lady called Maria. My new friend was about 40 years old but didn't look a day over 25. After a fun night, the girls went home, and Mauro and I went back to the beach for the day. When we returned to our apartment later, Maria and a another beautiful young girl were sitting on our staircase waiting for us. Maria told us that she brought her sister along, because she had liked the young man I was with from Colombia so much that she thought of introducing them. Another wild night of dancing and partying ensued, only for us to find out later that that girl Maria had brought was her 18-year-old daughter and not actually her sister.

I know that many readers will find all this unacceptable, and I felt bad supporting this kind of behaviour, but it is the reality of life in Cuba after 60 years of communism, and I would rather pay these girls something for a good time and see them make a little bit of money. I don't understand why Castro never legalized prostitution in Cuba, because he could have taxed it as they do in other countries like Argentina, Germany and Colombia. The Cubans at least have great doctors and a very good medical care which is sufficient to monitor the girls' health and try to limit the spread of sexual diseases. I think it's really sad what Castro did to Cuba, but it's a pattern common to many dictators. They start out as idealists, but soon however, the power goes to their heads and they create an evil one-party system in which a small elitist group surrounding the leadership clique makes a lot of money. This has been the case with tourism in Cuba where the non-tourist place and people starve. I saw that there were many similarities between Cuba and communist Poland. The shelves in the grocery stores were either empty – or full of only one or two products like Mango juice or something else. Sometimes one would see a huge line in front of the store, just because a pig had been slaughtered and there was some fresh meat for sale.

In the meantime I had also come across an interesting event originating in Malinalco, which is about 50 km south of Mexico City. I was really taken by the concept of the "Aerothlon" event because it was truly original, consisting of a relay race featuring segments of running, paragliding and mountain biking. A friend from Mexico, Pablo Lopez, had founded it. I then introduced Pablo to another of my friends, Benca Morales in Peru who ran the festival in Andes. Later, the Aerothlon became a favourite event at the Peruvian festival for which Benca gathered a lot of sponsors, making everyone happy.

We also tried to run an Aerothlon in Cuba. Unfortunately, there turned out to be too many hurdles involved in pulling off an event like this in Cuba. Just days before the event, somebody from the military cancelled everything on us. I guess we were just at a loss as to who was right person to bribe this time. This was, like everything else in the country, how everything worked in Cuba. It was particularly unfortunate because an Austrian pilot called Paul Gluschbauer, who is a well-known Red Bull athlete, had already arrived in Cuba, thinking that the event was on. I was once again holding a little film festival at the hotel Tropicoco that year, when I received word of the cancellation. It was here I first met Paul, who had come second in the prestigious Red Bull X-Alps race in Europe. I ended up taking Paul along with a few other friends to Vinales, where he managed to do some paragliding and had a nice high flight. My other friends and I were not such good pilots and only managed a few short sled rides or short little flights to the valley.

Afterwards everyone went horseback riding and skinny dipping in the wonderful caves found around the valley.

After spending time in Vinales, my good friend Simon Archimbault and I managed to get on a flight to Isla de la Juventud for some paragliding. Although all the flights were booked solid, one just had to pay a $10 bribe to get a seat on the plane. The plane was only about $20 each way. After a short flight we arrived on the island that was the setting for Robert Louis Stevenson's famous novel "Treasure Island". The island, the fifth biggest in the Caribbean, belongs to Cuba and, with a smaller military presence than on the main island, is a much cooler place to hang out. There are also 18 local paragliding pilots living there who were very happy to have some visitors coming to fly with them. We spent about 10 days there, six of which had great flying conditions. All the others we spent eating great lobster and hanging out on the beach. The best sex I ever had was probably on that island when I brought a girl home from a disco one evening and she did great things to me all night long. Although on several occasions I took advantage of the open sexual fringe benefits available in Cuba, I also scolded one mother who came up to me on the beach at The Isla de la Juventud and tried to sell me sex with her 17-year-old daughter. My own ethics were not of the highest standards, but I usually justified myself by saying I was supporting the local community. However I would never consent to having sex with a minor and I told the mother that what she was doing was very, very wrong.

By January 2015 I was back in Mexico, paragliding in one of my favourite spots – La Malinche, above the town of Tenancingo. It was on this occasion that I had another paragliding accident: I broke my leg in a sudden downdraft. The unexpected atmospheric effect left me no option but to turn downwind, towards the only available clearing to land in. I should have stayed pointing upwind and aimed for the bushes – instead of worrying about my glider. At first I didn't think it was a serious break. I even thought of recuperating by staying in Mexico. However, after a few more X-rays, it turned out to be much more serious. I again notified my insurance company that a claim had been set into place and they sent another male nurse down again to accompany me home for surgery.

I was in a wheelchair at the Vancouver airport with my male nurse, waiting to go through customs, when two Persian Canadian customs ladies decided to pick on us. I was in very significant pain for several hours while these ladies from Canada Customs hassled my male nurse. He was contracted from Los Angeles to come down to Mexico and then to accompany me back home to Canada. They insisted that he did not have a work permit to bring me back to Canada. Talk about runaway bureaucracy! Sometimes I wonder about our over-insured, over-bureaucratic system. Canada is an amazing place to live in and I wouldn't want to live anywhere else. Yet if one does not get to travel, one can go crazy with all the rules and regulations. After a couple hours of hassles a solution was worked out: the customs ladies finally let us into the country but my nurse had to pay the $150 work permit fee for the hour of time he would have to spend in the country while taking me to the hospital in Vancouver. I always had a problem with authority like police or customs officials in general. Sure, there are good cops out there but they number one in a hundred in my eyes. Most of them are there to be on a power trip. As far as customs, well I found a way to beat the system there as well. I would save all my dirty laundry for the customs agents, on purpose not doing my laundry before going home. Usually as the customs agents opened my bag and smelled and saw the dirty clothes, they would close my bags and breeze me through quickly, especially with dirty underwear. I made it a pointy to boycott visiting the United States during the times of president Bush or that moron Donald Trump. I found the whole attitude in the US of A – was an unpleasant right wing military one under those guys, unlike the times of Bill Clinton or president Obama when things were chill.

At the time of the accident I had been visiting Mexico during the winters. I had found a place near the town of Tenancingo, where a man named Daniel Pedraza had been manicuring a quite incredible paraglide launch site for over 18 years. A few Canadian friends had put their money together and bought a luxury villa which they had named "Casa del Piloto." Thus they had found a town which they would turn into a paragliding centre running tours in area. I had actually taken care of a few groups in the house and helped Daniel promote the area for many years.

At one time the Mexican ambassador, a certain Senor Angel, in Vancouver took a liking to me. He even gave me his paid assistant, Ligia Duenas, to help organize a race called X-AZTECAS, to be modeled after the Red Bull X-Alps in Europe and X-Andes in Mexico. I had tried to do that in Peru but it all ended with Xavier's death. Unfortunately, because of the corruption in Mexico City at the executive level of the tourism department in charge of adventure programming, the assistance turned out to be useless. Rich kids from privileged families were running the program, they did not really give a damn about tourism and couldn't care less about anything – except getting a regular pay check. The typical scenario featuring government tourism employees was playing itself out again here. This was a shame because I spent another year of my life, trying to get something going in Mexico with X-AZTECAS and I was just hitting a brick wall in the end. More recently the Oscar-winning Mexican film, "Roma" exemplified the problems of class structure in Mexico between those that have and those that do not. The situation and division between the classes is quite pathetic and it's evident in most of Latin America.

I even invested my own savings (which were not large) in a small place in Mexico, at Daniel's Flight Park at La Malinche. That location seemed the best alternative to get away from the dark and cold that is BC from November through February. It was also already half way to Colombia and Peru from Vancouver. Mexico had its problems but overall it was the best and closest option for a winter get-away for me.

I have found that, generally speaking, corruption is rampant in Mexico. My own research indicates that about five big families still run the country. In my opinion it is the most corrupt country in the world. One really cannot differentiate between the government and the Narcos – or, for that matter, between the government and the armed forces. Everything is intertwined in the drug trade. The Mexicans have learned how to grow better pot, although it is still full of seeds and stems. Plus Mexican plants don't come anywhere near the quality of the great marijuana grown in BC, although it has improved somewhat. At one time there was even a guy out of Toluca making great black hash – something of a real novelty in Mexico.

I should also mention that Mexico has a huge garbage problem. People just tend to drive and dump their garbage anywhere they can, including parks and any available land that is not being looked after. While Colombia and Peru have been teaching their kids in school about throwing garbage and about pollution in general, that has not been the case in Mexico which, compared to those two countries, is still filthy as far as garbage goes. One would think that with the importance of tourism to Mexico's economy, greater care would be taken in respect to the environment. Nevertheless, I still love the country and the people – except for those government tourism employees, who always seem in the end to be completely useless. One just has to be very careful in general.

Another accident; another opportunity: it was while I was recuperating from a broken ankle caused by a recent accident paragliding at La Malinche, Mexico that I got an interesting phone call. It arrived just as I was starting to go out of my mind in my mother's small two bedroom apartment in Vancouver. The call was from a good paragliding friend of mine, Brad Henry. Brad told me he had met another fellow, a producer from Radio America who had received a grant from the US government to make television programming in Cuba. The goal was to produce programs aimed to spread capitalism by teaching Cubans how to start up their own new businesses on the island. The producer was seeking a Canadian film crew rather than to send his American people to film in Cuba. The reason: Americans were still quite hated there, while Canadians were very welcome. Eighty percent of tourists in Cuba are from Canada, which explains the good reputation Canada has among Cubans. Most Canadian tourists come in droves to Cuba's beach resorts, spend a lot of money and pose no threat to Castro's regime or its revolutionary ideology. As a small Canadian crew, we would be able to just move around very easily – without the military bothering us. The 20% of non-Canadian tourists are mainly comprised of Europeans. American visitors are few and far between and, only recently, under the Obama administration did sanctions against Cuba get lifted. There was a significant easing of travel restrictions for Americans wanting to visit the island country.

I listened carefully to the proposal on the phone from my bed in Vancouver while nurturing my recently broken ankle. I agreed to take on the project with one important condition: "I would film the Cuban businesses and how they got their start, but these would have to be outdoor minded outfits as I did not want to get stuck in Havana filming start up restaurants, shops – or just the usual mundane stuff the Americans had been filming before." The American producer agreed to my terms, gave me a go ahead and laid on a pretty good start up budget.

I then went ahead and hired a friend, a Vancouver film producer who was also a great technician and cameraman as well as a sound man. Nathaniel "Nat" Tazner was great at multitasking and his skill set was perfect. We needed to move around fast and do it without a lot of notice. As the leader of a documentary crew, moving around without permits, I needed somebody who could wear a lot of hats. Nat had those hats. He had been producing a local cable show aimed at the Polish community in Greater Vancouver, for which I had done some programs. And so by April we left Canada for Cuba, where Nat already had a film company established so I thought he would make a great partner for the job. We first went to Santa Clara, where we hired a beautiful hostess who was also very multi-talented on radio and television – as well as being a gorgeous top fashion model.

We thus managed to produce 10 television segments with a budget of only $200,000 in Canadian currency. Nat ended up totally falling for and marrying the hostess, who was 24 while he was 56. I told him he might get three years maximum out of the relationship, as this was the case with many men marrying very young Cuban women. The truth of the matter is that such Cuban women really knew how to manipulate their men into submission. Nat's marriage actually lasted only a year so I had been somewhat over-optimistic in my advice to him. Cuban women are notorious for being ruthless with their spouses pretty quickly after marrying them.

Which brings me to another interesting story. A friend I know went to Cuba, met the woman of his dreams and brought her back to Canada. For 8 years they had a wonderful marriage, great sex and all that came with a happy union. Then my friend went away on a business trip only to come back and not find a trace of his wife. As it turned out the Cuban woman had a lover back in Cuba for whom she saved all her money so he could buy a jet-ski and escape to Cancun. This all happened while my friend was away. She never took a cent from him but just squirrelled away the money over the years. When the Cuban lover boy reached Cancun she left to join him leaving my friend still married and now miserable back in Canada. Now I hear the Cuban couple moved back to Vancouver and live not too far from his house. He has a new Cuban girlfriend now but leaves her there and only visits. I always thought as a filmmaker what a great story this would have made for a feature film. There are only a few characters and maybe a small shoot in Cuba and a guy ripping through the ocean towards Cancun. Here's a film with a great story to be made for only a couple million bucks rather than the overdone pointless 100 million dollar pictures coming out of Hollywood these days.

Nat's marriage ended badly but there was another, much more tragic situation that happened after our shoot in Cuba. A good paragliding friend, Les Snyder from Yelapa Mexico, had come out to Cuba to shoot some paragliding segments with us. He ran an SIV or towing service for paragliders out of his home in Yelapa, Mexico. Some local Mexicans were envious of his business and of the good time he was having. They broke into his house, tied him up and killed him by shooting him in the head two times. Everybody in Mexico knows who the killers were, but justice was never properly carried out for him and Les Snyder's killers are still on the loose. Yelapa had been so close to my heart and was also my first paragliding winter escape trip. I knew all the pilots there and Les's death really struck a cord there.

We shot six outdoor segments in Cuba, each half an hour long: a paragliding tandem operation, a kite surfing business, a scuba diving outfit, a rock climbing school, a mountain biking outfit and a horse riding business in Vinales. We also shot an adventure Mountain Festival segment in Peru at my friend's Benca's Festival later that June. That was totally my idea. I thought that, by hearing of us shooting a festival in Peru, the Cubans would be inspired by national pride and try to have one in Cuba. It was also the second year of the Aerothlon there so it was nice to see Pablo Lopez again. I also thought it would be useful and (again) inspirational to show the Cubans how a mountain festival is organized in Peru. My hope was that, as fellow Latin Americans, they might see it as totally doable. My fear, I guess, was that showing them some really big event in Canada or North America might give them pause for thought and lead them to think it was impossible.

Kasandra, whose father was a Cuban military officer, was rather loyal to Castro's revolution and always had excuses why Cuban shops had empty shelves. She had no hesitation in justifying bureaucratic corruption in the Cuban government. The Peru trip was a good lesson for her, as she was rather dumbfounded to see how goods were plentiful in all the stores, the economy was booming and the level of political corruption was nowhere near to that of Cuba. She stopped praising the revolution so much after that trip. So in June, in between the shooting and editing of our Cuban programs, we took a couple weeks with Nat and Kasandra to Cuba as we shot the television segment in Peru. Upon return to Cuba we finished editing all of the shows and by July I was glad to be back in Canada. Cuba had just become far too hot to enjoy at that time of year.

I spent the rest of the summer enjoying paragliding in Pemberton. I also made plans to return to Cuba in the fall to spend a month there from November on. After that my destination was Colombia, in January for about six weeks – and to meet up with Mauro, my good friend and flying partner. In the end I got ripped off in the whole filming deal. After marrying Kasandra, Nat went crazy trying to keep her, spending all OUR money on renovating her house – among other things. I ended up taking Nat to small claims court over all this. The entire situation became too tiring for me. After chasing Nat, who never responded to the calls from court, he was finally cornered with a warrant for his arrest. Again I lamented getting involved with the wrong guy. I had other filmmaker friends that would have been more honest with me during the job. Nat was a talented filmmaker but so were many other friends that I had. However, I ended up thinking that there was no use crying over bygones. It was not even over the money that I took the guy to court. I was just so angry over at the central issue of the whole situation – being ripped off by the guy I had hired in the first place. I ended settling out of court for half of what was owed to me but at least I think I made a point about honesty to Nat, or so I hope anyway.

I was now happy because a best friend, Troy Jungen would accompany me on a return to Cuba in November, 2015. Troy and I almost never made it out of Vancouver on our early morning flight to Cuba. Although he had insisted on going to a late party at some bar the night before, somehow – miraculously – my mother had awakened us in time to catch a taxi to the airport. The following day we were both really hung over and I had a lot of excess baggage.

West Jet, a Canadian airline that flies to Cuba, allows overweight luggage if it contains donations to Cubans. I had gathered seven paragliders for our impoverished Cuban pilot friends and I had them with us. It was a wonderful gift and our Cuban hosts really appreciated it. Virtually all of their gear is donated by pilots visiting from abroad. Later, upon returning to Cuba again from Colombia, I brought them another gift: a large tandem Swift paraglider given to me by my good friend Richi, from Colombia Paragliding School. It was a wing in very good shape and Richie had quite the argument with his girlfriend, because she did not want it just given away. However, Richi is a very generous soul though and really wanted to help his Cuban brothers.

I had also left my faithful Sigma 6 Advance paraglider, with which I had first flown in the Sierra and then in Nevada. The glider was so well-used that I warned the Cubans to only fly it occasionally and to use it mostly for kiting on the ground. When I came back the following year with my gear, I was surprised to find that about 30 pilots had been flying my Sigma for about a year. I noted with some unease that the nylon material would just rip if I tore it with my hands. As mentioned, I had gifted the glider to my Cuban pilot friends the year before.

On this fall's trip to Cuba, I had also brought (as mentioned previously) along seven paragliders which I planned to donate to the local paraglide club based in Jibacoa. The region had some areas with some amazing soaring potential along a 14 km escarpment which jutted out of the coastline, rising 200 feet above the Caribbean. The tandem pilots there were living in total poverty in the semi abandoned campsite, which was composed of concrete bunkers built by the Russians. These bunkers, like the rest of the country's current infrastructure, were in a deteriorating condition. Troy and I had an amazing time starting out at the little all-inclusive resort in Jibacoa. It was at this resort where, the year before, we had filmed our whole segment. This was the campground where the paraglide pilots got their clients for their tandem rides. We arrived on the night when the local pilots had a huge welcoming pig roast and that made for a great party. Troy and I really enjoyed the all-inclusive week of semi luxury at the Jibacoa Tropico hotel. Then we travelled to Vinales, where I introduced Troy to Yaroscal, the local rock climber who guides, teaches and does tours. Troy did some nice small rock climbs with Yaro, who was becoming busy organizing a climbing festival later – an event with which I would again help.

I left Vinales with Troy. In fact, for a brief time, for the beaches of Trinidad, the beach resort town in Cuba – camping in our Hannassy Hammocks, and snorkeling, swimming, drinking rum and eating at a beach side restaurant. The diner staff here guarded our camping stuff while we were gone – in exchange for us eating there. Troy was a good judge of character and, while on a side trip to Havana, we both met up with Nat and Kassandra. Troy knew right away that Kassandra would be trouble for Nat; his only comment was that she was one of those girls who believed that "her shit did not stink". It turned out that he was very right: Kassandra did indeed take Nat for a nice ride.

It was a great trip – except one night, when we went to this popular disco in a cave. I got drunk, even started dirty dancing and took home what I thought was a girl but "she" turned out to be a guy. I quickly kicked her/him out of my hotel room – realizing I had been tricked. I am not homophobic but I was born into a man's body – sorry – and just could not bear the thought of having sex with another man. This happened to me also in Thailand once when drunk in a bar I chatted up two sisters, went back to their place and had to make my escape – after finding one was a Lady Boy.

Turning my reader's attention back to Jibacoa, Cuba: Troy and I often helped to feed the paraglide tandem pilots. These guys were so poor that they often had very little money to live on or even buy food with. We helped them by loading up on free hamburgers, pizza and hot dogs at the outdoor bar of the all-inclusive resort we were staying in. Then we would complement the food by filling up a couple cups with drinks of rum and carry everything to the beach, where we handed it all over to the waiting Cuban paraglide pilots. It was quite easy for us to do, because all beaches in Cuba have an 8 meter stretch from the seashore inland where local Cubans can hang out on, even at these all-inclusive resorts. This became common practice for us after a while. We just wanted to help feed our poor Cuban friends. When the winds were bad or they had no clients, they had to go out skin diving and harpoon fish for food. Later on I ended up spending at least three weeks living in one of the abandoned Russian-built bunker-like cabins. I snorkelled alongside them, picked coconuts and just relaxed because we could not fly during that time. The El Niño, the tropical weather front, was once again that year ruining the whole weather system on the island during that trip.

I also watched horrified one day when the Cubans brought home a farmed live rabbit for dinner. In order to kill the animal they took it by the hind legs and just whacked it against the palm tree really hard. I guess it was a quick way for the rabbit to go. However I must admit that I hesitated before I ate the rabbit stew they had cooked up that night. Unfortunately, the intricacies of Cuban corruption i.e. not knowing who to bribe! - prevented me from ever organizing the festival on Isla de la Juventud or Treasure Island that year. We tried everything! We even worked with an elderly professor of extreme sports at Havana University. Everywhere up the bureaucratic ladder we found that, unless we had the direct connection to Castro's Mafia ruling the country, we really could not overstep the bureaucratic process and we simply did not know who we had to bribe!

Instead I worked helping my good friend Yaro, who ran an incredible rock climbing festival in Vinales. He really put a great rock event together there. He and his group first spent weeks removing the vegetation from the climbing routes they had selected for the contest. Then they invited some world-class rock climbers, many of whom were already around and climbing in the vicinity. Even Sasha DiGuliann showed up from New York. The hottest thing in rock climbing, she arrived with an entourage and a film crew provided by Red Bull. Yaro even arranged for a huge truck to be converted to a bench-equipped bus to transport the climbers from town to the climbing site every day.

Exploring around Vinales, I also ran into my friend, Julie Vance, and her boyfriend from Haines, Alaska. I knew Julie well from the world extreme skiing championships, held back then in Valdez. Just as I had been taken by paragliding, Julie was now a kite surfing fanatic.

While exploring around Vinales, I came across a lake or a big water reservoir where I knew the trees around its edges had been stunted by the wind. I took Julie and her friend out to the lake which was not that far away. We travelled by a horse-drawn cart with all their kite surfing gear. It turned out the lake was an amazing spot for practicing the sport. Julie ripped up the whole lake in the wind and said it was an amazing place to kite. Being also fresh water it could have been an excellent place to start up a kite surfing school. I even proposed the idea to Oscar, a Cuban guy who ran a hostel-like operation, "Casa Oscar" for rock climbers. He was a real businessman and I'm pretty sure that, if I would have stayed around Cuba longer, I'm sure I would've talked them into buying a bunch of kiting gear and starting up a kite surfing school. He would have had a lot of clients from those people coming to Cuba to kite surf and who were checking out Vinales for its great mountain vistas.

While in Vinales, I took a room in yet another "Casa Particular", one where the owner had a rather peculiar job on the side. He slaughtered pigs that the locals had brought him, as a means of making extra money. It was rather unpleasant hearing the whining and screeching of the pigs every other day as they met their fate under the knife of the butcher. The man had a beautiful daughter who I took out and shot many photos of, which I then gave to her to fill her portfolio to help her get some modelling work. I just wanted to help the family which had been very kind to me. Besides rock climbing, there was also much good mountain biking, hiking, spelunking and horseback riding in the area. It was a great location that contained lots to do for more active tourists – not the whales that just stayed on the beach at the all-inclusive resorts.

I went to Colombia from Cuba, where I spent a good six weeks driving around the whole country with my friend Mauro and his beautiful sister Madellin. We discovered various flying sites from outside Bogota, Villa Vicencio, Bucaramanga, San Gill, Chilcamoya Canyon, then on to Roldanillo. We travelled in a Ford Bronco, powered half by propane and half by gasoline, which made fuel costs quite reasonable. The propane was used when we were travelling on the flats or the valleys while, on the mountain passes, we would throw the switch forward to use gasoline, because the car needed more power. It turned out to be an incredible trip and I also set up Pablo Lopez with good contacts to start up an aerothlon event in Roldanillo, Colombia the following year.

Roldanillo is an incredible little town with a population of only 30,000 people, where some of the best paragliding in the world takes place. Great thermals for flying were discovered there and, just before our arrival, the town had just held the "Paragliding World's Championship" in 2015 – a competition which was really the culmination of paragliding contests on the planet. About 600 paragliders from around the world now visit for about three months of the year. Colombian cuisine is not the greatest, so as soon as the town started to get a lot of tourists, better restaurants opened up – including an amazing Argentinian one that served delicious steaks. It's funny that, although Colombia has some of the best food as far as vegetables, fruit and anything else on the planet, it does not yet have the cooking expertise of Argentina or even Mexico. Roadside diners offered little beyond burnt, hard and overcooked meat with rice and beans. Compare this to the culinary expertise of the Argentines, who just know what cuts of meat to use – and how to properly prepare them.

It's clear that in Colombia, the paragliding activity has brought a lot of money to the local economy, a situation from which many people now benefit. There are dozens of cars, trucks and taxis designated just to take pilots to separate launches. There are now four launches above the town itself and more going southward, as well as on the other side of the valley in Chinche. This latter city was an excellent afternoon flying site, where my friend Mauro had tandem flying friends. This was also a place where Pal Takats, a world renowned Redbull athlete and Acrobatic paraglide pilot, had bought his dream property along with his lovely Austrian girlfriend. I had actually met Pal in Pemberton several years previous when he held a special SIV manoeuvre clinic over Lilloet Lake one summer.

A good friend from Vancouver, Ted Ingham, had bought a speed boat specifically for the use in such clinics. We would spend a couple summers going to the lake and being towed up by a special winch Ted had installed on his boat. Unfortunately there are so few paraglide pilots in Canada that, apart from it being a great hobby, the endeavour could never make a proper business for Ted with his boat and later he had to sell it. We did have some memorable times camping on the beach, being towed and watching each other do aerials then landing on the beach. Pal Takats, who was a great pilot, managed to get towed up one day at the far end of the lake. Once aloft he caught a thermal and flew all the way back to Pemberton which was 20 some kilometers away. Pal, along with another famous Red Bull athlete, Horacio Lorenz, also managed in recent years to climb and fly from the summit of the nearly 6,000 metre Pico Bolivar in the Sierra Nevada of Santa Marta, where I had previously done two memorable films and expeditions.

I really fell in love with Colombia on that trip and vowed to come back the next year. Colombia is such an amazing country, diversified by its many mountain ranges which contain, lying between them, deep plush green valleys. The paragliding potential, which is still just being discovered, is endless. I'm sure future world records will be achieved there in the sport. While there, I also met about 300 people in person with whom I had only been acquainted on Facebook and other social media. One such meeting seemed especially nice: a couple, Katarzyna and Marcin from Poland, who were living in Vancouver. Somehow we had never met while flying in Pemberton – meeting instead in Roldanillo. I felt a certain satisfaction from such encounters since some people had often chastised me about the sheer numbers of Facebook friends I had. They sometimes wondered aloud at the meaningfulness of keeping all those names, saying they were really just people I had never met and might never meet. Certainly I agree that Facebook can indeed be a lot of wasted time if you do not use it for the right reasons. You can just pass your time forever sharing with your friends what you might have had for breakfast. But if you have an event, a festival or a cause to promote, there really is no better free advertising or promotion available in the world.

From Colombia I returned came back to Cuba again for a month, hoping to fly. My mother once again joined me in Jibacoa at the all-inclusive resort for two weeks. However, as before, El Niño was still in, so the weather was not that great but we enjoyed each other's company (as I had missed Christmas back in Vancouver with her again).

After she left, I moved in with the paraglide pilots in the Russian huts for my last weeks in Cuba, but again the weather was uncooperative and I was unable to fly.

I went through a bit of stress on the trip to Cuba and Colombia. A week before my departure to Colombia from Cuba I made a big mistake. I usually hide my passport where I am staying. This time I hid it under an old one burner electric stove that was never used in the bunker where I was staying. Then, my worst nightmare happened. While I was out, the security guard lady decided to fry some fish on the never used stove in my hut. When I got back home after the fish fest was done I looked under the stove where I hid my passport. The hot grease used to fry the fish had spilled and burnt my passport. I was horrified since I needed it in 2 weeks to fly to Colombia. The Canadian Embassy did miracles for me and my new passport arrived Friday afternoon a half hour before the embassy closed for the weekend. I flew out to Bogota on Sunday. That was too close for comfort! The embassy staff must have been quite amused.

1

2

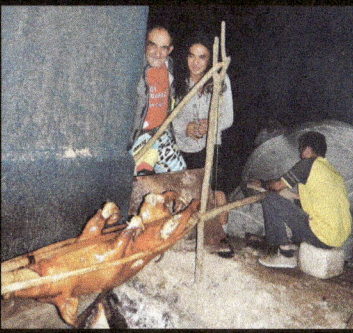

3

Interesting times in Cuba

1. Views around Viñales.
2. Basic local transport.
3. With Troy Jungen at a pig roast in Jibacoa.
4–5. Julie Vance from Alaska, kitesurfing on a new lake found near Viñales.
6. Paragliding over an old Russian built campground in Jibacoa.

4

6

5

In the air

1. Paragliders above Roldanillo, Colombia during competition.
2. View from the flight above Tenancingo Mexico.
3. Big air over the road near Pemberton, BC.

CHAPTER 15

MORE TIME SPENT SOUTH

I had enjoyed my stint in Cuba after visiting Colombia. However, thinking about it now, I feel I will not make a habit of going back there anymore. It was fun and everything, and I took in a lot of culture, especially with the Havana film Festival. Here we even had a sneak preview showing of the Paracinderella film at a special night club venue. It had been a nightmare dealing with the Havana Film Festival, trying to find a venue for our film. As before, it was unclear who we had to bribe to have our film officially entered or properly considered. So, avoiding that whole problematical situation, we found a restaurant and night club popular with the film crowd and arranged a showing there during but not as a part of the festival itself.

Again, concerning those who attended the Havana festival, I saw only the presence of an elite film community. They were quite arrogant, spoiled and rude. In my experience, this is how many in the upper classes behave in Latin America. They get preferential treatment from the government and the best cushy jobs in general, or so I felt. I was done with Cuba and had had enough. In the long run, I had discovered that, although the people were friendly, everybody had an agenda with you. Why? Because they really are prisoners of the regime and see every tourist as a potential ticket to get off the island. In the meantime the Castro family estate is said to be worth $900 million, or so says Forbes. There's an example of socialism at work for you.

There are a multitude of stories of Cubans flying to Ecuador – one of the few countries that grants them visas. From there they would walk overland through Colombia's Darien Gap – the perilous crossing between Panama and Colombia, where a road has still not been built. Then, whole families, thousands in numbers, would continue walking up through Central America – aiming to reach the US border with Mexico and hoping for asylum there. There are still thousands of Cubans left stranded in Central America after President Obama changed the laws allowing Cubans asylum status if they reached the US border by whatever means. Previously, once they reached US soil, they could apply for asylum. And they would probably receive it, given that it was a US policy meant to show America's determined and lasting opposition to Castro's Cuba. Mind you, America is no Angel and, as in Cuba, the CIA was busy disrupting Venezuela's politics whenever it could, ever since Chavez got in power there. Communist paranoia still prevails in the US of A and raises it's ugly head all too often.

Lately I heard an interesting tale from Bolivia. Since Morales the once popular Bolivian president was removed from office, Tesla shares skyrocketed. That is because American based interests wanted the minerals and especially Lithium from the Lithium abundant country. Morales, a dire socialist probably tried to block the exploitation of Lithium by foreign corporations and thus the States helped to organize a coup and have him removed.

Yes, the desperation in Cuba got to me after a while! I ultimately realized that almost everybody I had been dealing with was hoping I was their contact to somehow get off the island. It just got really tiring because of that. This is why it was so sad to see a carbon copy of Cuba emerging happening in Venezuela, a country which had been so affluent due to its huge oil reserves. I still remember this from our trip there in 1972 by VW with my parents. Hugo Chavez may have had good intentions when he nationalized the oil industry. At the time the industry was in the hands of the elite and there was a huge gap between the few that had and the rest of the impoverished country – who didn't. Power went to his head eventually, he saw himself as a new age Simon Bolivar and he became a dictator. Then after Chavez's death in 2017 from cancer, new President Maduro totally bankrupted the country. Over the years I watched this happen in Chile, Cuba and now – to my utter despair – Venezuela. Regarding Chile, I considered it especially sad, because I felt strongly that Allende really had been an idealist – not simply someone hungry for power.

In the fall of 2017 I attended an ARCTERYX party back home in Vancouver's trendy Kitsilano neighbourhood. The company makes very fine outdoor clothing and other outdoor gear very popular with upper scale people in Vancouver. My cousin John Hayto told me about a VIP party that was being held, which was by invitation only. But – hey! – "Once a dirt bag, always a dirt bag!" went our motto. So, we decided to crash the party in our regular nonchalant way. At the entrance our good friends Troy, Simon, Doris and myself got raffle tickets at the door. To our pleasant surprise, I won the $900 expensive Gore-Tex jacket and Simon, my good paragliding buddy, won the avalanche course. Unfortunately the folks at Arcteryx were not impressed. We were even told that by the organizers, "Some of our clients should have won that!" But it was too late, the dirt bags had scored again!

The year 2017 turned out to be another interesting one: I got an unexpected call for assistance that spring from a ghost from my past – the French extreme skier Sylvain Saudan. Returning to my somewhat usual naiveté, I invited Sylvain to my Pemberton home. After listening to his idea, I told him I would see what I could do about getting his name back on the famous Saudan Couloir run. Older readers will recall that it used to be named after him, before being changed to Couloir Extreme some 30 years back. Everyone still called the run "the Saudan", so I thought it was worth a try to officially get the name back. Unfortunately Vail Resorts had just bought Whistler and Blackcomb. My initial attempts were stymied because of a mix-up in the administration – as in nobody was answering my phone calls. So I did what I do best in these sort of situations and I went straight to the top.

I phoned Vail's CEO's executive assistant, Linda, and described what an asset it might be for the resort to get the Saudan name back for Blackcomb. Happily, the new CEO of the combined Vail/Whistler conglomerate agreed after Linda explained my idea, and he sent the message back to the powers at large in Whistler. From then on they welcomed us with open arms. In order to make that happen, I also organized two film showings for Mr. Saudan – one at the prestigious Millennium Place theatre in Whistler (where all the ski film premieres are usually shown). For the second event, I organized another show for Sylvain in Vancouver at the classic Rio Theatre on Broadway later that fall.

In Whistler, my bad boy reputation has followed me and – contrary to my expectations – I was offered a discount rate on my ski pass. I had been hoping for a lifetime ski pass for making the Saudan deal happen. I kind of shake my head at the effort I made – and the little appreciation I got from the Vail Corporation. Luckily the Whistler locals and my skier friends all know who brought the name back for them, so I guess that has made it worthwhile after all.

The beneficiary of my efforts, Sylvain Saudan, was not an easy fellow to deal with either – and I suffered for it. Always apprehensive, Saudan was usually worried that somebody was trying to steal from him. For example, he thought I may have made some money that he was unaware of from his film showings at Millennium place. He did not realize how expensive the theatre was to rent and he exploded in fury at me one day. My poor 86 year old mom had to step in and calm him down with a lecture. I felt obliged to ease his suspicions by showing him all the accounting information. I pointed out that I had actually lost a lot of time and money trying to organize the film showings for him. The whole ordeal must have made me so exhausted and stressed that on my first free day of the next skiing season, I fell and broke my leg quite badly on what is virtually a beginner run, the ski out called Highway 86 on Whistler Mountain. I was hospitalized in Vancouver while my poor mother cooked for and entertained Mr. Saudan for two weeks. In other words – during and after my accident, until it was time for him to go home, she was cooking. As for my leg, it had sustained a bad break. Not only that, it had been broken twice before in paragliding accidents and seemed to take so much longer to heal on this occasion. In the meantime Blackcomb fully exploited the Saudan name and brought back the spectacular Saudan Couloir race to the mountain again. Blackcomb and Vail Resorts even had Sylvain signing posters at the top of the couloir during the race itself.

By now Cuba had lost its lustre for me and I decided going back to that revolutionary paradise was of no interest to me anymore. By now in 2018, Colombia was becoming the place to frequent and enjoy. The Colombian government had recently signed a real peace deal with the FARC guerrillas and suddenly the country became an incredible place to visit. Up to now only real hard-core travellers and backpackers were the ones traveling around Colombia. In fact, the US still has a travel advisory for those visiting Colombia – leaving regular tourists still very hesitant to visit the country. However, once there, travellers found that the Colombian people were just happy to have you visit their country.

The locals were so welcoming that sometimes we would land our paragliders on someone's field or orchard and the whole family would come out to greet us, offering us fruit, drinks, and often dinner, before driving us back to town to our hotel. This re-opening of the tourism industry was helped by renowned author and ethno-botanist, Wade Davis, was quick to mention in all his lectures how Colombia had opened up to tourism lately. The country had been through so much violence from FARC as well as paramilitary groups, he said, that it was time for everyone to visit the wonderful country, which really deserved our tourism dollars. Wade, who had inspired me with his writings on the Sierra Nevada de Santa Marta, told me that last year, in 2019, 20,000 Colombians ventured out of their homes for the first time to travel around and explore their own country. Before that, they had been deeply terrorized by both the FARC and the paramilitary guerrillas. Kidnapping, for a while had become one of FARC's greatest revenue streams.

Colombians, as in most Latin countries, tend to have pretty large families. So FARC would just kidnap a child, and the family would raise money together in order to get the child released. For years FARC also waged a brutal campaign against the government, making bombing attacks in Bogotá and many other cities, and the public was terrorized. Peru is different again. Tourism is the second biggest economic factor after mining. The people remain proud. The Quechua Indians go about their daily lives with a normalcy, despite the tourists around them. Sure they try to sell us things but it's not out of desperation. Rather, it's a „take it or leave it" attitude as they go about their day. Mexico in general is the same, except when you get into the big resorts which have been overwhelmed and spoiled by tourists. In the town of Tenancingo, where I have spent a lot of time paragliding, the Mexicans wouldn't even glance at us. In this locale the only tourists were the occasional paragliders.

In general we all agree too much tourism spoils places – as is evident in the big beach resorts like Puerto Vallarta or Cancún. However, as soon as you get off the beaten road, people are much friendlier and not really expecting anything from you. One area that has changed, Valle de Bravo, is still the most popular place to paraglide in Mexico. But as soon as the „campesinos" (the local villagers) got wind of all the tourists visiting Valle de Bravo, businesses were created to capitalize on the opportunities. They started cashing in on all the visitors and inevitably things started to change. Taxi prices started going up and landowners were demanding fees for landing on their property. The locals started thinking that there would be a huge influx of money with these visitors, but this wasn't really true at all. Paragliders in general do not spend that much money and are they are always looking for the best deal – whether it be accommodation, rides to launch, or food in the restaurants. Unfortunately human nature is driven by greed, and gradually Valle de Bravo, once a great and cheap place to fly, became two or three times as expensive as other less known locations.

Whenever I travel to a new site in Mexico, Peru, Colombia and elsewhere, I try to teach the local children how to fold paragliders:. Kids in Valle de Bravo charge about two dollars to fold a paraglider once you have landed. It is a useful service as often one is quite tired after flying – and it's just nice to land and have your glider folded for you, while you drink a beer. Also it is great as a local micro economy. These kids actually make more money than many of their parents do working as labourers or in the fields. I have taught more than 100 kids how to fold gliders – from sheep herding Peruvian kids in Cuzco or Huaraz to Mexican youngsters in the distant fields near Malinalco or Tenancingo.

In all these cases I can proudly say, "I taught these kids how to fold gliders and make a decent amount of money for their families." I always wanted to do this with the kids from our local Mt Currie or Lil-Wat band. But here with minimal wage and all, they would have to charge at least 6 bucks for the folding service.

I just visited my dad lately. I had not seen him in person for over 20 years, although we are in touch by phone and email. I jumped on a plane to Fredericton, New Brunswick for a visit. We spent three glorious days together. This was something we had never done in one stretch, just the two of us. His wife, Hannah, was away in Europe and there was nobody else around. We went out for lobster, a New Brunswick specialty then we enjoyed never ending conversations about many topics, ranging from politics and science to media and the arts. I am so happy we did this together and hope for many more similar visits.

I returned to Colombia for three winters in a row, from 2016 to 2018. On my last trip there, I had a particularly horrendous bushwhacking experience from which I did not think I was going to come out alive. But somehow I managed to survive. I had launched at Los Tankes takeoff point that day. We had to wait a little longer for our launch window that morning, as the clouds had not yet parted over where we takeoff with our paragliders. When finally they did, I was the first to launch. I then proceeded to fly left to the house thermal. Suddenly I was hit by a rotor from the wind, which came in early from the Pacific that day. All at once the wind had me doing acrobatics and suddenly my glider was right below me – and very close to a mountain ridge or a bump on it. I had no choice but to do a huge pendulum swing – a manoeuvre in which I first turned over – and then under – my wing. I was fortunate: I somehow managed to top land the glider on the ridge below me. The grass was only up to my ankles at this spot. It would only have been an hour hike up to a road above me but, as lazy human nature would have it, I thought it would be easier just going down to the village below me.

It turned out to be a potentially fatal mistake. As I started scrambling down the steep slope, the jungle and the foliage intensified and grew taller. While flying over the landscape, it had all looked like an expanse of small grassy vegetation all around. How little did I know how different it was on the actual ground! It was like an impenetrable spider's web of cacti and every other type of vegetation equipped with spines. Sometimes it would be two meters in height. I used several techniques to go through the stuff. On the steep slopes I would just roll down, holding my paraglider in front of me and crushing the foliage as I descended. Down on the flats I would take my glider, throw it in front of me, crawl on top of it and then do it all over again. What made it worse is that I fly in the protective pod – a cocoon-like harness – in which I usually wear shorts. So my legs were getting a real beating on this expedition. Sometimes I would try another technique such as crawling on my belly below the major foliage and pushing the glider in front of me as I went.

I was definitely seeking a way through this vegetative mess. On my way down, I had spotted a small building way down below me. I learned later it was a water reservoir. It was further down the slope and over some flats – an estimated five hundred meters away. So I tried to stay on course towards that marker. Luckily I reached it and found a very rough machete-hewn trail which I followed. It finally took me into the village by dusk. Here, I virtually collapsed in the backyard of somebody's house and just cried out for help. Luckily somebody heard me and got a friend with a motorcycle to drive me back to my hotel in town. I have never encountered a harder bushwhack and I've been on a few before. It had taken me six hours to travel about 500 meters – about half a kilometre – in the cacti foliage to that water reservoir from hell. It nearly killed me. Luckily my cell phone worked from there and I was able to let my friends know the rough vicinity of where I was at, in case they had to send out rescue party for me the following day. Also a good Polish paragliding friend, a ship captain by trade, Stefan Piasecki, had launched shortly after me, spotted and identified me from the air, and let my friends know that I was all right. He saw me making my way down towards the village of Santa Rita. I spent the next entire three days curing my legs which were really swollen from all the cacti and spines in them. This was another hard lesson learned about being lazy and going down. It would've been much easier and faster to walk up to the road above me in the first place. Although I was deadly tired and my legs were swollen and full of thorns, looking back on the experience, I am kind of proud of myself – at my age – for somehow gathering the strength to crawl out of my terrible plight to safety. Again Polish climber Kukuczka's words come to mind here as he always said:

"The human organism is a lot stronger than we might anticipate."

But perhaps Kukuczka pushed it too far in the end as he died on the South face of Lhotse in 1989. He had already completed climbing the "Crown of the Himalayas" during his other alpine-styled ascents of all fourteen eight-thousanders. Yet that achievement did not seem to have been enough for him. He left a wife and two young children behind.

I have not dabbled in heavier drugs – or even cocaine for that matter – for many years. The Colombian laws are rather liberal towards drugs, and Colombians can legally possess 27 grams of marijuana as well as two grams of cocaine. The Aerothlon event had gone so well in Roldanillo, Colombia and I had worked hard to make the event happen – helping out Pablo Lopez in promotion and getting more athletes to enlist. My near death experience of crawling out through the jungle also convinced me that a good party now would be in order. It was a wild night at that downtown apartment above Roldanillo's main square that night. Nostalgic thoughts came back from old times in Peru and I do not regret the experience and will probably reflect on it for a long time.

In good company

1. Sylvain Saudan in front of his poster in Whistler, BC.
2. Saudan on the first ski descent of 8,000m+ Gasherbrum I or Hidden Peak in Karakoram.
3. Saudan taking it easy on skis in Whistler.
4. With Ptor Spricenieks in Whistler.
5. Dining on lobster with my father in Fredericton, NB.

Mountains and valleys

1. High flights over Pemberton.
2. My flight off Birkenhead Peak.
3. Above my favorite lake, Lillooet.
4. A carnival parade in Roldanillo, Colombia.
5. Native girl during parade in Roldanillo, Colombia.

CHAPTER 16

MORE ACCIDENTS, LIABILITY, AND NOSTALGIA

I love living in Pemberton although, like any village with a grand total of 3,000 people, it does lack the cultural perks of Vancouver and the bigger cities that I have so gotten used to. Whistler has a lot going on and is only 45 minutes away by car from our house, but I have begun to like my home's solitude. There are times when I don't venture out for days or even weeks when I am wrapped up in planning a new filming expedition, or involved in something like editing this book. Sometimes I have missed the social and intellectual stimulus that cities have to offer. I must say that although I have loved the action involved in my expeditions, with all the flying and skiing, I also still get huge pleasure from actually producing something whether it is writing an article, making a film, or organizing an event. I am a storyteller at heart, and in this way my personal ideology differs from that of other extreme athletes. For me, it is not enough to just go on a trip, carry out a ski or flight, and be fulfilled. In my dreams I find I am often chased by something, and so perhaps in my life I feel I am also being chased, as I dive into a new project so fast. I think I have to produce something from the experience to truly feel content. In actual fact my projects give me virtually the same satisfaction as the original expeditions in the field.

While most of my friends and neighbours in Pemberton were carpenters, mountain guides, or worked at the ski hill, I became a close friend and ski partner with a British fellow named Simon Bedford. Simon was an avid skier from London, who had done a lot of interesting broadcast camera work for the BBC. He had actually been a photographer in the 1970's and photographed many of the London bands like the Who. He made the bold move of moving to Whistler on the strength of its reputation alone, having skied for many years in the Euro places like Chamonix and La Grave. It must have been quite the culture shock for his wife and son after big city life. Simon and I have ended up doing a lot of work together on various films and projects. Simon's a great photographer and he did portraits of all the native elders and band members of the Mount Currie or Lilwat Nation tribe nearby, which ended up in a lot of galleries. Whenever I feel the need for intellectual chitchat on current affairs and politics I go over to Simon's house and we have some great talks.

During the early times of President Trump we got together, Simon and me, once in a while and would have a great laugh about him. I particularly remember coming to Simon's house one morning, having a coffee together and wondering -"What did that idiot do today– who did he piss off, or what new enemies can he make abroad?" It really was a good form of entertainment for us. Simon and I did a lot of skiing together, shot some great YouTube videos, such as hiking up the Goat Path in Whistler for great powder turns. Simon turned out to be a true friend as well: he was always there to help out when I would come home broken up from a paraglide crash or something. He's kept me entertained. I wish I had met him earlier as he would have made a great co-producer, friend and mentor on many of my productions. Sure I had lots of other good neighbours and friends around but the conversation was always limited with them. It revolved around paragliding, other sports and more local chit chat. My talks always went deeper with Simon and I really appreciated that.

The Paragliding community in Pemberton liked to be called the "Pemberton Flying Monkeys". Most of us are long time pilots who are largely self-taught, and had been flying long before the arrival of HPAC paragliding insurance. The maturity of the sport brought all the various other bureaucracies out of the woodwork populated with people trying to regulate the sport. Jim Orava was one of the oldest flyers here, and has been given the name of „Master Monkey". He is married to a Swiss paraglide pilot named Corinne Stoltz Orava. When he is not flying he works in the film industry here in Hollywood North, aka the Vancouver film industry, doing stunts and rigging, specialized jobs for which he was paid very well. Because Jim and Corinne had no children or large family expenses, Jim could manage to work only a few months of the year, and then travel to paraglide all over the world the rest of the time. Corinne used to join him on all these trips but later she purchased two horses, which made her unable to leave for longer periods of time. Jim is an amazing pilot who was the Canadian Champion in several competitions. He still competes in competitions around the world, such as the famous Monarca race in Mexico's Valle de Bravo every year.

Jim actually motivated and started out teaching many of the great local climbers and mountaineers how to paraglide. Some of them have since done incredible record flights, and have flown triangles over 200 km in length around the valley surrounding Pemberton. Jim was also responsible for securing the tenure for our paraglide launches above the Pemberton Valley. He was "the master monkey" who motivated all the others to help make the launches the reality that they are now – as well as getting the government grants to pay for the official designations. Although I was not the greatest hands-on guy in physical labour, I did my best to promote tourism and invite more paragliders to Pemberton using my social media pages. Personally I would much rather have those type of visitors than the church groups the municipality brought in as their contribution to tourism in the area. The town was still a little backward given how the Jehovah's Witnesses still commandeered most of the staff at one bank and at the town's medical clinic. Other members of the "Monkeys" were Jim Orava, Alastair Collis, Brad „Dingho" Murphy, Chris Kettles, Mel Scardoni, Tye Trand and a myriad of other monkeys paragliding there. Our community numbered about 20 to 30 pilots at one time. We were self-taught simply because there were no paragliding schools around at that time.

There never seemed to be a dull moment as the Pemberton flying monkeys progressed in their aerial adventures. Accidental tree landings were common and I had a few of my own. It doesn't take much to take your concentration away for a moment when flying: just look the other way and suddenly you are in the trees. It just takes one line to hook a branch and that takes you and your glider down. We had a lot of monkeys hook trees right upon takeoff from the lower launch, or while crossing the first ridge to the left where the thermals were. There was also a hollow between lower and upper launch which was easy to get trapped in. I remember once being in there and knowing I had to go down in the trees. I looked at all my options and tried to find the biggest clearing between the tall cedars. During the last moment as I cleared the last tree I put my hands out as far as I could, grabbed all my lines in my clenched fists. This gave me a couple extra meters falling through the branches – probably saving me from being hurt a lot more than I was.

A short list of some of my near-misses would have to include stories like:

Years ago, still on my old Wild Things glider, I was flying in the Chilliwack Valley. We launched off Mount Thurston and there was a sea of clouds only a couple hundred feet above the valley. As I penetrated the clouds I came out above a vast forested area without any clearing to land on, except for this one small gravel pit about the size of a small house. There was a road running through the pit. I started spiralling down towards the clearing and somehow out of sheer luck my last spiral took me right into the road, which was like going into a tunnel surrounded by tall trees and branches above me. I landed safely and thanked those angels again for taking care of me.

Another time in Hedley, I was stuck back in the valley's box canyon because a big wind came up. I could just not penetrate flying back out of there into the valley. Below me was a forest but, in one place, I saw a rock fall. I decided to chance it and land my paraglider in there among the boulders. I decided to go into spiral mode, then swooped in and somehow softly landed on top of one of the boulders in the rock fall. It was the size of a Volkswagen beetle. Miraculously, I touched down lightly and only bruised my hip slightly; otherwise my poor, already-battered body was okay. I packed up my glider and hiked out of there.

There was the time near Vancouver's North Shore that Dan Redford and I climbed up from Mount Seymour to Goat Mountain above the Capilano watershed. It was a precarious cliff-like takeoff but we both managed to launch okay. I managed to land on the gravel road in the Capilano watershed itself, while Dan was not so lucky and landed on a rock in the middle of the Seymour River, in the process breaking only his wooden seat board harness. Luckily the board protected him from any injury and we both managed to hike out of there all right without being caught by the authorities, as it is not allowed for anybody to venture in to the Vancouver watershed.

When talking about paragliding, I must mention my friendship with two individuals back in the early 90s. Max de Yong and Francis jointly ran a shop called Extreme Mountain Gear on W. 4th Ave. in Vancouver and were pioneering a lot of the paragliding in British Columbia. Max and Francis are renowned for their many paraglide adventures and close calls in the early days of flying around the lower mainland of BC. Back in those early days of flying, when the gear and safety protocols were not as developed as today, the tandem passenger sat behind the pilot. Paragliders never carried reserve or emergency parachutes for solo flying. I accompanied the two quite often on flights off Mount Thurston and other locations in the Chilliwack Valley. They drove a 4x4 Russian Lada vehicle which was our transportation up to the launch. One of our precarious launches was off the very peak of the West Lions near Vancouver. I launched off it twice, including once with Francis. The Twin Peaks of the Lions are clearly visible from Vancouver as they jut out from the northern horizon like two prominent bread cone-shaped mountaintops. It takes about 3 1/2 hours to hike up to the Lions from Lions Bay and the very last bit of the climb up to the West Lion consists of a few technical rock moves. The top of the Lion is barely the size of a modest living room – giving a pilot a good heartthrob, before taking off the cliff launch. The best place to fly to from this location happens to be a nude beach near Lions Bay, because it is big enough to land on when the tide is out. I frequented the beach often during the summer, given it is a very shielded bay, into which the usually cold Pacific extended, making it a pleasant swimming cove. I made two flights off the Lions landing on the beach over a few years.

Speaking of the Twin Lions, I also recall another adventure, this time one of the skiing kind, when we tried to publicize a first ski descent from the mountain. The idea was to film it from a BCTV News Hour helicopter, as part of creating another media spectacle for ITV.net as William was still trying to get something going with skiing projects. Several of us had climbed the Lions early one May morning. It was hard to predict what time of year it would be possible to ski the rock encrusted bread cone but that particular year there was a lot of snow and we felt justified in giving it a try. Although we reached the summit, we could not find a way to ski safely down the mountain, and I nearly died in an avalanche during our descent. The story: I usually take care to stay far away from the edge of a corn-iced slope like the one on the high pass that sits between the Lions. I was at least 50 feet from the edge of the cornice when I took off my backpack and put it down to take a rest before I put my skis on after the climb to continue my descent. Just then the entire slope gave way a foot below my backpack, sending an enormous chunk of the cornice, at least the size of Vancouver's City Hall, down into the ravine below. It was one of the closest calls and scariest moments of my life, seeing nature's power so close to me. One of the other skiers that day, a friend of Troy's called Eren sadly died a few years later attempting a descent of Mt St Elias, the second highest mountain on the US-Canadian border. Troy and I had stayed with him in Lake Tahoe years before and it was really sad to lose another brother.

Sometimes our paragliding mishaps were just plain stupid rather than dangerous, and here is a prime example: one day I asked my tenant drive me up to our lower launch – after which he was going to drive my car down. Unfortunately, it was only after I launched that I realized I had forgotten to give him the keys to my Delica. So I started circling around the launch, screaming at him and trying to throw my keys to him. Unfortunately, I lost my concentration with the flying bit, hooked a branch and came down yet again – however this time luckily rather softly right below launch.

Another time I had another flying misadventure, or rather, I made a bad choice of landing field. I got caught in what was a convergence of winds coming from Whistler and from the Northwest. I had lots of altitude but the Whistler wind was driving me eastward towards Mount

Currie. Occasionally I would turn into the wind to determine whether it was slowing down enough so I might attempt a landing. Finally, when I felt it was safe to do so, I landed but I didn't realize how far I was from the nearest road. I had landed in the field all right, but it was horrendous getting out. After struggling through the tall grass for several hours I finally reached a ditch. It was too wide to jump over and filled with water, but I didn't think it would be too deep, so I just braced myself for the ordeal and decided to wade through it, thinking it might come up to my knees. It turned out to be deep enough to reach my armpits, but I somehow managed to get to the other side, as it felt sort of like a quicksand underneath my feet. I emerged soaking wet with a very heavy wing and finally got to the village of Mount Currie, and eventually some friends gave me a ride home.

Paragliding is so interesting because of the eclectic and varied crowd that practiced the sport. My flying friends come from many walks in life. One of my friends is a 70 year old Polish Canadian engineer, Roman Karas. He worked for an international construction company, and managed to take his paraglider along on a many of his contracts. He flew in some exotic places such as the ex-Soviet state of Chechnya, where he needed bodyguards to fly and land, or exotic Madagascar in the Pacific. On one contract in Turkey he managed to crack some vertebrae in a rough landing and was flat on his back for four months as a result. But he continues flying and comes up to Pemberton as often as he can. It gives me a lot of confidence to see pilots who are older than me still flying into older age. One famous Polish paraglide pilot nicknamed "Praszczur" or "Grandpa" started flying at 78 years of age and the last we heard was that he did a tow flight when he was over 90. I would love it if I could keep flying into such a ripe old age.

But our fate comes in mysterious ways and besides losing Judd and Grampa Dave to paragliding accidents, we have also lost other great friends and pilots here in Pemberton. Rudi Rozsypalek, the pioneering glider pilot died when his glider was in a collision with a small Cessna which was off-course. Four people and a dog died in that crash. Rudi's son Thomas now paraglides with us. Jim Orava taught him. There is also a celebration every Solstice in June in memory of Marty: a "Marty Day." Oni Ajo, another Reid Road local and Marty's best friend, organizes the party each year faithfully for his friend. It usually takes place on either the upper or lower launches here in Pemberton as an all-night rave. Marty loved to dance, but sadly he died of cancer when he was only 34 and it is way too young to die.

I spent the spring and summer of 2018 battling the bureaucracy here in Pemberton trying to get support for an Aerothlon event to happen in my home town. That year marked an important milestone in my life. I made a return visit to Peru again at the end of June, which was the 40th anniversary on my first ski film „Ski Peru" of which I was the associate producer. It also marked the 40th anniversary of my ski descent from Huascaran.

My old friend Benca's "Festival del Andinismo Cordillera Blanca" was on again, so my friend Doris and I flew to Lima and then took the bus to Huaraz. Thinking that this trip might be my last big pilgrimage back to Peru, I felt it had a meaningful significance. I had done a lot of things in Peru in the last 40 years and so I thought that this trip would be a sort of culmination of all my trips here. I also wanted to get over the demons which still lingered in my head from my most serious paraglide crash to date – the one off the Barig Mine launch back in 2012 which ended in a broken femur. The Aerothlon had been held there for several years by then.

As a community we now talk a lot about battling fear, and a lot of attention is being paid to the subject now. Everyone has a personal way of coping with fear. Some will use faith or religion. Whatever, it seems I successfully exorcised my demons, and it felt great to overcome my fears and lift off once again from this location. I enjoyed a great flight, but 10 minutes after landing I realized that our flight path to the designated landing zone had crossed the flight path of the commercial airline route to the local airport. To my utter horror, just 10 minutes after I had landed, a small turboprop airplane went through the same airspace we had just been flying in.

Benca had asked me to give an hour-long presentation on my life at his festival, especially my Peru adventures. Ivan Canturin had also brought Inkafest again to Huaraz and my presentation was scheduled in between the films at the festival. It was a great opportunity to retell my 40 year history of adventures in that country. My presentation captured a full house – on the same night that the Inkafest Film festival also taking place at the same time. I got a lot of laughs and it seemed my presentation went really well. I was also very pleasantly surprised to find that Benca's father, Benjamin Morales, was there as well. After all, I had met him back even longer than 40 years ago – in 1972 on my first trip to Peru with my parents, in our family's Volkswagen van. It was so nice to see him again after knowing him for all these years. I sensed I had really come full circle here: I felt I had fully earned the moniker Peter Peru given my long relationship with this wonderful country.

Benjamin Senior was an incredible man. He was a devoted glaciologist who was very worried about what climate change was doing to the glaciers around Huaraz. He described to me how the villages and the rivers below the glaciers were drying up, thus depriving the people living below of water. He had devised an ingenious method of carrying by hand, by donkey and by mule, bags of sawdust, which he would then spread over the tongues of the particular glaciers. His technique was proving successful. One of the glaciers where we had skied and raced on snowboards was proof of it. The evidence was before our eyes: the ice fall where we have ladders placed to get up on the glacier passed points where the sawdust covered ice was meters higher than the rest of the glacier. Sure, this "sawdust solution" is not applicable to all of the Andes but you can choose and pick a few places – especially when the water supply is in peril. When I came back to BC I proposed Benjamin's idea to Blackcomb, as a way to preserve the little glacier there which was shrinking rapidly year by year. Sawdust is easy to obtain especially in BC, and one helicopter load would have done the job. My idea was spurned by Blackcomb, who told me that they were already consulting with Europeans about using plastic tarps. In my view the situation can be summarized as follows: tarps will look pretty terrible on the glacier, compared to some natural sawdust which would just wash away with time. But what are my opinions compared to expert European consultants?

After enjoying Benca's Festival, Doris and I, decided to visit Cajamarca. It is the northern capital of the Inca people in Peru and I had always wanted to visit. I had met a wonderful young woman at the festival in Huaraz called Leona Noriega. She is an expert climber and had promised to show us around the place. A lawyer and avid outdoors woman, she really wanted to get a similar festival started in her hometown and so I said I would gladly check out the area for its multi sport potential and would bring my paraglider along. Doris and I took the slow local bus up to the town, where Leona met us and showed us all the sites. There was only one local paraglide pilot supposedly residing in Cajamarca so this was unexplored territory for flying. I was very happy to be in this town, because my parents and I had missed it on our VW trip 1972/73. This town has a sad history: it was here in 1533 that the last Inca ruler Atahualpa was tricked and taken hostage by the Spanish Conquistadors. The invaders told his people that if they filled a whole room full of gold, their emperor would be released unharmed. But it turned out to be a deception and the last Inca ruler was killed anyway. The actual room that was filled to the seams still exists, and now is a major tourist attraction in town.

Unfortunately, the only paraglide pilot in Cajamarca was working in the USA. However, thanks to his help via Facebook, I found the paraglide launch site and was able to take a beautiful flight over the whole valley. Everyone was very keen to get something going in town and had great plans to start paragliding business there – as well as getting other sports going. Many Peruvian towns tend to lose all their youth, if there is nothing left in the city to attract them to stay. Doris and I had a wonderful time in Cajamarca. The town, unlike many in Peru, had never been destroyed by an earthquake and was still full of old colonial Spanish architecture, which Doris really enjoyed discovering. There were very interesting old burial sites in caves above and around the town, which were also very special to visit. Leona turned out to be an amazing guide and she knew the area very well.

Later that fall back in Pemberton, I got a surprise visit from a gentleman named Javier Cabrera. He came to my home in Pemberton and gifted me several bottles of Pisco Liquor and some great organic Peruvian coffee. He was working for a large Canadian gold mine that was located near Cajamarca. He told me he was tired of his job at the mine and wanted to get into tourism work. Leona had told him about my expertise and willingness to organize various festivals, as I had done in

Peru and Cuba. Javier's plan was to get a festival similar to Benca's going in Cajamarca. I suggested hosting an Aerothlon event there as well, given that it was near the border with Ecuador, a country which had a lot of paraglider pilots very eager to make the trip to Peru for the event. Unfortunately I learned later that the one and only paraglider pilot, a guy named Nery based in Cajamarca, had been terribly injured in a flying accident. He ended up in a coma for a few months. Nery's accident kind of put a damper on any future plans for a future paragliding festival there. It was somewhat similar to the accident in Huaraz with Xavier, which had postponed my X-Andes project indefinitely. However, time heals all so maybe the atmosphere will change in the future, because I would love to go down there and help organize something with my new friends in Cajamarca.

By July 2018 I was back from Peru in Pemberton when I got word that a 39 year old Polish skier, Andrzej Bargiel, had made the first ski descent from the summit of K2, the second highest mountain in the world at 8,611 m (28,251 ft). It was an impressive descent from the very peak down to the base camp at 5,000 meters. It was an incredible feat captured on drone by his brother who filmed the entire descent from the base. Others have died while attempting to ski down this mountain, but many more have perished just trying to climb the very technical peak.

Once again I find I am proud of my Polish heritage, and my sentimental attachment to my roots reborn again. Polish Himalayan climbers have had so many great climbing achievements over the years, and now a young and unknown skier from my country has taken the greatest prize in ski descents. I wish I could feel pride for the rest of the country but I find it hard. I think the Church and State have gotten out of hand ruling Poland, and on that subject, I am a Polish Patriot and I honour Polish history and it's peoples' fight for independence from invaders from the east and west for centuries, but sometimes I am ashamed of what is going on now in Poland. The far right is now rampant in both my home country of Poland and Hungary. They refuse to let refugees in, unlike the rest of the European Union. In Poland the same church and State try to impose their own like-minded judges on the high courts and a big dispute has arisen with the EU because of this. I call this 'Catholic Fascism' as the Church is orchestrating all this in cahoots with the Polish government. At least in the climbing and skiing world I have something to be proud of being Polish. The Polish skier Andrzej Bargiel's accomplishment on K2 overrides all the bad politics and I am so proud of this guy.

Meanwhile I continued working on my Aerothlon event: because it comprised of running, paragliding and mountain biking, and I was now in Canada, I had to deal with three different insurance policies for the three separate sports. I also would have loved to start the race right in the middle of downtown Pemberton, as happens in the Peru, Mexico or Colombia editions of the race. But here in Canada this became Mission Impossible. Canada's love of litigation, as in the US, means that the costs of putting on an event becomes so high that only large corporate-backed events can be held.

I soon found out that for my Aerothlon, I would need to position a flag person at every intersection to stop traffic as the athletes raced through, and these people had to be paid at least $200 a day. These marshals alone would have taken over half of my budget. I also received what I considered nothing but bureaucratic hurdles from the Squamish Lillooet Regional District (SLRD) – our local government entity which is in charge of the agricultural lands around Pemberton. It seemed to me that the bureaucrats have nothing better to do but try to block me from doing my event by inventing excuses.

The Aerothlon race did indeed take place in September, 2018 as planned, but the stress and effort of the entire exercise almost killed me. I had also tried to enlist the support of the current mayor of Pemberton. Two important people were planning to attend – the Mayor of Malinalco, Mexico where the Aerothlon had been founded, and Benca, from his festival in Peru. Both had reached out to our Pemberton mayor, hoping for some cross-cultural action like a reception to welcome the event to Pemberton, given that our Aerothlon was being held in all three countries. Unfortunately, too much must have been happening elsewhere because the reception never happened.

In the end, I did manage to pull it off by the skin of my teeth with the help of many friends who turned up to help out on the day. My old sponsor Intuition Sports, who make the best ski-boot liners in the business, kindly provided much needed support as did Cariboo Beer, a local

BC brewery who provided the post-race event with some great beer. The Pemberton Rotary Club also helped enormously.

The race was made up of three legs: a 12kms hill climb up to the Paraglide launch at 4,500', a speedy glide back to the valley floor, and a gruelling 25 kms mountain bike course through the legendary Pemberton bike trails. Athletes could compete in all three legs, or be part of a relay team as a runner, flyer or mountain biker. I hosted the event out of my house, as by then we did not have the budget to rent a proper venue. It turned out to be a lucky choice, with a great awards ceremony and the party afterwards went on through the night. Any event has to have a video, and local camera people helped out. Of course, as on any day paragliding, for the filming we had two drones flying and one of them hit a tree. My friends Harvey and Barry showed up to help film the event, as did Simon and another drone operator I found on facebook from Squamish. Another old friend of mine, Paul Guschlbauer showed up at my house in Pemberton with his new wife Magdalena. Paul is a celebrated Red Bull X-Alps athlete, who has won both the Mexican and Colombian Aerothlons. He also placed second and tied third in two Red Bull X-Alps races in Europe. We first met in Cuba when the Aerothlon was cancelled in 2016. I had taken him to Vinales where he had some great free flights instead.

Paul and Magdalena were flying a Super Cub small airplane from Alaska to Argentina in short stages. Paul kindly checked out the Aerothlon course, completing the run and subsequent flight, and gave a nice endorsement on camera for our video.

In order to rest and recuperate from the whole Aerothlon ordeal, I decided to go back to Mexico. I wanted to try some flying from near my new base, which was a little cabin I had bought. Paragliding politics was involved too: because I was not a fully accredited flyer back home, without the all-important P2 paraglide rating, I needed to get that lack of qualifications addressed. I am old enough to have flown before any of these regulations were introduced and the hole in my resume is catching up with me. Instructor friends told me I if could do all my required launches and flights down in Mexico, then after reviewing them, they would count towards the required level as part of my exam. I had already passed the written part of the exam back in Canada and now I had to do the actual flying. So I spent six marvellous weeks logging 70 hours in the air. Then on the last of my 25 flights, I was doing a final cross-country leg from our La Malinche launch site to Malinalco, a town about 30km away, when disaster struck me yet again.

I was easily making the landing approach above the small field I had chosen with no problem. I was using the figure 8 approach method above the road and the power lines to lose altitude in a controlled way. The field I had chosen was not very big and I wanted to make sure not to overshoot it. Such places often have barbed wire and other obstacles at the end which I didn't want to hit. So I tried to make it safe and land near the middle, I started my landing approach from well back over the wires and the road. Suddenly, during my approach manoeuvre, I was hit by a strong gust of wind which threw me back further towards the power lines. Sitting back in my pod harness and looking upwards, I was blinded as I faced the sun for that one critical moment, and tried to correct the flight so I could make my landing, which had now moved away from me.

I hit the power lines in a big explosion of sparks, and then bounced backwards, glider and all, coming loose from the wires, and fell through the trees. I had come down in a graveyard of all places, which certainly added a little black humour. Luckily my fall to the ground was slowed by tree branches breaking under me. I can imagine what the two grave diggers thought as I interrupted them working, but they recovered quickly enough to get help. I was numb from the shock, and I thought I was dead for sure after this one, as I had hit the two power lines, one with my butt and the other with my ankle. The electricity had entered my body through my legs at thigh height on the first power line, and had exited – blowing a hole out of my ankle in an explosion of sparks, where the ankle had touched the second power line. Sitting on the ground waiting for help as I gathered my senses, I noticed I could not feel anything in my right leg. Luckily, my panic receded after about 20 minutes as I started getting the feeling back in my toes. Later at the hospital, my whole leg was coloured purple, and in the two places where the electricity had entered and exited my limbs it looked more like hamburger meat than living flesh.

Some readers will find it strange that as a result of this crash, a campaign against me was started, trying to get me banned from the launch so I would not be able to paraglide. I feel that this was really unfair, as that last crash was truly a freak accident, and had happened when I had exceeded nearly all the P2 requirements I needed to fly legally in Canada. I had been flying a total of 33 years and I had four major accidents in that time. However, every one of them had a reasonable explanation – including one that I admitted was caused by my own my pilot error.

Odd encounters seem to occur after this latest accident:

As I was writhing in pain and at my most vulnerable lying in my hospital bed two individuals who had taken over the operation of running the La Malinche launch, and the new company that had been established to run paraglide tours in the area came to visit me in the hospital. I have never been more insulted in my life than by this visit. One of the visitors claimed I had brain damage and that I was a sociopath with a death wish. OK, this was not the first time I have heard this, but it is always from people who have no real clue about me. My visitors had even brought down all my belongings and said I was not welcome at La Malinche anymore. Some people just lack any sense of decency or compassion. Could they not have waited until later to scold me, rather than just while I was hurting so much already.

Even worse, another visitor threatened to cut up and destroy my paraglider if I ever appeared at our paraglide launch in Pemberton ever again. I could not bear the thought of not flying again in my backyard! After all, one of the reasons I had built my house there was especially for its proximity to the launch areas.

Apart from the ban on flying I was also sad not to be able to help promote the local Daniel Pedrazas Flight Park or the La Malinche launch site as I had done for the previous 13 years. Daniel Pedrazas has worked hard for last 18 years, investing all he has on creating one of the greatest flying sites in Mexico. He is a true visionary who is driven by passion and not just by money. His wife Marta turned out to be a true friend who visited me every day and brought me food and drinks as I recuperated in my hotel room in Tenancingo. Two other friends from home, Jim Orava and Stefan Piasecki, came over from Valle de Bravo, and had found me a small hotel and helped me move there from the hospital. Except for the visits from Marta and my Polish paraglide friends I spent a lonely two months. Most of my time I spent productively writing these words. Paragliding is a dangerous sport and accidents are a part of it, so I felt I was being really picked on as several people took it upon themselves to try to stop me from flying again.

I had had such great plans for Daniel's Flight Park. I had already helped him make some money by arranging some good tenants from my circle of friends for the little apartment he had made at the launch. I also thought there was a real potential of bringing other athletes, such as rock climbers from Squamish and mountain bikers from Whistler, during those harsh Canadian winters. I had already written to Yaro, my rock climbing friend in Cuba, and invited him over to Mexico to help scout new routes for rock climbing at La Malinche.

I had actually started writing these memoirs while flying at La Malinche, continued in the hospital, and then my little hotel. Having to move out of the hotel for cost reasons I carried on while recuperating at my friend's Pablo Lopez' cabin in Malinalco. My travel insurance covered my stay in the clinic for only one week and after that I stayed in the hotel, and then finally moved into Pablo's house. I knew I had six weeks of real solitude to really focus and get the bulk of my book written here. After that I planned to just edit and add small sections to it later when I was back in Canada. When I finally caught my plane back to Vancouver, I was just starting to be able to put weight on my leg.

As I have mentioned before in this tale, if one gets almost famous and has a certain notoriety in the media, one meets a lot of new "friends" but among such friends there are also a few ass-holes – as has been the case here. I will just leave it at that, amen.

Luckily, writing my life story had kept my spirits up during the nearly six weeks that have now passed since the accident happened. As of this writing, the experience has turned out to be a great "make-work" project – and one has helped me pass the misery of rehabilitation.

I actually began to write my book two months before my accident, but I really did not have the discipline to write every day because I was often too tired from paragliding all day long. I also lost the first 12,000 words, as I am really not that computer savvy. In fact, I accidentally deleted the whole beginning part and was unable to ever recover it.

Then a visiting French paraglide pilot named Tristan, who had arrived at the La Malinche launch site, helped me out a great deal by finding me a software that allows me to just dictate my book to the machine and then just edit on my word document. As I still type with only two fingers, I often punched the wrong keys on the computer and that's how I had deleted my text in the first place.

I am happy to admit that I have been inspired by the famous British climber and author Joe Simpson to write my book. At first I tried to emulate Joe by writing 2,000 words a day – as he had done during his writing career. Later on and thanks to the accident, I had a lot of spare time and some days I wrote as much as 8,000 words daily. In total, I first spent a week in the hospital, next moved in to the little hotel room in Tenancingo for three weeks, and finally moved to Malinalco, where my good friend Pablo Lopez was kind enough to let me stay in his little cabin, surrounded by pristine Mexican wilderness. This turned out to be an ideal place to recuperate as well as finishing writing a general draft of my book.

I am again reminded how much I love living in Pemberton. I think Canada is probably one of the best places to live in the world out of all the countries to which I have travelled – up to 57 now, I think. That number seems funny to me – a weird kind of correlation perhaps – because that is also the amount of women I think I have slept with in my entire life. Although seeing the numbers, I realize that they really have nothing to do with each other. Besides being a matter of apples and oranges, the majority of the women I had been with were probably during my first trip to France when I was 18 and 19, and sex was plentiful then. I count the women sometimes to amuse myself, while trying to fall asleep. It's sort of like counting sheep. I know it all sounds rather crass and a lot of feminist-minded women would not like what they read here. However, I'm just telling things, as it is, from my heart. I truly do not think I am a chauvinist. I love women but just not found that elusive soul mate yet.

Sometimes I wish society in general, the one that wants to regulate every human activity for health and safety, would just leave us risk-takers alone. In my case it's my personal obsession with paragliding. I know it's a dangerous sport as are many other extreme sports that we choose to participate in. With paragliding the best way of putting it is that it is 'dangerously easy'. It's a sport that requires a lot of skill and patience while waiting for the right winds and weather. Making the wrong decisions can easily result in death or severe injury, as has been the case for me several times. I know I am also not the most careful person when practising sports like paragliding or skiing. For that reason, I never wanted to do tandems or take passengers flying. I just did not want the responsibility. It is one thing if I break myself up but it would be totally unacceptable to me if I was to hurt a passenger.

This makes me actually recall another incident flying in Pemberton. My radio had died during my flight so I didn't know what was happening at the launch. Another Pemberton pilot, a neighbour actually, was advising people not to top-land but I didn't get that info. I came in for my landing, prepared and flared and landed a bit hard, but on my feet and no big deal. The next thing I see was this guy running up to me and making slashing moves on my paraglider's lines. At that moment I was a bit zoned from flying all day and really did not realize what the guy was doing. Well, it turned out he ran up to me and cut a bunch of my lines with a knife as punishment for not heeding his advice about top landing that day. My radio had died so I knew nothing of his worries, and yet more bs is thrown in my direction.

Since I have no kids or family, except for my 88 year old mother, I think it's really up to me alone if I want to take risks. All my paragliding accidents were a result of my own pilot error – mine and only mine. But I managed to survive them and can only hope that I learned from each one not to repeat the same mistake ever again. That's all we can really do in life when we practice these risky sports. I do not think it's for society to dictate to us individually how we should lead our lives. I still smile when I think of my time in Alaska in the 1990's and the risks taken there by the locals, when they put on the world extreme skiing championships. The people of Valdez forged on with their dream to hold the contest, despite the huge liability risks involved. We don't get banned buying a ski lift ticket although we've had a few accidents skiing. Or, we do not often have our car insurance denied after an accident, although our premiums may go up. So then, what gives the right to people along with HPAC to prevent me from flying?!

Whistler and Blackcomb have lost over a dozen mountain bikers annually to spinal cord injury, and it makes the local doctors really angry having to mend these cases all the time. Yet, since the sport brings such good revenue to the resort, the injuries are hushed up by WB and now the Vail Corporation. When I do a count of dead comrades these days, I find I have lost most friends to avalanches – a lot more than to paragliding.

Such have been the losses in my social life. Physically, there have been costs too: my body is a bit too beat-up to enjoy the hard core work outs of the past any more. Whether it is on ski tours, long treks or even mountain biking, my carcass has been through the mill. I think that as long as I do not crash anymore while paragliding, I could keep flying into my 80's – as long as I can manage to run the few steps at takeoff.

I am amused when I see all these guys my age re-discovering their youth and pushing their bodies to the limits. Well, I have no desire to push my body like that anymore – in any of the sports I do. I know I can do whatever it takes if I have to survive, as I did on my last bushwhack in Colombia. I have been doing this all my life and feel the flying is now my reward for all the abuse I subjected myself to in my younger years. I am sixty some years old now, and rather tired of too much physical exertion. I did all that when I was younger. We ski-toured back when it was just starting to be popular in BC in the early 80's. We mountain-biked with the first bikes that showed up in Canada, and we bushwhacked till the end of the world. Now, it's time to relax, to look down on it all from a paraglider – from the third dimension, as it were. That's how I feel anyway. I still love to ski, go for a hike or take a bike ride. I even tried surfing recently and am thinking of learning how to kite surf for the times when one cannot fly and the wind might be across the launches at coastal sites.

I doubt that I will be doing any more first ski descents as my reflexes and technique are just not there anymore. But who knows? In fact, I may still surprise everyone with another ski adventure yet.

I tallied up my first ski descents recently, and, according to my best knowledge and recollection, they are as follows:

FIRST SKI DESCENTS by Peter "Peru" Chrzanowski

1. Huaytapallana – unnamed glacier 5,000 meters, July 1977.
2. Huascaran – first ski descent from 6,200 meters, July 1978.
3. Tsurup Glacier, 5,000 m, July 1978.
4. Ishinca – first ski descent, July 1979.
5. Ranrapalca – first Canadian on summit, ski fall, 1979.
6. Andromeda – Columbia Icefields, September 1979.
7. Peyto Chutes – (above Peyto Lake, Icefields Parkway, August 1979).
8. West Couloir – Wedge, July 7th, 1980.
9. North Face of Mt Athabasca, October 1980.
10. Popocatepetl Volcano, Mexico – Ventorillo Route, December 1982.
11. Mt Robson – Furher Ridge, Kain Face, August 1983.
12. Mt Serratus – North Face, July 1984.
13. Mt Currie – Diagonal, May 8th, 1985.
14. Mt Waddington – Angel Glacier from below summit knob to Combatant Col, September 1985.
15. Mt Atwell – Siberian Couloir, April 1990.
16. At least 5 first ski descents and foreruns WESC (World Extreme Skiing Championships), i.e. a mountain we dubbed Cauliflower Mountain (from it's ice formation on it) was one example; April 1991–98.
17. Mt Diamond – North Face, Chugach Range, Alaska, April 1993.
18. Nepal, Three first ski descents down three glaciers, 2 near Gokyo, one in Chola Pass, October 1997.

I want to emphasize again that there is no reason for people around us to try to protect us from ourselves, or from the activities we choose to do. I think the whole question of liability paranoia and litigation in our country has really gotten out of hand. Canada is the most over-insured country in the world. To my mind the whole concept of third-party liability insurance is kind of ridiculous in a sport like paragliding. I mean: who are you going to hurt but yourself? Unless, of course, you are unlucky and crash into a kindergarten class playing soccer, or cause an expensive racehorse break to his leg, when you perhaps suddenly startle him in a field. But the chances of those kinds of mishaps really are one in a million! So, for God's sake people, let us live and practice our sports.

Hitting a power line is one of the most stupid things one can do in paragliding and I am ashamed of it. Yet it was really a true freak accident! Yet I do remember a rather humorous moment in Peru when I snagged a power line with my wing while landing. Luckily, I failed to electrocute myself, but I managed to cut the electricity to the whole village. I was escorted to Huaraz by two Quechua natives, where I had to buy a new transformer for the village, but luckily the whole ordeal only cost me about $40. Power lines in Peru are often strung diagonally across fields, which makes them virtually invisible from the air. Also my friends tell me that now since I have been electrocuted I am more susceptible to be hit by lightning. Oh no – yet another thing to worry about!

I still love putting in my time on skis, but I prefer to do it in March and April, when the weather is warmer, the sun comes out more often but we still have good dumps of powder (which often come at night). I have told many people that I started paragliding and got taken by it so much because I love powder skiing and was looking for something that gave the same buzz. Flying then became an extension of the powder skiing feeling – seeking that floating sensation which later leads to free flight.

While I thought we were quite good in our day, I marvel at the things kids are doing on skis these days. One of our Pemberton locals, Kye Petersen, who is my old friend Trevor's son, has made a real mark in the sport of free-riding, first acting as ski talent in other peoples' films, and now producing his own ski films. His films are almost like pieces of art. It's just good skiing put to music, but the views are so spectacular and the skiing is really so out of this world; these are the reasons that Kye's film is such a pleasure to watch.

Another Pemberton local who has done well is Eric Pehota's son, Logan, who has also reached rock star level in the world of free-riding on skis – and was a world champion last year. His dad really took care and skied with him a lot when he was younger. Both boys had big shoes to fill as both their fathers were some of the best extreme skiers in their day.

Sometimes I'm envious that I did not produce a son to carry on with my own adventurous ways. But, on the other hand, I'm just so happy I didn't marry the wrong person either, which would have meant just a lot of suffering for everyone involved. I still run into a lot of people from my ski bumming days in Whistler during the 80s and 90s – and the memories are fun to reminisce over sometimes. One of those friends, Florian, a Romanian-Canadian, used to ski with us in the early Whistler years but then moved to Toronto and married a doctor and now he helps her run the administration for her practice. He has since started paragliding. Imagine our joy and utter surprise when we met again thirty years later flying in Mexico and Colombia.

I still think it is our choice as to which sports we get involved in, as well as the lives we choose to live. It is not society's duty to protect us from ourselves. Regulation and litigation have gotten out of control in Canada as a result of our lawyers learning from the lawsuit-crazy legal system south of the border. The free-spirited ways enjoyed in our small paragliding community by The Pemberton Flying Monkeys have also finally come to an end. Along with the formation of the Hang Ginding and Paragliding Association of Canada or HPAC, which brought in many regulations, other things have also changed. For example, a new paragliding operation has moved into our free flying community in Pemberton in the last seven years or so. Although the newcomers had done a good job taking over the shuttle service to the launches, A certain amount of the charm was also taken out of the sport as it became little more than business as usual. That always seems to be the case when money starts driving things instead of just passion. I reached out to the newcomers but my ban still remains, so what else can I say?

In the old days and for many years local flyer Judd had run the shuttle, and it was a friendly if somewhat ramshackle operation. Later a Brit, John Lyon, took over the operation and bought a off-road Ford F150 truck and ran the shuttle very effectively for several years. Unfortunately, the bureaucracy surrounding the Canadian immigration system made it impossible for him to operate economically and he had to abandon the enterprise and return to England. The problem was that because he wasn't Canadian they insisted that a real Canadian had to work alongside with him, and such an arrangement could not make a profit. And so the newcomers had taken over the shuttle. To their credit they did bring the Canadian National Paraglide Championships to our valley. They run a great business venture but to me it has sucked dry the true spirit of camaraderie which had existed earlier within our "Pemberton Flying Monkeys" community. It was now all business and that is a shame.

Later the same people saw an opportunity in Mexico and began doing tours out of Tenancingo and the La Malinche launch. They eventually were the accomplices to the person who orchestrated to drive me out of my little home at La Malinche, Mexico for good. But it might be best in the long run. I just did not enjoy being associated with that type of company – one that was only driven by business and were not really my friends. I had tried my best to help and to work with the newcomers and their paraglide business. They truly sucked the spirit out of our beautiful sport.

I had worked very hard to help the newcomers promote the Canadian National paragliding Championships. I made videos and photos and spent countless hours on social media advertising their event. I also managed to get them national television coverage through a good friend from the CBC sports department in Vancouver. Since paragliding is still so obscure – unlike in Europe – with only several hundred active pilots in Canada, it is difficult to get major media outlets to cover our beautiful sport, and this was an achievement I had managed against all odds. Furthermore, when time came for running my own Aerothlon event in Pemberton, the newcomers conveniently skipped town that weekend, and no transport was available for the runs up to the high launch. I think they did this so they would not have any liability if my event ended in an incident. OK, I did have a colourful history, with stories like "The Curse of the Ski Traverse" which preceded me and did not help much with my reputation. But unfortunately the newcomers never seemed to make an effort to even get to know me. They just looked at my reputation.

Paragliding adventures

1. A flight over Pemberton valley.
2. Playing and skating with a paraglider in winter at Gates Lake near Pemberton.
3. Kiting a glider before strapping in and taking off at launch in Pemberton.
4/5. With new friends on a beach near Puerto Escondido, Mexico.

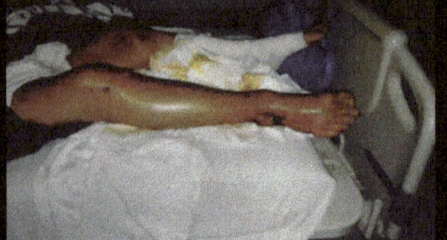

A variety of events

1. Steve Ogle and Chad Sayers on Pico Bolivar (5675) in Sierra Nevada de Santa Marta of Colombia.
2. Chad Sayers during first turns in the Sierra.
3. My rundown DOA (Death On Arrival) off Blackcomb peak.
4. Johnny Trash during his nude climbing escapades at Merlin's bar at Blackcomb base.
5. Paul Guschlbauer (left) with Pablo Lopez during Paul's flight from Alaska to Argentina,
with a stopover in Pemberton and my house.
6. My burnt leg after crashing into electric lines in Malinalco, Mexico with my paraglider.

EPILOGUE

Sometimes people ask me: "If you were live your life over again, what would you do differently?" I respond by saying that I am very happy the way my life has turned out in the end. Thinking about this question, as I finish off this book, I have some further thoughts. Perhaps finding a proper partner or soul mate in flying and in doing my projects would have been even better. If I had met that perfect partner and she had wanted a kid, I probably would have complied. Otherwise I was never driven to have kids. Having grown up with a single mother, who is a strong character anyway, did not help either. I could not imagine handling two powerful women in my life. Maybe that fear contributed as well to my staying single? Also I might have taken a little more care of myself and spent less time being hurt. Whatever, I am very content with what I have achieved up till now for many reasons. I was perhaps too often naive and much too willing to believe what people promised. That has got me in trouble several times through choosing the wrong partners to join me on my various trips.

As I have said I would love to be able to carry on flying in my own backyard as I have done for over 30 years. I built our dream home in Pemberton largely due to the great flying. I will continue paragliding despite the obstacles of official rules. Luckily I can fly in the back country without a permit, since Canada has such vast spaces. I want to be able to continue flying into old age with my friends as I have done for decades. I am a survivor and I will somehow manage the ugly politics and legal issues to the best of my ability. I suspect I will have to probably travel more in order to get the flying that I seek to do in the future. But I refuse to be intimidated by all this and I have many friends, who I know, will stand by me on this subject and I thank them in advance as I write my final words in this book. As my good friend Ptor Spricenieks always said "What will not kill you, will make you stronger in the end", and let's face it, paragliding is a dangerous sport.

For instance, Mexico's La Malinche is famous for how gentle its Restitution wind is in the evenings, but nearly everyone I have known there has been injured flying during the strong heat of the day. If I was to be banned from flying there because of my accident, then so should everybody else who has injured themselves in that place. I don't think I should be singled out. There were 13 paragliding accidents this year in Roldanillo, Colombia, and of those three were fatal, so we are fooling ourselves if we think we can ever make the sort safe. I said earlier that the best description I have heard is that paragliding is "dangerously easy," meaning that it is not just easy to fly, but also dangerously easy to screw up. It is too easy to forget something in your pre-flight check, or make a pilot error as I have done several times. But the feeling of free flight is unequalled by any other sport. Once you get the bug to fly it's like a shot of the finest drug and so difficult to leave behind.

Regarding the danger of flying, at least 80 people die each year from participating in extreme sports in Chamonix, France. But in that country if people choose to go into the back country terrain and die in an avalanche while skiing, or crash paragliding, nobody else is held liable. Athletes do not get banned from resorts just because they have accidents which end up harming only themselves. La Grave, France, is the epitome of this attitude and is a truly free ski resort with just one groomed run. There is no official ski patrol, and everything is wild and 'savage'. That is a far cry from what Vail Resorts and the others are trying to achieve. As the push for new customers from countries like China increases, and since they are not a very mountain-savvy bunch, things will only get more industrialized. I wish things would have stayed less uptight here in Canada, but we are so strongly influenced by the United States, with its lawyers and the suing craze down there.

My feelings about HPAC (Hang Gliding and Paragliding Association of Canada) or their third-party liability insurance are not positive. As far as I am concerned, and of course this is only my personal opinion, HPAC is nothing but a business proposition that wants to control everything to do with paragliding in Canada. It is a guild or monopoly which holds us prisoner just to collect our dues. Although I do appreciate the business agent from HPAC provided a document which one of our local landowners had insisted on having before she approved our landing the Aerothlon athletes on her field. But on the other hand, if things had remained as they were before HPAC was formed, landowners would have never asked for anything in the first place. Now that awareness and fear has been instilled in them by insurance companies, I guess the old days of 'outlaw' flights has gone from Pemberton forever.

When it is my time to return to the "land of blue lights," I would rather do it as a result of my own choosing, rather than dying out of boredom at some dreadful old age home. I have no kids or family, and this perhaps makes me willing to take more risks as an individual. This is another reason why I have never wanted to carry the responsibility of flying tandem or carrying passengers. It is one thing if I hurt myself, but I could never bear the thought of injuring somebody else if it was because of a faulty decision of mine.

When I had my most recent accident I chose to stay in Mexico to recuperate because I did not want Nina, my 87-year-old mother to even see my badly burnt leg. I thought after leaving the hospital that it was best to rent the little hotel room. I could then do some work on my manuscript until I healed a little more before going home. Also my prefered diet consists probably 80% of fresh fruits and vegetables, and I thought I would fare much better resting in Mexico. I find that I prefer fresh fruit more than the produce that is available during the winter months in Canada, where everything ripens on boats under artificial lights. I truly feel that I made the right choice due to the healthier drier climate to recuperate here – and just write my book.

In my dreams I would love to go back and fly again in the Sierra, but my body does not really allow any more serious exploits such as those of my friend Ptor Spricenieks.

I recently learned that Ptor and a couple of his friends had managed to return to Colombia and the Sierra Nevada mountains of Santa Marta to climb and attempt to ski some of the peaks. This dream was finally fulfilled when they hiked for 13 days, first through the jungle, then along granite spines to the snows and peaks beyond, and I am so happy for them!

I have lost many friends over the years. It probably numbers over a dozen who have died in avalanches or falling accidents on skis. In paragliding I find I mourn fewer friends, but at least a half dozen have perished flying. But our beautiful flying sport is much smaller than skiing in numbers of participants, so that must say something about the dangers as far as ratios and numbers go. Two years in a row now I have attended wakes or celebrations of life for skiers I knew from Whistler and Pemberton. The most recent ski accident was of Dave Treadway who tragically fell 30 metres into a crevasse near Pemberton. So even as I write and edit this section, I find I am still losing friends. Dave's accident happened in conditions where the temperature rises quickly and a snow bridge gave away on him while skiing on a glacier. Dave was a true rock star in the ski film celebrity world and as experienced as anyone in back-country travelling, so his accident was particularly hard to take. It was so sad being in that room again at the Fairmont Chateau in Whistler for another friend. The year before we had gathered for Lisa, a friend and skier who died in an avalanche. She was a professional guide, but also a mother who left a son behind. I had survived a dreadful 900 metre fall into a crevasse, and I had managed to crawl out of back in 1979. Why was I spared then, and Dave and Lisa had not? After all I was the sinner who had left the Catholic church, yet the Universe, or my private angels, have shown me mercy so many times now. Cats have nine lives, but I seem to have more!

The next generation of athletes are continuing to break barriers in all sorts of extreme sports. A young Swiss skier called Jeremie Heitz specializes in skiing extreme faces at incredible speed, and I was honoured when Jeremy thought to call ME to find out the conditions on Mt Robson's north face before attempting a descent of that incredible slope. The face had finally been conquered by my friends Troy and Ptor in 2010.

Much as I criticize the insurance industry for it's money grabbing ways, I also have to say I am very grateful to my travel insurance and our Canadian medical system. Perhaps now is the time to apologize to my poor mom, who has had to deal with bad news so many times and helped me mend on so many occasions.

By mid-October 2019 I bought my plane tickets to Mexico and Colombia. I would be gone from November 10th until February 26th 2020 again. I hoped to do some more cheap dental work in Mexico on the way. The mission is to try to summit Cerro Kennedy by 4x4 and enjoy the Sierra Nevada de Santa Marta again. Then with a few friends we hope to paraglide off before mid-December if all the stars line up. It will be my 20th and 10th anniversary of two films in "The Heart of The World".

Otherwise, I was just trying to lead my life and keep pursuing a few more dreams – and hoping that my body can still somehow keep up with my mind. I was flying again and got my P2 certification in Revelstoke from friends Chris and Brad who run a paragliding school over there. That way I did not have to deal with the newcomers here in Pemberton that were giving me such a hard time. Now, with paragliding as my main sport still available to me, there are yet so many places I want to visit and fly over. I still do not have my HPAC Insurance for paragliding and the red tape is just getting worse as the Newcomers are trying to block my P2 certificate and my insurance. They have really divided our once tight paragliding community with all this. I really do not need HPAC to use our launches which are on crown land. I guess I will not be landing at the school or the official HPAC landing LZ, but hell, I can land on my friends fields all over the valley instead. I do not want the school to be jeopardized for others to land in and local muni authorities are always looking for an excuse to hassle someone. I am back editing my book in Pemberton and it's just so nice to be home again.

* * *

Another Autumn came and went. We held a 2nd annual successful Aerothlon in Pemberton again. We had a bit of sponsorship from the SLRD (The Squamish Lillooet Regional District). These were the same people that tried so hard to block the event the first year. That made me resort again to a desperate letter writing campaign then. I wrote to the BC premier, the Attorney General, the ministers of tourism as well as BC lands and housing. I also reached out to the ALM (Agricultural Land Commission) which governs over the SLRD. This appeared to do the trick because the SLRD came up with $2,000 in funding. We were doing miracles here. My eternal sponsor and maker of the world's finest ski boot liner, Intuition Liners, came through with $1,000 towards the budget and another $1,000 in prize money. Together with some $1,200 in athlete registration fees we now had a little over $4,000 to pull off the event. Conventionally, it would easily have cost $100K in the Corporate world if it was supported the way it could have been. Again I turned my house into the Aerothlon headquarters and this was where the many friends, sponsors and volunteers slept.

By November, 2019 I was once again on a plane to Mexico to help Pablo Lopez produce an Aerothlon at Temascaltepec, which is a minuscule town near the Penon, a popular site used mostly by pilots from Valle de Bravo. Unfortunately, nasty politics rears its head at paragliding sites in Valle de Bravo where various tandem operators work. Pablo managed to circumvent these politics by having the Mayor of the actual town of Temascaltepec, which is only 10km away from the Valle, lend his support for the Aerothlon. The town is eager for tourism and would love a piece of the paragliding action Valle gets. I chuckle now as I feel Pablo and I were doing similar stunts to the "Beyond The Steep" debacle, which Chuck Hammond engineered the 1980 Mt Robson spectacle, when he proclaimed "I own this town", speaking about the 'municipality' of Valemount, where the ski Mt Robson circus had appeared. It was a different situation in the details, but it reminded me of the innocence and naivety some small towns presented sometimes to new ideas which were so fresh and invigorating to all. We brought tourism value to the town through a social media campaign for the Aerothlon and this generated some paraglide traffic. This is beneficial to all initially, because in general paraglide pilots are small spenders, and the town was still inexpensive and unspoiled by tourists. In time prices are hiked up everywhere tourists visit. I was also in Mexico to start some major dental work to do the initial surgery needed for the 6 implants I was to have. The plan was to continue on to Colombia for three months after the dental work, then return and complete the implants in Mexico. Unfortunately the dental experience became rather intense and at a moment's notice my dentist decided to anaesthetize me, thus moving me to a hospital to finish the surgery. The anesthesiologist arrived, I was put under and woke up with the all work completed. It never ceases to amaze me how situations like this seem to get quickly resolved here in Mexico, while in Canada it would have been difficult to make quick arrangements like this for surgery again due to over regulation.

I looked at this trip to Colombia with Doris as a reprieve and a change from my regular filming expedition. It was to be a more pedestrian outing with Doris, who booked a series of hostels on a rather mundane tourist route from Cartagena to Palominio on Colombia's northern Caribbean coast. I had been here before and I was keen to revisit Tairona Park and it's marvellous beaches.

I had a lot to think about during this trip. The electrocution accident from the last January was certainly one of the most serious injuries I have had. I had almost lost my leg, as the doctors wanted to amputate it at the hospital in Mexico City. Luckily the doctor at the Tenancingo private clinic saved it with massive doses of antibiotics, and deep cleaning the wounds every day, and luckily I avoided picking up an infection. I thought the trip would bring me down to earth a bit, and I would enjoy all that more normal mortals in the hostel realm revel in so much. I had nothing really to prove although the idea of flying off Cerro Kennedy, and making a third film in the Sierra, had me really jazzed up.

Doris and I have travelled together on many occasions and she is probably one of the few people that can put up with moody or grumpy me sometimes. I had thus planned a whirlwind tour with Doris through Colombia's northern Caribbean coast from Cartagena. We started with visiting the outlying island group called Isla Grande. Then we would continue on, through the remote and wild Tairona Park to the town of

Minca, from where I could go for my only paragliding session off Cerro Kennedy. I had arranged 4x4 vehicles to take us up to the 3,000 metre peak which has a Military base situated right on the top. My good friend Mauro was here several weeks ago from Bogota doing a trail running marathon up the mountain and had secured permission for us to paraglide off the peak. I had therefore contacted a half dozen Colombian pilots to join us on the adventure. I had glorious things in mind: perhaps I could make a film about my return to "The Heart of the World". But Cerro Kennedy also was to became a symbol of my age and inability of my body to perform as it had years before. There was no way I could hike up "gnarly ridge tops" for 13 days, as Ptor had described on his trip up there the previous year, after I had spent all that time in a hospital bed in Malinalco Mexico, then again after my power line incident. Yes, I was going to make the trip back to the Sierra again, but I was going to do this "old timer style", or by Toyota 4x4. Apparently the launch was supposed to be easy, Mauro had said. So I was a bit preoccupied with finding a good spot to land in Minca, but I had found a farm field cut out of the jungle that was nearer to the take-off. There was a cable running down one length of the field but knowing where it was made it alright, or so I thought. Another option I had found was a soccer field in the middle of Minca itself. Mauro had come back with a friend from Bogota, and they hiked up to the top of Kennedy. Mauro's friend was also a paraglide pilot and I hoped they would know of alternative landing fields between us and the beach at Santa Marta. They had been fooling around and enjoying each other's company and really had not done any reconnaissance for good landing spots. I was a bit bummed by this but reality slowly sank in to my addled brain. These guys were in their late twenties and thirties, and it was not much of a "mission" for them to fly off Cerro Kennedy. I had come with pre-conceived ideas of what I wanted but now the current state of reality finally dawned on me: "You are getting to be an old fuck, Peter", was my conclusion from all this. I was not going to make my third film here twenty years after my first, because nobody cared but me about this rather ad-hock filming expedition. It turned out Mauro and his friend were too intimidated by the soccer field landing because it was lined with a ten meter fence. Another friend of mine, Willi Garcia, had landed there ten years ago but he said it was not the easiest of tasks. On the other hand the farm field I had chosen as our alternative landing zone in Minca had an intimidating wire running across part of it. My compatriots reluctantly bailed on flying off the peak. I must be getting wiser in my old age and I also decided not to attempt the flight as I was alone now. So I turned back down towards the coast. Doris had got eaten by mosquitoes in Minca and gave me a really hard time about coming here in the first place. Funnily enough, I kind of enjoyed the town because it was set in the foothills of the Sierra where it was cooler than our times at all the beaches we had just visited recently. I too suffered from Minca mosquitos bites but I guess my body was just more resilient to the pain of their bites. How things change in ten years. Yes, just twenty and even ten years ago I had managed to hike up religiously in the 40 degree heat and 80% humidity here. Now, I had been the only one paragliding in our crew of 8, here in the same Sierra. And now I am too intimidated to go at it alone, out of the comfort of a Toyota 4x4 Land Cruiser and not having to hike hardly at all!

It was a big moment for NOT DOING something in my life for a change. Was it fear or just common sense that had me make a decision – a voice of reason perhaps? I have no family, unlike Ptor, who made a film a few years ago on deciding to scale back his risk taking projects due to a family consisting of a relatively new wife and two kids now. Before this trip I had consulted with Ptor via email about paraglide landing options and he claimed there were fields between Santa Marta and Minca, but I really could not see anything on the cab ride up to Minca from Santa Marta. Everything felt so different on this trip. I had taken so many chances before. Was it having all those serious paragliding accidents between 2010 and now that were having a final impact on me, making me take the risk free option? I had recently changed the working title of my book from I SURVIVED AGAIN to I SURVIVED MYSELF. A friend in Mexico, Gerardo Moran, had suggested it to me and I liked it right away. The name sort of insinuated, or so I thought, that I had blundered myself into all the predicaments and accidents, which I had. It was a more humble title, not one of momentous heroic achievements but rather one of blunders trying doggedly to achieve something in the ski mountaineering and paragliding worlds.

Was my body finally saying STOP Peter... STOP before you finally kill yourself! Yes, you have "Survived Yourself" but don't ever take it all for granted because in the end it can be anywhere around the corner.

Thus, with my tail between my legs I gave up on my goal of flying one last time from Cerro Kennedy, and Doris and I continued our rather pedestrian tourist trip through Palomino on the northern coast again. It was from here we had hiked with the help of mules twice into the Sierra. The first time was in 1999 with Monuno, with the mule driver and his two sons. We were staying at the Faro hostel in Palomino when out of the blue I decided to ask the local lady cooking breakfast if she had heard of Monuno's family. To my surprise she had known them well. Teresa was the name of Monuno's daughter still living in town and Monuno's son Juan was now 32 and living nearby in Santa Marta. Juan had been 12 years old when he accompanied our group when we intended to ski the Sierra back in 99. I ended up meeting both Teresa and Juan, showing them our JOURNEY TO THE HEART OF THE WORLD film where Juan even sang a song about the Sierra Nevada. Teresa had tears in her eyes upon seeing the film, which I gave to her on a memory stick later.

The Guajira peninsula in Colombia is the most northerly point of the South American continent, had always attracted my attention as a place to visit. I was really beginning to miss flying on this trip so I thought it would be great to talk Doris into visiting the peninsula, which was famous as a lawless desert land inhabited by the exotic Guanu indigenous peoples. Transportation is the main problem in travelling through the Guajira and Doris was hesitant at first, reading the various travel warnings covering the area. Unfortunately, Doris then got sick in Palomino and I ended up being able to join an adventure tour operator on a three day tour into the Guajira. Once she had recovered, Doris also managed to do the same trip a few days later and our paths crossed at Punto Cayan when our separate groups met up at a restaurant en route. Visiting the Guajira was both humbling and fascinating. The last part of the trip to Punta Gallinas, the northern most point of the Guajira the road ran through Sahara-like country, a Martian landscape with a few shrubs and towering Cacti. The place was more like Morocco or the edge of the Sahara Desert. The locals wore colorful robes which resembled the clothing of northern Africa than South America. It is so rough that there was not one defined road and the trip by faithful Toyota Landcruiser was spectacular, to say the least. The colourfully clad Guanu natives were so minimalist in their life style that they really showed a sense of humanity living on the edge of nothing. Their shacks were constructed from small flat board-like planks which came from the core of the many Cactus plants growing around them. They were so well adapted that they even managed to find wood within the cactus. I thought that alone was fascinating as to the scarcity of anything here. The people lived off herding goats (as only goats found the scarce food here) and the spoils of the sea.

As our Land Cruiser passed a series of shacks which was their version of a village, kids would hold up a string across the track in the road, hoping visitors might stop and examine their wares. I had been with quite a few 'primitive' tribes like the Arhuacos, the Kogis, the Quechua and other Indigenous cultures but the lack of water, and the dire existence of these people on what really seemed nothing was striking to me. It helped to re-evaluate my own existence and made me reflect about myself and the things I may have deemed so important at one time. I managed to stay for a couple of extra days in Punto Cayan and tried to absorb this wild environment. I found I loved it here, in this frontier town, right on the edge of nowhere and truly at the end of the world as we know it.

The rest of the trip took us through New Years in Bucaramanga where my friend Ricardo Mantilla runs a paragliding school called Colombia Paragliding. I have known Richi for over ten years and I had sent him a number of pupils to learn to fly as I really believe his location and climate makes his school one of the best in the world. Doris, who does not paraglide, had become a bit bored with the location of our hostel, which was far out of town and on the side of a mountain. So she decided to visit a few nearby towns she had heard were interesting, and I could just relax and enjoy myself flying for a few days. We did enjoy a great New Year's Eve celebration with a fireworks spectacle going on over the entire city of Bucaramanga, with its two and a half million inhabitants watching below. While back in Canada we have some great fireworks displays in Vancouver, these are all so regulated and take place in one safe designated location. Here in Colombia the whole city puts on a fireworks display as everyone in all parts of town tries to out-do everyone else with the pyrotechnics. For myself, it's just another pleasant reminder of the joy of travel to lands which are not so over regulated as Canada and have such spirit and soul.

After having a week of paragliding, which is my true salvation, Doris came back and it was time to visit Medellin, the city that Pablo Escobar made so famous through his clandestine deeds. We met up with Natali Vasquez, a good friend whom I first met in Santa Marta 20 years back during the making of my "Journey To The Heart of the World" film. I had mentioned earlier how Natali had been sought out later by Ptor with whom she left Colombia for Canada and ended up living in Chamonix, France. Their own relationship did not last too long but in the process Natali took up skiing, paragliding and later skydiving and even wing suit flying. She is a truly free spirit. I found her in Medellin recovering from two injuries, a knee and a hip and was unable to even walk very far with her cane. We had not seen each other for at least 10 years and it was great to catch up. Natali is one of those few souls out there that understands me and my tumorous lifestyle. She had always been so supportive and that meant so much during all those misadventures I have had along the way. We hence enjoyed each other's company, laughed, reminisced over great Colombian Coffee in various trendy Medellin cafes.

While in Medellin I was contacted by a filmmaker called Leo back in Whistler, BC who was working on a film with Kye Petersen, Trevor's son. I was honoured to find out that they were making a film featuring some of us "old school boys" again and wanted an interview with me. They emailed me the questions and I had Natali film me at our Medellin hostel giving commentaries on what they asked for. I then transferred the footage to them by internet. "Aaaah, the joys of modern technology" I thought. I wish we had options such as these available to us when we were making films. It was nice of Kye to remember me and I did my best in the interview. I still wanted to keep one foot in the ski world which I had sort of left behind due to my obsession with paragliding more recently.

After several days of hip cafes and restaurants in the trendy Medellin neighbourhood and some sightseeing in the city, an impressive cosmopolitan centre complete with innovative commuting gondolas and an advanced train/ metro system, I had enough and just wanted to paraglide again.

I had learned a lot about Colombia over the years I had visited the country. Although the major "Violencia" or the killing grounds had ended in Colombia after the peace deal the Colombian government made with the FARC, there still was a lot of mistrust out there. The people of Colombia were not that pleased with the deal their government had made with the FARC. Many felt the government gave them too much and pardoned a lot of killers, which Natali said now roamed the country freely. Colombia was an intriguing case study. Here was a country that gained hugely economically from the world's, but mostly North America's, addiction to cocaine. Since the end of FARC the cartels still produced a huge amount of cocaine but managed to stay out of the limelight compared to the 80's or the Escobar years. By now they had laundered and reinvested their money in other legitimate businesses. In most places in Colombia the people remain humble and do not flaunt their wealth. Often their houses or facades facing the street seem just like regular houses but once inside one sees incredibly lavish mansions outfitted with the world's best amenities. One Colombian friend explained to me how in Colombia the Cartels invested, not terrorized their communities. It seemed like such a wiser move than in Mexico, where the Cartels massacred their own, as was the case in Iguala or Guadalajara. The Colombian drug lords had big families which they wanted shielded and protected by the authorities which were gingerly paid off at all levels of government, so instead they poured billions into the infrastructure of their home towns and villages. Yes, Colombia is certainly interesting now as everything seems to flow, the people all seem well fed and dressed. Tourism is beginning to thrive and we are all kind of inclined to forget where all the money initially came from. It is kind of sad realizing Colombia's wealth had come from the world's but mainly America's drug addiction but the world order is not always that fair. I had always felt safe in Colombia, even during the times of the "Violencia" because the Cartels were always smart about trying not to inflict damage to visiting foreigners. This was so they did not get the wrath of foreign embassies having to come to the aid of their nationals and thus giving grief to both the cartels and the Colombian government so intertwined with them. Don't get me wrong, I love Mexico and will probably make my winter headquarters there (that is if I ever retire, haha!) simply because it's only half the distance to Colombia and there are easy and cheap direct flights to Mexico from Vancouver. I prefer the dry hot climate of 28 degrees during the day, with it going down to 10-15 centigrade or so at night. Roldanillo, Colombia is great, having the great flying and so many friends there too but the humid heat of 36 degrees is just too much after you land in the afternoon. The climate in Medellin and Bogota is nicer, as these cities are at higher elevations but I still prefer the little town of Malinalco above all. The beaches of Acapulco are only a three hour drive away if one needs a dose of the ocean. I am working with Pablo Lopez here to see if we can develop a spa-type resort here as an Aerothlon training camp. It can be a spa or a yoga spiritual retreat for North Americans to escape their winters and do rentals to a huge market base of 25 million people a few hours away from Mexico city the rest of the time. I think on the whole, Colombia may be safer than Mexico now but I still love the people and the country there as well. Both Colombia and Mexico's lower classes still have big overpopulation problems although I think Mexico is far worse off with the capital, as Mexico City alone having 25 million people. Colombia also has that problem but not quite to that extent. I still blame this on the Catholic church refusing to promote birth control to the less educated masses which they hold an iron grip on. I also found the poorer people in both countries to be the friendliest while the rich elite show a lot of bias and racism to their less privileged neighbours. I have had a lot of delusions and was often disappointed trying to do business with those in power in both countries where broken promises are common.

Back in Medellin I made the rather complicated trip up to the St Felix paraglide launch site. It was a beautiful launch. High above the northern part of the city. It was early, before 10 am as I laid out my glider in the light conditions. Then, while trying to launch, I took a few steps and the glider over shot me. It spun me around and as I fell I felt my already dislocated shoulder get whacked out of position. The pain was excruciating. I moaned for help and as a pilot ran down to me I asked him to yank hard on my arm to get it back in place. Aaaaaargh!

– I had done it again, I thought. I had hurt myself despite the promises I had made to myself on this trip not to. The ambulance came and the paramedics yanked some more on my arm making sure it was in its proper place. As I writhed in pain in the back of the search and rescue vehicle we drove for about half hour to some small town hospital nearby. They were unable to tend to me so we ended up driving for another hour all the way down to Medellin where I spent five hours getting X-rays, painkillers and my arm put in a sling. There was no damage to bone evident on the X-rays and the doctors told me to wait at least five days to see how it would feel. In the meantime my arm was swollen like a sumo wrestlers. We rested an extra couple days in Medellin and decided to continue our trip as I optimistically thought my arm was feeling better. Doris had to catch a flight out from Bogota, and I would continue down to Roldanillo where we had another Aerothlon scheduled for February 2nd where I had a lot of work to do. I loved Doris as a true kind hearted friend but had come to the conclusion that the hostel scene had been enduring and really was not my style of trip. Doris spoke no Spanish so the hostels were her way of meeting other English speaking travellers and the staff usually spoke some English as well. I met a few interesting people at these hostels but in general I found it a rather boring crowd with little passion or direction outside of shopping and sightseeing usually taking safe organized tours and rarely going off the well beaten tourist track. I guess I just preferred paraglide pilots for company as the risks in the sport provided mutual comfort and camaraderie for our rather small global community. They were just more interesting company and even outside of the flying found more variety of fun to do things on the ground as well.

When I got to Roldanillo my arm was still humongous in size, a paraglide pilot, and also an American emergency doctor advised me to get an ultrasound done of my arm. Roldanillo was a small town yet due to all the paraglide accidents there someone bought an ultrasound as a good business venture. The doctor also told me the best way to get the swelling down was to keep it up as high as possible. I managed to hang my arm off some tv wires above my head a few nights in a row while I slept and got the swelling down considerably. I went to take that ultrasound only to confirm my biggest worry – that I had indeed torn a tendon which prevented me from raising my arm to eye height. I was devastated, it meant no paragliding while I was in this flying mecca where at least 600 pilots converge each year. My good friend Roman from Vancouver was arriving as well as many friends from Poland and overseas. AND I COULD NOT FLY! I was in utter misery. All I could do was occupy myself with getting more athletes to enter the Aerothlon and take pictures at launch of the various other paragliding competitions taking place. I had no choice but to stay here and enjoy my time aside from flying. I was booked into my last round of dentist visits in Mexico before flying home to Canada so I had no other choice without very expensive schedule changes. What made it worse was now being pre-occupied as to whether surgery could be done right away or when I was to be back in Vancouver on February 26th. I dreaded the thought of waiting months for surgery and losing a whole year of flying as a result.

The Aerothlon went off really well in Roldanillo, Colombia. Michal Gierlach, a well known Polish pilot won the individual division. I had corralled at least 10 pilots to enter the competition and most of them were Polish. I was happy because we were planning an Aerothlon in Poland next August 2nd. By having the top Polish pilots compete here will help get the whole Polish flying community excited about the event and help spread the good word about it. I was so happy being able to go back to Poland again after 12 years of absence. I feel a lot more Canadian than Polish now but I still yearn for the old country which must be in my blood still. I also look forward to meet more beautiful women there, something which always excites me. This all helped my psyche from the flying withdrawal but overall I was not in the best of moods. By chance, I met an Austrian girl called Alina in the main square and talked her into registering and competing. To all of our surprise, Alina came third in the entire individual division as she ran the arduous 800 metre vertical course up to the launch, then flew the 6 km to the stadium in downtown Roldanillo and then completed the 14 km XC bike ride. Dominika came third in the women's division as well, with Polish pilots Pawel Chrzaszcz and David Krasewski making the top finishers as well. It was all rather exciting. I felt happy and fulfilled in Colombia even though I did not get to fly in Roldanillo. The owner of a paragliding school in Telluride, Colorado even approached me about producing an Aerothlon event there, and there was talk of doing one in Switzerland and even Austria, the home of Red Bull X-Alps.

A few days after the Aerothlon in Roldanillo I flew to Mexico city and on to Malinalco where I continued the work on my teeth and made more revisions for the book. I am again living at Pablo Lopez's house writing as I had done a year ago. Unfortunately I could not be in Whistler and I would miss Johnny Trash's 50th birthday party with "The Day Glow Abortions" playing a 30-year anniversary gig at the GLC bar in Whistler. The Abortions was a legendary hard rock band which in the late 80's could only be silenced by cutting off the power at our notorious Whistler's A-frame.

My main concern right now will be to have surgery on my shoulder as soon as I get back to Vancouver, so that I can raise my arm high enough to reach the controls for paragliding. Maybe some things are just meant to stay the way they were, although it was a good exercise on my behalf to look at safer options from flying on this last trip. I had tried. Although I may philosophize on this subject for a while, not much has changed except now I am in my mid-sixties I have to look a lot more realistically at what my body do, and not only in flying.

As far as my own ideology and belief system goes – Well, I just hope I will be a bit wiser and more careful in my older age now. I guess I have learned some important lessons in life. I never really paid attention to having a lot of money and was sometimes a bit careless in my spending. This characteristic may have come from my father's side as he was always generous in his spending with everyone. My mother, however, was more careful and knew how to save money. Consequently we now have a beautiful home in Pemberton. I still believe money is not the most important thing in life and having the free time to spend it is more important. Your health is most important of all. Throughout my whole life I never had an abundance of money yet somehow managed to live comfortably and still follow my passion. I have been around big money lots of times as my stories have told and was never really impressed by any of it, although it was fun and weird to me. I find a lot of rich people are not that happy and always have a fear of losing that wealth or having to always watch out that someone does not take it from them. We need money to live and survive but there has to be a balance between having it and the time to spend it. In some ways I am sorry that I never had kids but treat my films as my children. It would have been nice to have a steady partner, to make love and films together.

As far as women go in general I have never meant to be disrespectful to them. True, I like sex but often I preferred a good early morning deep powder run, or a great paraglide flight over spending time courting a woman at some bar the night before. None of the girls I have been involved with have changed my mind and: I AM SO HAPPY THAT I NEVER MARRIED ANY OF THEM IN THE END GAME. (Except for Jenny from Peru...)

I guess I will have more time due to the rehab physio for my arm to keep editing my book in Pemberton and it will be nice to be home again. I am finding out about the hard work involved in publishing a book. It is so difficult to get a publisher since everyone and his dog is self-publishing these days making the established publishing business very difficult and cutting into their sales. Every publisher has a different set of criteria, which makes you jump through a lot of hoops just pitching your story. Some publishers make it easy for you to submit on-line. Others want a brick of paper printed out and sent to them by snail mail. Still others make you summarize every chapter with a one pager as they do not have time to read your whole book.

April 3rd, 2020. Chaos has struck the world with the arrival Coronavirus-19. In Canada we are all living in fear and wondering what is really going on. I try to keep an open mind, but I just don't believe everything the government here and elsewhere on the planet are telling us. I recall the fears of the Kogis of the Sierra Nevada de Santa Marta. They warned us, the "little brothers", a long time ago that we are bringing nothing but grief, war, pollution to them. And now a virus? Who do we believe? It just seems too perfect, too smooth as if it is being orchestrated by the mainstream media in each country. Living here in the wilds of Canada we feel very lucky compared to those stuck in cities. Spring is here now so if the electricity goes out for a while we can survive by hunting, cooking on fires and making do without a refrigerator. I guess my biggest worry is if things get really bad in the USA, they will come up here and just take over our land and precious natural resources. Arm sales are up in the US and here in Canada too. Already vigilante groups are forming as armed local tribes of sorts are created to guard their respective communities. And so the virus has ignited so many conspiracy theories.

In a way I am back to my routine of raising sponsors and promoting the event again while doing final revisions on this book. Recently, I was invited to join an overland expedition with a group of Polish adventurers. The goal is to drive from Poland to Pakistan's Hunza Valley in the Karakoram, which is another place I have always wanted to visit. But the question is can I manage a trip like this now? I am getting older after all and my body is quite battered. Yet something inside of me is telling me to go for it again. Should I listen to those inner voices and my intuition or take it easier in life now? In the end, I turned down the offer.

Our Aerothlon turned out to be a great success in Pemberton, but the gargantuan effort to organize it nearly killed me. To make the event possible I had to create a whole COVID safety plan in place for the BC Health department. Somehow we pulled off the race, with a social distanced start and no big award ceremonies. That same day in Austria, Paul Guschlbauer had embraced the Aerothlon concept and held an event in Wagrain Austria with organizer Simon Vargas. Another event, in Poland was cancelled due to the virus situation in different parts of Europe that August.

I still hope to be able to paraglide into my eighties, and I managed to get my rotator cuff on my shoulder operated on in Vancouver. My doctor, Tym Frank, had some empathy for my condition and asked why I needed to have my arm repaired. I was honest and told him that now, all I really had left was flying for pleasure. As long as I can take a few steps to launch, and control my wing, "Peter Peru" should be able to fly again. Dr Frank understood and managed to get me a CT scan within a week. I was operated on in mid May and had been doing physio ever since.

Another good friend, James Oroc disappeared during a flight in Nevada in August 2020. James was such an accomplished flyer. He was my age and was known worldwide. When he went off radar on his cross country flight his friends immediately organized a fundraising platform on line which paid for his search and rescue, and looked for him for a whole month. First, his paraglider was found wrapped around a bush, then a few days later his body was found nearby. It is still a mystery what happened. James was a part of our X-Andes crew when we lost Xavier back in 2011, and we had just enjoyed a few beers together beers in Roldanillo, Colombia eight months earlier!

On a happier note, it was great at this time to finally watch Andrzej Bargiel's full documentary film on his first ski descent of K2. It took two years for the film to come out even for such a feat. Bargiel appears as a mild mannered humble guy. The viewers learn that he comes from a family of 11 siblings from a village between Krakow and Zakopane. He gives credit to his feat of skiing K2 as nothing compared to his mother having to birth 11 kids. Two of Andrzej's brothers accompanied and supported him on the trip. The Polish Himalayan tradition is renewed by this feat and documented properly for ever. Well here you have it folks, two stories, one of success on K2, the other of death in Nevada. Life rolls on...

As part of the production of another film, Kye Petersen, Trevor Petersen's son and his DOP, Leo Holmes dropped by my house in Pemby to shoot an interview with me. It was nice to catch up with Kye, as he and I never really spent much time together. We talked about the old school days of skiing with his dad and our many adventures. The equipment has changed so much both for skiing and filmmaking since those days. I was honoured to be featured in the final edit.

My old age haunts me now. I have never been a fitness freak in the way that younger athletes are these days. I have always preferred to get into form whether it was skiing, biking or paragliding by doing it and acclimatizing that way. I suffer for the first week or so ski touring or hiking, after spending time on the computer too long, but then I would be OK.

Sometimes, I feel almost embarrassed to see many friends my age, many early retired, others older, yet most in better shape than I am. However I comfort myself with a simple answer – it really is pure laziness on my part. I want to be in shape but I do not have to try to relive my 20's. It hurts too much now! Many of these other guys were so busy with their jobs and families all their lives that only now can they break out and r e a l l y take the time to enjoy the natural world around them.

Not so long ago I had crawled out of a Colombian jungle, and I really did not enjoy it, although even then I marvelled how I survived the ordeal. I keep reminding myself of my limitations and my body now as it will never be like in my twenties, thirties or forties again.

I have no brothers or sisters being an only child, with little family except my wonderful 89 year old mom, my cousin John, and his kids. Then there's the remnants of my dad's family; a step-sister Klara, her doctor husband, and their grand-children and mother on the other side of Canada in Rothsey, St John. Therefore, my own immediate family is rather small and I have to look towards my friends more. So "Fred Beckey style", surrounding myself with young friends.

September 2021, and for the last year and a half the COVID-19 virus has played out around the world and here in Canada.

The toughest part of the COVID travel restrictions was that few of my lady friends from abroad turned up to visit. I usually enjoyed a few such visitors a year which makes a single guy's life a little happier. Some of my friends were more paranoid about the disease than others, and some thought it was a political hoax. Whatever our beliefs, I think we were all careful not to slobber all over each other, to keep a safe distance, to wear masks where needed and follow the rules as dictated by our local Health BC, and the government in Ottawa.

My father's funeral has not yet taken place in Poland, and so I am on standby for that if it happens suddenly. A memorial was held for him in St John New Brunswick, organized mainly by and for his second family and his colleagues at UNB. I was not invited and was a bit upset by that snub. I wrote a nice tribute for him anyway and posted it on social media.

I wanted to write a tribute to my father who passed away in June 2020 last year. Due to COVID everything was delayed as far as a memorial for him and I was not informed of the recent ceremony at UNB: https://blogs.unb.ca/.../Mourning-the-passing-of.... I spent the first 18 wonderful years with my father and mother. We came to Canada in 1967 from Poland and moved to Fredericton, New Brunswick where my Dad received a post Graduate scholarship. I remember both my parents as very outdoorsy and sports minded. They took me skiing, hiking and even some rock climbing in Poland until the age of 8. It was my father who molded me into the person I became. In 1972 we did an incredible 14 month overland trip to Tierra del Fuego by VW camper from Canada. You can see a bit of that here in my film SACRED FLIGHT. https://www.youtube.com/watch?v=UH293IcazqI.It was an experience which totally changed my life. Upon my return to Fredericton I could not relate at all to my friends at the age of 15. My father came to my rescue and helped me obtain a summer job in Peru, where I worked from age 18 to 22 as a research assistant in The Andes, first in the town of Huancayo, then Huaraz. It was here where I fell in love with high mountains and began climbing and skiing nearby glaciers near our earthquake research high camp at over 4000 meters elevation. The job lasted four summers. On my third summer there I organized my first big mountain ski expedition, combining resources from UNB Surveying Engineering Department and my sponsors to climb and ski Huascaran, Peru's highest peak. It was from these projects I earned my nickname as "Peter Peru". I never looked back and continued my lifestyle in adventure and making mountain documentaries. My parents got divorced in 1977 and he remarried and started a life with a new family. Although I missed not seeing my father that often over the next thirty years, he was always there for me supporting my often arcane projects both spiritually and financially when I was in dire need.

RIP Adam Chrzanowski!

Besides posting the tribute on social media, I also emailed copies to the UNB Surveying department and the local newspaper, and sent copies to MacLeans magazine and the Globe and Mail newspapers as obituaries. I had worked in Peru for UNB, and many older folks would still know me, and I will not be silent! I thought I should have been invited, being the old rebel I put my tribute out there anyway. I was proud of my Dad and hoped he was equally proud of me, and nobody was going to deny my existence as his only son and blood child.

The winter of 2020/21 was brutal on my broken and worn out body, and I managed to ski for a paltry thirty days on Whistler and Blackcomb. I had a strange foot infection which I think I got from my ski boot liner. The sore has never really healed, and was located on my electrocuted leg, which is partly numb above my toes still. It has been broken four times now, and there is so much hardware in it that I really need to take good care of it. For the last ten years or so, I have gone south to Mexico or Cuba or Colombia between the months of November and March, so my body was just not used to the brutal cold and short dark days of my mountain home. What cheered me up considerably was that my good friend Troy Jungen stayed with me for several months to keep me company. He was ski-touring every day off the countless routes along the nearby Duffy Lake Road with it's many peaks. He achieved his goal of ski-touring for 53 days this winter, and thus matched his actual age. By April '21, I had also managed to paraglide for the first time in eighteen months. I won't deny that it was hard to get back on the horse again because of the demons in my head. Of course, these were from the many previous accidents which I have had.

Unfortunately, I have put my Mother Nina through so much anguish with my accidents throughout my life. I would hate to put her through the stresses and dramas of yet another mishap again. That turned out to be a huge psychological strain that I was dealing with every time I was getting ready to fly. But something inside of me forced me to get over my hesitation. The situation was made worse because the Newcomers in Pemberton, who had blocked the issuing of my P2 Pilot accreditation and HPAC Insurance, had also banned me from using their shuttle and had poisoned my chances of getting rides up to the launch with others. This gave me yet another emotional hurdle to get over before taking off. I was nervous at first during every launch, and one time on take-off I got sucked into a bad sink and hooked a tree just below the launch. I was hanging there uselessly until my friend Roman came to my rescue and helped me get down. My glider was not so lucky, so I had to hire an agile young chap to retrieve it out of the tree the next day, but hey, that's pretty common in paragliding. The worst outcome of that incident was that my wing was damaged. I had three gliders but they were all now in need of fixing. But, since the summer was drawing to a close and we had classic conditions with good thermal flying, I bought another glider to use while the others were being fixed, and soon I was flying again!

I got around my access problem with the Newcomers by using my Delica and driving with my friends up to the paraglide launches. This worked fine, but without the convenience of a shuttle service we had to retrieve the Delica at the end of the day. So I bought an e-bike for that purpose, and it is easy to persuade a friend to ride up and retrieve the van. The only problem with this is that it became a chore trying to find drivers as we gradually exhausted all the neighbours and friends. Luckily (but not for him!) Jim Orava broke his foot while riding on his motorcycle, so we had to have him do the driving for a while. The Newcomers have really taken over the flying scene here now. They can have 60 paraglide students at a time, with tandems lined up galore, and now the shuttle has been farmed out to yet another company. I feel sorry for Jim Orava because he worked so many 12 hour days up there building the launches, cultivating and irrigating the grass so it would grow well and we would have a nice surface to take off from. But Jim is such a Buddhist at heart that he has just watched without rancour as everything was taken over by the Newcomers.

My friend Roman Karas set an incredible example to all of us last year. At 74 we taught him how to ski tour. He was an OK skier but had never ski toured. He was enjoying his time off after working for Lavalin International all those years and I think he really enjoyed skiing and flying with us. I think he blames me for telling him to resign from his job, hehehe. One day we took a helicopter to ski up on Ipsoot Mountain where I had not skied in over 30 years. It was a glorious early April day with crisp cold -13°C temperature and a fresh snowfall the night before. We were dropped off at the peak, from where we skied down over the vast glacier, ski toured back up and retraced the best slope, then we had a pleasant lunch before being picked up and whisked back to Pemberton at the end of the day. Simon Bedford was with us, and edited a nice short film from all the various videos and pictures we had shot. Another friend on this short adventure was my good friend, and ski and paraglide partner Krzys Ryczkiewicz, who now lives in Victoria on Vancouver Island.

With global warming and everything, the forest fires this year were not too bad here for us around Pemberton, but the interior of the province was really hurting as smoke filled the air. We experienced the new phenomenon called a Heat Dome, and there were heat waves with a record breaking 49.6°C temperature reaching nearby Lytton, which gained worldwide notoriety after a fire destroyed the entire town in thirty minutes.

September '22. We keep flying as long as the weather is favourable. Unfortunately, another good friend of ours, Fish Boulton, has just crashed in Hedley while speed-flying. He cracked a couple of vertebrae, but luckily did not lose feeling in his feet, and is on the road to recovery. He was the tree-rescue expert, who got my glider out of the trees with no damage earlier this summer. Yes, paragliding is a dangerous sport. But in spite of the risks, the rewards of free flight are just too tempting, and we keep flying. However, fall is coming in here in the North-West. The thermals are getting weaker, and I have to start thinking about heading south again.

I am itching to travel so I hope the world opens up soon after the Covid pandemic.

Faith is a curious thing. My father once told me that he believed once we die, the candle just goes out and there's nothing more – the candle is out– it is all over. I guess it is like going under with anesthesia before surgery – then just never waking up. I always hoped that there would be more to life and death. Even the idea of the world of blue lights which I felt I experienced seemed a nicer scenario than just a plain black end.

To turn to a lighter note, the seasons are changing and I'm hoping to manage a paragliding trip to Mexico and Colombia before December, if travel opens up again. But first I have to finish publishing this book. Hopefully it will be published in Polish, as I continue to look for an English publisher. I am still hoping that I don't have to self-publish and therefore be responsible for all the marketing and distribution of the book. I had to go through that process to sell my documentaries, and after so many years it becomes too much of an arduous task to contemplate.

By fall of 2022 I have finished editing and publishing my book in Polish, under the cover and title "Szusss" with Roman Goledowski and Annapurna Publishing. My good friend Jedrzej Jaxa-Rozen had done a great job translating my rambling into Polish. Romans' great editors at Annapurna, who incidentally are nearly all women, have also really helped add life and colour to my narrative.

So now I am 65, and just as I thought that I might be able to start to relax in my "Golden Years" a new, rather intensive book adventure started.

Back in October '22, I was in Poland enjoying an intensive thirteen city and festival book-signing tour. It was fantastic to be back in the country of my birth after a 14 year absence. I criss-crossed the nation by trains and buses from Zakopane in the Tatra Mountains in the south, to Gdansk on the Baltic Sea in the north, giving a 90 minute slide and video presentation. I was lucky from the promotional point of view, as I appeared to come out of nowhere to be parachuted into the Polish mountain book genre. All of a sudden I was getting attention from the Polish national media and all the mountain film festivals. I appeared on everything from TV breakfast shows to radio interviews, featured in magazines and online on YouTube book presentations. This surprising exposure was not really because of my own exploits. A lot of the attention that was being given to extreme skiing was because of Poland's own Andrzej Bargiel, and his historic and extraordinary first ski descent of K2. Before him it was the big Himalayan climbers that took the centre stage and were the rock-stars of the Polish public. I freely admit I used this popularity as leverage to get publicity for my book and as an opportunity to drum up support for the planned Aerothlon in Bielsko-Biala and the ski resort of Szczyrk, which will be held next May.

I had the chance to meet a lot of fantastic people on my trip and the hospitality and food was really the best. Surprisingly, I find the frenetic pace of life in Poland and its consumer-driven lifestyle unmatched in any other country I have visited. I thought the Poles had got over their desire to be clones of America but it seems that the drive to outdo their neighbours still really dominates everyday life. Perhaps this lingers from the years of communist deprivation, and the attitude seems to have become imbedded for yet another generation. But Poles will be Poles, always unpredictable in their habits, lures and woes. So the media in Poland embraced my whole "Ski Bum" culture thing which was so foreign to Poles. How can one just exist to ski? Soon some of Poland's biggest online portals and print media latched on to the "Ski Bum" phenomenon brought to them from Whistler in Canada. I was often pleasantly surprised that after some of my presentations parents would come to me with their ten or twelve year old children in tow, and tell them the wisdom of choosing a life like mine as I signed books for them. If they only knew the hardships that went with the fun along the way. I had no intention of creating some twisted motivation of any sorts with my book, or my life, but it seems that this was the direction it was heading! I soon started playing along and added a motivational theme to my presentation. I often referred to the maddening pace of business in Poland and how it compared to my own lifestyle, and this became something I could use in my talks.

I returned to Canada after the Poland trip and was home for Christmas in December. By late January 2023, I was once again in Mexico to meet up with my good friend Krzysiu Buczkowski. He had not paraglided since our last meeting four years earlier in Colombia, so it was nice to enjoy the easy flying around Malinalco for ten days together.

After saying goodbye to Krzysiu, I continued south to Cali in Colombia, and then on to Roldanillo to meet other paragliding friends and fly with them for a month. While we were there, we held the best Aerothlon yet, with great participation by everyone in February with perfect flying conditions.

By early March I was once again back in Canada for a short recharge before heading to New York to attend the annual Explorers Club meeting. It took me two years to be invited, but thanks to my sponsor Chris Nicola, the renowned American cave-explorer, I was accepted as a member into the prestigious club by April. At first I felt a bit like a fish out of water, arriving direct from the wilds of Pemberton. I was soon acclimatized however, mingling with two thousand other explorers and having cocktails in the Explorers' imposing clubhouse in downtown Manhattan. At other times I met really interesting people at the opulent breakfasts and lunches held during the weekend.

By May '23 I was off to Poland again for yet another two-month book tour. Once again I teamed up with Ewa Michalak, who helped me so much on my earlier tour and she took the reigns again in organizing the Aerothlon in Szczyrk and Bielsko Biala for May '23.

Ewa really has made me appreciate Polish women so much again. She was independent, well-organized and yet still had that wonderful feminine touch which was so nice to be around. She made me realize that perhaps I belonged with a Polish partner in life, which is something I neglected to pursue properly all my life. Some will say I have not treated women well in this book. Some even insinuated that women were really just accessories in so many of my stories. Spending time with Ewa and other Polish outdoor-minded gals now made me realize how I missed out on female company overall, culturally, socially and intellectually, and only really related to the more physical parts of a relationship (i.e. sex) in the past. I had found myself always going south to Mexico and Colombia seeking an encounter or an 'exotic' relationship, yet here in Poland the bond between me and the women I met seemed to be so much more genuine.

The first Polish Aerothlon turned out to be a great success, thanks to the logistical hard work by Pawel Faron and his crew. Luckily we had a two-day weather window and on that Sunday in May the wind gods were with us, and the breeze died down providing us with that perfect sunny day. The flying element of the three discipline Aerothlon is always questionable, while the running and biking elements are not so weather dependent. The sponsors and everyone involved seemed happy with the way things went and we hoped for an even better event in 2024. After the Aerothlon, which was work of a kind, I got to go paragliding for fun in Italy and Slovenia for 8 days on an organized road trip as one of Pawel Faron's clients. I enjoyed the flying and the chilled atmosphere of Slovenia the most. This guided trip was a first for me but I really enjoyed the experience. Pawel runs a class operation with his company FLY-LITE doing trips all over the world from his home in Zywiec, Poland. Upon returning to Poland from this little vacation, I stayed in a pension in Gora Zar and flew there a for few days. Gora Zar had some nostalgic value to me because 14 years earlier I had spent a week there staying at the glider pilots hotel. Also it was here that I had met up with my good friend Troy Jungen in 2008, and we had started our Polish road-trip together.

On one visit to Zakopane, I also had a wonderful three hour chat with Andrzej Bargiel, the man who skied K2. Because of the publicity of his descent, he had made my extreme skiing tales more interesting to Polish readers. Andrzej was about to leave for the Karakorum, to attempt to ski both 8,000 metre+ peaks; named Gasherbrum I and II. He later managed to ski both peaks. It was wonderful to immerse ourselves in an inspiring conversation spanning many years and people in the extreme skiing game. And I wanted to congratulate him on his record breaking descents which he made in August 2023.

By the end of July 2023 I was again back in Canada and at home in Pemberton. It's nice to be home but again it is a busy time as I have to get this book out in English now.

Meanwhile, Beat Steiner, my original film partner, just gave us an amazing invitation to his world-famous Bella Coola Heli Skiing lodge. He has invited all eight original cast from "Search for the Ultimate Run", for four days heli-skiing in January 2024. This is a fantastic idea, and we are so stoked and pumped to go! It is our 40th anniversary of the film shot during the Christmas holidays back in 1983/84. It will be an incredible reunion, but first I plan to take my 92 year old mom for a month to Mexico as the hot dry weather is so beneficial for her arthritis and I can paraglide with Pablo Lopez and Gerardo Moran, my friends there.

Then, of course, there's the bucket list of places left where I want to fly; New Zealand, Australia, Indonesia, India, South Africa, Brazil, Spain, Bolivia and Argentina, and, "phew", there's more places still... I just hope I can still get to some of those dream locations while continuing to "Survive myself in my Lifestyle" and to just be true to the many good friends I have gathered in life.

So on to the next adventure; Maybe I will have to gather my friends with some good pilots and go back to Cerro Kennedy in Colombia to make that special flight and another film perhaps... So – just let them bring it on and I hope to keep surviving it all!

Is there a moral to my story? Not really. Maybe, like those parents of teenage boys in Poland, you might be inspired to look at some alternative choices in life. I made my choices early back in 1982, and by no means did I expect to end up writing a motivational book here, but if you find my story interesting and giving you some kind of incentive to follow your passion then all power to you.

Magical Colombia

1–2. Beaches of Tayrona park near Santa Marta, Colombia.
3–4. The Guajira peninsula is more like Morocco and the Sahara.
5. Colorful dress of the Wayu tribe in the Guajira.

The Aerothlon

1. Logo and poster of an Aerothlon in Pemberton.
2. At the starting field.
3. A good takeoff requires running and skill.
4. Flight above Pemberton valley.
5. A Canadian girl from Quebec celebrates Bastille Day in Pemberton, in French colors.
6. Polish friends after Roldanillo Aerothlon.

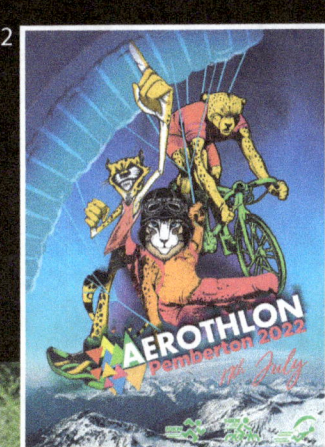

Aerothlon continued

1. Start of the Aerothlon in Temascaltepec, Mexico.
2. Aerothlon Pemberton poster.
3. Aerothlon crew in 2022 in Pemberton.
4. Team Poland Victoria in the Aerothlon 2022.

Aerothlon memories

1. The first Aerothlon in Pemberton, 2018.
2. Aerothlon winners in Malinalco, Mexico where the Aerothlon idea began.
3. Ptor Spricenieks with his wife and two sons and a painting of The North Face of Mt Robson, my gift at his wedding.

Polish Tour 2022

1. Peter on popular breakfast TV talk show in Warsaw, fall 2022.
2. Full house at Peter's presentation at Krakow Mountain Festival, Dec 2022, part of 18 city Polish book tour.
3. Peter at his best, Krakow Mountain Festival. On the picture: summer 1979, above Peyto Lake, Canadian Rockies, a first ski descent of unnamed couloir.
4. Peter with his Explorers Club sponsor, Chris Nicola in Manhattan, NYC, April 2023.
5. Peter with Andrzej Bargiel (First ski descent of K2, 2018) in Zakopane, June 2023.
6. Peter with Michal Gurgul, Outdoor Magazine, Poland.

Aerothlon 2023 Polish edition Szczyrk

1. Entire crew and athletes at award ceremonies for Aerothlon, Poland, Szczyrk, May 2023.
2. Aerothlon running start in Szczyrk.
3. From left: Peter, Ewa Michalak and Pawel Faron, organizers of Aerothlon Poland.
4. Agata Sarna takes tandem flight with pilot Dominik Kapica at first Aerothlon in Poland at Szczyrk/Bielsko-Biala, Poland, May 29, 2023.
5. Peter with Agata Sarna, fifth overall in her first Aerothlon in Poland.

Acknowledgments

In the first place I wish to thank my Mother, Maria for enduring everything I put her through. I also thank my father Adam for showing me an alternative way in life and forgiving my rebel ways sometimes. It is thanks to my parents that I am the person I am today. The trip by VW camper, all orchestrated by my father, to South America and later my summer job in Peru made me pursue many dreams and have other priorities.

Here are more people that helped me with my book;

Simon Bedford, Thank you Simon for all your help with photography, drone work, editing videos and this manuscript as you have been an incredible help.
Pablo Lopez from Malinalco Mexico where I wrote most my book in his little cabin.
Peter Shrimpton, Thank you for the copy editing in the manuscript.
Jedrzej Jaxa Rozen, for the beautiful translation to Polish.
Evelyn Stypolkowski for some copy editing.
Rod Drown, The original editor of the English version.
Chris Lockhart, good friend and additional editor of the English book.

Troy Jungen, one of my best friends for help with my house and so many trips and films.
Dominika Chylinska, editing Polish version and general consulting on story line.

Arthur Makosinski for inspiration and many ideas that I used in life.
Roman Gołędowski from Annapurna publishing for his help and patience in the whole book process.
Krzysiek Ryczkiewicz, good friend that really helped me with many tasks to help with the book.
Doris Spika for her great help as a travel companion.
Jim Orava, my dear neighbor and good friend that gave me so much valuable advice in to paraglide safely.
Lukas Kott, my good friend that kept my spirits up during my gloomy days.
Cauleen Bridges, I thank my dear friend for so many great ideas and giving me that name, „Peter Peru".
Roman Karas for all your help on so many fronts!

John Hayto, who was always there when I needed him.
John's son, Matthew Hayto for editing help on English book.
Cindy Hayto for putting up with John and I, and many great dinner parties.
Gerardo Moran for coming up with the title „I SURVIVED MYSELF"
Daniel Pedraza for your kind help when I was paragliding at La Malinche, Tenancingo Mexico.
Benquello Morales for all your help in Huaraz, Peru.
"Chepe" from Aerothlon Roldanillo, Colombia for all your help organizing the event.
Hector from the hotel "Vientos del Norte" in Roldanillo for all your help in Aerothlon Roldanillo, Colombia and lots of good times.
Pawel Boryniec for help in so many expeditions together and films.
Krzysiu Buczkowski for your help in Mexico and Colombia.
Adam Balut for help in organizing an important presentation for me at AGH in Krakow.

I thank a long list of doctors and surgeons in Canada, Mexico, Colombia and Peru that helped put me back together again.
Megan Hanson for being my first long term girlfriend.
Jenny Altamirano for being a partner and friend on X-Andes and other projects in Peru.
Heather McDevitt for help and putting up with me around the world on ODYSSEY 86 DC-3 airplane trip.

I thank all the women in my life for companionship and some beautiful romantic times.
Maryna Badzioch for her help and accommodation in Krakow.
Crystal Maguire, INTUITION liners, my loyal sponsor for so many years.
Ian Waddell, my lawyer and Executive Producer on "Goldenrush" film.
Curtis Petersen from PPI who helped me in so many film projects.
Ptor Spricenieks for being there always as a friend.
Harvey Zlataritz, my partner in many film projects that had such patience with my antics.
Barry Backus, for editing help and much more in advice.
Scotty (Heber) Fullmer for all these years filming together.
Jurek Badzioch, my cousin in Krakow for your help.
Robert Jungman for all that great hemp clothing sponsorship with Jungmaven, his company.
Zbyszek Fedyczkowski, for place to stay and help in Krakow.
Ewa Michalak, for all your help with the Aerothlon and my Polish book tour.
Pawel Faron from FLYLITE, his company for running the Aerothlon Poland and great flying advice.

Last but not least I thank anyone I may have omitted in this list.

Photo credits

Cover photo Peter skiing: Lockhart Chris
Comic book 6a, b, c, d, e, f by Smith Stu Mackay
Bac Dominik: 12a-5
Bedford Simon: 12b-3, 14b-3, 15b-1, 15b-3
Clarke David: 3a-3, 3a-4, 5b-5
Duffy Mike: 11b-4
Frazee David: 5b-2, 5b-5
Goledowski Roman: 18c, d
Huynh Mylinh: 18a-2
Jorgeson Blake: p. 10
Lawson Todd: 13a-5, 13a-6, 13a-7
Makosinski Arthur: 3b-2
Maurer Greg: 7b (1-4)
Orava Jim: 16a-1
Smith Sarah: 10b (1-5)
Spricenieks Ptor: 9a-3, 16b-1, 16b-2, 18b-3
Tordoya Americo: 3b-2, 3b-3, 3b-4
Vasquez Natali (obraz): 13b-4
All the rest off the photos are by Extreme Explorations and Peter Chrzanowski.

INTERESTING LINKS – VIDEOS

AIRHEAD DIARIES 1:
https://www.youtube.com/watch?v=LfjLwiS1sME

AIRHEAD DIARIES 2:
https://www.youtube.com/watch?v=A5I6nFxuJjQ

AIRHEAD DIARIES 3:
https://www.youtube.com/watch?v=A5I6nFxuJjQ&t=85s

CUBA COLLAGE:
https://www.youtube.com/watch?v=of3ATwnWzk0

JOURNEY TO THE HEART OF THE WORLD:
https://www.youtube.com/watch?v=yamJXfHjV-U

GOLDENRUSH:
https://www.youtube.com/watch?v=XFnwdsGCl1M

MT WADDINGTON:
https://www.youtube.com/watch?v=R7NzhsGCQYs

PARACINDERELLA:
https://www.youtube.com/watch?v=VNr5ByPGbhc

PARAPENTE CUBA:
https://www.youtube.com/watch?v=K14BuHdU8MI

PEMBERTON AEROTHLON:
https://www.youtube.com/watch?v=ZBJMsARjRwk&t=46s

PEMBERTON PARAGLIDING:
https://www.youtube.com/watch?v=leeIOqYvY5I

PEMBERTON PARAGLIDING 2:
https://www.youtube.com/watch?v=QHlwg5tvGmk

SACRED FLIGHT CLIP 1:
https://www.youtube.com/watch?v=6oIHPUgox2c&t=81s

SEARCH FOR THE ULTIMATE RUN:
https://www.youtube.com/watch?v=fshQ_q7k9h4

THE GOOD LIFE:
https://www.youtube.com/watch?v=_OuRZGKwt5Q

SACRED FLIGHT CLIP 2:
https://www.youtube.com/watch?v=UH293IcazqI&t=13s

SKI PERU:
https://www.youtube.com/watch?v=VSYmBvloxME

THE NORTH FACE: SEVEN YEARS ON MT ROBSON:
https://www.youtube.com/watch?v=5GmWVd_wUmg&t=22s

THE SPIRIT:
https://www.youtube.com/watch?v=uWOm39KXw0Q

VALDEZ GOES EXTREME:
https://www.youtube.com/watch?v=JgwXfXUQh6o

WHISTLERS GOAT PATH VD CHUTES:
https://www.youtube.com/watch?v=Ji8A5iWXCc0

INTERESTING LINKS – NEWS/ARTICLES

PETER PERU:
www.peterperu.ca

GRIPPED ARTICLE:
https://gripped.com/gripped-outdoors/the-first-ski-descent-of-the-north-face-of-yuh-hai-has-kun/

MOUNTAIN FILM FILMOGRAPHY:
https://www.mntnfilm.com/en/filmography/peter-chrzanowski

NEW YORK TIMES:
https://www.nytimes.com/2007/12/16/movies/16brow.html

POWDER:
https://www.powder.com/stories/classics/influential-skiers/

SKI THE WORLD:
https://skitheworld.com/2019/11/heli-ski-mystery-mountain/

SYLVAIN SAUDAN CBC STORY:
https://www.cbc.ca/news/canada/british-columbia/sylvain-saudan-godfather-of-extreme-skiing-lends-his-name-again-to-blackcomb-mountain-1.4395230

SYLVAIN SAUDAN VANCOUVER SUN: PIOTROWICZ ARTICLE:
s/octogenarian-ski-daredevil-ready-to-give-his-name-to-extreme-blackcomb-run

ZBIGNIEW PIOTROWICZ ARTICLE:
http://zbigniewpiotrowicz.pl/peter-chrzanowski/

OPINIONS ABOUT THE AUTHOR AND HIS BOOK

Peter Chrzanowski is the kind of wonderful character that gives one faith that everything is going to work out just fine.

Wade Davis
BC Leadership Chair in Cultures and Ecosystems at Risk
Professor of Anthropology

"Certainly in the world of extreme sports, Peter is by far one of my favorite storytellers. It's almost unbelievable, what his life has been like, but if you ask around everything he tells you is 100% true. These things really did happen! And the fact he's still alive to tell these tales means clearly, his life is now meant to be shared for the enjoyment of us all!"

Kristen Ulmer, former #1 in the world athlete, extreme athlete/skier/writer and author of "The Art of Fear"

"Growing up watching Peter's big mountain and ski exploits in the late 1980s, I remember thinking those missions sometimes seemed loose, and weren't always "successful"; in their goals, but man, did they ever look like an adventure. To think what Peter has accomplished, and survived through, since then is mind-boggling. Few in the mountain kingdom will have lived the kind of DIY-adventure life that Peter has, and if he has a book coming out... I wanna read it!"

Feet Banks, editor. Mountain Life Magazine

I SURVIVED MYSELF is an author's story about passion, emotion and a yearning to document his adrenaline stories as he goes close to the thin red line. Peter did fantastic things in the mountains and paragliding as well. This of course came with a lot of risk and accidents. Therefore Peter's rich life becomes an inspiration for today's youth.

Krzysztof Wielicki
Polish top alpinist,
First ascent on Mount Everest in winter
He is the 5th man to climb all fourteen eight-thousanders

Peter has an hour to hour and a half audio visual presentation from his life displayed in this book. He wants to motivate youth to take an alternative route in life, if they wish. Yes, it is OK, if you wonder about taking the less travelled route, perhaps without family or perhaps with, in order to follow your passion. You can also do it without a lot of money, being creative instead.

Please feel free to contact Peter if you have an organization, that may need a great presentation.